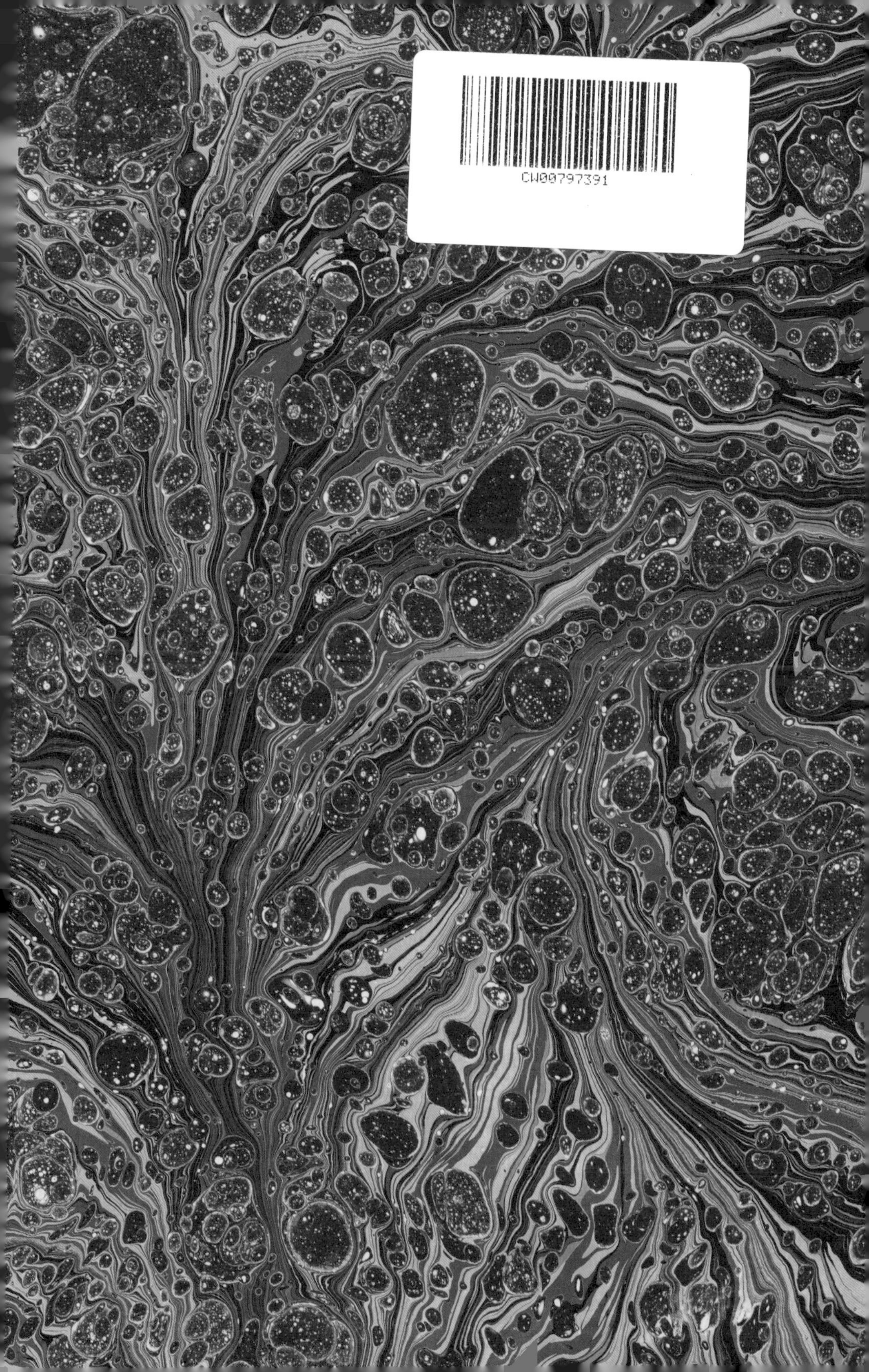
CW00797391

KAMPFGESCHWADER 51 “EDELWEISS”

KAMPFGESCHWADER 51 "EDELWEISS"

The Complete History of KG 51 in World War II

Wolfgang Dierich

4880 Lower Valley Road • Atglen, PA 19310

Copyright © 2014 by Schiffer Publishing Ltd.

Library of Congress Control Number: 2014944372

All rights reserved. No part of this work may be reproduced or used in any form or by any means—graphic, electronic, or mechanical, including photocopying or information storage and retrieval systems—without written permission from the publisher.

The scanning, uploading, and distribution of this book or any part thereof via the Internet or via any other means without the permission of the publisher is illegal and punishable by law. Please purchase only authorized editions and do not participate in or encourage the electronic piracy of copyrighted materials.
"Schiffer," "Schiffer Publishing, Ltd. & Design," and the "Design of pen and inkwell" are registered trademarks of Schiffer Publishing, Ltd.

Designed by Robert Biondi
Type set in Times New Roman

ISBN: 978-0-7643-4739-9
Printed in China

Published by Schiffer Publishing, Ltd.
4880 Lower Valley Road
Atglen, PA 19310
Phone: (610) 593-1777; Fax: (610) 593-2002
E-mail: Info@schifferbooks.com

Translated from the German by David Johnston.

This book was originally published under the title,
Chronik Kampfgeschwader 51 "Edelweiss,"
© 2011 by Motorbuch Verlag, Stuttgart, Germany.

For our complete selection of fine books on this and related subjects, please visit our website at www.schifferbooks.com. You may also write for a free catalog.

This book may be purchased from the publisher. Please try your bookstore first.

We are always looking for people to write books on new and related subjects. If you have an idea for a book, please contact us at proposals@schifferbooks.com.

Schiffer Publishing's titles are available at special discounts for bulk purchases for sales promotions or premiums. Special editions, including personalized covers, corporate imprints, and excerpts can be created in large quantities for special needs. For more information, contact the publisher.

Contents

"War is no adventure, war is a sickness ..."
— Antonie de Saint-Euxpéry, from Flight to Arras

To Jagdbombergeschwader 34
in Memminberberg/Allgäu

Foreword

This chronicle of *Kampfgeschwader 51* (Edelweiss *Geschwader*) was compiled from documents and reports. It is one of the first accounts ever of the employment and operations of a German *Kampfgeschwader* during the Second World War. For this reason, adequate space is dedicated to the development of aerial warfare and the bomber in particular.

The author, Gencral Staff *Oberstleutnant* Wolfgang Dierich, is not of the wartime generation. But as the *Staffelkapitän* of the *Bundesluftwaffe*'s 2. JaboG 34 based in Memmingerberg, the prewar base of III./KG 255/51, his young airman's heart desired to tell the story of KG 51, which became famous as the "Edelweiss *Geschwader*" during the Second World War. On his own initiative he made the edelweiss the emblem of his *Staffel* and the airmen of the *Bundesluftwaffe* in Memmingerberg also wear it on their service uniforms.

Since then a good comradeship has linked it to the KG 51 Veterans Association in Landsberg/Lech, the peacetime base of KG 255/51, whose three Kampfgruppen in Landsberg, Leipheim and Memmingen employed the alpine rose, gentian and edelweiss as *Gruppe* emblems and which became known as the "Alpine *Geschwader*." From it the "Edelweiss *Geschwader*" emerged during the war.

By voluntarily taking up the task of writing the wartime history of KG 51, Wolfgang Dierich is deserving of thanks and appreciation, which I, as the first *Kommodore* of the *Geschwader*, would like to express on behalf of all the members of the *Geschwader*, both the living and the fallen and missing.

The airman has never sought the heroism of his actions, thoughts and feelings. He was and is reserved in his descriptions. The hard experience of war has marked him.

Nevertheless, through countless conversations and extensive and, in some cases sadly disappointing, correspondence, I was able to convince the surviving members of the *Edelweiss Geschwader* and also the families of the fallen and missing, despite their understandable reluctance, to contribute to this effort. Only thus could this chronicle begin and grow.

The "Edelweiss *Geschwader*" was assigned the *Luftwaffe*'s most modern equipment on almost a regular basis. Whether it was the Do 17, far ahead of its time and allocated to the *Geschwader* during its formation, or later the Heinkel He 111, the Junkers Ju 88, or the Messerschmitt Me 262, the *Geschwader* always flew aircraft that were at the forefront of technical advancement. With it this brought temporary advantages over an enemy with massive material superiority and all the disadvantages and difficulties always associated with the introduction of new aircraft types.

The *Geschwader* was always committed at the points of main effort and earned the reputation as a "fire brigade." 1,500 killed and missing testify to the toughness of its operations.

The "Edelweiss" enjoyed a good reputation, whether in France or over England, in the Balkans or in the expanses of Russia.

After the release of this chronicle many voices will surely be heard, complaining that they have not been heard. One must always expect that. Despite all inquiries, there will still be gaps due to a lack of information. Additional information can be added to the text of future editions.

At this point I would like to thank General Staff *Oberst* Dr, Gundelach of the *Bundeswehr*'s Military Research Office in Freiburg and the Central Archive in Kornelimünster for his tireless assistance.

Messrs. Arz, Felles, Dierich, Feldmann, Hoiß, Maser, Pflüger, Poetter, Schwachenwald, Dr. Stahl and Widmann provided the critical review of the manuscript along with valuable advice and guidance. Thanks to the publisher, especially Mr. Wolfgang Schiller, who encouraged this project, for the book's generous layout.

May this book bring the young reader closer to part of the history of the German air force.

Willibald Spang
Generalleutnant (Rtd.)
first *Kommodore* of KG 255/51

Chapter 1
Creation of a New Weapon

Balloons and Airships

When the Montgolfier brothers' hot-air balloon made its first ascent on 5 June 1783, thought was already being given to possible military use of this "lighter than air" vehicle. Ten years later, in 1793, the French formed tethered balloon battalions called *Aérostiers*. Eight years earlier, in 1785, Blanchard and Dr Jeffries had successfully crossed the English Channel in just two hours. On 26 June 1794, during the Battle of Fleurus, a tethered oxygen-filled balloon was used to observe enemy positions and direct artillery fire, the first time such a vehicle had been used in warfare. A French tethered balloon also played an important part in the siege of Mainz in 1796, where it helped demonstrate French power.

The day of military photo-reconnaissance arrived much later, during the Battle of Solferino (24 June 1859), when French forces photographed Austrian positions from a tethered balloon. For years the military significance of these vehicles went unrecognized, however this changed during the siege of Paris in 1870. Sixty-six spherical balloons, five of which fell into German hands and two were blown out to sea, left Paris carrying 147 persons, 363 carrier pigeons, 9 tons of dispatches and 2.5-million letters. Léon Gambetta, the organizer of French resistance, also left the city by balloon and was able to continue his political efforts.

One year later an invention by the German captains von Sigisfeld and von Parseval – the wind-resistant "kite balloon" (called the non-rigid airship) – enabled even better observations, because by then a method of propulsion (Daimler gasoline engine 1883) and a steering system had been developed. Before long, further technical improvements turned the airship into a flying machine that, to the people, became the symbol of technical advancement. The "rigid airships" of Count Zeppelin – father of the idea and its realization (LZ 1 took to the air on 2 July 1900) – became a household name. With his wooden frame "ships" kept aloft by "ballonets" (gas bags), Schütte-Lanz selected another – perhaps cheaper – design method.

When the First World War broke out, the army command (OHL) had nine Zeppelins, one Parseval and one Schütte-Lanz. The navy initially had one, later three, Zeppelins. In keeping with their strategic purpose, all of these airships were used for long-range reconnaissance. Thanks to their considerable payload of about 8.5 tons in the beginning, airships had an advantage over aircraft of being able to carry significant bomb loads. On the night of 5-6 August 1914, Zeppelin Z-6 carried out the first bombing raid in history, attacking the Belgian fortress of Liège. Further attacks followed against targets on the Western Front, such as Manon-Viller, Antwerp, Ostende and Calais, and on the Eastern Front against Mlawa and Lodz. In early 1915 German airships made large-scale raids on Paris, London and English ports. The French carried out an attack on the open city of Karlsruhe on 9 August 1915.

Even though the Zeppelin's possible payload had risen to 52 tons by the end of the World War, the vulnerable airships had suffered heavy losses and were no longer suitable for strategic bombing. Though also highly vulnerable, only the tethered balloon survived as a relic of this developmental period, protecting important targets during the Second World War. Many bomber pilots had unexpected experiences with barrage balloons, particularly over England in 1940 and 1941.

The Aircraft

Otto Lilienthal (died 9 August 1896) developed and researched the foundations for the "heavier than air flying machine," although many before him, men like Leonardo de Vinci, Henson, Penaud and Langley, had strived to realize the dream of manned flight. Building on Lilienthal's research and experiments – especially in the field of gliding flight – enthusiastic aviation pioneers carried on the work all over the world. Powered flight was born on 17 December 1903, when Orville Wright took to the air in his flying machine, remaining airborne for 13 seconds and covering an impressive distance of 36.6 meters.

Further developments followed quickly. Some of the resulting aircraft were unusual and curious-looking. For years France played a leading role. On 25 July 1909 Blériot crossed the Channel in his powered aircraft, to the horror of the English, who saw their "splendid isolation" threatened. In 1912 Garros established a world altitude record, climbing to 5,600 meters in his powered aircraft.

Because of its anticipated performance and maneuverability, the aircraft appeared to be a war machine with development potential. Military authorities recognized it as a means of significantly extending the reconnaissance activities of the cavalry deep into enemy territory. In assessing the aircraft as a new weapon of war, the general staffs were most interested in operational and strategic long-range reconnaissance.

Once again France showed the way in the use of the aircraft for other military tasks. They used it for artillery observation, correcting fire and also for dropping bombs. The installation of radio equipment simplified air-ground communications, largely eliminating the use of signals for command and control.

While the use of aircraft in the Italian-Turkish War (Tripoli and Libya in 1911) and the Balkans War (1912-1913) was certainly of significance in the history of warfare, it had little military value. In those theaters it had largely a moral effect.

The German Fliegertruppe in the First World War

The first German military flying school was established in Döberitz in 1910. A modest establishment, in its first course civilian instructors trained four officers to fly. Soon other young army officers volunteered for training.

An officer who volunteered for the air corps in those days was seen by many superiors as an adventurer, whose transfer request was approved in order to prevent him from doing something stupid in other areas. The potential of German aviation was underestimated by the broad mass of the people and all branches of the army.

Despite a lack of recognition, the officers of the young *Fliegertruppe* happily set about expanding their arm, despite numerous setbacks. An appeal for contributions to the National Aviation Fund provided the financial means, and on 1 October 1913 four aviation battalions, each of four companies, were formed. France, on the other hand, had 170 warplanes in service by 1911. 150 officers were qualified pilots, 73 of these had a military diploma, and among them 40 had a field rating, which signified that they were fully qualified military aviators.

When the war broke out, there were 254 qualified observers in the entire German army. The French had at least twice as many. With mobilization, the Germans formed 34 aviation battalions, each with six aircraft and crews (pilot and observer), as well as seven fortress aviation battalions, eight rear-echelon air parks and five aircrew replacement training battalions. The aircraft were produced in ten small factories. The operational aviation battalions were subordinate to the army high commands or general commands; there was no supreme command of aviation in the OHL. The army high commands also lacked an office for practical and organizational communications and coordination between airmen and the troops fighting on the ground.

The first operations in the World War were reconnaissance flights behind the enemy front, which enabled the army command to make vital decisions. Airmen discovered and reported enemy troop movements in both the Battle of the Marne and the Battle of Tannenberg. The observer aircraft became the eyes of the army. The first reconnaissance flights were by no means harmless pleasure flights. With a cruising speed of about 100 kph, the aircraft were tempting targets for the accurate enemy anti-aircraft guns.

Little progress was made in aerial bombing because of the poor prospects of hitting the target. The use of aircraft concentrated on reconnaissance. The unarmed German aircraft soon had to deal with enemy combat aircraft armed with machine-guns. The obvious consequence was the arming of German aircraft.

With the onset of aerial combat, the struggle began for air superiority, which soon became a part of overall military superiority. Not until 1917, with Germany suffering from a shortage of trained pilots and equipment, did the Allies regain superiority in the air. This demanded extraordinary feats on the part of the German *Fliegertruppe* and a maximum effort by every single airman.

When the war began, the airman had to carry out a wide variety of tasks. He was an intelligence gatherer, directed artillery fire, photographed the front and the enemy rear, dropped bombs, and in isolated cases even intervened in the ground fighting. Though they initially lacked mobility on account of their extensive support system, thanks to the initiative of their leaders the aviation battalions were soon not only capable of keeping pace with the advancing units, but also rushed far ahead of them with their reconnaissance flights. During the Battle of the Marne, German aircraft ventured as far as Paris.

All of these circumstances resulted in the development of an unbreakable bond of comradeship in the still young *Fliegertruppe*. From the moment of takeoff until landing, the crew, consisting of a pilot and an observer, was inseparably connected, forced to rely on one another, and alone with their mission and the enemy. The fitters (mechanics), who looked after the aircraft, engines and weapons on the remote forward airfields, played a major role in the success and fate of their flying crews and squadrons. On their knowledge and care depended the engines of the day, which were not very reliable, and the handling characteristics of the aircraft. A very special relationship of trust developed. The comradeship between the flying and non-flying personnel was stronger than any formal command relationship between officer and enlisted men.

As the commanders of army corps and armies came to recognize the potential benefits to be derived from aerial reconnaissance, the airmen received growing support in their call for a unified command for front-line aviation. *Oberstleutnant* Siegert played a major role in *Major* Thomsen being named "Commander of Front-Line Aviation" on 11 March 1915. He was placed at the head of all aircraft and airship aviation as well as the army's weather service. Thomsen was directly subordinate to the Quartermaster-General. The air forces left the ranks of the transportation units and became independent.

At home the "Inspector of Aviation Forces" implemented directives and suggestions from the front-line aviation commander. By strictly organizing the aircraft industry he ensured that the increasing qualitative and quantitative demands from the front were satisfied and stopped the front-line aviation battalions from procuring aircraft directly from the factories! The position of "Aviation Staff Officer" was created in every army high command, in order to introduce and maintain practical cooperation between the air corps and other branches of the armed services. The army airparks, which had become independent, were also under their command.

By then the number of *Feldfliegerabteilungen* had more than doubled (25). As well, the supreme army command had an air corps with 36 aircraft under its immediate command for strategic tasks.

The strength and ability of the field aviation battalions grew steadily. As many as 2,000 aircraft reached the front each month. New aircraft were capable of reaching altitudes of 6,000 meters and were twice as fast as older types. Improved bombsights made it possible to bomb effectively with bombs weighing from 10 to 1,000 kg. Low-flying close-support aircraft supported the infantry. Losses rose as the demands became greater. Often only one of three aircraft that took off on an operational sortie came back. Combats between individual aircraft developed into breathtaking, large-scale air battles.

The strength of the *Fliegertruppe* grew by another fifty percent between April 1915 and April 1916. That year was marked by an expansion of the organization, fundamental training of the crews and further technical advances.

Whereas formerly the crews had been required to carry out a variety of tasks with one and the same type of aircraft, a proccss of specialization now began. The aviation industry created long-range reconnaissance aircraft, close-support aircraft, day and night bombers, two-seat training aircraft and, in particular, fighter aircraft, which were organized into dedicated aviation battalions and *Staffeln*.

The air corps formed:

— reconnaissance battalions
— artillery observation battalions
— close-support *Staffeln*
— OHL long-range reconnaissance battalions
— OHL bomber *Geschwader* (BOGOHL)
— fighter squadrons (*Jagdstaffeln*, or JASTA) and wings (*Jagdgeschwader*)

The enemy had greater resources, and the German aviation corps had to compensate with improved performances by individual aircraft and crews while using available resources and personnel in a cost-effective way.

In this time of such fundamental developments, the aircraft crews were called upon to achieve the near impossible.

The pilot or observer badge could only be obtained by serving at the front. The Airman's Commemorative Badge, probably the most coveted decoration among airmen, was only awarded to those who had served at the front for a long time. It was not unusual for airmen, after completing their daily reconnaissance program, to land on their own initiative far behind the front to destroy railway embankments, for example.

How critical the airmen were of their own guns is illustrated by the following poem:

Airman Palström

Peevish anyway, Palström
was shot at by German guns
while flying in German
zones.

How – he thought, taking evasive action
and resolutely flying on –
how was it possible, indeed,
that it ever happened?

Is the artillery of no use
when it comes to field guns?
Or do the gunnery regulations
give shrapnel free rein here?

Muffled in wet clothes,
he checks the service manuals,
and soon he finds it:
Germans are not supposed to shoot here.

And he comes to the conclusion:
the conclusion was only a dream,
because – he concludes trenchantly –
There cannot be what is not supposed to be.

In the summer of 1916, the fighting at Verdun and on the Somme became a battle of materiel, and on 8 October the air forces took on their ultimate form and organization.

From then on the "Commanding General of the Air Forces," *Generalleutnant* von Hoeppner, would be at their head, with his own aviation general staff that would organize and oversee the strategic and tactical employment of the airmen.

His subordinate in each army corps was the "Commander of Aviation." It was their job to liaise with the various battalions and squadrons and coordinate operations with the troops on the ground. In addition, there were special aviation units for use by the supreme command of the army through the "Commanding General of Air Forces" (KoGenLuft).

Boelcke was the master teacher for fighters in the air. When he fell victim to a tragic accident, his place was taken by Manfred von Richthofen, the "Red Baron."

In this brief account numbers may sound dry, however sometimes they say more than words.

By the end of the war more than 47,000 aircraft were delivered to the German Army Administration. In autumn 1918, just before the end of the war, there were about 5,000 aircraft at the front. France built approximately 68,000 aircraft and 85,000 aero engines between 1914 and 1918, England about 50,000 aircraft, the USA approximately 11,000 aircraft and 29,000 aero engines. Thus without Russia and Italy, the enemy built almost 129,000 aircraft and 114,000 aero engines, while Germany was only able to deliver 47,000 aircraft. The following numbers comparison illustrates the job of expansion that was necessary.

When the war began, Germany had eight small aircraft factories. By 1918, however, 83 aircraft and engine factories had to work constantly to even come close to meeting the demands of the front. During the war the engine industry delivered 40,500 aero engines. In 1918 the 5,000 German aircraft on the Western Front faced far more than twice the number of enemy aircraft.

The following figures may round off the outline of the history of the German *Fliegertruppe* in the First World War.

Monthly fuel consumption:

1914	600 tons
1915	3,000 tons
1916	4,500 tons
1917	5,500 tons
1918	7,000 tons

The total wartime consumption was thus 230,000 tons of gasoline and 30,000 tons of oil.

Each German *Bombengeschwader* dropped 100 tons of bombs per month during the last year of the war. In 1918 there were about 7,000 aircraft machine-guns installed in the 5,000 aircraft and later also many small-caliber (20-mm) aircraft cannon. By the end of the war, the German side was using about 2,000 aircraft cameras with focal lengths of up to 1.20 meters and about 100 optical cameras. In May 1915, for example, approximately 400 photographs were taken per day, whereas in May 1917 the number of photos taken behind the enemy front was about 1,500. A cautious estimate suggests that in 1918 alone, an area of more than 25 000 square kilometers on the Western Front was photographed each week. This is an area roughly equal in size to Hesse. Altogether, during the war approximately 3,000,000 square kilometers of ground was photographed, under wartime conditions, with of course come duplication.

In 1918 there were 5,000 aircrew – officers, non-commissioned officers and enlisted men – at the front, with an equal number in training in the homeland. Each month the front required approximately 15% of its flying personnel as replacements, equal to 750 pilots, observers and gunners. From January to September 1918 alone, 1,099 aircrew lost their lives on the Western Front.

The humiliating ceasefire terms of Compiègne (8 November 1918) ended the war and sucked the *Fliegertruppe* into the maelstrom of revolutionary events.

On 16 January 1919 the position of the Commanding General of Aviation was dissolved. When the war ended, the *Fliegertruppe*'s casualties (killed, wounded, missing) stood at: 13,100 of 17,000 trained pilots (71%).

According to the terms of the Treaty of Versailles, 15,174 operational and training aircraft, 27,000 aero engines and immeasurable quantities of materiel had to be surrendered or destroyed. The only aviation units left were a few police squadrons attached to the police administration.

Air War Theories

A variety of air war theories developed from the operational experiences of the First World War and the conflicts in the period between the world wars. In hindsight, knowledge of these theories makes it easier to understand and explain the air war from 1939 to 1945.

(1.) The Italian General Douhet created a new doctrine of strategic air war, which became the topic of heated discussion in military circles. Douhet was the first to clearly emphasize the decisive role of air forces in war.

According to his theory, the first objective was to gain absolute air superiority (destruction of the enemy's air force in the air and on the ground). Only then were strategic bomber fleets supposed to ruthlessly and without pause carry the air war to the enemy's military, industrial and political centers until the populations' will to live and resist was broken.

Just how prophetic these ideas were is shown by the success achieved by the Allied bomber fleets in resolutely pursuing them, especially towards the end of the Second World War.

The enemy had achieved air superiority. Germany had become a fortress without a roof.

The "air cruisers" envisaged by Douhet had been created by the Americans in the B-17 Flying Fortress and the British in the Lancaster and Halifax. England in particular had made plans for the possible strategic bombing of Germany in its master plan of 1939.

(2.) Another group of military experts thought that cooperation between air forces and the earth-bound elements of the army and navy offered the best possibility of success in wartime. They saw the aircraft as nothing more than a means of supporting the army through tactical operations. They attributed no independent role to the aircraft.

Thoughts in this direction could be found in German specialist literature in the 1930s and were reflected in part in the organization of the air fleets of the *Reichsluftwaffe*. They were small, independent air fleets with fighter, reconnaissance, dive-bomber, heavy fighter, close-support and bomber units, born of Hitler's blitzkrieg concept. The positive experiences of the Spanish Civil War played a significant role in the conception of these organizations.

Despite these ideas and tendencies, a decree of 26 February 1935 created the *Reichsluftwaffe* (a title that was never to catch on – it remained *Luftwaffe*) as a third, independent branch of the *Wehrmacht*.

(3.) The group of so-called "moderate Douhetians" called for the waging of strategic air war and cooperation. They envisaged that air forces would have both strategic and tactical or operational roles. The parties had very different ideas about the primacy of strategic or tactical operations.

The Royal Air Force (RAF) made a clear distinction between strategic and tactical conduct of aerial warfare and this was reflected in its organization and equipment. It had strategic long-range bombers, fighter units for home defense and aircraft to support the navy.

Similar considerations determined the planning and equipment of the American army air force (USAAF), however with respect to potential cooperation with the army it benefited from experience gained in the first two years of the war. For the *Luftwaffe*, operations in direct or indirect support of the army obviously took priority. The *Luftwaffe* had neither the personnel nor equipment with which to wage an independent strategic air war, something the political leadership had not envisaged. The "blitzkrieg concept" implied only operational and tactical use of air forces.

The "cooperation" between the Soviet air force and army was particularly outstanding. Apart from nuisance raids, during the Second World War the Russian army air forces never engaged in operations that were of an operative, much less strategic nature. Nevertheless, in some cases the Russian close-support aircraft and fighters inflicted significant losses on elements of the German military with their "pinprick" tactics. The 285 missions flown against the port of Costanza by naval aircraft of the Black Sea Fleet from 22-30 June 1941 were an exception with an operative character.

What Is A Combat Pilot?

The notion of the "combat pilot" has undergone a great change since the First World War.

Initially units equipped with single-seat fighter aircraft (*Jagdstaffeln* – *'Jasta'*) were called combat units – one only has to think of Richthofen's "*rote Kampfflieger*."

Soon, however, there developed a differentiation between the special roles in air warfare. So it was for those units specially envisaged for the bombing role – the *Bombengeschwader* of the Supreme Army Command (BOGOHL). Their creation and rapid development were a direct result of the First World War's shift to positional warfare. After the front became frozen, both warring parties installed large ammunition dumps and supply depots behind their trench systems beyond the range of enemy artillery. These areas were also used to assemble and train reserve personnel, in order to acquaint them with conditions near the front. Rail and road traffic to these areas was so extensive that the railway stations and towns were packed with troops and materiel.

All of the warring powers understandably sought means with which to attack these tempting targets, and the bomb-carrying aircraft turned out to be the most effective. Whereas, at the end of 1914, 3.5-kg bombs and flechettes were simply dropped by hand with no bomb racks or sights, reconnaissance aircraft began carrying 10- and 20-kg bombs in early 1915. Not surprisingly, however, their effectiveness was limited.

In the meantime specialized bombing aircraft were planned, built and tested, initially for tactical missions only as so-called "vertical artillery." Their underlying idea included both vertical envelopment as well as reconnaissance, and units equipped with these aircraft came to be nicknamed "vertical cavalry."

Whereas the bombers of 1916 (G Type = large aircraft, or GL Type = light large aircraft) were capable of carrying a bomb load of about 200 kg a distance of 400 km at a speed of 110 kph at an altitude of 1,000 meters, by 1918 they were able to carry a bomb load of 800 kg a distance of about 800 km at a speed of 130 kph at an altitude of 4,000 meters. The small number of four-engined, multi-place "giant aircraft" produced by Handley-Page, Sikorsky and the Staaken Flugzeugwerft were even capable of carrying up to 3000 kg of bombs over long distances.

The German aerial offensive against the southeast coast of England, Dunkirk and Paris, begun in the spring of 1917, had a clearly strategic character, as did the enemy raids on German factories in the Upper Rhine and Ruhr regions.

The designations "light," "medium" and "heavy" appear repeatedly in the development history of the bomber aircraft. These terms are confusing, as they only indicate how heavy a bomb load and aircraft was capable of carrying and how heavily armed (defensive positions) a bomber was at a particular period.

General Douhet called for an "air cruiser" carrying a heavy bomb load with a powerful defensive armament that was later realized in the American and British multi-engine heavy bombers.

In his enlightening book *L'Aviation de Bombardement*, however, French engineer Camille Rougeron expressed the view that a "fast bomber" would be much less vulnerable and more effective and would also need a smaller crew.

The famous De Havilland Mosquito probably came closest to this concept. In the Dornier Do 17, which achieved spectacular success at the 4th International Air Meet in Zurich in 1937, proving to be faster than any of the participating fighter aircraft and winning the International Alpine Circuit for Military Aircraft, the *Luftwaffe* potentially had a high-speed bomber.

This specially modified aircraft caused a sensation and showed in which direction development could and should proceed in Germany.

The Reich Minister for Aviation's order for the third development phase (1936) of 25 May 1934 saw the term "*Bombenfliegerverband*" (bomber aviation unit) replaced by the designation "*Kampfverband*" (combat unit).

The *Fliegertruppe* included the *Luftwaffe*'s flying units and the flight training schools. Its personnel were divided into flying, technical and general personnel.

As a rule, a *Staffel* consisted of nine aircraft, three *Staffeln* and later two airfield operating companies (FBK) formed a *Gruppe*, and three *Gruppen* made up a *Geschwader*. Each *Staffel* also included three spare aircraft for the aircraft park.

The Role of the Kampfflieger

German *Kampfflieger* (bomber airmen) were trained according to the following principles:

> *"The role of the Kampfflieger is to carry out bombing attacks. By striking the sources of strength of the enemy's armed forces and by interrupting the flow of power from them to the front, including all means of transportation and routes, it attempts to defeat the enemy military. These sources of power include all enemy installations and safeguards that serve to strengthen or augment the fighting forces. For the most part these are location-bound, fixed installations.*
>
> *The goal of the air war, to break the enemy's will to fight and his fighting strength, cannot be fully achieved if air operations are limited to daylight and the enemy is able to catch his breath at night. The effect of daylight attacks must therefore be augmented by dusk and night attacks.*
>
> *The list of potential targets include the following groups of targets:*
>
> *— the enemy air force*
> *— the enemy army*
> *— the enemy navy*
> *— the enemy army's sources of strength*
>
> *During decisive operations within the overall conduct of the war, the use of bombers to provide direct support to the army or navy is possible and necessary.*
>
> *The goal of every bombing mission is to destroy the targets being attacked. Even the most powerful enemy defenses must not prevent the bombers from completing their missions.*
>
> *The air force must also strike the enemy people and nation at their sensitive spots. Unintentional secondary effects during attacks are unavoidable. Attacks on cities for the purpose of creating terror are fundamentally to be avoided. If, however, the enemy carries out terror attacks against defenseless open cities, reprisal raids may be the only means of deflecting the enemy from this brutal style of warfare.*

Aerial photos are important aids to operations by bomber units.

Careful tactical, technical and mapping preparations are necessary for a successful attack by the bomber. Bomber crews operate day and night, at high and low altitude, and in formations of no less than three aircraft (Kette) in daylight. The bomber unit is more vulnerable to flak and fighter defenses during daylight attacks than at night, unless cloud cover is used during the approach to and withdrawal from the target.

Although orientation is more difficult at night, the aircraft have the advantage of flying under cover of darkness. High- and low-level attacks are dependent on:

— general enemy situation
— type of target to be attacked
— type of aircraft available
— weather, time of day, terrain

In conditions of good visibility, high-altitude flight simplifies orientation and reduces the crew's workload. A high-flying unit will be detected by the enemy sooner than a low-flying one, which almost always achieves the element of surprise and considerably reduces the effectiveness of the enemy's ground and air defense. Low-level flight places increased demands on the crews and requires a higher level of training and experience."

The general heading of *Kampfflugzeug* covers a wide variety of aircraft and roles, differentiated by purpose and mission, as follows:

Purpose:
Medium bomber, long-range bomber, torpedo-bomber, mine-layer, pathfinder/target illuminator, balloon destroyer, glider tug, "Mistel" aircraft, transport aircraft, aircraft for dropping of parachute troops and agents, search aircraft, courier and weather reconnaissance aircraft.

Role:
Bomber *Geschwader* (KG), bomber *Gruppe* (KGr), bomber replacement training *Gruppe* (EKGr), special purpose bomber *Gruppe* (KGr.z.b.V.), train-busting units (Eis), coastal aviation *Gruppen* (Kü.Fl.Gr.), transport *Geschwader* (TG), glider tug *Gruppen*, weather reconnaissance *Staffeln* (Westa, Wekusta), bomber schools, central bomber schools, Luftdienstkommando (LD), courier *Staffel*, air communications *Gruppe*.

Legends about German Bomber Development

Even today, in literature and verbal commentaries, one can find statements about the *Luftwaffe*'s equipment that are wrong, either due to a lack of knowledge or intentionally false statements. Now, thanks to extensive documentations by K.H. Köllner of the Military History research Institute in Freiburg, we can attempt to briefly illuminate and clarify the "ifs and buts" of several legends.

1. It is false to claim that the creation of a strategic bomber fleet died with the tragic death of *General* Wever, head of the *Luftkommandoamt* (general staff), on 3 June 1936.

It is correct that:

The prototypes of the four-engined Do 19 and Ju 89 bombers were incapable, particularly with respect to engine performance, of meeting the military requirements for the conduct of an operative to say nothing of strategic air war, even by the standards of the day. There were no engines capable of providing these heavy aircraft with sufficient power.

Göring ordered development halted on 29 April 1937. The three Do 19 prototypes were scrapped, while a civilian version of the Ju 89, the Ju 90, was developed and saw service with *Deutsche Lufthansa.*

In autumn 1936 the General Staff called for the development of another heavy bomber type (later dubbed the "Ural bomber"). The contract was given to the respected Heinkel company.

The He 177 "*Greif*" (Griffin), as the type was named, was conceived as a four-engined long-range reconnaissance aircraft and bomber. Its novel feature and at the same time its Achilles heel was its system of power plants, in which paired engines each powered a single large propeller. These power plants were not entire reliable and tended to overheat, resulting in fires. The further insane requirement for dive-bombing capability doomed this large, heavy bomber to mediocrity and its operational career was less than successful.

Vast quantities of valuable materials, hard-to-get parts and production capacity flowed into this project, diverting them from much-needed fighter and medium bomber production.

Given the constant shortages of raw materials and especially the chronic fuel shortage that existed during and even before the war, the requested production figures could only have been achieved at the cost of other aircraft types and classes of armaments.

The *Luftwaffe* chose the second-best solution, the construction of a large fleet of medium bombers with the best possible range.

2. It is false to claim that Udet introduced the dive-bombing method to the *Luftwaffe*:

It is correct that:

When the secret "Stahr Flying School" at the Lipetsk airfield in Russia began operations (in 1925), dive-bombing was already part of the tactical training program. It was not by chance that the experiences of the infantry and close-support units of the First World War were evaluated.

Dive-bombing increased the chances of scoring a hit as it was possible to bomb more accurately in this way than from horizontal flight with the bombsights of that era.

Orders for the formation of a dive-bombing unit were issued on 12 October 1933, just prior to the secret expansion of the *Luftwaffe*, even before Udet joined the service (Reichswehr). Udet later promoted the "dive-bombing idea" base don his own experience, perhaps too much (see the fiasco with the He 177).

3. It is also false to claim that von Richthofen (head of the Technical Office's development department) ordered development of the Junkers Ju 87 Stuka halted in June 1936.

It is correct, however, that:

Only the head of the Technical Office (Udet) could have brought this about.

The Heinkel He 50 and Henschel Hs 123 were ill suited to the dive-bombing role. Benefiting from its experience with the K 47, Junkers designed the Ju 87, a robust dive-bomber, which in December 1936 entered service with the "Legion Condor" and proved itself in action in Spain. It is unlikely that von Richthofen had such a change of heart within the space of just five months. Rather his directive for the continued development of the Ju 87 was misinterpreted – and eagerly circulated.

The Bow Was Overdrawn

The *Luftwaffe* was simply overextended in terms of personnel and materiel by the political leadership's demand that it achieve full war readiness in just six years. The bow was overdrawn.

Shortcomings, weaknesses, defeats and failures by the *Luftwaffe* in the Second World War can be explained by the mistakes, inconsistencies and failures of the short expansion period. For the most part, improvisation – combined with conjurer mentality in many circles of the National-Socialist leadership – took the place of leadership skill during the war. The resulting cost was high, and not just among the flying personnel.

A strategic bombing campaign against the sources of power in England and Russia was beyond the *Luftwaffe*'s ability, as it lacked usable four-engined bombers. The *Luftwaffe* was forced to commit its twin-engined medium bombers at all the critical spots in the front, especially in the east, and they suffered heavy losses in operations near the fronts. The bombers nevertheless made a significant contribution to the success of the blitzkrieg campaigns.

The strategic concept was consciously absent from the air force manual of 1936 (LDv 16), as there was no political directive for it. The operative *Luftwaffe* was condemned to operative tactics – direct and indirect support of the army. Or were the effects of the directive issued by the head of the *Reichswehr*'s army command of 24 February 1932 still being felt?

It stated in part:

> *"The air forces and air defense forces are support weapons for the army and navy. Their combat operations are an integral part of the land or sea war. This does not exclude the air force bombing units from being used in combined operations if the situation requires."*

Creation of a Kampfgeschwader

Even though the *Reichswehr*'s budget lacked funds for the training of a cadre for future bomber units, apart from a few observers, in Lipetsk, Russia, a change did come about in October 1933 when orders were issued for the creation of the "Deutsche Lufthansa Transport Inspectorate," the cover designation for a so-called "interim bomber wing" which was to use converted Lufthansa aircraft in the event of mobilization as well as its personnel and equipment.

As future bomber crews, the members of this interim bomber wing were trained in long-range navigation, instrument and night flying. Operating by night, they flew along special "RB (German State Railway) routes."

Soldiers who in 1936 left the *Reichswehr*, often under curious circumstances, and came under the State Minister of Aviation formed the core of the future *Luftwaffe*'s personnel. Their departure was a mere formality. For reasons of secrecy, in addition to the suffix "*a.D.*" (retired) after their rank, they were incorporated into the German Air Sports Association (DLV, a cover designation for the air force) with a corresponding rank.

Comparison of Army and DLV Ranks

Generalleutnant	*DLV-Fliegerchef*
Generalmajor	*DLV-Fliegervizechef*
Oberst	*DLV-Flieger-Kommodore*
Oberstleutnant	*DLV-Fliegervizekommodore*
Major	*DLV-Fliegerkommandant*
Hauptmann	*DLV-Flieger-Kapitän*
Oberleutnant	*DLV-Schwarmführer*
Leutnant	*DLV-Kettenführer*
Oberfeldwebel	*DLV-Obermeister*
Feldwebel	*DLV-Meister*
Unteroffizier	*DLV-Flugführer (Oberwart, Bordfunker)*
Gefreiter	*DLV-Hilfsflugzeugführer*
(Ober)Flieger	*DLV-(Ober)Flieger*

With its modern cut, the blue-grey (airman's blue) uniform was similar to the later *Luftwaffe* uniform, a similar version of which is worn by members of the Bundeswehr-*Luftwaffe* today.

In matters relating to personnel and discipline, the "former" soldiers were still guided by the current *Reichswehr* manuals. The Do 11 and Ju 52/3mg3e (with retractable "dustbin" ventral turret) interim bombers were envisaged or introduced as equipment for the interim bomber wing in 1933, however they were ill-equipped in terms of radios and other equipment.

The formation of six *Luftkreiskommandos* (air force district commands, cover name: Senior Air Offices) was ordered on 1 April to provide territorial *Luftwaffe* command authorities:

Luftkreiskommando I	Königsberg
Luftkreiskommando II	Berlin
Luftkreiskommando III	Dresden
Luftkreiskommando IV	Münster
Luftkreiskommandos V	Munich
Luftkreiskommando VI (See)	Kiel

As Commander of Army Aviation, *Oberst* Sperrle (later air fleet commander) commanded all land-based aviation units then available (including KG 154 *"Fliegergruppe Faßberg"* and KG 252 *"Fliegergruppe Tutow,"* each with two to three *Staffeln*).

Thanks to the general enthusiasm for air sports, in 1934 powered- and glider-flying groups were formed in many places in Germany, much to the joy of the country's youth. As

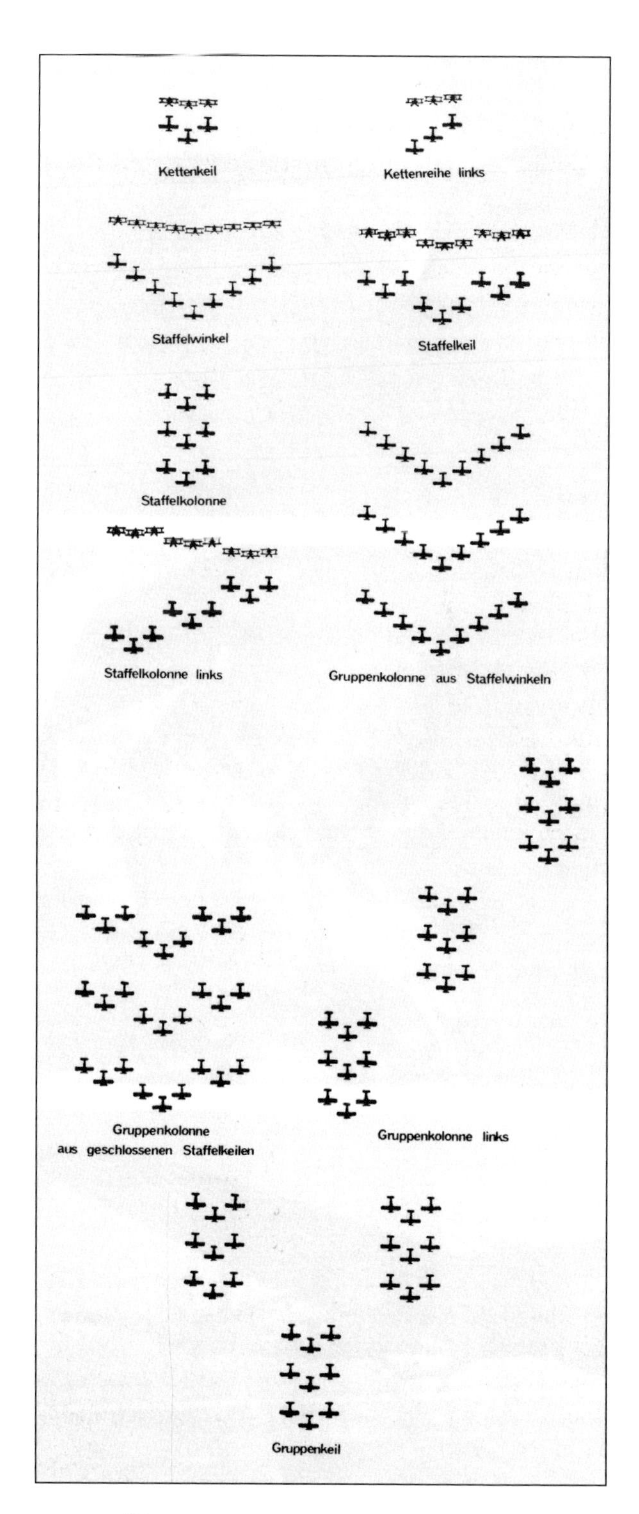

The types of formations used at the beginning of the war.

at all times, this group of sports lacked the necessary funding. The Reich provided financial, material and organizational assistance as best it could and with purposeful farsightedness with respect to military plans. The German Air Sports Association with its installations used the opportunity and, as a welcome cover institution, it offered a basis for expansion of the *Luftwaffe*.

Sport flying airfields were built, including some in central Germany, and in most cases their dimensions were in fact too large for small sporting aircraft. "Sports airfields" were also established in Merseburg, Finsterwalde and Altenburg. They were built to the latest standards, with large hangars and spacious quarters. The "High-Altitude Flight Center of the German Weather Service," in reality a bomber school, was created in Lager-Lechfeld south of Augsburg. The "Hanseatic Flying School Registered Association" was created in the Luneburg Heath as KG 154 Fassberg, and the "Radio Direction Finder Research Institute of the Reich Association of the Electronics Industry" as KG 252 Tutow south of Greifswald, the "Forestry and Agricultural Flight Research Institute" as Bomber School Prenzlau southeast of Neubrandenburg, along with other similar government installations with innocuous designations.

The *Geschwader* and *Staffel* numbers were only used in internal *Luftwaffe* correspondence as "Secret Command Matters" (the highest secrecy level). Their three-digit numbers were supposed to disguise the unit designation, which was only partly successful. Brief explanations of these appear chronologically in the appendix.

The Air Force Is Revealed

The *Luftwaffe* was officially revealed to the world on 1 March 1935, even before the introduction of compulsory military service (21 May 1935). Its activities could no longer be concealed in any case – even to the outside world.

On the air sport uniforms the shoulder boards and patches were replaced by those of the *Reichsheer*. The "flying badge" became the *Luftwaffe*'s nationality emblem on uniforms and standards. Branch-of-service colors were introduced on collar patches:

white	*generals*
black	*State Aviation Ministry (RLM) and attached units*
crimson	*general staff*
gold-yellow	*aviation units*
bright red	*flak artillery*
gold/pale brown	*signals troops*
dark blue	*medical personnel*
dark green	*nautical corps and officials*
pale green	*air surveillance/air police*
pink	*engineer corps*

Airmen from the First World War and crews of *Deutsche Lufthansa* formed the core of the new air force. Other personnel for the new service came from units of the *Reichswehr*, the state police and from the powered- and glider groups of the DLV.

The primordial cell of our *Geschwader* was the "*Kampfregiment Merseburg*" (first mentioned on 1 October 1935) with the Merseburg and Finsterwalde "*Geschwader*" (RLM order for the third formation phase 1936 of 25 May 1934; at that time *Geschwader* still had battalion status and after the *Luftwaffe* was unveiled in spring 1935 was equivalent to a *Kampffliegergruppe*).

On 28 March 1935 the RLM issued orders for the formation of several units on 1 April 1935, including:

Kampfgeschwader* (553) Merseburg
Kampfgeschwader* (652) Finsterwalde
*Temporary numbers only with Table of Organization No.162 (Fl) for the headquarters and No. 163 (Fl) for the flying Kampfstaffeln, equipped with Ju 52s.

For reasons of secrecy, the *Geschwader* numbers continued to be withheld and the units were only referred to by "*Fliegergruppe*" with location, as in "*Fliegergruppe Merseburg*."

The *Geschwader* commanders were directly subordinate to the air district senior air commander.

In terms of organization, a regiment was equivalent to a *Geschwader* with three *Gruppen*; a battalion a *Gruppe* with three *Staffeln*; and a company a *Staffel* with three *Ketten* each with three aircraft.

New Geschwader Are Created by "Cell-Division"

1936 went down in *Luftwaffe* history as the year of cell division. The "mother units" had to form their "daughter units" by 1 April 1936. This questionable procedure of "making two from one" saw one bomber *Staffel* (48 aircrews, as per table of organization) become two new ones. Headquarters followed a similar procedure.

Table of organization for a *Kampfstaffel* including reserve on 1 April 1936:

12 pilots	(3 officers, 9 NCOs)
12 observers	(9 officers, 3 NCOs)
12 radio operators	
12 flight engineers/gunners	
48 men	

The mother *Staffel* had to divide itself into two parts, as follows:

1st Part	*2nd Part*
6 pilots	6 pilots
(2 officers, 4 NCOs)	(1 officer, 5 NCOs)
6 observers	6 observers
(4 officers, 2 NCOs)	(5 officers, 1 NCO)
6 radio operators	6 radio operators
6 flight engineers/gunners	6 flight engineers/gunners
24 men	**24 men**

To avoid personnel manipulation (the good stay, the bad go), the air district command or, at his direction, the senior air commander, decided which part was to be sent to the new location and which would remain at the old. No consideration was given to families. The objective was to ensure that all units received roughly the same complement of personnel, which later proved correct thing to do.

Chapter 2
Peacetime and Expansion

Merseburg

On 12 October 1935 the newspaper *Merseburger Zeitung* reported the official welcoming of the Merseburg air garrison with its first commanding officer *Major* Schwabedissen.

As told by Herbert Meyer, at that time a variety of aircraft types were flown, including the Junkers W 34, Ju 52, Ju 86 and Dornier Do 23. Among the pilots he knew were Ruthmann, Vohs, von Lösch, Diekötter, Katzberg, Schlüter, von Schroetter, Schmidt, Grunewald and Weiner.

On 1 April 1936 the units of *Kampfgeschwader 153* were based as follows:

Geschwaderstab and *I. Gruppe* in Merseburg (emblem: Thieving Magpie)

II. Gruppe in Finsterwalde and the newly formed *III. Gruppe* in Altenburg (emblem: Altenburg Playing Card). From this *Gruppe* the *7.*, *8.* and *9. Staffel* of KG 3 were formed by cell division.

By June 1936, in addition to the aircraft already mentioned, each of the *Kampfgruppen* also received 27 Ju 52 bombers.

After receipt of these aircraft, the parade square drill that had been standard dwindled and intensive specialized training was begun in all areas. The individual *Staffeln* and *Gruppen* were quickly brought up to strength with young troops who had already completed several months of their service commitment. Uniforms of every branch of the *Wehrmacht* were represented at the air bases until all personnel had been issued their kit.

Observer Turich described in detail the training in Merseburg. Between 13 December 1935 and 4 February 1936, there was probably no German airfield or landing strip that was not visited by the "Merseburgers" in their Ju 52s, Do 23s and W 34s (aircraft code number 32 and civilian registrations). They also flew circuits and carried out navigation, cross-country and gunnery flights. Situated beside the warm waters of the Baltic Sea, Stolp and Kolberg were popular weekend destinations because of their friendly populations and even friendlier girls. Of course these visits were made as part of the flying training program or sporting activities.

Early Casualties

For many reasons, the ambitious training program came at a high cost. From June to December 1935 the *Luftwaffe* experienced an average of 48 aircraft crashes per month, 12 of them fatal! Half of these accidents were the result of a lack of flying discipline that was probably timeless. Breaches of flying orders, inadequate flight preparations, instrument and bad-weather flights despite the lack of specialized training, reckless aerobatic flight, and carelessness on the part of crews – especially pilots – during technical checks of the aircraft, which were often not easy to handle (the terms "flying coffin" and "widow maker" have always been part of aviation slang) appeared regularly in the accident reports by *Oberstleutnant* Ritter von Greim, the Inspector for Flight Safety and Equipment (In S). He took over this less than enjoyable position on 4 February 1936. It was a crisis situation that threatened to seriously endanger the operational readiness of the units and supply system.

The hasty formation of five more *Kampfgeschwader* headquarters with eight *Gruppen* in 1935 probably did little to improve the flight safety situation.

Move to New Bases

At the end of 1936, rumors began to circulate that, after the cell division process, elements of *Kampfgeschwader 153* would soon be leaving their bases and moving to southern Germany. Such beautiful large cities as Nuremberg, Munich and Stuttgart were mentioned, but nobody believed it! Experience suggested that new air bases were usually situated far from large cities.

In November 1936 a crew flew their Ju 52 from Merseburg to Lechfeld. From there the men continued in a rickety old Hansa automobile through unfamiliar towns. They soon arrived at a, for the times, enormously large construction site.

Excavation pits, large, half-completed housing blocks and hangars, and a long, wide, firm and freshly laid-out field suggested that this was to be the site of a new air base. The images were familiar. Perhaps it was Memmingerberg, where the planning and grading work had begun in the summer of 1935, and where, as all over Germany, workers of all kinds labored day and night to literally create the air base from the ground up. Before their return flight the next day, the crew was advised to maintain the strictest silence. Maintaining secrecy was everything!

While the *Kampfgruppen* continued their usual varied training in Merseburg, Finsterwalde and Altenburg, companies with specialized personnel from all elements of the *Wehrmacht* were formed, which would later become airfield operating companies, headquarters companies and air base companies. Industry provided trained and capable specialists for employment in the maintenance facilities, administration, handcraft workshops and other important positions.

The veil of secrecy was finally lifted in 1937 and the existence of the new bases was revealed. The elements of KG 153 earmarked for the formation of the new *Geschwader* were transferred to southern Germany.

The *Geschwaderstab* and the *I. Gruppe* (Merseburg) were sent to Penzing near Landsberg. The *II. Gruppe* (Finsterwalde) would move to Leipheim near Ulm/Günzburg and the *III. Gruppe* (Altenburg) to Memmingerberg near Memmingen/Allgäu. Six months earlier, the *III. Gruppe* in Altenburg had been forced to send experienced cadre crews to the "Legion Condor" in Spain as part of "Air Exercise Rügen," something that was not seen as a beneficial to the training program.

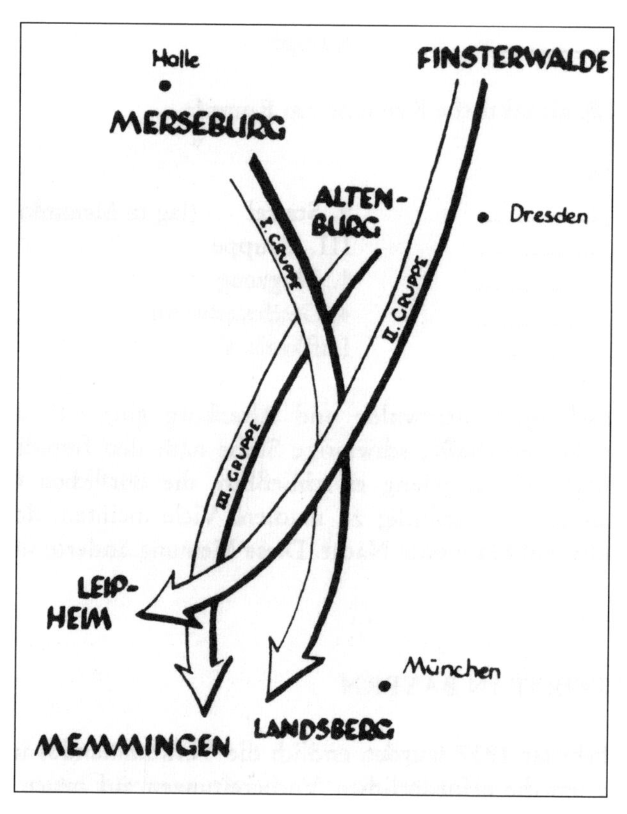

Transfer from Thuringia/Saxony to Bavaria, 1937.

In a short time, a new unit, I./KG 77, was formed at the old base in Merseburg.

While the exact timing of the transfers was not yet known, it was revealed that the new title of *Kampfgeschwader 255* "Alpine *Geschwader*" was to apply following arrival at the new base. The tactical code "54 +" soon dominated the skies over southern Germany. The numbers were simple codes that could be deciphered as follows:

KG 255
Air District V (Munich)
Code number 5 (for Kampfgeschwader)
2nd
Geschwader
Kampf (bomber)

or, for example, as a tactical code on the fuselage:

54 + A39

9. Staffel (based in Memmingerberg)
III. Gruppe
1st aircraft
4th *Geschwader* in Air District V

In Merseburg, Finsterwalde and Altenburg there began a feverish search for the unfamiliar locations on maps. The rural towns were finally located on ordnance maps. Many observed that they were miles from anywhere. This opinion soon changed, however.

Bases in Bavaria

Finally, in mid-February 1937, the advance parties were despatched to make preparations at the new bases, where the air base companies had already done good preliminary work. Such was the case in Landsberg under *Major* Völk and *Oberleutnant* Fath as detachment leaders and in Leipheim under *Gruppenkommandeur Oberstleutnant* Dr. Hans Fisser and his adjutants *Oberleutnant* von Schroetter and *Hauptmann* Brückner.

Kitchens, handcraft shops, administration and the all-important canteens were already hard at work, despite ongoing construction work on buildings and infrastructure.

The official transfer order was issued on 1 March 1937. The bulk of the unit arrived at its destination on 15 March after a four-hour train ride. On arrival at the new garrison, the airmen received a mixed welcome from the local populace. Some were friendly, others reserved. Each man got used to his new surroundings, which coon became a second home, and the hearty, friendly Swabian population. Even though none of the bases were completely finished, at least the clean, well-tended quarters, which fit comfortably into the style of the landscape, were quite to the taste of the enterprising soldiers. The landing fields were usable for limited flight operations, at least during dry periods. The *III. Gruppe* arrived in Memmingerberg on 7 March 1937.

When the *4. Staffel*, *5. Staffel* and the headquarters company under their commanders *Major* Petzold, *Hauptmann* Otto Pilger and *Hauptmann* Miczek arrived late in Leipheim, the place no longer looked quite as desolate.

The cooks were excellent, but their dishes were not to everyone's taste. The duty officers made simple entries in the mess logs, such as:

"Food sweet enough," "food very good and plentiful; but can the cooks also prepare some northern German dishes." These entries did not go unnoticed. From then on, every Friday for lunch there was pumpkin with rice, and in the evening "beer radishes" with tea. Both were probably harvested at the railway embankment or on the landing field. The cursing that resulted probably needs no further explanation. The men got used to the new food and out of necessity learned to slice and salt the radishes before eating them.

Soon after establishing themselves at their new bases, the units resumed training with more vigor than before. Like the repair and servicing personnel, the aircrew could hardly complain about under-utilization.

New officers, recently promoted on 20 April 1937, joined the unit:

I. Gruppe (Landsberg) Oblt. Pflüger
Lt. Redenbacher †
Lt. Pfordte
Lt. Hauser, Hellmuth
Lt. Sommer, Joachim †
Lt. Klein, Richard
Lt. von Hippel, Eberhard
Lt. Sorg †
Lt. Baron von Dalwigk zu Lichtenfels, Egon

II. Gruppe (Leipheim) Lt. Joachim, Günther †
(later to KG 77) Lt. zu Nedden †
Lt. Liebler †
Lt. Jacobs, Rolf †
Lt. Lauth †

III. Gruppe (Memmingen) Lt. Wicke, Heinz †
Lt. Brandt, Kurt †
Lt. Jüsgen, Hans †
Lt. Rath, Wilhelm †
Lt. Ziegler, Kurt
Lt. Schnez, Viktor †
Lt. Müller, Gerhard
Lt. Simon, Erich †
Lt. Häberlich, Klaus
Lt. Küchle, Fritz †

Of these 24 officers from one age class, during the war 14 were lost in action (equal to 59%). Everyone was kept busy with instrument and DF homing flights, formation flights, night and low-level flights, especially the *5. Staffel* under *Hauptmann* von Greiff in Leipheim, plus overland flights to Tripoli and Rome (spaghetti at Alfredo's) with regular gunnery and bombing flights in every type of aircraft flown by the *Geschwader*, including the Do 17, Ar 66, Do 23, Ju 52, W 34 and Fw 58.

This led to races to see who would be the first to loop a Ju 52 or undertake a dive in the notorious Do 23 and survive.

The pride of the *Geschwader* was the Do 17 E (later M), or "Flying Pencil," then the fastest bomber aircraft in the world. Everyone wanted to fly the aircraft and experience its performance for himself.

The maintenance and repair personnel were familiarized with the various technical innovations. The remaining personnel on the bases – whether civilian or military – were also kept busy and stood ready to achieve the construction targets that had been set and achieve a high standard of operational readiness. Comradeship grew and everyone felt part of a team regardless of rank or whether he was a member of a *Staffel*, company, repair facility or administration office.

An expression took hold that would survive the war: "The individual is nothing – the team is everything!"

The sonorous drone of aircraft engines could be heard day and night. Low-level and transfer flights and practice moves to forward airfields demanded constant readiness from every member of the *Geschwader* in order to achieve maximum performance. Air gunnery and practice bombing were carried out in Unterschlauersbach, Achmer, Parow and Manching.

Flying his two-seat Arado Ar 66 accompanied by his observer Turich, the first *Geschwaderkommodore*, *Oberstleutnant* Spang (1/3/37 – 15/11/38), one of the "old eagles," scouted 21 airfields in southern Germany in two days. He did so in order to have sufficient alternate and forward airfields for his large unit, which had almost 120 aircraft, in the event of mobilization.

On 25 May 1937, he took off from Landsberg at 04:55. After stops in Bad Aibling, Fürstenfeldbruck, Memmingen, Leipheim, Giebelstadt, Würzburg, Schweinfurt, Kitzingen, Illesheim, Fürth and Ansbach, he landed in Ainring at 15:16. The next morning he took off again at 07:34 and flew via Friedrichshafen, Freiburg, Karlsruhe, Herzogenaurach, Böblingen, Ansbach, Neuburg, Schleißheim and Neubiberg, arriving back in Landsberg, his headquarters' and *Geschwader*'s home base, at 18:49.

Soon the *Geschwader*'s *Ketten*, *Schwärme* and *Staffeln* began landing at all these airfields to familiarize themselves with them. The crews flew to bases scattered to the four winds, stayed there temporarily and of course, in the nature of all soldiers, explored the surrounding areas.

On 1 July 1937, the *6. Staffel* was formed in Leipheim under its commander *Oberleutnant* von Schroetter. Towards the end of the year a reorganization of the bomber units was carried out, in which the flying *Staffeln* were reduced in size and the airfield operating companies were created, in part from personnel from the headquarters companies.

First Operations

By then the *Luftwaffe* had a total of eleven *Kampfgeschwader* headquarters with 30 bomber *Gruppen* each with three *Staffeln*. During "Case Otto," the incorporation of Austria into the Reich on 12 March 1938, the *Geschwader* received its first mobilization order and had to carry out "paper flights" (leaflets on Vienna instead of bombs). This was a common practice at the time as a demonstration of air power intended to exert pressure on the powerless political leadership and population of a country. It is a demonstration of power that is still occasionally used today.

The *Luftwaffe*'s Inspector of Bombers (*Luftwaffe* Inspectorate 2) assumed responsibility for caring for and supervising all bomber and dive-bomber units on 12 July 1938. He was technically responsible for the bomber schools, the air weapons schools (E), the navigation school in Anklam, and the overall navigational and bombing training of the air force with the goal of achieving a uniform level of training of the flying and participating ground personnel. After Austria became part of the German Reich, the crews of the *Geschwader* finally had a legal opportunity to admire the Alpine peaks between Innsbruck and Graz, which until then had been images on the frosty horizon, and experienced mountain flying.

Preparations for the big autumn maneuvers in 1938 demanded the utmost of the flying and technical personnel.

Generalmajor Hugo Sperrle, the commanding general and commander of *Luftwaffe* Group Command 3 in Munich, had made a name for himself in Spain and later continued his association with the *Geschwader*, commanding the air fleet to which it was attached.

The *Geschwader* had the opportunity to demonstrate its flying discipline and its skills in navigation and formation flying on 12 September 1938, when a massed formation of the unit's Do 17s flew low over the grounds of the Reich Party Congress at Dutzendteich near Nuremberg, to the astonishment and enthusiasm of the Germans and also the critical foreign observers.

The Commander-in-Chief of the *Luftwaffe* expressed his appreciation and awarded field emblems, plants of the Alpine flora, to the *Gruppen* of the fastest *Kampfgeschwader* in the *Luftwaffe*, KG 255 "Alpine *Geschwader*":

I. Gruppe	Alpine Rose
II. Gruppe	Gentian
III. Gruppe	Edelweiss

These emblems marked the aircraft of each *Gruppe* when they began their return flights and soon became well known throughout Germany. The shield on the staff of the *Geschwader* flag bore the inscription:

"Your life is bound to the life of your people."

Oberst Wolfgang von Stutterheim, one of the bravest officers of the *Garde du Corps* and a wearer of the *Pour le Mérite* from the First World War, assumed command of the *II. Gruppe*, replacing Dr. Fisser, who was promoted to *Oberst* and became *Geschwader*kommodore (Feb. 1939 – 26/3/1940). He replaced the unit's second *Kommodore*, *Oberst* Ritter von Lex (16/11/1938 – Feb. 1939). *Oberst* von Stutterheim went on to command III./KG 77 – which was created from II./KG 55 – during the Polish Campaign.

Following the measures contained in "Plan Study Green," on receipt of the coded signal "*Geschwader* Day, day, time," the *Geschwader* moved to airfields near the border. On 10 October 1938 the codeword "*Sternflug*" (rally) was received, and the *Geschwader* flew missions over Czechoslovakia as part of the annexation of the Sudetenland. Here, too, leaflets were dropped instead of bombs.

Afterwards *Major i.G.* Korte took over the *I. Gruppe* from *Oberstleutnant* Mälzer. As the pattern unit for the *Luftwaffe*, the *Gruppe* carried out special missions, entraining and movement practice for the newly created airfield operating companies. Airfield operating company commander *Oberleutnant* Fritz Uhl received praise for his efforts.

At 15:25 on 8 March 1939, the crew of a Ju 52 with the code 54 + 25 took off from Frankfurt/Rhein-Main airport on a training flight with seven radio operators on board, bound for Landsberg. It was a beautiful, cool spring day with only a few harmless cumulus clouds in the sky. After the Danube appeared "somewhere," the aircraft encountered a few snow showers. This did not cause the crew any problems until contradictory radio bearings from Stuttgart and Munich caused the instructor radio operator Puls to become unsettled and instantly wide awake. Munich reported that they were in the Linz area, or east of Munich, while Stuttgart radioed that they were south of the airfield at an undetermined distance. It was thus a typical flying mishap that always happened when a pilot followed a familiar "oil slick" back to home base without paying too much attention to navigation.

To cut a long story short: they suddenly found themselves in the Inn Valley, flying between high mountains and low-lying clouds. The faithful old Ju shook heavily as it encountered increasingly heavy icing. By then the aircraft's position had been worked out. It only had to clear one more peak, dusk was coming, and everyone believed they would soon reach the fields of home.

At 17:25 the winter stillness on the Hochmiesing in the Rotwand Mountains was suddenly shattered by the crash of the completely iced-up Ju 52. The engines separated from the airframe and tumbled down the steep slope, while the crew, some of them badly injured, only succeeded in freeing themselves from the deep show with swimming motions. Thanks to the alertness of *Wehrmacht* personnel in a nearby mountain hut, all were rescued that evening. Unfortunately a young radio operator later died of severe internal injuries.

On 1 May 1939 the *Geschwader* was diminished by yet another "cell division." The *II. Gruppe* "Gentian" in Leipzig was taken from the unit, disbanded and sent to Königgratz, in order to become the *III. Gruppe* of the future Kampfgeschwader 77. In Königgratz the *Gruppe* was surprised by mobilization and subsequently played a full part in the Polish Campaign.

From 15 to 25 May 1939, I./KG 255 took part in a major exercise from the operational base in Bad Wörishofen. The spa town, which relied on tourism, provided a pleasant diversion for everyone. It was pleasant to occasionally get away from the austere barracks. Everyone was astonished when, on 1 May 1939, new *Geschwader* designations were assigned, "en bloc," to the existing air fleets. The aircraft had to be repainted.

The *Geschwader* assignments:

Luftflotte 1 *Geschwader* Nos. 1 - 25
Luftflotte 2 *Geschwader* Nos. 26 - 50
Luftflotte 3 *Geschwader* Nos. 51 - 75
Luftflotte 4 *Geschwader* Nos. 76 - 100

The renamed *Geschwader* headquarters were KG 1 "*Hindenburg*," 2, 3, 4 "*General Wever*," 26, 27 "*Boelcke*" 51, 53 "*Legion Condor*," 54, 55, 76 and 77. The headquarters of Lehrgeschwader 1 also counted as a Kampfgeschwader headquarters. Among these 13 *Geschwader* headquarters, to each of which was attached a permanent Headquarters *Staffel*, there were 30 *Kampfgruppen* with a total of 90 *Kampfstaffeln*.

They were:

Location	**New Title**	**Name**	**Old Designation of Parent Unit**
Neubrandenburg Kolberg	I./KG 1	"Hindenburg"	IV./KG 152
Sprottau/Liegnitz	I./KG 2	"Holzhammer"	II./KG 252
Liegnitz	II./KG 2		II./KG 252
Elbing/Heiligenbeil	II./KG 3	"Blitz"	II./KG 153
Heiligenbeil	III./KG 3		III./KG 153
Gotha	I./KG 4	"General Wever"	I./KG 253
Erfurt	II./KG 4		II./KG 253
Nordhausen	III./KG 4		III./KG 253
Lübeck-Blankensee	I./KG 26	"Löwen"	I./KG 257
Lüneburg	II./KG 26		II./KG 257
Hanover-Langenhagen	I./KG 27	"Boelcke"	I./KG 157
Wunstorf	II./KG 27		II./KG 157
Delmenhorst	III./KG 27		III./KG 157
Gütersloh	II./KG 28		III./KG 254
Landsberg	I./KG 51	"Alpengeschwader"	I./KG 153/255
Memmingen	III./KG 51		III./KG 153/255
Ansbach	I./KG 53	"Legion Condor"	I./KG 355
Schwäbisch Hall	II./KG 53		II./KG 355
Giebelstadt	III./KG 53		III./KG 355
Fritzlar	I./KG 154	"Totenkopf"	I./KG 254
Langendiebach	I./KG 55	"Greifen"	I./KG 155
Gießen	II./KG 55		II./KG 155
Wiener-Neustadt	I./KG 76		I./KG 158
Wels	III./KG 76		III./KG 158
Prague-Kbely	I./KG 77		I./KG 153
Brünn	II./KG 77		II./KG 158
Königgratz/Olmütz	III./KG 77		II./KG 255
Schwerin	II./LG 1		II./LG 1
Greifswald	III./LG 1		III./LG 1
Neubrandenburg	I./LG 3		I./KG 152

As one can see, the *Gruppen* were divided almost equally among the air fleets. Not long afterwards, on 1 August 1939, the unit received another surprise during the quiet period that typically precedes a major storm. The "Alpine *Geschwader*" was unexpectedly forced to give up its Do 17s, of which it had become fond, and reequip on the He 111 at short notice and as quickly as possible. This rapid conversion within just two weeks (15 to 30 August 1939 I./KG 51 in Landsberg, III./KG 51 in Memmingen) placed great demands on the personnel of the entire *Geschwader*, especially the flying and technical personnel. The conversion program also included leaflet missions over the Dijon area of France after the outbreak of war, which provided something of a thrill. When mobilization came, the *I. Gruppe* was again at *Luftflotte 3*'s disposal with 36 crews fully operational on the He 111. Everyone in the area of the *5. Fliegerdivision* Munich under *Generalmajor* Ritter von Greim asked the same question: "Why the rush?" The answer came in that same month of August 1939, on the day of mobilization for the attack on Poland, which began the Second World War, as we now know. No one dared think about the terrible consequences that this decision would later bring.

On that fateful day the title KG 255 "*Alpengeschwader*" with the tactical code "54 +" was finally struck off and changed to KG 51 "Edelweiss" with the code "9K +." The emblem of the *III. Gruppe* in Memmingen was thus the shared *Geschwader* emblem, which the units would employ throughout the entire war in almost every theater and which gave it its generally used name of "Edelweiss *Geschwader*."

The Black Day of Neuhausen ob Eck

It was blistering hot at the remote frontline base in Neuhausen near Tuttlingen, where the *III. Gruppe*'s *9. Staffel* was stationed with the 3rd Platoon of the 7th Airfield Operating Company, on 27 September 1939. A loading exercise was supposed to take place during the afternoon. At 14:00, twenty 50-kg bombs with *Zünder 15* fuses stockpiled beside the field were loaded onto a truck and carefully driven to aircraft 9K + LT. The helpers were especially careful when handling the bombs. They were not particularly familiar with them and surely had a typical unwell feeling in their bellies. The words "fuse unusable" were printed in chalk on the tail of one of the bombs. In addition to the twenty bombs for aircraft 9K + FT, which was parked about 120 meters away, on its next trip the truck also brought a 21st, which a man then carried to 9K + LT.

Upset, the man in charge of the ammunition, *Obergefreiter* Kropp, arrived on a bicycle and said: "Where are the four bombs with the unusable fuses?" He wanted to stop them from being put in the aircraft. As they weren't with 9K + FT, they could only be with 9K + LT. The truck followed. They found the bombs, shouldered them and placed them on the bed of the truck. When the third bomb was tossed onto the bed it exploded with an ear-shattering bang. It was exactly 14:30.

At that moment *Obergefreiter* Schaale of the *9. Staffel* was checking the two automatic bomb dropping systems (RAB), while *Unteroffizier* Held was lubricating 9K + LT's locking plates. In addition to them, men of the airfield operating company were also killed or wounded. The port fuel tank was struck by fragments. The escaping fuel immediately caused the aircraft to catch fire and it was completely destroyed.

Alerted by the explosion and the cloud of black smoke in the sky, men from every unit rushed to the scene and tried to save what they could, risking their lives in doing so. Pilots and mechanics pushed nearby machines to safety. *Hauptmann* Brandt, the *Staffelkapitän*, called the men back, because the extreme heat made extinguishing the fire impossible and there was still danger of further explosions.

At 15:00, seventeen more bombs detonated at short intervals, causing further devastation. All bombs in Neuhausen, Memmingen, Baltringen and Landsberg were immediately checked and some were found to be defective. They lacked the fuse retaining screws or the springs of the fuse contact rods were weak or corroded.

The first wartime casualties in home fields hit the unit hard. Killed that day were:

Oberfeldwebel Schaale	9. Staffel
Unteroffizier Wittmer	7th AOC
Unteroffizier Albrecht	7th AOC
Unteroffizier Hering	7th AOC
Gefreiter Reichel	7th AOC
Gefreiter Fischer	7th AOC
Flieger Bergmann	7th AOC
Flieger Schwitz	7th AOC
Flieger Grünsch	7th AOC
Flieger Hank	7th AOC
Obergefreiter Kropp	Air Base Company (E) Neuhausen o.E.

Chapter 3

The Air War in the West and over England

Sitzkrieg

At the western end of the Memmingerberg airfield there was a small wood surrounding a grey water tower. It seemed that nature had placed it in the most inappropriate location, regardless of any aviation requirements. No one could suspect that, to many returning from long-distance flights or combat missions, the Memmingerberg would later become a welcome signal that they were home again. During night flying operations, however, the airmen on watch beside the takeoff flag were often horrified to see the navigation lights of "birds" turning onto finals disappear into the depression that extended west towards Freien and the city of Memmingen as they approached to land. This same phenomenon can still be seen today with modern jet fighter-bombers.

We had come from the excellent air base in Altenburg, whose buildings blended so harmoniously into the gently rising slope of the Leina Forest. It is no wonder, therefore, that we regarded the confusion of the Memmingerberg construction site with a certain degree of skepticism. But our wandering and searching eyes were soon reconciled. Here the many distinctive spires of the free Reich city rose from the valley, there the Ottobeuren abbey peered over a nearby small wood near the village of Hawangen, a variety of fresh greenery stretched uphill to the silhouette of the mountains, which many had never seen before. All in all, it seemed a good place to pitch our tents. In scarcely two years one of the loveliest air bases anywhere was created there; who didn't think his air base the best! It's said to be the same today. Among the quarters and hangars, trees and shrubs found good soil in which to grow. Purely by chance, thanks to its enterprising designers the pond that provided water for the firefighters had the shape and dimensions of a large swimming pool, and on the sports field many football goalposts had fallen. Gatherings of airmen from northern areas and lovely maids from Memmingen at the church door and the registry office had long since ceased to be a novelty.

The crews had exploited the charming countryside from Säntis to the Salzburg area. The faithful and roomy Ju 52 with its retractable ventral observer's position had given way to the Do 17E "flying pencil." This was an aircraft that appealed to the hearts of the young airmen. Who can forget the exiting flight over Vienna to Innsbruck, when we came home on our last drops of fuel? Who can forget "air force day," when the population of the city and surrounding district came to the airfield, ducking as the formations flew low overhead, pressed to examine the aircraft on static display, paid 50 *Reichspfennigs* for a photograph in flying suit and parachute, and fell on their knees before the Fieseler *Storch* whose tailwheel had snagged the telephone line and associated apparatus when it took off. They were days filled with the joy of flying, even though we now and then had to provide a final escort for good comrades.

War Breaks Out

For many of us, the outbreak of war on 1 September 1939 came as a surprise. Despite the intensive preparations for war, most probably hoped that the *Luftwaffe* – because it was so potent – was there to guarantee the peace, as a sort of "fleet in being."

Then the mobilization schedule was taken from the safe and suddenly determined the starting point and schedule of all our actions.

As it did not take part in the fighting in Poland, for the *Geschwader* the first months of the war were filled mainly with practice wartime movements, bombing practice, camouflage and formation flying.

Our aircraft were extremely well concealed on the forward bases. On one occasion the commanding general, *Ritter* von Greim, abandoned plans to land at Neuhausen ob Eck because he thought that his transfer order had not been carried out. He had been unable to see the aircraft hidden in the forest.

The moves to and camouflage efforts at the previously selected operational airfields at Biberach, Bad Wörishofen, Reichenbach, Unterschlauersbach and Baltringen were intended to forestall French attacks on our peacetime bases. In Landsberg, for example, beautiful dark fir trees were painted on the hangar doors to simulate a forest. One evening a jokester painted a colorful, larger than life Red Riding Hood and wolf in one such "forest." This was much to the amusement of the surprised soldiers and to the dismay of the air district, which reacted sourly. The prankster was the *Kapitän* of the *7. Staffel*, *Hptm*. Joachim Poetter. The incident is now covered by the statute of limitations and may therefore be mentioned!

The missions flown by the *Geschwader* in this first phase of the war were somewhat unusual. They were the so-called "paper flights." Because of extreme meteorological conditions, one of these missions brought us valuable and sad experiences. The following account is by the *Staffelkapitän* of the *7. Staffel*, *Hptm*. Poetter:

KG 51's Propaganda Mission on 17 November 1939

In order to erode the French enemy's will to fight and to demonstrate the range and power of the German bombers, from time to time propaganda material was dropped over France, specifically during the period between the Polish Campaign and the start of our offensive in France on 10 May 1940. KG 51 was selected for this mission, because during the fighting in Poland it had been the sole bomber Geschwader to remain in the southwest of the Reich to defend against the western enemies.

In mid-November, the III. Gruppe was at the operational base in Bad Wörishofen. We had received a large quantity of propaganda material, which was supposed to be stacked for hanging in the bomb cells. After they were dropped, a small barometric fuse blew the packet retaining straps. The wind then carried the many thousands of leaflets over large areas of enemy territory. Among the leaflets were a series of tactful large postcards. Beneath a white central field that showed a dead French soldier hanging in barbed wire. Above the white field in large letters were the words: 'Où le Tommy est-il resté?' (Where was the Tommy?). If the whole thing was held up to the light, one could see in bright colors English soldiers amusing themselves with attractive nude French women. Of course these pictures were also very popular among our soldiers.

On 17 November 1939 the meteorologists forecast weather conditions that seemed eminently suitable for a long-range daylight propaganda mission. Twelve of the Geschwader's He 111s were sent. The target areas included Marseille, Bordeaux, Nantes and Brest.

From the 7. Staffel, Oblt. Oechsle took off for Marseille, and Oblt. Nölken and I headed for Bordeaux. Our planned flying altitude was 6,000-7,000 meters, above a solid cloud deck with a wind of about 70 kph from the west to northwest – at least that was the forecast.

Our machines took off at 08:25. We climbed through the cloud to 7,000 meters and, after overflying the radio beacon in the Black Forest, set course straight for Bordeaux. Soon afterwards I began having serious doubts about the accuracy of the back bearings. My observer Lt.d.R. Stärk was certainly not very happy that I didn't trust his bearings. Ultimately I found the bearings so absurd that, assuming that we were possibly sitting on an incredible 'Alpine effect,' I decided to rely on dead reckoning from then on.

After several hours the solid layer of cloud broke up. We then tried to orientate ourselves using features on the ground. But instead of seeing the sea ahead and to our right as expected, to our left we discovered the Golf du Lion, the Mediterranean. Over the coastal lake at Sête we were able to determine our exact position. An enormously strong wind must have blown us to the left, far off course. In view of the still uncertain wind conditions, our remaining fuel and the fact that Marseille was among our targets, I decided to drop the leaflets northwest of Marseille.

During the return flight we took bearings from the transmitter in Sotten in Switzerland and thus confirmed that an unusually strong wind had to be blowing from the northwest. With an excessive amount of crab – the nose of the aircraft was pointing roughly towards Paris – we headed north to avoid infringing on the Swiss border.

After some time I requested another bearing from Lt. Stärk but he didn't respond. I glanced to the side and saw that he was sitting half slumped over, his face blue. He was suffering from altitude sickness and would undoubtedly die if he did not get oxygen soon. (In fact the oxygen line had iced up.) At that time we didn't have much experience with high-altitude flight, but I knew that a rapid descent to an altitude of about 3000 meters was perhaps the only way to keep him from dying of altitude sickness. While I was not completely certain that we were not possibly over the Alps, I did feel a certain sense of security because of the huge wind correction angle towards the west we had been maintaining.

And so we began a steep descent into the clouds. Heavy propeller icing suddenly began shaking the machine, but at a height of 3,500 meters our 'patient' woke up. I maintained the same course for a while, all the while trying – vainly in my opinion – to obtain 'reasonable' bearings from Switzerland and the Black Forest. Finally, by now also concerned about our fuel state, I decided to acquire ground contact – cost what it may. A decision that, looking back, I would advise any instrument flyer against.

At 700 meters we sighted the ground from wisps of heavy rain clouds. I descended, followed railroad tracks, and on a station sign read the name Mirecourt. We located Mirecourt 60 km west of the Vosges. Heading east, we flew over the Vosges and the Black Forest and, after 6 hour and 50 minutes, landed back in Wörrishofen in clear skies. Soon afterward, Oblt. Nölken returned after more than 7 hours in the air, almost out of fuel. He had been the only one to reach Bordeaux and, though skeptical, had still relied on the bearings.

The evaluation of all of our flights led to the conclusion that, instead of the forecast 70 kph, the wind must have been out of the northwest at a speed of 210 to 230 kph.

Of the 12 aircraft that took off, almost all violated the Swiss or even the Italian border. One aircraft landed in Italy, another in Slovakia. The Staffelkapitän of the 8. Staffel, Hptm. Plischke, had crashed in the Alps on the Austrian-Italian border. His crew, including pilot Oblt. Henne, came down by parachute, some in Austria, some in Italy. Oblt. Oechsle had encountered such heavy turbulence over the Swiss Alps that his flight engineer sustained a serious head injury.

That the Mistral could produce such high wind speeds was largely unknown in our air force. I was subsequently sent to various bomber units to speak to the crews about the experiences of our flight. The two outstanding crews of my Staffel, Oblt. Nölken's and Oblt. Oechsle's, were later killed near Portsmouth and Odessa.

Conversion onto the Ju 88

In March 1940 the *I.* and *II. Gruppe* of our *Geschwader* – one of the most modern in the *Luftwaffe* – began converting onto the new Ju 88 bomber in Greifswald and Barth. Each *Staffel* spent approximately one week there becoming familiar with the new aircraft. The rest of the training was carried out at the units' own bases. The *III. Gruppe*, however, was forced to wait a while. Operational readiness would have suffered if the *Gruppen* had all been withdrawn to reequip simultaneously.

It was not unusual for three pilots to board one of the new Ju 88s without an observer, radio operator or gunner, in order to practice the new technique of dive-bombing. As the aircraft was extremely robust in order to withstand the g-forces encountered after pulling out of the dive, it was easily capable of aerobatics. Everyone tried his hand at loops, rolls, Immelmann turns and steep climbs, even though this was not strictly legal, which ultimately meant that the pilots were flying "indecently." But who worried about morale when seized by the urge to fly!

The rushed training on the sensitive "race horse" came at a cost. Pilots *Uffz.* Stretz, *Feldwebel* Bier and *Uffz.* Müller were killed during dive-bombing training at Lechfeld when their aircraft crashed near the church in Bobing.

Oberst Kammhuber was well aware of the difficulties involved in converting from the He 111 onto the Ju 88 when he arrived to take over as *Kommodore* on 27 March 1940. KG 30, the "Eagle *Geschwader*," which was primarily an anti-shipping unit, was then the only land-based unit equipped with the new and heavy dive-bomber. He quietly hoped that the *Geschwader* would have sufficient time to familiarize itself with the new machine before it had to undergo its baptism of fire at the front.

This hope was partially realized. The first new aircraft arrived at the beginning of April. The flights already equipped with Ju 88s had to move to airfields with longer runways and night lighting. The *Geschwaderstab* moved to Lechfeld, while the reformed *II. Gruppe* went to Fürstenfeldbruck. The units earmarked for night operations settled in Munich-Riem. The *1.* and *2. Staffel* of the *I. Gruppe* plus the *III. Gruppe*, with their veteran crews on the He 111 H, initially remained in Landsberg and Memmingen, while the three *Ketten* (Pflüger, Schallenberg, Graf) of the *3. Staffel* only completed their conversion training on the Ju 88 in Lechfeld at the end of May.

Events on the other Fronts

The *Geschwader* took no part in the campaigns in Poland and Norway. Events in those theaters will be described briefly for the sake of continuity and as a lead-up to events in the Balkans and Russia. Without a declaration of war, Germany invaded Poland at 04:45 on the foggy morning of 1 September 1939. The Second World War had begun.

Fifteen minutes before X-hour, *Oberleutnant* Bruno Dilley, *Kapitän* of the *3. Staffel* of *Stukageschwader 1*, led his *Kette* of Ju 87s in an attack on the bridges over the Vistula in Dirschau. German bombers flew deep into the Polish rear areas. Within days German fighters and destroyers achieved total air superiority over Poland.

Luftflotte 1 under *General der Flieger* Kesselring and *Luftflotte 4* under *Generaloberst* Löhr supported the divisions of the German 3rd and 4th Armies, which crushed all resistance on the ground.

Warsaw, the capital of Poland, capitulated on 27 September 1939 after massed air and ground attacks. One day later the fortress of Modlin fell during the final fighting east of the Vistula. Despite a heroic effort by the tough Polish Army, the last resistance was broken on 6 October after just five weeks of fighting.

Though technically inferior, until 16 September the crews of the Polish 1st, 3rd and 4th Air Regiments attacked German troops flying their obsolescent Potez 25 and P-37 aircraft.

"Cooperation" (direct and indirect support of the army by the *Luftwaffe*) contributed decisively to the rapid progress of the campaign. The enemy was crippled less by bombing raids on his production facilities and airfields than by the severing of his supply and transportation routes and lines of communication. With *short* supply lines to a *front*, the concept of a "lightning war" restricted in time and scope proved successful.

For the sake of completeness, it should be mentioned that Warsaw was not an open city and only capitulated after five demands to surrender and one massive air attack by 1,150 aircraft (25/9/1939).

The *Luftwaffe* lost a total of 78 combat aircraft and 734 personnel.

The fighting in Poland was followed by a long breathing space for the German military that lasted until the spring of 1940.

Only in the "wet triangle of the North Sea" did German bomber units began attacking warships in British ports and off the extended coast of eastern Great Britain.

The air battle over the German Bight took place shortly before Christmas 1939, on 18 December, when a formation of Wellington bombers conducted an armed reconnaissance mission to Wilhelmshaven.

In February 1940, from bases in the northwest of Germany and the North Friesian Islands, German bombers penetrated to the lair of the Home Fleet in Scapa Flow and the Firth of Forth (Scotland).

KG 26, the "Lion *Geschwader*," and KG 30, the "Eagle *Geschwader*," had the best-trained Ju 88 crews for these missions, which demonstrated to the British fleet that it was not invulnerable to attack.

Despite a claim to the contrary made in the *Wehrmacht* communiqué of 27 September 1939, the British aircraft carrier *Ark Royal* was not sunk by a 500-kg bomb. Despite his properly submitted negative reports, the pilot involved was immediately promoted from *Gefreiter* to *Leutnant*.

The Soviet-Finnish Winter War, which began on 30 November 1939, was ended by the Moscow peace treaty of 12 March 1940. Following this, the *Wehrmacht* High Command was unsettled by the Allies' aggressive political activities in Scandinavia.

On 28 March 1940 the supreme allied war council decided to mine Norwegian waters and land troops in Narvik, Trondheim, Bergen and Stavanger in order to gain control of the Swedish iron mines at Gallivăre.

Germany responded to this threatening development by forming the Special Staff "*Weserübung*" in Hamburg. The supreme command was aware that the occupation of key points in Denmark and Norway would decide the success or failure of the operation.

Early on the foggy morning of 9 April 1940, at the specified "Weser time 05:30," the first transport units under *Oberstleutnant* Baron von Gablenz, the "Air Transport Commander Land," who had a fleet of about 500 aircraft, took off.

On 3 April the ships of the German task force and the fleet under *Admiral* Günter Lütjens were already at sea, as was a fleet of British warships under Admiral Sir Charles Forbes.

Aided by hazy weather, all of the German units reached the Norwegian coast, however German troops encountered heavy resistance in Oslo, Stavanger and Bergen. Faced with the threat of bombing, Denmark surrendered without a fight.

The battle for the Oslo-Fornebu airport finally ended in the Germans' favor after heavy fighting in the air and on the ground. By the evening of that day Oslo was in German hands.

Initially delayed by weather, German paratroopers jumped over Stavanger-Sola, revealing for the first time the secret of the German parachute corps.

The Allies put their expeditionary corps ashore on either side of Trondheim and near Narvik. They were driven out of Trondheim, however. Only at Narvik did the fighting continue, with the German forces commanded by the popular mountain troop *General* Dietl. On 13 May 1940 ground contact was established to the Dietl group and the fighting at Narvik was brought to a successful conclusion.

The Norwegian forces surrendered on 10 June 1940. Prior to this, the British forces had embarked between 3 and 7 June. The British cabinet had decided to abandon the failed Norwegian operation.

These operations were completely overshadowed by the events of the early days of May 1940, when the whole world held its breath. The campaign in the west had begun.

The French Campaign

By 9 May 1940 crews of the *Geschwader* had already crossed the French border on hostile missions. Reconnaissance missions and "paper flights" (leaflet raids) to future combat zones such as Besançon, Luxeuil, Lure, Epinal, Bourges and even to Bordeaux and Marseilles enabled the crews to become familiar with operations over enemy territory under near wartime conditions. They also gave the crews practical experience in navigation and permitted them to become familiar with their new equipment. Most missions were flown at high altitude under cover of darkness or cloud.

On the evening of 6 November 1939, the *III. Gruppe* flew its first mission over France. The following crews took part:

He 111 9K + BD
Oberleutnant Schwegler, *Oberstleutnant* Stoeckl, *Oberfeldwebel* Lubrich, *Unteroffizier* Görres

He 111 9K + AT
Hauptmann Brandt, *Feldwebel* Müller, *Unteroffizier* Herrmann, *Unteroffizier* Müller.

Fourteen bundles of leaflets (600 kg) were dropped from a height of 4,000 meters over the Bourges – Monluçon – Râonne – Autun area. The crews encountered light and ineffective anti-aircraft fire. By the evening prior to the start of the new Blitz campaign, the crews of the *III. Gruppe* had flown just 18 sorties over France. Losses had been negligible. Despite the ongoing reequipment and training measures associated with the Ju 88, the *Geschwader* was probably prepared for its coming tasks in the west, although serviceability (He 111 – 63%, Ju 88 – 53%) was below the general level of the *Luftwaffe*. Operating two types of aircraft, 67 He 111s and 75 Ju 88s, a total of 142 machines, from five different bases (Landsberg, Bad Wörishofen, Lechfeld, Fürstenfeldbruck, Munich) was no easy task, especially with the small number of fully trained personnel at the unit's disposal.

On 17 April 1940, the *Geschwader* headquarters issued the "Order for the Start of the Defensive Battle." It consisted of ten closely spaced typewritten pages and was probably the first and last such extensive order issued by our *Geschwader* during the war; they still had time for such things then.

There were three possible operational plans, Cases A, B and C. Given the available information, it was likely that Case C would be carried out.

As all members of the *Geschwader* did not normally see such operational orders, which were issued by the operations officer (I a), extracts of the order issued by the *III. Gruppe* are published here for the first time:

KG 51 **Command post, 17/04/1940**
Section I a (Memmingen)

Gruppe order for the start of the defensive battle

1. Ground and air situation unchanged.
2. The German Armed Forces will repulse a Franco-British attack by counterattacking immediately.
3. Luftflotte 3 will support the army, concentrating its operations at the points of main effort.

Success depends on:
a) Preventing the Franco-British air forces from conducting systematic operations over our army,
and to this end the French air force is to be struck first.
b) Preventing the French and English from sending troops into northern France.

4. V. Fliegerkorps will commit the bulk of its forces in a first strike, without preparatory reconnaissance, to destroy a series of important French peacetime bases. Elements will be committed against enemy aircraft discovered on airfields (especially fighters).
5. Combat sectors: for KG 51:
Right border with KG 55: Dachau (55) – Laupheim (55) – Lahr (55) – Epinal (51) – Chatillon s.S. (55) – Clamency (55).
Left border: Reich border with Switzerland.
Depths: Aisy (30 km SW of Chatillon) – Beaune – Pologny – Monthe.
6. There are three different cases for the 1st mission:

a) Case A
Code word: "Express, Day, Time."
Simultaneous crossing of border by day, attacks partly against fortified positions, partly against airfields identified as occupied.
b) Case B
Code word: "Free to overfly western border."
As soon as the code word is received *Geschwader* will attack strongpoints immediately. If code word is received at night: dawn attack by first wave, followed immediately by daylight attack by a second wave.
c) Code word: "Execute Spessart Blue." Dawn attack by first wave against fixed strongpoints.

Simultaneous overflight of the border by the 2nd wave for daylight raid, partly against fixed strongpoints, partly against airfields identified as occupied.

7. The following additional three code words are applicable to all three cases:
a) "Practice Alert": This code word initiates preparations as per the *Gruppe* order of 6/2/40. The aircraft will be loaded as per directions for loading for practice alerts of 17/4/40.
b) "Stop Practice Alert": This code word means: There will be no attack, aircraft already in the air are to be recalled, all preparations are to be halted, the alert is over.
8. Reconnaissance: In addition to the special reconnaissance orders contained in the attack orders for Cases A, B and C, the following applies:
a) After the *Gruppe* returns from the first mission, one aircraft is to be assigned to maintain contact. Take off immediately if enemy bombers appear in greater strength than a flight of three.
b) In addition to their other duties, all crews flying with visual reference to the ground are to observe airfields, roads and rail lines on their route of flight for traffic and troop movements. Of particular importance during the first days of fighting are all transport movements towards the north from the Vosges area and the Dijon area.
c) Important information concerning occupied airfields, which represent a lucrative target for bombers, as well as fighter and balloon defenses, is to be reported by radio. Earliest report by radio during outbound flight about 60 min. after takeoff, after crossing the border. Radio reports by *Staffelkapitän* or *Kette* leader.
d) Immediately after landing, the observer (aircraft commander) is to personally report observations for lucrative targets for a bomber unit as per Para. C to the *Geschwader* commander. If he is not present, report shall be submitted by telephone directly to the *V. Fliegerkorps*.
   Subsequent immediately report to the *Gruppe* commander verbally or by telephone. In case of doubt, *Gruppe* commander will decide if an immediate report to superior offices is necessary.
9. Signals Orders: to be issued separately.
10. The commanders of remaining serviceable aircraft report to the adjutant.
11. The Staffel commanders are advised that, immediately after landing, they are to make a report to the *Kommandeur* (or in his absence the adjutant) concerning the conduct of the attack, quantity and type of bombs dropped, observations, special occurrences etc. If necessary, interim report by telephone pending return of all aircraft.
12. Preparations for next mission are to begin immediately after landing using all available resources. Fuel load 2,000 liters.
    Loading: per *Staffel* 1 a/c SC 10, 1 a/c B 1 El, rest SC 50. HQ and recon. a/c SD 50.
    If insufficient SD 50s are available, they are to be replaced by SC 50s.

Case C

Mission order: Dawn attack by 1st wave against strongpoints, simultaneous overflight of border by 2nd wave for daylight attack against airfields known to be occupied.

1. Code word: "Execute Spessart Blue"
   Attack order for the first wave.

Night flight by as many crews as possible, but only those that are night-qualified. Crossing of border with engines throttled back, dawn attack. It is vital to surprise and destroy the enemy.

2. Attack force:
   III./KG 51: Lyon-Bron (10318) 7 *Ketten*
   I./KG 51: Luxueil (10247) 2 *Ketten*
   Besançon le Valdahon (10260) 2 *Ketten*.
3. Alternate targets:

Every occupied airfield in the *Geschwader*'s area of operations, especially fighter fields. If necessary, decision by *Kette* leader as per previously arranged method. Specifically, the following airfields are worthy of consideration:

Amberien (10320)	7 hangars	Besançon (10259)	2 hangars
Bourg (10287)	4 hangars	Luxueil (10252)	3 hangars
Besançon (10260)	4 hangars		

The targets : Dijon – Longvic (10247)
Belfort – Chaux – Sermamagic (10255)

will be attacked by Ju 88s of I. and II./KG 51 after sunrise. To avoid interfering with or prematurely betraying this attack, it is not to be attacked by III./KG 51 as an alternate target.

4. Execution of the attack:
   a) All *Ketten* must drop their bombs between dawn and sunrise.

Kette or individual takeoff:	1st *Kette*	03:30	Landsberg
	2nd *Kette*	03:33	Landsberg
	3rd *Kette*	03:35	Landsberg
	4th *Kette*	03:42	Wörishofen
(Takeoff times will be ordered	5th *Kette*	03:44	Wörishofen
after receipt of the code word.)	6th *Kette*	03:46	Wörishofen
	7th *Kette*	03:48	Wörishofen

b) Formations: details of *Kette* makeup at issuing of orders.

c) Assembly: On the route segment Landsberg – Memmingen, marker lights positioned until 20 km from the border, *Kette* leaders turn on landing lights until *Kette* has formed up. If necessary, stagger aircraft vertically to help aircraft in the *Kette* stay together.

Efforts are to be made to keep the *Ketten* together, however individual aircraft separated from the formation are also to attack the target at the scheduled time. As many *Ketten* as possible are to rejoin during the return flight.

d) Altitudes: After Memmingen begin climbing at 2 m/s to 7,000 m ASL, then – prior to the reaching the front – descend at 1½ m/s and IAS of 380 to attack height of 3,000 or 2,800 m ASL, if possible cross border at 6,000 m ASL during return flight, then descend to 500 m AGL.
e) Route: Memmingen – radio beacon Fritz – Macòn (attack height – 3,000 or 2,800 m ASL must be reached) – target Lyon Bron (1st *Kette* low-level attack, rest 3,000 or 2,800 m ASL) east of Besançon – Mühlhausen – Wörishofen or Landsberg. Bear in mind proximity of Swiss border during flights to and from target, ensuring no infringements of the border.
f) Attack direction: 3 *Ketten* high-explosive and 1 *Kette* incendiary bombs from 3,000 m ASL on X in target photo on heading of 180°, rest on heading 225°.
g) Target assignment: 3 *Ketten* to drop high-explosive and 1 *Kette* incendiary bombs from 3,000 m ASL on X in target photo, rest from 2800 m ASL on "O" in target photo. Drop bombs as per bombing template. Assignment of targets to low-level *Kette* during issuing of orders. Beware of high-tension wires.
h) Bombing: Payload as per order for loading during practice alerts of 17/4/40.

Bombing interval.

Aircraft which will drop on X in target photo:

50-kg bombs and incendiary clusters	50 m
250-kg bombs	100 m

Aircraft which will drop on O in target photo: 30 or 60 m.

The aircraft of the 1st *Kette* will attack at low level. After ... hours they must cease overflying the target at low level. (If necessary seek alternate target.) The high attack aircraft must not drop the first bombs before ... hours. (Danger to the low-flying aircraft.)

i) Landing: Land at departure airfields.
k) Alternate airfields: Kaufbeuren, Neubiberg, Schongau, Reichenbach, Munich-Riem. If necessary due to low fuel state Freiburg or Neuhausen.

5. Pickup: by a *Staffel* of I./JG 54 (Bf 109) in area north of Thann in the southern Vosges. Altitude: 6,000 m ASL.
6. In case of bad weather: special order to be issued. Anticipate rolling attacks by fully instrument-qualified crews.
7. Reconnaissance:
   The reconnaissance flight (*Schwarm*) is to ready:

a) 1st armed reconnaissance aircraft:

Mission: Determine the aircraft present on known airfields, locate as yet unknown occupied airfields. Of particular importance: where are fighter airfields? They are suspected to be in the areas around Chaumont, Luxueil, Gray, Besançon and Belfort. Special attention is to be paid to surprise attacks on fighters taking off. Take target strike photographs.

Transmit evaluation of results as quickly as possible, first verbally to *Gruppe* and then by telephone directly to the *Geschwader*.

Reconnaissance area: Aisy (30 km SW Chatillon) – Semur – Besaune – Pologny – Monthe – Pontarlier (10259) – Langres. As well, outside the reconnaissance area determine effects of attack on target, at the earliest ½ hour after the last Kette has bombed.

(b) 2nd armed reconnaissance aircraft:

Mission: Similar to Para a, however determination of effects of attack on target (outside reconnaissance area) deleted. Pay particular attention to fighters returning from first mission. Where are they landing?

Reconnaissance area: as per Para a.

Takeoff: Independently 2 hours after takeoff by last *Kette* of first wave. If possible, nuisance attacks on targets of I. and II./KG 51, or the second wave of III./KG 51 should they already have been attacked. Apart from targets already specified, *others, identified as occupied airfields, are not to be bombed.* Nuisance attacks during the reconnaissance mission only permitted if they do not interfere with its completion.

Attack order for the 2nd wave

Remaining crews to cross the border simultaneously for daylight attacks on occupied airfields.

8. *Probable Targets:*

III./KG 51 Montbeliard Arbonas (10257)

I./KG 51 Luxueil (10252)

Lure (10253)

Malbouhans (10254)

Targets will be confirmed on a timely basis.

9. *Alternate Targets*:

In case no enemy aircraft are found at primary target, for III./KG 51: Belfort-Chaux Sermagny (10255).

For I./KG 51: Belfort – Chaux Sermagny (10255)

10. *Execution of the attack*:

a) The timing of the joint crossing of the border remains to be ordered (X-Hour).

Takeoff readiness at dawn.

Kette takeoff times: 1st *Kette* at x – 76 min. (Landsberg)
2nd *Kette* at x – 75 min (Landsberg)
3rd *Kette* at x – 70 min. (Wörishofen)
4th *Kette* at x – 69 min. (Wörishofen)
5th *Kette* at x – 68 min. (Wörishofen)

b) *Formation*: The remaining crews will be reorganized into *Ketten* and *Staffeln*. Assignments during issuing of orders. *Staffel* column formation with *Staffeln* in visual range. Return flight in formation if possible.

c) *Assembly*: 1,000 m to 1,500 m ASL on the leg Landsberg – Memmingen.
d) *Altitudes*: At Memmingen begin climbing at 2 m/s to 6,000 m ASL, attack height 4000 m ASL, overfly border at 5,000 m ASL on return flight, then descend to 500 m AGL.
e) *Route*:
f) *Direction of attack*:
g) *Target allocation*:
h) *Bombing*: The bomb load as per order for loading during practice alerts of 17/4/40 to be changed as follows:
Second wave payloads:
2 aircraft with B1 EL
2 aircraft with SC 10
rest with SD 50 without delay fuses
The excess aircraft with B1 EL and aircraft with 250-kg bombs to be unloaded and loaded with the missing SC 10 or SC 50. If sufficient SD 50 not available, SC 50 with delayed action fuses to be loaded.
i) *Landing*: At departure airfields.
k) *Alternate airfields*: Kaufbeuren, Neubiberg, Schongau, Reichenbach, Riem.

11. *Fighter escort*: One *Staffel* of I./ZG 52 will escort the 2nd wave. For this purpose Neuhausen o. E. will be overflown en route to target (approx. 4,500 m ASL), where fighters will join up to escort the 2nd wave until the return flight. *Gruppe* Dept. II will report takeoff time and successful takeoff directly to JG 54 (location Hechingen via Vulkan) and I./ZG 52 (operational base Neuhausen o. E.)
12. Special orders will be issued *in the event of bad weather*.
13. I will be flying with the 1st wave. In my absence the adjutant will deal with operational questions for the 2nd wave.

signed (Stoeckl)
Oberstleutnant and *Gruppenkommandeur*

The German offensive in the west began at 05:35, X-Hour, on 10 May 1940, the Friday before Pentecost. The signal for our *Geschwader* was: "Execute Spessart Blue."

In 1942, *Oberleutnant* Hermann Bräck, a young pilot of the *9. Staffel*, wrote the following in his commemorative booklet *Bomber Crewman over France*:

> *"Then the Kapitän's telephone rang again and a moment later the order came: 'Wake the entire Staffel immediately, crews to flight briefing at 00:30, duty NCO report to me at once!' Seconds later the entire barracks was alive. After the Kapitän (Hauptmann Brandt) had issued his final brief instructions, he wished us good luck and left the room.*

I then joined my crew at the table, reviewed all the details of the coming attack once again and made the navigational preparations. 'Well Herr Leutnant," observed my radio operator Obergefreite Lerique, 'we can get started. Our captain will show us where to bomb.' He was right, we could follow our Kapitän blindly; he would lead us correctly, for he had gained a year's experience as a bomber pilot and demonstrated his ability with the Legion Condor in Spain. Around us the other bomber crews had also completed their preparations. As we weren't supposed to take off until 03:56, there now began a lively exchange of opinions about the likely events of the coming hours and days. We spoke about the possible strength and capabilities of the French defenses and the chances of hitting the target. Suddenly someone shouted: 'We also have to expect that our French colleagues will also honor us with a visit! After all we are the most southwesterly bomber unit. Hopefully we will be able to see with our own eyes how well our airfield flak artillery can shoot!' — 'I hope instead that a group of destroyers from our airfield intercepts the incoming Frenchmen. I would rather experience an actual aerial combat as an observer, for if we are attacked by fighters ourselves it probably won't be much fun for us!' observed one of the others. We were all aware that we would soon be taking part in a bombing raid, even if passively. A few years ago the French air force had still been the strongest on the continent! It was unlikely that they would idly observe our 'efforts' over there. With such and similar contemplations, the hours passed. At about 03:00 we wished each other good luck and walked out to our aircraft. Thousands of German airmen in the west were probably making their way to their aircraft at that moment, ready to demonstrate the power of the German air force to the enemy. I thought of my parents, who were probably still sleeping peacefully and suspected nothing of the great events.

Everyone felt the seriousness of the hour. A proud, happy feeling took possession of us. Now at last it was our turn!

At our 'Kurfürst' the crew chief reported the aircraft ready for action and wished us luck. We helped each other put on our parachutes and made our way to our positions. I quickly rechecked the fuel load and the armament. The bomb aimer busied himself with his bombing equipment and the radio operator tuned his set. Then I started the engines. Both roared their droning song. Much would depend on their flawless operation in the coming hours. We could rely on them. The instruments showed that everything was in order. A final wave to the comrades staying behind and we taxied to the assigned takeoff position. The 7. Staffel was just taking off. Kette after Kette left the ground in formation. Then our Kapitän's Kette raced across the landing field and it was our turn. My Kette leader was Leutnant Klischat. I was the left 'Kette dog' in this last flight of three.

A brief flash of his landing light, our engines roared to full power and we took off on our first combat mission. This was our first night formation flight ever and I had my hands full maintaining the correct distance from the leader's aircraft. All went well, however. Unfortunately, after some time the panels of our cockpit glazing began to fog up. At times I could barely or not at all make out the lead aircraft's navigation lights and had to rely on my radio operator, who had a clear view forward from his position up above and called out course and distance changes to me. As well, the earth was covered by thick, impenetrable ground fog. There was therefore no trace of the French defenses to be seen. Still unable to see anything after flying on a westerly heading for some time, I decided to turn back.

Fate had played a cruel trick on us. I therefore decided to bring my precious bomb load home with me, for blindly dropping these bombs on French territory was forbidden but also completely pointless.

It slowly began to get light. We couldn't be seen from the ground, but could also not see anything apart from the tops of a few church spires and the odd treetop sticking out of the dense fog. After a few minutes I received a base radio bearing and was thus able to set a precise course for home.

We landed at our home base at 06:34; our spirits were low as one can imagine,. When I learned that the other two aircraft of our Kette had landed an hour and a half-hour earlier and had likewise brought their bombs home, I felt a little better. A trouble shared is a trouble halved! We discussed our unsuccessful flight in detail. We were expecting the first Kette from our Staffel to be back from its mission in about one to one-and-a-half hours. Our spirits low, we awaited the landing of our Kapitän.

His two 'Kette dogs' landed first and about 20 minutes later he himself arrived. When we had reported our failure to him, he eased our minds somewhat by telling us that we had acted correctly given our situation. The first Kette had reached its target and had been able to carry out its mission. The results had been outstanding. One airfield and an arsenal had been destroyed.

Our comrades were besieged with questions about the details of the operation. Two French fighters had intercepted the Kapitän on the way home and our Staffel had suffered its first casualty. The flight engineer had been hit in the head by two bullets and was dead. The aircraft itself looked in very poor shape. We counted 78 bullet holes. Skillful maneuvering and good defensive fire from the remaining gunners had prevented the fighters from shooting down the aircraft. The other two aircraft of the Kette returned without encountering fighters. Over the target they had encountered furious anti-aircraft fire but it caused no damage."

The young and in some cases inexperienced crews had to fly as many as three sorties per day. Anyone who is an airman can only imagine what it means to spend almost four hours of flying time in a cramped cockpit under the stress of enemy action.

The crews had gotten up at midnight that day, and it was not until after their last flight eighteen hours later that deceptive quiet returned.

"Freiburg!"

A tragic event hung over this first day of combat and it is linked to the history of our *Geschwader*, especially the *III. Gruppe*.

German bombs were accidentally dropped on Freiburg in Breisgau. So much false information, including unwarranted personal attacks, was published after the war that it is fitting to clear the record and relate "how it really was."

The mission order for the 22nd combat mission in France by the *III. Gruppe* of *Kampfgeschwader 51* (10 May 1940) specified the Dijon-Longvic airfield as target, with the fighter base at Dôle-Tavaux as the alternate.

Twenty He 111s, heavily laden with bombs and flown by already overtired crews, took off from Bad Wörishofen and Landsberg between 14:30 and 14:41.

The aircraft formed up into a *Staffel* column, with visual contact between the *Staffeln*, on the Landsberg to Memmingen leg at an altitude of 1500 meters AGL. It was very warm for the time of year, and billowing storm clouds hung over the Black Forest and the Vosges. The specified border crossing altitude of 6,000 meters AGL took the *Ketten* through turbulent, impenetrable banks of cloud. Even in close formation flight, it was almost impossible to see the next aircraft.

Dijon was bombed with good effect. Two French fighter aircraft, Moranes, were certainly shot down, another probably.

Kette leader *Oberleutnant* Schiffering's 9K + DR was forced to make an emergency landing in Friedrichshafen after it strayed off course and found itself over Solothurn in Switzerland. Schiffering's machine was attacked by two Me 109 fighters. Believing that the two daring pilots were German – they were almost certainly members of the Swiss *Flugwaffe* – his crew did not return fire. The Swiss pilots' aim was excellent (7 cannon shells and 50 machine-gun bullets struck the aircraft and *Unteroffizier* Schäfer was badly wounded).

A single *Kette*, led by the relatively inexperienced *Leutnant* Seidel, became separated from the formation in bad weather over the Black Forest. Off course, the crew became nervous and, flying on instruments, headed west in an effort to locate the target.

The following entry appears in the *III. Gruppe* war diary:

> *"This Kette attacked the airfield near Dôle alone from an altitude of 5,000 m. The crew identified 3 hangars and several quarters or workshops. Hits were observed on the hangars, quarters, on the airfield and in an anti-aircraft position."*

Kette leader *Leutnant* Seidel, of the *8. Staffel*, who was later killed near Portsmouth on 12 August 1940, wrote:

"After taking off from Landsberg, I was forced to fly on instruments some of the time. In the process I obviously strayed off course. Based on flying time, I estimated that I must be near Dijon, but although I had visual contact with the ground I could not determine my position. I then made a number of heading changes in an effort to orient myself through holes in the cloud. Suddenly a large city with an airfield appeared before me. I recognized Dijon and at X-hour I dropped my bombs on the airfield. Because of the poor visibility I was not able to observe the effects. After dropping the bombs I set course for Landsberg, at first again on instruments part of the time, then visually below cloud."

The *Kommandeur* added:

"The amount of time from the when the bombs were dropped until landing was insufficient for a direct flight from Dijon to Landsberg, but it would have been enough to cover the Freiburg to Landsberg segment.

While a comparison of aerial photos of the Dijon and Landsberg airfields revealed a certain rough similarity, Leutnant Seidel admitted that the airfield he had attacked could also have been that of Freiburg. In any case he could not say with certainty that it hadn't been Freiburg. In particular, however, calculation of the flight time after the dropping of the bombs led Lt. Seidel and me to the shocking conclusion that, after wandering about and searching for a long time, when the city of Freiburg suddenly appeared before him he had wrongly identified it as the city of Dijon. Lt. Seidel was stunned when this theory became a certainty."

Author's note: the above statements are from testimony given after the war and obviously confuse Dôle-Tavaux with Dijon. As the layouts of the Freiburg and Dôle-Tavaux airfields are almost the same in 1970 as they were in 1940, apart from new construction in their surroundings, from his own experience the editor cannot rule out mixing up of the two air bases. In similar weather conditions, with constant knowledge of his position, from 5,000 meters it was difficult for him to make a positive identification even though he was intentionally following this route.

As a result of human error by a qualified, honorable man and the combination of unfortunate circumstances, 22 children, 13 women and 22 men were killed, while another 20 children, 34 women and 47 men were injured.

For various, and at the time understandable reasons, the truth about this tragic error by German aircraft was concealed and turned into an Allied terror raid.

It is not the task of the participants and posterity to assess blame and guilt. Despite the pain it caused, it was and is a serious case of human error and not a "crime by the fascist *Wehrmacht*" as history writers in the east would still like to see it. A moral statement of accounts is probably not appropriate in our time.

In the international history of aerial warfare there have been hundreds of cases of bombs mistakenly dropped on friendly troops and civilians in the period up to the present day. This is not intended as an excuse, but to create awareness of the special circumstances and factors to which men and aircraft are always exposed in combat situations. Often this nullifies previous training and precise planning. For the historically more interested, Dr. Anton Hoch wrote an objective and professional examination of our first day of fighting in the *Quarterly for Contemporary History* (Volume 4, 1956).

Breathtaking Advance

Whereas the initial blow had fallen on the French air force, in the days that followed, the units of *Luftflotte 3* under *General der Flieger* Hugo Sperrle received orders to support the panzer divisions of the 1st, 4th, 12th and 16th Armies of Army Group A during its breathtaking advance through the Ardennes. For the most part, our *Geschwader* operated ahead of the southern wing of the German front advancing toward northeastern France, as part of the *V. Fliegerkorps* (*Generalleutnant* Robert Ritter von Greim).

The initial focus of operations by our *Geschwader* lay in the Sedan area, where we attacked lines of communications and troops in the French positions on the Meuse. The usual route led from Landsberg or Lechfeld to Mannheim and Trier, and then from there at extreme low level over Neufchâteau to Sedan. Low fuel usually meant that the return flight ended in Frankfurt/Rhein-Main or Giebelstadt, where the aircraft refueled for the flight back to base.

On 18 May elements moved to Gerolzhofen to reduce the time lost through en route stops and shorten the distance to target. This did nothing to alleviate the supply problems. *Kommodore Oberst* Kammhuber, who celebrated his 75th birthday on 19 August 1971, described these actions, which were supposed to be the new Ju 88's baptism of fire:

> *"On 16 May 1940, six days after the start of the western campaign, I was telephoned by the Commander-in-Chief of the Luftwaffe. He ordered me in the most urgent manner to immediately commit the Geschwader against railway targets in the Nancy – Epinal – Vesoul area. Göring added that great importance was being placed on these operations and told me that, because of its new equipment, he expected KG 51 to achieve the maximum possible success in dive-bombing. And he was justified in expecting that, provided the attack could be flown in good weather and clear visibility. But what happened?*
>
> *The call was received in the morning. I immediately consulted the meteorologists, who made the following forecast: at noon about 7/10 cloud cover over the Black Forest, extending to about 5,000 meters, after overflying the Black Forest 2/10 cloud cover, good visibility. It would therefore be necessary to find the 'duty hole' over the*

Black Forest, for crossing it in a lengthy instrument flight seemed extremely risky. There had been no time for instrument flight training on the Ju 88 because of the short interval between its entry into service and going into combat. It was quite clear that flying the entire Geschwader through a solid, high-topped cloud deck must result in unacceptably heavy casualties. Just two days earlier, while passing through a harmless-looking cloudbank, the left 'wingman' in my Geschwader command Kette had crashed and the entire crew died in the resulting fire. In my mind I can still see the machine to my left, emerging inverted from the clouds and immediately afterwards disappearing again into cloud below.

At about noon I took off with the Geschwader Kette and the I. Gruppe, which was based in Lechfeld. Over the field we joined up with elements of the II. Gruppe coming from Fürstenfeldbruck, those that were equipped with the Ju 88, and set course toward the west. Even from a distance one could see that the weather situation must have worsened considerably, for nowhere could one see a hole in the black curtain hanging over the Black Forest. Nevertheless, I flew as close to it as I could.

I had meanwhile reached an altitude of 5,000 m, in the hope of perhaps getting over the solid cloud cover, but that too was impossible – above there was no end in sight. But for the Ju 88s, each carrying four 500-kg bombs, 5,000 meters was the upper limit. What to do? If I led the entire Geschwader into the clouds, given the state of things I would have to anticipate serious crashes before we reached the target, while the casualties during the return flight might turn out to be a disaster for the Geschwader if the weather continued to deteriorate. Should I turn back and abort the mission? Why had the Luftwaffe's Commander-in-Chief put such great emphasis on this particular mission by calling me personally?

A difficult decision for a Geschwader commander given the mentality of the highest levels of command, which I knew only too well. Before me I saw my men, whom I had gathered around me before departure to give them their mission orders and assign targets; I thought of their families at home, who would be overcome by sadness if their loved ones failed to make it back. I decided to turn back. Let those in higher places rage as they wished – the men of my Geschwader meant more to me and were worth more than all the anger and raging if such an urgently-issued order was not carried out.

So that I could not be accused of personal cowardice – which they were quick to do in those days – I decided to fly on alone. I had the Geschwader turn around and gave orders for it to drop its armed bombs blind over a prepared site in the Lech alluvial area and then land its home bases. I myself flew on alone through the clouds on instruments. As I had earned an instrument instructor rating in the summer of 1939, I could fly on instruments with confidence, even in the Ju 88, even though I had not previously had the opportunity to practice on the type.

After about 30 minutes of instrument flight the cloud cover broke up abruptly. I was over the Rhine Plain at an altitude of 5,000 meters, and before me the Vosges lay beneath an almost cloudless blue sky. If only the entire Geschwader had been with me! At that moment I was very angry at myself over my earlier decision. But it had happened!

We flew towards our target as trained, went into a dive, dropped our four 500-kg bombs over the target, photographed the hits, and then remained a while over the target area calmly watching the fall of the bombs and the results. After taking additional photos and making notes, which might be of value to higher command, we turned onto a heading of 090 degrees. The whole time we were not the least bothered by any sort of defensive measure. I have to admit that we were a little embarrassed that everything had gone so smoothly.

When we arrived over the Rhine Plain again, the wall of cloud was still over the Black Forest, just as dark and threatening as before. What harm would it do? We had reached the target, now nothing more could happen, so we entered cloud and set course for our base in Lechfeld. It was extremely turbulent in the clouds and the Ju 88, now without its bomb load, was tossed roughly here and there. We had been flying on instruments for about ten minutes when it happened: the autopilot failed. I wasn't prepared for that. It happened too suddenly and the struck the machine just as it was recovering from an especially heavy bump. I was therefore unable to find the switch to change from autopilot to manual control. Turn and bank indicator left – ball right – artificial horizon over the line. Before I could react, there was a roar, the altimeter needle began spinning rapidly, and the indicated airspeed needle reached the stop at 720 kph. I thought we were finished.

From the rear seat the radio operator, Leutnant Lüderitz, yelled: 'Great flying! Get out!' Like me, the observer, Leutnant der Reserve Krösch, stared at the altimeter as if spellbound, and the flight engineer, Uffz. Schneider, tried to open the ventral gondola. But he was unable to do so. In the dive we were pressed so firmly into our seats that we couldn't leave them. At that moment the thought went through my head: if the same thing had happened to the poor 'wingman' two days earlier, the failure of his automatic pilot, then I now knew why he had crashed. But what good was this knowledge to us now, when we ourselves were in the midst of crashing?

Yes, now we waited for the death that must come in a few seconds. But it didn't come. Just before we reached the ground the cloud cover broke up. I was able to bring the machine out of its dive, albeit through the use of brute force.

I'm not sure how this was possible. When we regained our senses we were flying low over the ground along a rail line. We roared over a train, from which the people waved up at us enthusiastically. It was pouring rain and to the right and left the clouds hugged the ridges on either side of the valley. We had been lucky to have come down in the lowest part of a valley in the area of Donaueschingen. From there to Lechfeld, where we finally landed safely, the clouds hung low. I had to fly on instruments most of the way.

Now I was no longer angry at myself for having sent the Geschwader home, for how many have made it back if I hadn't ordered it to turn back?

My crew and I were grateful to chance – or should one call it fate? – for having gotten home alive.

This experience taught me two lessons that were of value to the Geschwader:

The autopilot originally installed in the Ju 88 (Ascania two-axis autopilot) was too weak for the aircraft. Based on our experience it was immediately beefed up and to my knowledge there were no more accidents of this kind.

The second lesson was a very encouraging one: the Ju 88 had demonstrated the strength of its wings in convincing fashion. In any other aircraft the rough handling during a manual recovery, which is what one must instinctively do, would probably have 'folded its ears back,' meaning they would have come off, and it would have broken up. The only damage to my Ju 88 was extensive wrinkling. The normally smooth skin of the wings displayed severe wrinkling – but otherwise it had remained intact. Several days later, after the wings had been replaced, I was able to fly further sorties in the same machine."

"Operation Paula" saw the *Luftwaffe* launch large-scale attacks against airfields in the Paris area. On 3 June a technical problem forced Kammhuber to fall behind the other aircraft of the *Geschwader* as they flew away from the target (Étampes airfield). The crippled machine was shot down by French fighters over Meaux on the Marne. The crew survived the crash and became prisoners of war, however they were soon freed.

Oberst Dr. Fisser took over as commander of the *Geschwader*.

Leutnant Bräck described another mission by He 111s on 20 May 1940:

"At 17:00 we took off again to attack the rail triangle south of Compiègne. I was flying the aircraft on the left of our Gruppe's command flight. There was an almost solid layer of thin cloud at 2,500 meters, and so we flew above the clouds. Our escort of destroyers picked us up just before we crossed the front. After overflying the city of Soissons, several minutes prior to the target the entire Gruppe descended through a hole in the cloud. We then leveled off at an altitude of 1,800-2,000 meters and continued the flight. A few seconds later the French anti-aircraft artillery opened up with a show of fireworks as big as the one we had encountered that morning. Not long after we descended, two Moranes shot out of the clouds and flew towards me, guns firing. They whizzed past not ten meters beneath us. 'What nerve!' grumbled my observer disapprovingly, for he had been unable to reach them with his machine-gun fire. It had happened too quickly. The radio operator reported that our escorting destroyers had engaged the Frenchmen, who immediately dove away. We took a few

bullets in our starboard wing in the exchange of fire, but they were in a spot that posed no danger. Meanwhile our duel with the anti-aircraft artillery had begun. I could see the tracers from my observer's weapon racing towards the earth like tiny sparks, each trying to overtake the others. Then our target, the rail triangle, appeared before us. We could clearly see that the area was studded with medium anti-aircraft guns. There were incessant muzzle flashes. Apparently this link was of great importance to the French. Never before had I seen such a concentration of flak artillery at a target. The bomb run began. While the observer was issuing a steady stream of course corrections, I happened to look down through the glazing and saw the beginning of a salvo of medium anti-aircraft fire. It rushed straight towards our bird's cockpit. More out of instinct than deliberation, I applied hard left rudder. This all happened in an instant. Two short, hard blows shook our machine. 'That hit us, but where?' observed Sepp drily. In that moment I couldn't see anything either, but I had no time to look closer as we were almost at the bomb release point. Another jolt shook my bird, and in the same instant I heard a dreadful clatter from outside: heavy anti-aircraft artillery, and close! The bombs were gone and the formation began a left turn. An uneven howling of the engines suddenly caused me to prick up my ears. I got such a fright that, for fractions of a second, the blood froze in my veins. Engine failure – forced landing – captivity! At that moment these three concepts combined in my thoughts to form an unpleasant outlook for the future. I had no time to look at my instruments, instead I had to concentrate fully on the movements of the lead aircraft so as not to ram it. I tried to equalize the engine rpm by jockeying the throttles but was unsuccessful. The terrible rising and falling howl of the engines continued, a sound that was probably capable of waking a pilot from a sleep of death. Below we had sighted a column of trucks on a road and it opened fire at us. 'The bombs are right on target, Herr Leutnant!' shouted Sepp from below in the ventral gondola, and in the same breath: 'We're losing all our oil! Everything liquid is running out!' We continued flying straight and level and I now had time to check the engine instruments. I found that the oil and coolant temperature gauges had already far surpassed the maximum. A glance at the starboard wing revealed the cause. What a sight! I was amazed that the wing was still attached. Right beside the engine, near where the bullets had struck earlier, it was little more than a sieve in a strip approximately one meter long and half a meter wide. That must have been caused by a direct flak hit or at least a near miss. The starboard engine was still running, albeit at reduced revs. The temperature was still rising, however, and I had to shut it down to reduce the risk of fire. I left formation and radioed the lead aircraft: 'Starboard engine out – am trying to reach departure airfield.' The Gruppe passed me. Four destroyers stayed with me as escort. They circled round our bird, whose speed was greatly reduced. I must probably reach our own lines in about 40 minutes. There! What was that? The port engine had begun running irregularly. That's all I needed. I reduced power slightly and listened intently to the drone of the engine. It was running smoothly again, but I had lost too much speed and was forced to slowly and steadily lose altitude. It was the beginning of a battle for every hundred meters of altitude. By then the starboard engine had cooled off. I started it again, applied full power to both engines and climbed with both engines shaking until the temperature gauges again reached their limits. Then I had to shut the engine down again. We had gained 600 meters of altitude. And so it went in turns. Up – down! Our own lines lay behind us. My escort circled one last time in farewell and disappeared for home at full power. I thought things over. I didn't want to force-land here in occupied territory. With the situation on the ground it would have taken us more than eight days to get back to our base. I decided to carry on until both engines failed for good or we reached the first air base in Reich territory. If the engines held up, I could reach our departure airfield. From there our travel prospects would be quite good. It was already obvious to us that it would take quite a while to repair our aircraft, it if was possible at all. Finally, it was after 21:00, by which time my comrades must already have landed at home base, we saw an airfield below us. From a height of 1000 meters I looked closely at the airfield, fired two red flares to signal an emergency landing, and began my approach. After some difficulties, I succeeded in lowering the undercarriage. I was unsure if it had been damaged and feared it might collapse on touchdown. Just to be sure, we carefully strapped ourselves in tightly. The field wasn't very big. Everywhere on its edge, fighters and destroyers were parked in several rows one behind the other. I crossed the perimeter but my speed was too great, for the landing flaps suddenly refused to move. Shot up! Not until the middle of the small airfield did the wheels touch the ground. At breakneck speed, more than 150 kph, we raced towards a group of parked Me 109s on which several mechanics were still working. The thought raced through my head: 'This is going to be a big crash, if not worse.' 'Slide on the belly, the undercarriage has to go!' my brain commanded me. By then we were 120 meters from the aircraft. Now – I gave the port engine full power and applied full right rudder. The undercarriage could not stand this abrupt course change and must collapse. Our bird made a sharp right turn of about 60 degrees and ... headed in a new direction, straight towards an empty spot at the edge of the airfield. There I couldn't endanger any people or other aircraft. I steered through this gap and finally, after jumping several ditches, came to a stop in a potato field in front of a small swamp, about 300 meters beyond the airfield. The undercarriage was still in one piece! That's always the way it was. If something isn't supposed to come apart it surely breaks, but if ever something is intended to break, it withstands every test.

We climbed out, breathed an audible sigh of relief and inspected our 'Heinrich' from all sides. Meanwhile several crews from the destroyer Gruppe that had escorted us, which was based at this field, plus an engineer, arrived and also examined our battered bird. Now we could see that we had been hit by two 40-mm anti-aircraft shells about three-quarters of a meter from our starboard engine. They had shattered the main spar and shredded more than two square meters of the skin on the bottom of the wing. The heavy anti-aircraft shell that had detonated right next to the engine had riddled the entire engine cowling plus the oil and fuel tanks. We also found several machine-gun bullet holes in the wing and several shrapnel holes in the underside of the fuselage! That same night I called my unit and reported my landing and the damage to our aircraft. We had come through once again. It seemed a miracle to us that no one had been even slightly injured. This strengthened our belief that the bullet had been cast that had our name on it.

At noon the next day we received orders to make our way home by train and there take over another aircraft. So far we had 'only' gone through three aircraft. Now it was the fourth aircraft's turn. We arrived at our base on 23 May and to our joy we were reunited with our old 'Kurfürst.' It had just come out of the hangar after having had its damage repaired. My crew and I immediately took off for the forward airfield where our Gruppe was now stationed. To my dismay, after our arrival I had to give 'Kurfürst' to another crew who had recently joined the unit and had yet to fly a combat sortie.

The next day the 9. Staffel, which had suffered the heaviest casualties so far, was ordered to immediately proceed to an air base in the home area. There we were supposed to retrain on the Ju 88. For us this meant the end of operations in this campaign."

Oberleutnant Bräck and his crew were later killed in Russia on 11 January 1943.

Dunkirk

At about noon on 24 May 1940, Hitler gave the order for the German armored forces to halt outside Dunkirk on the line Gravelines – St. Omér – Béthune. Despite the fact that his air units were exhausted, Göring pompously declared to his *Führer*: "*Mein Führer*, leave the job of smashing the enemy encircled near Dunkirk to me and my *Luftwaffe*!" As a consequence *Geschwader 51* once again had to revise its plans at short notice. Its operations against French airfields and lines of communications were halted and it was given a new target: Dunkirk.

The *Geschwader* subsequently struck repeatedly at British troops retreating in disarray from the Flanders front towards Dunkirk. The Allies had launched "Operation Dynamo," an attempt to save the British Army.

An unbelievable fleet of small ships, fishing boats, tugs with cargo cranes, private yachts and motor boats, interspersed with destroyers and torpedo boats, all loaded with troops, moved across the Channel. For the first time, 200 Spitfires, which had previously been held back, joined the action. They inflicted heavy losses on the German bomber units, which had been attacking without pause since morning.

III./KG 51 flew its 53rd mission in France on 27 May 1940, sending twelve He 111s against troop concentrations near Dunkirk.

At 10:09, *Gruppenkommandeur Major* Kind took off from Landsberg in his 9K + BD to fly reconnaissance, followed by six aircraft of 7./KG 51. At 10:10, led by *Staffelkapitän Hauptmann* Schenk von Schweinsburg, five aircraft of 8./KG 51 took off from Bad Wörishofen.

Powerful defenses, heavy flak and numerous British fighters were unable to prevent them from dropping 160 SD 10 and 204 SC 50 bombs over the target.

The crew of *Leutnant* Gild, with *Gefreiter* Kassegger, *Unteroffizier* Kannewurf, *Gefreiter* Bartelt and *Feldwebel* Göttlicher, failed to return and was reported missing. It was later learned that they had been killed near Dunkirk.

About five hours later the He 111s, some of them riddled by splinters and machine-gun bullets, landed in Frankfurt-Main, where preparations were made for the second mission of the day. Holes were patched and wounded crewmen received medical treatment.

Two hours later eight He 111s of the *7.* and *8. Staffel* took off again and dropped 215 SC 50 bombs on their target, the port and city of Dunkirk. The *9. Staffel* had already left on 23 May and was training on the Ju 88 in Regensburg-Obertraubling, the first unit of the *Gruppe* to do so.

From far away, the crew of *Oberleutnant* Berger of 2./KG 51 spotted the giant mushroom clouds of smoke hanging over their target area. The unit's nine Ju 88s had taken off from Lechfeld at 12:23. Berger and his observer *Oberfeldwebel* Blumhofer concentrated tensely on the ship that was their target. The initial dive looked good. The ship began taking violent evasive action and slipped out of the sight. The attack had to be aborted. The heavily loaded machine pulled out of its dive and maneuvered for a second attack. Manning their MG 15s, *Unteroffiziere* Puls and Smotzek scanned the sky. As Puls replaced an empty magazine and began firing again, he noticed five lurking Spitfires positioning themselves for their first attack. After firing one burst, his machine-gun suffered a burst barrel. At the same time the Ju 88 was hit. An engine was knocked out and Berger immediately turned towards the safety of the coast. When the Spitfires realized that the crew of the crippled aircraft was no longer shooting back, they approached one last time and positioned themselves off the bomber's wingtips. The British pilots waved and escorted the shot-up bomber for a while. The air war was still being fought under certainly tough but chivalrous rules.

Berger and his men wanted to bale out, but the canopy refused to jettison, and he decided to make an emergency landing in Brussels. When he flew over the airfield a red flare was fired from below. The aircraft's undercarriage refused to lower. Berger was bleeding from the shoulder, Puls had been wounded in the arm and eyes. Without hesitating, Berger put the bird down on its belly. The crew spent weeks in hospital near Brussels.

That day the *I.* and *II. Gruppe* committed a total of 43 Ju 88s.

The inferno went on. Dunkirk burned, resembling a smoldering chaos, but it did not fall.

On 28 and 29 May the weather was so bad that few bombs fell on the bridgehead. Only in the afternoon were several missions possible. Sea fog kept the *Luftwaffe* grounded until 31 May.

The weather cleared on the morning of 1 June. The bomber units resumed their relentless attacks. The devastating results caused British Admiral Ramsey to order his rescue fleet to only sail at night.

Dunkirk fell on 4 June 1940. 40,000 French troops became POWs, sacrificing themselves so that the British expeditionary force of 215,587 men and 123,095 French troops could be evacuated to Great Britain to form the core of new armies.

Luftwaffe commander-in-chief Hermann Göring failed to deliver what he had promised and irresponsibly allowed his arm to bleed. The strengths of the *Geschwader* in personnel and equipment fell 30 to 50 percent below authorized. The *Luftwaffe*'s confidence in victory received its first setback.

Paris was occupied without a struggle on 14 June, and on 22 June the German-French ceasefire was signed in Compiègne Forest, the historic site where the Treaty of Versailles had been signed.

Move to France

After the rapid advance, which in places had encountered stiff resistance, all of the units needed time to rest and restore their strength.

But there was no time for rest. Everyone knew that they were supposed to move to airfields in the Paris area. It was time to implement practiced movements and refined plans in order to move from the units' home bases to new operational bases in foreign territory with no loss of time.

Meanwhile crews still had to retrain on the Ju 88 in Regensburg-Obertraubling, Greifswald or the bomber school in Anklam in the short period of just three weeks. Aircraft had to be overhauled in the maintenance facilities, transfer packages put together. The organization of the overland trip for the ground personnel, who were already used to being taxed to their limits, was carried out with little inkling of the difficulties that awaited in recently-occupied France because of the wrecked transportation system in the country.

During this time the 7th Airfield Operating Company, which had been assigned to the unit, got to know the roads and railway stations in Germany and France all too well. It was a foretaste of what was to come when it accompanied the *Geschwader* to the east.

This type of company turned a forward airfield into an air base. It consisted of about 150 men and was led by a reserve officer, usually with technical qualifications, as company commander. He was assisted by a senior NCO, pay officer, fourier/cook, NCOs in charge of the clothing stores and armory, and about 15 general office personnel. Each operating platoon had 25 NCOs and men. With an experienced *Oberfeldwebel* as platoon leader, they serviced our aircraft day and night. A workshop platoon with about 35 NCOs and men took care of the difficult, major repairs, while the *Schirrmeister* (maintenance technical sergeant) with his 22 drivers maintained the company's extensive motor pool.

This included:

1 Mercedes automobile
5 Mercedes three-axle trucks with trailer
4 Mercedes extended personnel trucks
3 other trucks
4 tractors
2 motorcycle-sidecar combinations

A brief mention of how the airfield operating company was moved around in just six weeks: when the French Campaign began from Reichenbach near Schussenried to Landsberg to care for the *III. Gruppe*:

23 May transfer back to Reichenbach, to service a *Gruppe* of KG 26 "Lion *Geschwader*."
27 May moved back to Landsberg.
2 June move to Regensburg-Obertraubling for a brief indoctrination on the Ju 88.
9 June arrival in Lechfeld.
12 June move via Stuttgart – Mainz – Trier.
14 June to Sedan.
15 June in Villers Cottre.
23 June in Mondésir near Étampes (south of Paris).

Like most major French airfields, Étampes had been badly damaged by bombing and artillery fire. With the help of prisoners of war, the company set about preparing it to receive the flying units – removing debris from wrecked hangars, leveling the airfield and clearing out living quarters. Senegalese prisoners of war were willing and good-natured helpers.

The first aircraft of I./KG 51 arrived in Paris-Orly, which had not been so badly damaged, on 18 June. Lack of fuel prevented large-scale flying operations, however, and the unit had to move to Villacoublay with its large runway.

Finally, at the end of June, the unit was able to move into its assigned quarters.

The *Geschwaderstab* and the *II. Gruppe* were quartered in La Fontaine castle near Brétigny, the *I. Gruppe* initially in Château Villemain near Grisny-Suisnes and later, together with the *III. Gruppe*, in the castle barracks of Château Grand Yard near Voisenon. From there it wasn't far to the air base at Melun-Villaroche, which was extremely well equipped, and to Villacoublay, Brétigny and Étampes-Mondésir.

When the last retrained crews arrived at the beginning of July, they found their comrades well established. The historic surroundings of Paris offered tempting tour destinations like the Versailles and Fontainebleau Palaces or more distant attractions on the Loire, even as far as Orléans.

The young dancers in the Place Pigalle and the topless bars of the Montmartre provided diversion. Given the abundance of excellent French wine and champagne, it is not surprising that the airmen's wallets were usually empty. *Gruppe* and *Staffel* commanders were often more than a little worried about their enterprising men.

During a visit by *Generalfeldmarschall* Hugo Sperrle, commander of *Luftflotte 3*, the first decorations and promotions were handed out to deserving crews and personnel in the huge, architecturally unique airship hangar in Orly in the presence of *General* Ritter von Greim. The period of relative quiet and rest was short-lived, however.

The next objective was obviously England. This campaign went into the history books as the Battle of Britain.

Overview of Operations against France

(1/9/1939 – 19/6/1940)

(*III. Gruppe* only due to missing documents)

59 missions with 434 aircraft (He 111 only), including 18 leaflet missions by 32 aircraft.

		Flying hours:
Reconnaissance Schwarm:	65 sorties	265 h 24 min.
7. Staffel	148 sorties	614 h 18 min.
8. Staffel	139 sorties	572 h 40 min.
9. Staffel	82 sorties	321 h 59 min.

Quantity of bombs dropped: total 373,480 kg
including:
SC 10............................956
SC 50.........................3,287
SD 50 3,779
SC 250..............................6
incendiary..................7,920
SBe 50............................24

Ratio of incendiary to high-explosive bombs approx. 1 : 1
Enemy fighter aircraft shot down: 14
Casualties:
Killed: 35
Wounded: 20
Missing: 4

Operations against England

The ground organization and the ultimate locations of the units of *Luftflotte 2* (Kesselring, Brussels) and *Luftflotte 3* (Sperrle, Paris) were by now in a tolerable state. As usual, however, much had to be improvised. The *Kampfgeschwader* were based along the Loire, in the Paris area through Brussels as far as Amsterdam; the dive-bomber and fighter *Geschwader* on the other hand were based mainly around Le Havre and Calais on account of their limited range.

Our *Geschwader* formed part of the *V. Fliegerkorps* (*Ritter* von Greim), whose headquarters were in Villacoublay, along with KG 54 (*Oberstleutnant* Höhne, Evreux) and KG 55 (*Oberst* Stoeckl, Chartres).

The historical analyses of the battle differ in their division of its phases; the author is aware of a total of eight different interpretations of the battle. He favors the Swiss interpretation (Dr. Theo Weber), which in his opinion comes closest to the entire process of the air battle.

The *contact phase* began in July 1940 with armed photo-reconnaissance, attacks against merchant shipping and nuisance raids on British ports. These were conducted as per air fleet orders, as no instructions had been received from the OKL. Powerful bomber forces struck the island nation for the first time on 10 July, their objective being to draw the British fighters into battle.

The *III. Gruppe* contributed just three crews flying the new Ju 88 A-1 against targets in the Portsmouth area, which lay under thick cloud and showers.

In France the freshly retrained crews continued to train intensively on the new type at the *Staffel* level. They were familiarized with dive-bombing techniques, dropped practice bombs to improve their accuracy and practiced cooperation with KG 100 (pathfinder unit). The ground personnel were given the opportunity to get used to handling, arming, caring for and servicing the Junkers bomber. Some enterprising observer pilots scoured the countryside in the search for suitable alternate airfields.

Slowly they became used to the new area of operations. Just three major operations were flown by the end of July. The last, on the 29th, struck armaments and aero-engine factories and refineries as far away as Liverpool and Southampton.

Main Battle Phase I began on 8 August 1940, which was dubbed '*Adlertag*' (Eagle Day), after Führer Directive No.17 finally gave the *Luftwaffe* an operational objective.

The Royal Air Force was supposed to be defeated as quickly as possible. A variety of targets had to be bombed. Armaments factories, the new and surprisingly effective radar stations, air bases and troop camps. Terror attacks were expressly forbidden.

At first, bad weather hampered large-scale air operations. The majority of our pilots and those of the other *Geschwader* were not yet sufficiently familiar with night operations and there was no time or opportunity to train.

So-called "destroyer crews" were sent to attack particularly important targets. For their dangerous, often reckless missions, in addition to their flight pay they received a special bonus of 400 *Reichsmark*, a substantial sum in those days. The "destroyer crews" were outstanding airmen, the pick of crews from every *Geschwader*. They were assigned their targets with all available target information, without being tied down to the timing or special tactics and orders of their unit. They answered only to the air corps in carrying out their attacks. The commander of a crew assessed the weather and the air situation on his own, and he ultimately decided when and under what conditions the attack would be made. There is no need for further explanation of the dangers associated with these operations, when one considers that these crews operated without fighter escort, flying their missions alone.

Leutnant der Reserve Dr. Karl-Heinz Stahl and his crew (Schröter, Nömeyer, Motes) carried out one of these special missions on 23 August 1940. Their target was the RAF training camp at Aldershot.

The following account is based on the work of *PK-Sonderführer* Wolfgang Küchler:

> *"The clouds hung low over our French forward airfield of Villacoublay, almost as if they wanted to touch the ground with their wisps. The crews were sitting around disgruntled. They had been expecting a 'short hop' to England, but the mission had been called off on account of weather. But no one left the Staffel dispersal. Perhaps something might still be up? Correct, for scarcely two minutes had passed when the adjutant came running from the command post, a note in his hand. The Geschwader had called with orders for one crew to take off immediately for Aldershot airfield. A crew with instrument flying experience was to fly the mission. The men were abruptly roused from their rest. Tensely they looked at their Gruppenkommandeur, Hauptmann Kurt von Greiff, who was to make the difficult selection. After a long pause his gaze fell upon the small, wiry Leutnant der Reserve Karl-Heinz Stahl. 'You're flying!' A few minutes later 9K + Ida Heinrich lifted off the airfield with its heavy bomb load. The crew, which had just been selected from so many for this special mission, felt a quiet pride.*
>
> *Soon after taking off, Leutnant Stahl climbed into the clouds. The engines of the Ju 88 droned monotonously as it climbed calmly and steadily, meter by meter. The aircraft broke through the tops and the crew was presented with a fantastic sight. The sea of clouds swelled and seethed, but the four men alone in 'Ida-Heinrich' had little time to observe the spectacle. They had to concentrate on the task at hand. The French coast lay far behind the German bomber and they must already be over England. The clouds not only obscured the ground but would also prevent British fighters from intercepting the Junkers. That was reassuring.*
>
> *Leutnant Stahl looked at the clock and reached for his big airman's map of England. Ten more minutes, then they would be there. The tension grew. Would the*

English anti-aircraft gunners be on their toes? Will we have fighters? With a quick look, gunner and observer Oberfeldwebel Schröter carefully checked the bombing control panel. The dorsal gunner, Gefreiter Motes, squatted intently behind his machine-gun. Radio operator Feldwebel Nömeyer had also exchanged his radio equipment for the machine-gun. Everything was ready for the attack. 'Ida-Heinrich' descended through a hole in the clouds – the 'duty hole' perhaps? To their surprise, not only was the target, Aldershot airfield, below them, but also forty Spitfires, flying tirelessly in a tight circle. Alerted by radar, they were patrolling over the airfield.

Light anti-aircraft guns welcomed the intruder with an initial, inaccurate salvo. A pair of Spitfires turned to attack the lone bomber. Leutnant Stahl calmly maintained his heading on the bomb run, the only way to place the target squarely in Oberfeldwebel Schröter's sight. The first bomb fell. Three more slight jerks followed as the other bombs left the aircraft.

When 'Ida-Heinrich' pulled out of its dive there were eight Spitfires diving after it. They came in from two sides. Feldwebel Nömeyer opened fire. One British pilot fired and his aim was excellent. Bullets struck the aircraft with a clattering, splintering sound. A second burst just missed the head of Oberfeldwebel Schröter. Luckily for him, he was still lying on his belly at the bombsight and thus escaped death. After the British attack, Feldwebel Nömeyer was slightly wounded, but this did not stop him from giving the Spitfire, which had closed to within thirty meters, his iron response. Hits! The Spitfire reared up and slowly rolled onto its side. A burst from Gefreiter Motes finished it off. It went down in flames behind a banner of dark smoke. Another fighter came from above left. Anticipating the enemy's actions, Leutnant Stahl applied full power and turned into the attacker. The British fighter whizzed past the German aircraft, missing its tail by scarcely five meters. Only with difficulty and full power did 'Ida-Heinrich' reach the safety of the clouds. Peace at last. But what about 'Ida-Heinrich'? The instrument panel was shattered, the electrical system shot up, the radio unusable, even the intercom was out. The men were happy to have escaped the mess still in flying condition.

The danger was not yet over, however. After three minutes of instrument flight in the clouds, the starboard engine suddenly began to shake. Leutnant Stahl shut it down. The aircraft continued its flight on one engine. The pilot had to push hard on the rudder pedal to stay on course. Soon he got a leg cramp and Oberfeldwebel Schröter had to step on the pedal. With the aid of the backup compass they flew a zigzag course towards the French coast, steadily losing altitude because of the lack of engine power. Caen lay far ahead of them. It was high time to land, their fuel was almost gone. Suddenly the port engine shook and quit. All was still. Leutnant Stahl summoned all his strength one last time and concentrated on a belly landing, which always entailed considerable risks, in Caen. The aircraft approached calmly and steadily, the only noise from the slipstream, and touched down safely. All hands immediately came to help the crew and ten minutes later even the commanding general, who happened to be in Caen and observed the emergency landing by 'Ida-Heinrich,' congratulated them."

The Kommodore Is Killed

Wettererkundungsstaffeln 1 and *161* (weather reconnaissance units) and KG 40, in which *Major* Petersen, former *Staffelkapitän* of 1./KG 51, was serving as *Gruppenkommandeur*, reconnoitered the weather over the Atlantic and the British Isles. A large Azores high meant that it promised to be good.

The British radar stations, especially those on the Isle of Wight, had to be rendered "blind" if the German forces were to reach the English ports undisturbed.

The attacks on the radar stations were led by *Erprobungsgruppe 210* under Rubensdörffer. At about 11:00 on 12 August 1940, over the French coast near Cherbourg, KG 51 with almost 100 Ju 88s rendezvoused with *Zerstörergeschwader 2* and *76* (120 Me 110s) and JG 53 (25 Me 109s).

Leading the big formation, *Kommodore Oberst* Dr. Fisser waited impatiently for the *Schwärme* and *Staffeln* to join formation. The principal target was the public shipyards in Portsmouth. The *Staffelkapitäne* led their units towards the target at 5,000 meters. The bombers were carrying SC 250 and a few big SC 1000 bombs.

There was little opposition from fighters prior to the target. The raiders weren't detected by the Poling radar station until 11:45. A rising barrage of 50 balloons, which suddenly swayed in the sky at heights up to 1,800 meters, announced an imminent attack by flak and fighters.

German fighters tried to lure the British into battle. The Ju 88 unit split up. 70 aircraft turned towards Portsmouth. Horizontal and dive-bombing attacks struck the port, main railway station, fuel tank farm and small ships. At almost the same time, twenty Ju 88s began attacking Ventnor radar station on the Isle of Wight.

The anti-aircraft guns began to fire. At 4,000 meters the salvoes were still inaccurate, more of a nuisance. At 2,000 meters and lower they were heavy and accurate. More and more of our comrades sheared out of formation, hit by flak or fighters. Thirteen crews from our unit failed to return. At 12:30 a Hurricane of No.213 Squadron shot down the *Kommodore*'s aircraft. *Oberst* Dr. Fisser was killed. His observer, *Oberstleutnant* Lüderitz, and *Leutnant* Schad were badly wounded and became prisoners of war.

The *I. Gruppe* lost four crews, the *II. Gruppe* two, the *III. Gruppe* six. Only a handful of men survived to become prisoners of war.

When the formation turned for home, Spitfires, Hurricanes and Defiants dove on the bombers like hawks. Apart from the thirteen aircraft shot down, almost all of the rest had sustained varying degrees of damage from machine-gun and cannon fire. The crews of *Major* Marienfeld, *Kommandeur* of the *III. Gruppe*, and *Oberleutnant* Lange of the *9.*

Staffel each shot down a Spitfire. *Leutnant* Unrau's aircraft (9K + HL) was pursued over the Channel by three Hurricanes. His radio operator, *Feldwebel* Winter, shot down one of the British fighters. With one of its engines shot out, the Ju 88 just managed to reach the French coast. There the second engine failed and, displaying his flying skill, Unrau put the aircraft down on the outer edge of the coastal bluffs. The crew, none of whom had been wounded, climbed out and counted 180 hits on their machine.

On 14 August the *Kommodore* of KG 55, *Oberst* Alois Stoeckl, formerly *Gruppenkommandeur* of III./KG 51, was shot down and killed by fighters of No.609 Squadron while attacking Middle Wallop airfield.

The other bomber units also suffered heavy losses, as a result of which *Luftflotte 5* (Stumpff) was forced to join the battle from its bases in Norway beginning 15 August.

Thanks to its radar stations, RAF Fighter Command was in the advantageous position of being able to deploy its forces sparingly but effectively. For its part, the *Luftwaffe* tried to engage all four British fighter groups simultaneously by launching deeper penetrations and spreading out its targets. On 16 August the *Geschwader* attacked British airfields. The *I. Gruppe* was supposed to strike Redhill, the *II. Gruppe* Brooklands and the *III. Gruppe* Gatwick. Dense fog made it impossible for the *III. Gruppe* to locate its target. The formation leader decided to bring the bombs home and drop them on the designated bomb jettison area west of Étampes, thereby possibly avoiding dropping them on a densely populated area.

A *Gruppe* of *Zerstörer* from ZG 76 picked up the bombers at St. Aubin and escorted them home, clearing the Eastbourne – Horsham – Worthing area of enemy fighters. This daylight operation was unusual in that there were no casualties. Further daylight raids were made against enemy airfields and Portsmouth, now too familiar, until 25 August. *Jagdgeschwader 53 "Pik-As"* provided fighter escort.

Among the SC 250 bombs that were dropped, for the first time some were equipped with LZZ (delayed-action fuses), which delayed detonation of the bombs for hours or even days. The new 250-kg incendiary bombs also proved effective.

Some crews made the unwelcome acquaintance of the "brook," as the English Channel was referred to condescendingly. Fortunately many were saved by the well-organized German air-sea rescue service.

From then on, the fierce air battles at high altitude were regular occurrences as the bombers stubbornly fought their way to their targets. Receiving timely warning, the enemy fighters were rarely caught on the ground. They scrambled as soon as an incursion was reported, in order to intercept the German aircraft before they dropped their bombs if possible.

By the second half of August the air battle had reached a critical stage for the British. Since 8 August the Royal Air Force had lost 1,115 fighters and 92 bombers, whereas the *Luftwaffe* had lost just 254 fighters and 215 bombers.

The objective of gaining air superiority over the island appeared to be within reach, but at the end of August the offensive tactics of the German bombers were changed.

A change was made to night operations. Taking off at two minute intervals, usually at about midnight, all night-qualified crews – unfortunately, still not all – took part in the raids on Liverpool, Birmingham, Manchester and Bristol and, beginning on 8 September 1940, London. At this time the British night-fighter force, which later became so effective, was not yet a major threat. This would remain so until the beginning of 1941.

During one of the last missions against Liverpool-Birkenhead, five minutes after the first bombs were dropped a crew sighted a pattern of lights suddenly appear on the ground. South of Bristol, countless lights gradually came forming a strip 5 kilometers long and about 500 meters wide. Supposed to represent a huge fire in a city, it was easily distinguishable as a diversion. On 30 August 1940 the British employed a large-scale simulated fire south of Liverpool that was supposed to simulate a burning dockyard. Many German crews were deceived by this skillful deception and dropped their bombs on the Welsh heath.

Because of the relatively heavy losses, a steady flow of new, freshly trained crews joined the unit. Of course they could not begin combat operations immediately. For the combat *Staffeln*, training these new crews while conducting regular operations was a serious burden. In August 1940, therefore, the *Geschwader* command tasked *Hauptmann* Ritter with the formation of a replacement training *Staffel* in Orly. Its job was to systematically train the "newcomers" and slowly prepare them for their future tasks. Special emphasis was placed on night flying. The 7th Airfield Operating Company detached an operating platoon under *Feldwebel* Weiß to service the *Staffel*'s aircraft.

After about four weeks of training, the new crews were assigned to the individual *Staffeln* of the *Geschwader*.

So that the indoctrination could be carried out quietly and effectively, the Replacement Training *Staffel* with its four He 111s and six Ju 88s was later transferred to Lager Lechfeld.

In Wiener-Neustadt it formed the core of the *IV. Gruppe* (Replacement Training *Gruppe*), whose role was to prepare young crews coming from the flying schools for frontline operations. Experienced bomber crews from the *Geschwader* were both instructors and father figures for the "fledglings."

Flyer's Latin: Based on a report by Oberleutnant Hänel

Do you know what "wooden eye" actually is? Perhaps you would say some sort of medical-technical matter, or the fighting name of a bloodthirsty, moccasin-wearing, tomahawk-swinging Delaware Indian from a Karl May novel.

Don't be disappointed that it isn't, especially if you don't know how to tackle the second meaning of the title, for it is a modern expression, specifically one invented and used by our airmen returning from one of the operations they deal with on a daily basis.

"Aviation slang" is a treasure trove of the juiciest and most graphic expressions, a way of describing unpleasant or routine activities in such a vivid way that they come alive, or stating more pleasant matters in such a manner that it causes one to smile. I am convinced that, after the war, a professorship will be established for aviation slang.

But "aviation rhetoric" was not just created for humor, but also for the all too justified desire to use this secret code to make oneself understandable only to the initiated and mercilessly reveal laymen as such. I believe, however, that you will be astonished by how these expressions hit the nail on the head. For example: "I took a shit-kicking." It is dramatic and a little disrespectful; but how can one describe more concisely the situation that results when the enemy fires countless rounds into one's cockpit?

We're still not in the air yet, instead we are snoring in the beds of our "château-castle" because there is "airman's weather" (airman's weather is when he does not need to fly on account of fog and bad weather and enjoys his flight pay). Sudden alarm! The "weather frogs," who deal with wind, hydrometers and barometers and wave weather maps, have prophesized "flying weather" in their "rubber forecast."

And now you are with us in the milling mass unleashed by the magic word "alarm" in all of the segments of the well-organized operation for the destruction of the enemy, whether we see fighters, reconnaissance aircraft, bombers or transports, dive-bombers or strategic reconnaissance machines. The "boys," the aircraft mechanics, run up the engines of the machines, the "crates," or if one has developed a special relationship with them, the "old ham" or "government ship." Meanwhile the crew "climbs into the harness," or puts on their parachutes. We climb aboard, the bird taxis for takeoff, positions itself there and waits for the takeoff signal. Then off we go. The pilot "sticks the bottle in," urging the engines, or "gas cookers" to maximum revolutions, which in turn spin the "slats," the propellers, at high speed. After the unit, the "bunch," has formed up after "making a bend" around the airfield, it flies straight to the target, the *Kette* leader in front, his "*Katschmareks*" or "*Kette* dogs" to the sides and a little behind.

Especially popular, by the way, is being present in the last *Kette*, which acts as "wooden eye," lookout against hostile enemy intentions, and as "backstop" against attacks from the rear. (As the old saying goes, "The devil take the hindmost!")

Just look at the fighters, flying like a swarm of hornets after they shoot into the sky like rockets in a "cavalier takeoff," or the bombers, which drone along in an iron phalanx. In contrast, "the old auntie" or "the old lady Ju" of course looks a little clumsy as it wobbles past on a reciprocal course; but this "tired bird" also has its merits. How often may it have brought supplies, stuffed full "to the collar." Yes, and now "we are hanging in the sky." The radio operator "pushes gas into the antenna," establishes radio contact, the "stoker" or "grease monkey" (flight engineer) caresses the engines in his thoughts; for it would be unpleasant for them to "puke" or "bitch" now, especially as the crate, with its load of fuel and "eggs," is more or less a "load of porcelain." It is the observer's aim to put the "eggs" to good use, while the gunners "spy to the rear" to prevent an enemy from "getting on our neck." Meanwhile, after passing through the "muck" or "garbage" (clouds), it is time to begin "sucking" oxygen. This is roughly how the "gang" makes its way towards the enemy, providing mutual cover and protection, with the "bunnies," the still young and inexperienced crews, in the middle.

The long-range reconnaissance crews, the "eyes of the command" (the bombers, by the way, are its "long arm"), have a much more difficult time of it, flying all alone to take photographs with their "sunshine traps." Of the course the entire crew are "wooden eyes" to prevent the enemy from "administering a shit-kicking," which they undoubtedly would like to do by "pressing the buttons" that activate his weapons. The reconnaissance flyers are only supposed to see, not fight, and bring their observations safely home.

Therefore, as difficult as it may seem, better to "turn the crate around," "tails up" and "take up the slack" and "row away" than to allow one's "ass to be kicked," with the possibility of catching fire and "reeking and coming apart." For black smoke pouring from the machine, "smoke from the kitchen," is an indication that "something is crackling in the cardboard box," illustrates a situation that is made no more comfortable by "getting off," abandoning the aircraft by parachute, especially if there is a possibility of "landing in the brook" between England and France. Apart from the associated sniffles, this is also not good for the film cassettes. It is a little different for the other aircraft under enemy fire. Tracer from the enemy's machine-guns, the "corpse fingers," "whiz past one's ears," soon causing one to have "full trousers" or "a copper bolt" or "colored pencil in one's rear." Putting his crate "on its nose" and getting out of there "at breakneck speed," crying softly because "it stinks to him" and "flatirons," or anti-aircraft shells, are coming up at him. Such a "row" is a very exciting business. The actions of the reconnaissance and transport crews are not reported on, their efforts are known only to the staffs. The flight home still remains. The "old man" gives the signal for the formation to break up, for below he can see the white "commander's shirt," the landing cross, which is made of white cloth and shows the aircraft the wind direction and the spot where they should touch down. There is, of course, special joy when many crates "waggle their wings" on arrival, which is the same thing to us today as scalps were to the Indians.

The machines "sit down" one after another, perhaps there's a "belly landing" because the pilot failed to put down the "legs," the undercarriage, and in an "egg landing" one is particularly careful to avoid breaking up the battered crate, for after a successful flight it would be rotten to make "kindling" out of it or "spew out" the bird. The "boys" are soon there again, receiving our crates, helping the crews from the "crockery." They are very happy to have solid ground under their feet again, aware that their "battle pates," on which there are now light pearls of sweat, have not been damaged. After having held out so well during the flight, are they to "lose their breakfast" now? No, then they quickly walk behind a hangar in the direction of the mess to "fizzle" or "solder one up," then they "take a breather" or "eavesdrop on the mattress," which is the same thing, then all is well again. Something along the lines of "la bums, the landing, la bums Tara, the collision!"

London

A new phase of the bombing war developed from the actual "fighter battle." On 3 September 1940 Göring ordered the air fleet chiefs to The Hague to discuss changing the bombing targets. In his opinion, major attacks against the enemy's air bases, fighter control stations, radar sites and aircraft factories were no longer worthwhile.

Instead they would bomb military targets in and around London in order to force the English to commit their reserves to defend the vital metropolis. With the first German night raid on London (5-6 September 1940), the Battle of Britain entered a completely new phase: it was the beginning of the German air war against England's military potential. Whereas German air operations during Main Battle Phase I had largely benefited the plans of the admiralty, which was supposed to prepare a landing in England, the attacks that began on 6 September had no apparent connection to the Sea Lion planning. It was the beginning of *Main Battle Phase II*, which went on until 10 May 1941. Göring had ordered the start of the economic war at a time when the British fighter arm, especially its ground organization and personnel resources, had reached a low point, and when even a brief continuation of the campaign against the English fighter infrastructure would have had the most serious consequences for Fighter Command.

Without exaggeration, one can call this the strategic phase.

On the afternoon of 7 September Göring was joined by Kesselring and Loerzer near Cap Blanc Nez as German bomber and fighter units roared overhead. The radio correspondents who were present reported that he had "personally taken over command of the *Luftwaffe* in the battle against England."

625 bombers took part in raids on London that began in the afternoon and lasted well into the night.

That night approximately 60 aircraft of KG 51 flew towards London at an attack altitude of 4000 meters. Long before reaching their targets they could see the sky over the suffering city, tinted red by the many fires. Realistic diversionary targets (simulated fires) were discovered south of the city. Curiously there was no reaction from the anti-aircraft guns. As it was later learned, they were not allowed to fire to avoid endangering the population of the city. This was soon to change, however.

Night after night as many as 300 bombers were over London, which was given no rest. The night-fighters, mostly Blenheims, became more aggressive and proved an annoyance, although fortunately our aircraft suffered no losses. Meanwhile some bombers were sent against Plymouth, Portland or Portsmouth to divert the enemy, but as before London remained the focus of operations.

The occasional daylight raids, which had to be carried out without fighter escort, were nerve-wracking. It was not unusual for up to twenty Spitfires, which patrolled off the coast, to dive on the formation during the return flight. The bombers always hoped to find clouds in which to "sneak away crying softly." In most cases this trick was sufficient to shake off the pursuing fighters.

In October we began flying only at night or taking off into thc autumn and winter dusk so as not to arrive over the target before dark. Of course there could be no element of surprise, for the outstanding British radar network almost always detected the formation as it left the French coast and constantly "kept an eye on it through night and fog." By day the fighter-bomber *Staffeln* of the fighter units, ironically called "light Kesselringe," flew to their targets. They almost always suffered casualties and their attacks could not be seen as more than pinpricks.

In the operations against London, which remained the principal target until 14 November, the night attack tactic resulted in not inconsiderable losses through crashlandings and unplanned landings away from base.

The *III. Gruppe* alone flew 295 sorties in 49 operations. Just nine machines aborted due to weather or technical reasons, mostly engine trouble.

During the *Geschwader* parade on 12 November 1940 in the big Zeppelin hangar in Orly, *Generalfeldmarschall* Hugo Sperrle decorated battle-tested men of KG 51 with the Iron Crosses, First and Second Class. Many wore large bandagcs on their limbs, signs of wounds sustained in recent battles.

On Saturday, the 16th of November 1940, our target was the city of Coventry and English ports. These were attacked with the help of the navigation aid "Knickebein." It was not needed, however, because the glow from the burning city showed the way from a great distance. The day before a big raid, in which 500 tons of high explosive and 30,000 incendiary bombs were dropped, had taken the city by surprise.

The following example of *Oberleutnant* von Claer's act of comradeship illustrates how closely the crews were bound together and how they supported each other.

On 18 October our unit again attacked the city of London, which was defended by flak and fighters. When the machines returned, that of *Oberleutnant* Claer was missing. He had been forced to ditch in the sea with two dead crewmembers and *Feldwebel* Heinrich Märte aboard.

The onboard inflatable raft was deployed and the men put on their life vests. They just managed to get out of the aircraft in time, before it slid beneath the surface and sank. The two survivors paddled in the salt water of the stormy sea and realized that the riddled life raft was useless. The two men knew that difficult hours lay ahead of them. Would they be found drifting in the water? Would they reach land alive?

With difficulty they clung together, so as not to become isolated playthings of the waves. Hours passed. By nightfall their heavy flight gear was long since soaked with burning salt water and threatened to drag the two men under despite their bulky life vests.

Fw. Märte was married and had two children, while *Oberleutnant* von Claer was still single. Their life vests were now barely keeping them afloat. At this point von Claer said: "I'm single, you are married with a wife and two children. You must reach the shore of the Channel and survive. That's not important to me, so take my life vest. Farewell and give my greetings to the homeland and our comrades!" Von Claer slipped off his life vest and passed it to his comrade. Not until the *Oberleutnant* had drowned was Fw. Märte able to pull on the life vest. Early the next morning a German U-boat found the two and brought them aboard. Märte was unconscious, with severe saltwater burns over his entire body.

Oberleutnant Claer gave his life to save the life of his comrade.

Further large-scale night raids like the one on Coventry – but with lesser effect – were made that November against Birmingham (19-20), Southampton (23-24), Bristol (24-25), Plymouth (28-29) and Liverpool (28-29). As well, raids on London continued on a reduced scale; each lasted between four and ten hours!

In November alone, a total of 6,747 tons of high-explosive bombs fell on economically important targets in the British cities. These attacks went on into December 1940.

KG 100 and KG 26 often flew with our unit as pathfinders. Using illumination bombs, they laid so-called fire roads to the target, which could be seen from far away. This was necessary because the radio navigation aids ("Fred," "Knickebein 3," "Knickebein 4") were being intensively interfered with, making them unsuitable for navigation. The British used their signals intelligence very cleverly to break into our linking devices and radio aids.

At Christmastime the phrase "effect on the target as at Coventry" frequently crept into the military communiqués. From this later developed the macabre new word "coventryize."

The unit was given the New Year's holiday off and celebrated in Paris; bad weather made flying impossible in any case.

In January 1941, the effective jamming of the navigation systems by the British and their radar-guided night-fighters forced the German air fleets to switch to attacks on coastal cities – also at night – which could be located without radio aids, instead of attacks on industrial cities in the interior. It was a decisive defensive success by the English, as we know.

In his combat report of 10-11 January 1941, *Oberleutnant* Küchle described being attacked by a British night-fighter:

"Combat report by Oblt. Küchle concerning night-fighter attack:

Night sortie on 10-11 January 1941

The fires in Portsmouth could be seen even before we reached Fécamp. The attack took place from the southeast to the northwest. After dropping our bombs (21:08) from 4,800 meters ASL, I made a left turn towards Fécamp (compass heading 140°). I was flying with the superchargers on low with 2,100 rpm and boost pressure 0.8. There was a broken layer of cloud over the target at about 1000 meters, while the Isle of Wight was clear and could easily be made out in the moonlight. Between Portsmouth and the Isle of Wight, about 2 to 4 minutes after dropping the bombs, the radio operator spotted a night-fighter that was approaching our machine from almost ninety degrees to the right. Just before it reached us it pulled up and made a left turn, positioning itself behind our tail.

After the first pass, during which the night-fighter did not open fire, the pilot descended the aircraft at about 3 m/sec., with the autopilot still engaged. The radio operator and the enemy opened fire almost simultaneously at a range of about 100 meters. The pilot then descended the aircraft at about 100 m/sec., and even faster after bullets were heard striking the aircraft. At 4300 meters the airspeed indicator showed 450 kph. During the steep descent the pilot saw tracer from the night-fighter over the aircraft, exactly in our line of flight, whereupon he immediately broke left. The night-fighter climbed away to the left.

A second attack followed soon afterwards, this time from below and to the right. It was probably a different night-fighter, for the first was hardly in a position to make a second pass. Without autopilot, in a progressively steeper dive, at an indicated airspeed of 500 kph and 2,300 revolutions, the pilot turned onto a southerly course using the turn-and-bank indicator. The flight engineer fired off half a drum [of ammunition], then the fighter climbed away. The second attack was much briefer than the first.

The radio operator saw a night-fighter above to our left that did not attack.

We headed for Fécamp, making frequent heading changes between 180 and 100 degrees using the autopilot. By then our altitude was 2,000 meters ASL. As there was no indication from the starboard oil tank and the starboard engine was running roughly at times, we gained altitude over the Channel. No one in the crew was injured. As the hydraulics instruments were no longer indicating, the pilot tried lowering the flaps and undercarriage. This revealed that the hydraulics were gone. We advised that our landing gear was unserviceable and were told to land last. During the flight the pilot put on his shoulder straps, as did the observer prior to landing.

We reached the airfield at 22:10. Anticipating a crash landing, the pilot decided not to land until all aircraft were back.

We began our approach to land at 22:50, after the emergency lowering of the undercarriage and landing flaps. When the wheels touched down, the aircraft tried to swing to the right, which was prevented through the use of left rudder and brakes. Barely able to hold the machine and assuming that the undercarriage was going to shear off because of the steep slope to the right, the pilot ordered the canopy roof jettisoned. As it rolled out, the aircraft swung slightly to the right. As soon as it came to a stop, the engines were shut down, the electrical system switched off and the crew left the aircraft.

The aircraft was hit 38 times in the two attacks. The right tire had been shot up in the air. Eight to ten larger holes led to the conclusion that they must have been caused by explosive shells from heavy machineguns or cannon. Muzzle flashes from three guns had been observed in each wing. Perhaps one of them had been a cannon. The night-fighter fired green tracer. The armored cockpit roof (Opel model) had taken several hits but they failed to penetrate the armor. The starboard propeller had two bullet holes. The tail had also been hit a number of times, some of which may have been caused by the radio operator.

The mixture ratio of the ammunition that was fired was 1:1:1. There was no blinding effect and the path of the projectiles was easily followed.

signed Küchle
Oblt. and Schwarmführer."

The *Geschwader* did not take part in the last big raids on England:

On the afternoon of 27 March 1941 we flew our last attack in this theater, against Oxford-Cowly, in typical pre-spring weather. One last time we encountered the annoying, accurate English flak. There was already hectic activity at our bases. Everything was being packed up – we were pulling back to the Reich.

Operational Overview and Casualties

Before turning to another theater of war, a summary of the operations against England from 20 July 1940 to 31 March 1941. The published information is from the war diary of the *III. Gruppe* of KG 51, which has survived, and may be considered representative for all of the bomber units that took part in the battle.

The *Luftwaffe* lost 2,265 aircraft (25% fighters, 35% bombers alone). These losses could be replaced by new machines, although it is doubtful that production would have kept pace with the technical achievements of the enemy. Much more serious were the heavy losses in well-trained pilots and crewmen. Total casualties were 3,363 killed and 2,117 wounded, plus 2,641 aircrew either missing or captured by the British.

Many of the dead from *Geschwader 51* were buried in the cemetery in Meaux.

From then on, as an independent branch of the armed forces, the *Luftwaffe* was accorded secondary importance. For the rest of the war, the leadership never again dared to wage strategic warfare with it. Even in supporting the army and navy, it was unable to have a decisive effect at key points, revealing the limits of German power. The days of the Blitz campaigns were over.

Aircraft Losses KG 51 (Operations against England)

Period 1/7/1940 – 31/10/1940 (just four months)

Losses	**100%**	**70-80%**	**45-60%**	**25-40%**	**15-20%**
Stab	1	—	—	—	—
I.	13	2	3	12	4
II.	13	—	1	7	4
III.	12	3	2	7	7
Erg.-Stff.	1	—	—	2	—
Total	**40**	**5**	**6**	**28**	**15**

The following aircraft losses were suffered on 12 August 1940 alone, when the Kommodore, Oberst Dr. Fisser, was killed:

Stab: *1 (100%)*
I.: *3 (100%), 1 (30%)*
II.: *2 (100%)*
III.: *4 (100%), 1 (30%), 1 (15%)*

Note:
Aircraft losses were arranged depending on the degree of damage:

100%	*Total loss (crew usually killed).*
60-80%	*Aircraft unusable, still-usable parts were removed for subsequent use (cannibalization).*
45-59%	*Seriously damaged aircraft, with major components requiring replacement.*
40-44%	*Damaged aircraft in which the power plants or systems (e.g. hydraulics) had to be replaced.*
25-39%	*Damage requiring inspection of the aircraft by the unit.*
10-24%	*Moderate bullet/flak damage requiring only minor repairs.*
less than 10%	*Minor bullet/flak damage, which in some cases could be repaired by the crew chief.*

III./Kampfgeschwader 51 Cantonment, 31/3/41
Operations Officer Section (Wiener-Neustadt)

Summary of Operations against England
From 20/6/1940 to 31/3/1941

1. *112 missions with 648 sorties, including*

reconnaissance Schwarm	*118 sorties*
7. Staffel	*205 sorties*
8. Staffel	*180 sorties*
9. Staffel	*145 sorties*

2.	*Flying Hours:*	*1,603 hr., 31 min.*
3.	*Kilometers flown:*	*48 099 300 km*
4.	*Bombs dropped:*	*636 tons 270 kg*

5. *Losses:*

13/7/40	*9K + CR Werkn. 7074, 20% damage resulting from belly landing in Rouen.*
	Pilot Fw. Müller, injured: none.
30/7/40	*9K + ER Werkn. 7081, 100% damage resulting from crash near Nogent le Rotron.*
	Fw. Kurzweg, Fw. Oschließ, Gefr. Boenisch, Fw. Jörg (entire crew dead).
31/7/40	*9K + FT Werkn. 7068, 35% damage from belly-landing in Orly.*
	Pilot Lt. Höchstetter, injuries: none.
9/8/40	*9K + GS Werkn. 7052, 75% damage, crashed during takeoff from Mondésir.*
	Pilot: Fw. Weindl, injuries: none.
9/8/40	*9K + DD Werkn. 5064, 50% damage, crashed during takeoff from Mondésir.*
	Pilot: Obfw. Sonntag, injuries: none.
10/8/40	*9K + JR Werkn. 7071, 20% damage during landing in Beauvais.*
	Pilot: Oblt. Simon, injuries: none.
12/8/40	*9K + ED Werkn. 7073, battle damage caused by fighters.*
	Wounded: Lt. Schweisgut.
12/8/40	*9K + AT Werkn. 5042, 70% damage resulting from forced landing near Le Havre.*
	Pilot: Lt. Capesius, injured: Sdf. Engel.
12/8/40	*9K + KT Werkn. 7091, 100%. Missing during attack on Portsmouth.*
	Lt. Höchstetter, Uffz. Gottfried Noak, Uffz. Otto Noak, Uffz. Stahr, (entire crew missing).
12/8/40	*9K + LT Werkn. 5052, 100%. Missing during attack on Portsmouth.*
	Fw. Schuß, Obgefr. Storek, Gefr. Merker, Gefr. Nortel, (entire crew missing).

12/8/40	9K + FS Werkn. 5072, 100%. Shot down during attack on Portsmouth.
	Oblt. Wildermuth, Oblt. Stärk and Uffz. Droese captured, Uffz. Rösch missing.
12/8/40	9K + BS Werkn. 4078, crashed during attack on Portsmouth.
	Lt. Seidel, Fw. Lokuschuß, Uffz. Fischer, Sdf. Bigalke (entire crew killed).
12/8/40	9K + AS Werkn. 5063, 100%. Crashed during attack on Portsmouth.
	Oblt. Nölken, Obfw. Kessel, Fw. Gundlach, Fw. Velten (entire crew killed).
19/8/40	9K + FR Werkn. 7069, 100%. Crashed, missing during attack on
	Fw. Moser, Fw. Schachtner, Uffz. Bauchauer, Fw. Maak, (entire crew killed).
25/8/40	9K + BR Werkn. 7072, 100%. Crashed during attack on Portsmouth.
	Uffz. Maurer, Uffz. Schulz, Gefr. Pfaff killed.
30/8/40	9K + DS Werkn. 7076, 15%. Landing crash at Mondésir.
	Pilot: Fw. Lang, injuries: none.
7/9/40	9K + CD Werkn. 2167, 30%. Landing crash at Villaroche.
	Pilot: Oblt. Rath, injuries: none.
12/9/40	9K + DT Werkn. 5053, 100%. Shot down during attack on London.
	Uffz. Gutberlet, Obgefr. Luebe killed.
16/9/40	9K + JT Werkn. 7065, 25%. Belly landing in Orly.
	Pilot: Uffz. Franke, injured: none.
20/9/40	9K + MR Werkn. 7092, 45%. Landing crash near Lille.
	Pilot: Fw. Müller, injuries: none.
25/9/40	9K + FR Werkn. 4144, 100%. Crashed near Evreux.
	Fw. Eimers, Lt. Meiser, Gefr. Herich, Gefr. Altmann, (entire crew killed).
27/9/40	9K + IR Werkn. 2174, 100%. Crash near Pussay.
	Uffz. Bender, Gefr. Kienbauer, Gefr. Jung, Gefr. Israel, (entire crew killed).
27/9/40	9K + BR Werkn. 6153, 100%. Crashed near Oisonville.
	Fw. Brünningsen, Fw. Conrad, Uffz. Hartmann, Uffz. Maier, (entire crew killed).
10/10/40	9K + CD Werkn. 2104, 25%. Landing crash in Mondésir.
	Pilot: Oblt. Küchle, injuries: none.
10/10/40	9K + HS Werkn. 299, 100%. Crashed during attack on London.
	Uffz. Metschulat, Fw. Wollf, Uffz. Kafka, Uffz. Schragl, (entire crew killed).
12/10/40	9K + DR Werkn. 7075, 100%. Takeoff crash in Mondésir.
	Oblt. Simon, Obfw. Strauß, Fw. Baader injured, Fw. Torporzisseck killed.
28/10/40	9K + MR Werkn. 8040, 100%. Lost in attack on London.
	Uffz. Krämer, Gefr. Hauf, Gefr. Zimmermann, Gefr. König, (entire crew killed).
6/11/40	9K + KS Werkn. 5070, 100%. Missing during attack on London.
	Oblt. Mathis, Lt. Geilenkirchen, Uffz. Schütz, Gefr. Mader, (entire crew killed).

18/11/40	9K + GR Werkn. 7082, 100%. Crashed near Villeneuve/Paris
	Uffz. Meißner, Gefr. Wolf, Gefr. Effler, Gefr. Rothhäuser, (entire crew killed).
18/11/40	9K + AT Werkn. 7054, 80%. Landing crash in Brétigny.
	Pilot: Uffz. Pahl, injuries: none.
20/11/40	9K + GT Werkn. 7062, 80%. Landing crash in Brétigny.
	Pilot: Uffz. Franke, injuries: none.
31/11/40	9K + AB Werkn. 5050, 20%. Landing crash in Brétigny.
	Pilot; Uffz. Rabien, injuries: none.
31/11/40	9K + FS Werkn. 3189, 15%. Belly landing in Brétigny.
	Pilot. Oblt. Maletz, injuries: none.
21/12/40	9K + FT Werkn. 296, 100%. Crashed near Brétigny.
	Pilot: Fhr. Pahl, Uffz. Born, Gefr. Reibel, gefr. Bier, (entire crew killed).
30/12/40	9K + LR Werkn. 5045. 100%. Crashed while on approach to land at Brétigny.
	Lt. Lutz killed, Fw. Wagner, Gefr. Übel, Uffz. Bruns injured.
15/3/41	9K + BS Werkn. 7119, 60%. Forced landing near Bovoux.
	Obfw. Scherer, Fw. Thieme, Uffz. Plücker injured, Uffz. Hoffmann killed.
15/3/41	9K + HT Werkn. 2271, 40%. Landing crash near Borneville.
	Lt. Capesius, Fw. Öchsl, Uffz. Schulz, Uffz. Horch injured.
21/3/41	9K + BR Werkn. 6167, 100%. Crashed near Le Havre.
	Uffz. Unruh, Uffz. Heikes. Obgefr. Murra, Gefr. Niestädt (entire crew killed).
24/3/41	9K + KT Werkn. 6154, 100%. Crashed near Villacoublay.
	Uffz. Jenkel, Uffz. Selbert, Uffz. Knotz, Gefr. Glier (entire crew killed).

Summary:
Losses in flying personnel:
Killed: 4 officers and 47 NCOs and enlisted men
Missing: 3 officers and 16 NCOs and enlisted men
Captured: 2 officers and 5 NCOs and enlisted men
Wounded; seriously: 3 officers and 5 NCOs and enlisted men; slightly: 2 officers and 7 NCOs and enlisted men

Losses in aircraft:
100% 21 aircraft
70-80% 4 aircraft
45-60% 3 aircraft
25-40% 5 aircraft
15-20% 5 aircraft

Chapter 4
Interlude in Yugoslavia and Greece

Wiener-Neustadt

On the morning of 29 March 1941 the aircraft of our *Geschwader* took off from the Paris area in a generally southeast direction. They flew low over the now-familiar landscape of France. The cloud-shrouded Vosges lay below them. Not until the Zabern Depression did we see the Rhine. Near Karlsruhe we picked up the autobahn and followed it through Pforzheim, Stuttgart and Ulm before landing at Lechfeld to refuel. There we were looked after by the men of the *IV. Gruppe*, which was based there. From Lechfeld we flew over Munich, Rosenheim and Salzburg. Over Linz we descended and flew low over the rooftops and trees along the Danube to Vienna. From there we made our way to our new base in Wiener-Neustadt. By evening all aircraft had arrived safely. In the surrounding area, as in Wöllersdorf, we found good, comfortable quarters. We were astonished to find numerous units with aircraft of all types in the huge airfield area. Never before had we seen such a concentration of aircraft on a single field.

Italian head of state Mussolini reacted angrily when German sent a "military mission" to Rumania, by marching into Greece on 28 October 1940 from his starting point in Albania. One day later the English occupied the key position in the eastern Mediterranean – Crete. The Italian attack bogged down almost as soon as it began. The situation was made worse by the landing of British land and air forces in Piraeus and Volos on 7 March 1941. By 25 March an Italian defeat seemed unavoidable.

In Wiener Neustadt, meanwhile, the *Geschwader* retrained on the improved Ju 88 A-4. In fine spring weather, training and formation flights were carried out over the Danube Basin, Lake Neusiedler and Lake Balaton as far as Hungary and Rumania.

The military uprising in Belgrade on 27 March stoked the smoldering fire in the Balkans. On that day Hitler issued Directive No.25. Yugoslavia had become an enemy that had to be crushed.

The *Geschwader* prepared itself for a new campaign, for the signing of a friendship and non-aggression treaty between Yugoslavia and the Soviet Union on 5 April heated up the tense situation.

On the eve of the campaign, KG 51 had the following operational strength (Ju 88s only):

	Available	**Serviceable**	**Percentage**
I./KG 51	28	17	61%
II./KG 51	27	18	67%
III./KG 51	23	19	83%
IV./KG 51	10	6	60%
Total:	**88**	**60**	**68%**

Luftflotte 4 (*Generaloberst* Löhr) was given the following mission in the Führer Directive, Item 3.a.:

> *"As soon as sufficient forces are ready and the weather permits, the Yugoslavian air force's ground organization and Belgrade are to be destroyed by Luftwaffe in continuous day and night attacks."*

The air units of *Luftflotte 4 (*Vienna) on 5 April 1941, the eve of the Balkan war:

German Air Mission in Bucharest:	Air District Command XVII:
III./JG 52 Bucharest	Fighter Replacement Training *Staffel* 27 Götzendorf
	Replacement Training *Staffel* St.G. 2 Graz

a) Directly attached to *Luftflotte 4*:
4.(F)/121 (Seyring)

KG 2	Zwölfaxing (Do 17 R)
I./KG 2	Zwölfaxing (Do 17 R)
III./KG 2	Zwölfaxing (Do 17 R)
III./KG 3	Münchendorf (Do 17 R)
II./KG 4	Aspern (Heinkel 111 P-4) (mining Gruppe)
KG 51	Wr. Neustadt (Ju 88)
I./KG 51	Wr. Neustadt (Ju 88)
II./KG 51	Wr. Neustadt (Ju 88)
III./KG 51	Schwechat (Ju 88)

b) Air Commander Graz:
Kommodore St.G. 3

Stab II./JG 54	Graz (Bf 109)
II./St.G. 77	Graz (Ju 87)
Stab St.G. 3	Graz (Ju 87)
I./JG 27	Graz (Bf 109)

c) Air Commander Arad:
Kommodore St.G. 77

III./JG 54	Arad
St.G. 77	Arad
I./St.G. 77	Arad (Ju 87)
III./St.G. 77	Arad (Ju 87)
4./JG 54	Arad (Bf 109)
I./ZG 26	Szeged (Me 110)
JG 77	Deta (Bf 109)
II./JG 77	(with 5./JG 54) Deta (Me 109)
III./JG 77	(with 6./JG 54) Deta (Me 109)

d) *VIII. Fliegerkorps*: H.Q. Gorna Djumaja

2 (F)/11	Do 17 (Sofia-Filipovci)
St.G. 2	(*Stab* and *Stabsstaffel*) Belica North
I./St.G. 2	(Ju 87) Belica
III./St.G. 2	(Ju 87) Belica
I./St.G. 3	(Ju 87) Belica
I./St.G. 3	(Ju 87) Krainici
JG 27	Belica
II./JG 27	(Bf 109) Sofia-Vrba
III./JG 27	(Bf 109) Belica
I./LG 2	(Bf 109) Sofia-Vrazdebna
I./LG 1	(Ju 88) Krumovo
II./LG 2	(2 *Staffeln* Bf 109, 1 *Staffel* Hs 123) Sofia-Bozhurishte
7./LG 2	(Me 110) Sofia-Vrazdebna
10./LG 2	(Hs 123) Kranici
II./ZG 26	(Bf 110) Krainici-Vrazdebna

Air-Sea Rescue *Staffel* 7 Varna
IV./KG.z.b.V. 1 Krumovo

In total:
8 *Kampfgruppen* (bombers), 7 *Stukagruppen* (dive-bombers), 8 *Jagdgruppen* (single-engine fighters), 2 *Zerstörergruppen* (twin-engine fighters), 1 *Schlachtgruppe* (close-support aircraft), 3 *Fernaufklärerstaffeln* (strategic reconnaissance).

The Campaign in the Balkans

The attack on Yugoslavia (Operation No.25) and Greece ("Operation Marita") began at 05:15 on 6 April 1941 without an express declaration of war. The government quarter of Belgrade and all major bases of the Yugoslav Air Force were bombed.

Generaloberst Löhr (commander *Luftflotte 4*) personally selected the targets, whose elimination was supposed to make a unified national and military command in Yugoslavia impossible: the seat of the government, the buildings housing the military command, the transportation and communications network and purely military installations. He also gave express orders to use only experienced and reliable pilots in order to minimize civilian casualties.

Löhr even had the attack directives for Belgrade given verbally to his *Geschwader* commanders in advance, however in *Luftflotte 4*'s written attack order the targets to be attacked were given in the usual *Luftwaffe* manner based on grid squares.

In the early morning hours of 6 April, our *Geschwader*, together with other bomber and fighter units, took off from Wiener-Neustadt and Vienna-Schwechat and, in cloudless skies, headed for Belgrade over Lake Neusiedler and the north tip of the prominent Lake Balaton at an altitude of 3,200 meters. The bombers were carrying high explosive and incendiary bombs.

The Yugoslavia fighters bravely tried to defend their capital. Equal in courage and equipment (they had recently-acquired Me 109 fighter aircraft) but inferior n numbers, they fought stubbornly. The targets stood out clearly against the rest of the cityscape and were easily located.

The 469 aircraft taking part in the attack bombed successfully, and the city was soon shrouded in smoke and flames.

During the German advance, Yugoslavian army and air force installations in Novisad, Banja Luka, Gradiska, Mostar and Dubrovnik were attacked. The *Kapitän* of the *6. Staffel*, *Hauptmann* Berlin, was killed during one of these operations.

Many of the unit's personnel were wounded during the low-level attacks. Many of the aircraft came home with damaged inflicted by anti-aircraft fire and small arms fire from Yugoslavian ground forces.

From 7 to 11 April the weather in the Vienna area was poor, or "best QBI." During the return flight after an operation some thought often of this calming airmen's slang and "grew nervous."

On 13 April Sarajevo was subjected to waves of attacks on Hitler's personal order. It was suspected that representatives of the Yugoslavia government were present in the big hotels near Ilidza, due west of Sarajevo.

That day the *III. Gruppe* alone flew 29 Ju 88 sorties and dropped 28,750 kg of bombs.

The 15th of April. Theis first part of a brief campaign ended with attacks on ships and moles in the port of Dubrovnik and Fort Opus.

The Yugoslavia Army surrendered on 17 April 1941.

III./Kampfgeschwader 51 — *command post, 18/4/1941*
Ia Section — *(Wiener-Neustadt)*

Summary of the Yugoslavian Operations
from 28/3 – 15/4/1941

1. *Missions*
   14 missions with 148 sorties, including:

Reconnaissance Schwarm	*26 sorties*
7. Staffel	*45 sorties*
8. Staffel	*32 sorties*
9. Staffel	*45 sorties*

2. *Flying Hours: 482*
3. *Kilometers flown: approx. 144,600*
4. *Quantity of bombs dropped: 154,200 kg, specifically:*

1 Flam 250	*of 250 kg*
10 AB 36	*of 400 kg*
9 SC	*of 1000 kg*
51 SC	*of 500 kg*
394 SC	*of 250 kg*
170 SD	*of 50 kg*
70 SC	*of 50 kg*
24 Flam	*of 250 kg*
0 AB	*of 36 kg*

5. Casualties:

a) During flight to Schwechat:

9K + ET 70% crash	*(Lt. Capesius)*
9K + AS 20% crash	*(Fw. Rabien)*
9K + CS 100% crash	*(Obgefr. Müller, killed)*
	(Obgefr. Hinzpeter, killed)
	(Uffz. Emmert, killed) buried in
	(Gefr. Häberle, killed) Rastatt

b) During flight to Wiener-Neustadt:

9K + HR	*35% crash (Major Vehmeyer)*
9K + DT	*25% crash (Uffz. Evers)*

c) During combat missions:

9K + FS	*100% crash*	*(Lt. Voigtländer, killed)*
		(Lt. Teichmann, injured)
		(Fw. Tromm, seriously injured)
9K + AD	*30% crash*	*(Obfw. Müller, forced landing near Siklos)*
9K + AD	*30% crash*	*(Oblt. Wolff, forced landing near Bark)*
9K + DT	*20% crash*	*(Lt. Capesius, blown tire during roll-out)*

6. One enemy aircraft, type Hurricane, shot down by the crew of Fw. Gügel on 12 April 1941 during attack on Mostar.

Greece and Crete

Meanwhile, after breaching the Metaxas Line, the German forces had also advanced deep into Greece. Athens and Corinth were occupied on 27 April.

From the 14th to 16th of April the *I. Gruppe* under its commander *Hauptmann* Hahn had moved from Arad to Krumovo near Plovdiv. It was stationed there on the bank of the Maritza at the foot of the Rhodope Mountains with LG 1.

From Krumovo the *Gruppe* and the *Staffeln* of LG 1 immediately entered the battle for Greece. Meanwhile in Wiener-Neustadt the men of the airfield operating company converted the machines into close-support aircraft. The big *Vemag* (vertical bomb magazines) were removed and replaced by *Vemag 90* magazines for the carriage of SD 2 anti-personnel bombs. The SD 2 was a new weapon that had seen little use and had to be dropped from a maximum height of 28 meters above ground. The crews told the most incredible stories about the bomb's effects.

Some crews, who were in need of rest, were permitted to take a brief vacation in Mariazell in Styria. Others eagerly practiced the still unfamiliar ultra low-level flying in the still very new Ju 88, gaining proficiency.

At Wiener-Neustadt, the *IV. Gruppe* under *Hauptmann* Stemmler had also been settling in since 6 April 1941. With experienced instructor crews from every *Gruppe*, it prepared to begin its special duties as a replacement training unit. Away from the combat fronts, it would train crews arriving from the flying schools in special tactics and combat techniques under relatively peaceful conditions.

From a tactical point of view the Ju 88 was capable of four different types of attack:

Horizontal high-altitude attack: thanks to the excellent view from the cockpit, the pilot could see the target until the bombs were dropped and plan his approach to the target accordingly. The observer dropped the bombs using the Lotfe bombsight and the automatic bomb-dropping mechanism.

Low-level attack: The pilot carried out the bomb run and dropped the bombs himself by means of a button on the control yoke.

Inclined attack: The pilot aimed at the target using the reflector sight, approached the target in a shallow dive at high speed and dropped the bombs from close range.

Diving attack: Differed from the inclined attack only in being made from a greater altitude at a steeper dive angle.

Of course experienced crews did not rigidly adhere to these procedures. Often they used their experience and skill to tailor their tactics to the situation.

The *IV. Gruppe* was responsible for all training and there was a regular exchange of knowledge with the operational *Gruppen* and *Staffeln*.

Tactical experience was constantly collected and analyzed in order to be passed on to the bombing schools (Tours, for example).

"Operation Marita" was not yet over, however. The *Geschwader* was used mainly to attack the Greek ports – Volos on 15 April, Chalkis on the 19th and 20th, Chania on Crete on 21 April. These attacks seriously hampered British efforts to withdraw troops from Greece and land ships in Crete. The British naval units operated beneath a curtain of anti-aircraft fire.

In preparation for an airborne landing on the island, armed reconnaissance was carried out over the waters between Athens and the island of Crete, to where the British and Greek defenders had withdrawn. The defense was centered on the Maleme-Chania sector.

The island and the Cretan Sea had to be monitored constantly. Many crews returned with flak damage and were forced to land at other airfields or even make forced landings with wounded crewmen and shot-up aircraft. That was about the price for a sunken ship in Suda Bay.

The *Geschwader* stationed a detachment in Saloniki. The personnel of the 1st Airfield Operating Company patched up the battle damaged machines as best they could so that – even though not fully serviceable – they could later be flown back to Krumovo or Wiener-Neustadt. Simply the awareness of not having to make long flights over inhospitable territory with unpredictable weather gave the crews a feeling of security, indeed even safety. One just knew that comrades from one's own unit in Saloniki were watching out and standing by to lend assistance.

Operations went on for two weeks. The *Geschwader* did not provide air support for the airborne landing on Crete ("Operation Mercury"). Most of its aircraft were handed over to LG 1, which remained in Krumovo. On 13 May 1941 the unit's personnel returned by train to Wiener-Neustadt, where the staffs were already working on plans for the next movements.

Operational experience to date was summarized in reports by the departments of the operations and technical officers:

III./Kampfgeschwader 51 *command post, 25 May 1941*
Operations Section *(Wiener-Neustadt)*

Subject: Experience in low-level attack with the Ju 88 (loaded with SD 2)

Reference: Geschwader Order No.24/41

To
Kampfgeschwader 51
Ia Section
Command Post

I. ATTACK IN KETTE OR ROTTE FORMATION

1. The Rotte has proved its superiority as the most flexible type of formation for low-level attacks. The Rotte formation makes it possible to follow even tight turns in roads, enabling visual steep turns to the left, and also steep turns to the left and right as soon as the decision is made not to cross over the road under any circumstances. If this decision has not been made or cannot be made for tactical reasons, then the lead aircraft must climb in the right turn. In order to unmistakably advise the wingman (even without radio communication) that a right turn is being initiated and not to go from low flight into normal flight, the lead machine must indicate by banking to the right that the right turn will commence after pulling up.

When dropping SD 2's, it is advisable for the wingman to close to almost the same altitude; this will give the lead aircraft greater maneuverability, split the defenses and guard against fragmentation effect if the lead aircraft suddenly drops its bombs.

The disadvantage of the Rotte is that neither aircraft flies over the road itself and the necessary density of fragments can only be achieved if the cone of fragments from the two machines intersect over the road, which means that the lateral spacing of the aircraft must be 30 meters at greatest.

In addition, the Rotte must be flown so flexibly as to automatically fit the tactical situation and instantly exploit the situation as found. If, for example, a horse-drawn column abandons its vehicles to the left when the Rotte appears, the formation leader must attack the personnel to the left of the road, while the wingman attacks the vehicles and horses. Of course there cannot be plans for every situation encountered, although understanding can be created in the classroom and through map exercises. Not until the attack itself do the two pilots demonstrate their tactical understanding, grasp of fleeting situations and their ability to assess and make decisions, assisted by bomb aimers and standing gunners, just as the leader of an infantry squad has to act independently in leading a rifle squad in the attack.

2. Echelon right formation has proved itself to be fully usable, although its flexibility is far less than that of the Rotte. Climbing turns to the left will still be entirely possible for experienced crews. As in Rotte formation, a right turn is to be initiated by the lead machine banking and climbing.

The greatest advantage of echelon right is that the No.3 can attack the road itself, while the Kette leader and the No.2 cover the shoulders on both sides and formation flight is easily carried out with good visibility to the left. Here too it is advisable for the other aircraft to close up (wing chord spacing) during the attack.

The leader must, however, to some degree adjust spacing based on the No.3, as it is this machine's task not to leave the road. Command of the echelon right formation must not under any circumstances pass to the No.3, otherwise the leader loses command, which is passed to the weakest flyer in the formation, who usually also lacks the powers of evaluation and decision for tactical situations. Such an echelon right formation then represents nothing more than a badly flown Kette.

3. Though considered the best formation tactically, the Kette is to be consciously avoided for low-level formation flight because of its great inflexibility. When, in addition to the cannon, the observer or radio operator must man the forward upper machine-gun to increase firepower during ground attacks, the pilot's view to the right from the Ju 88 must be characterized as poor, making efficient formation flying difficult.

As well, when attacking targets not clearly identified, which must first be located in the target area, the Kette is too inflexible.

In areas where there are no enemy fighters, it must be left to experience to decide how advisable it is to break up the Kette and make individual attacks. Reforming must then take place at a position based on bearing and distance from the target attacked.

4. A spacing of 300 meters is suitable to avoid the effects of prop wash in low-level flight. With respect to the SD 2's safety distance, therefore, consecutive attacks by individual aircraft, Rotten or Ketten can safely be made at intervals of 800 meters.

TECHNICAL DETAILS

1. During landing the Ju 88 is somewhat nose-heavy because of additional installations such as armor, cannon, etc.
As per the manual, approach with some power and landing flaps extended, flare. The aircraft will then make a three-point landing, power off. Rollout is no longer than landing with engines throttled back.

2. Equipped with four drums for MG-FF automatic cannon. Total of 240 rounds. 2nd drum stored beneath observer's seat, 3rd and 4th drums in the ventral bath. Secured by leather straps.

3. The gunner's role during an attack is to use the upper machine-guns to suppress enemy defensive fire. The gunner stands in the bath, has a clear field of vision forward over the canopy and also covers the attack area with the cannon. For the best effect, machine-gun drums should be loaded with a B-ammunition to tracer ratio of 3:1.

4. Changing cannon ammunition drums must be practiced until it becomes automatic:
a. Transport the full drum to the observer's position.
b. Remove the empty drum.
c. Steady the cannon by observer and gunner (with left hand).
d. Install the full drum (observer).

5. The reflector sight is being removed to give the pilot a better field of view.

III. SAFETY REGULATIONS FOR THE CREW AND OUR FOLLOWING TROOPS

1. After the attack, the bomb release button is to be pressed several times over enemy territory away from roads and railroads.

2. In the event of engine loss on takeoff, the Vemag 90 is to be jettisoned with bombs. Do not forget to open the bomb doors.

3. In the event of engine loss over friendly territory in a loaded Ju 88, the Vemag 90 with bombs is to be jettisoned. Mark location on map.

Transfers and their Problems

The *III. Gruppe*'s war diary reveals very clearly the recurring problems associated with movements by the unit. Despite numerous rehearsals, there were often problems in many areas:

III./Kampfgeschwader 51 — *Command Post, 18/4/1941*
Technical Officer's Section — *(Wiener-Neustadt)*

EXPERIENCE REPORT CONCERNING TRANSFERS

The operational possibilities of the forward airfield in question must be thoroughly investigated prior to the move. If this had been done during the move to Parndorf, two further moves, which endangered the operational readiness of the unit both in terms of aircraft and equipment, would not have been necessary. In this way unnecessary crashes caused by soft ground or half-soaked airfields could be avoided. As well, such a move unnecessarily hampers training by the Gruppe.

The airfield operating companies and the Gruppe cannot move simultaneously if the move is covering a larger distance, for the Gruppe will find itself at its new location without equipment and can only carry out the most minor work if there is no appropriate maintenance facility at the operational airfields. It is therefore inadvisable for higher command to dispatch both airfield operating companies simultaneously. It would be much more appropriate to hold one airfield operating company back until the entire Gruppe has taken off.

The speed of movement, and with it the ability of the Gruppen to quickly achieve operational readiness, is hampered in that the airfield operating companies do not have the prescribed heavy prime movers, instead having only medium prime movers. If these are coupled to two trailers, their maximum travel speed is 25 kph. Furthermore, the airfield operating companies must be provided with an additional truck, as the capacity of the available equipment is inadequate, for example, to take along rations for 11 days per man as during the last move, which by itself would have required one truck.

The airfield operating companies must be dispatched on a timely basis so that at least the Staffel dispersals and refueling points can be determined prior to the arrival of the bombers.

During a transfer it is advisable to send the maintenance crew chief ahead with the Ju 88s and the dorsal gunner in the transport aircraft.

The units must assign a man to each transport to be responsible for the loading and unloading of equipment.

Strength of the advance party: 1 officer, 1 paymaster, 4 NCOs and 4 men (meaning each unit is to supply 1 NCO and 1 enlisted man).

It is scarcely possible to establish a general sequence for transport, as this depends on whether a Gruppe is assigned an adequate number of transport aircraft to carry out the move in a single flight, or the aircraft have to make three or even more flights.

A cleanup detachment must consist of the following: one officer and one Feldwebel per unit.

Chapter 5
Russia – The Verdun of the Luftwaffe

Preparations for "Operation Barbarossa" in Krosno

Preparations for the campaign against the Soviet Union were longer and more complicated than for any other operation of the Second World War. The military planning for "Operation Barbarossa" – codename for the campaign against the Soviet Union – were supposed to be concluded by May 1941.

After the campaign in the Balkans delayed the concentration of forces by five weeks, Hitler scheduled the operation to begin on 22 June 1941. Meanwhile, beginning in January 1941, 17,000 trains rolled east, including 106 supply trains per day in the final weeks before the attack. At the beginning of May, large formations moved up to the Soviet-German demarcation line under cover of darkness. Despite German efforts to conceal them, the Soviets could hardly remain unaware of troop movements on such a scale.

The German command was fully aware of the vastness of the second front into which they were supposed to advance. The Caucasus and the White Sea were separated by 3,000 kilometers, interrupted by the vast, inaccessible area of the Pripyat Marshes (600 by 200 kilometers) between Minsk and Kiev.

The only period suitable for operations was from May to October. Before and after that, the notorious muddy period hampered major movements. The difficulties associated with the long Russian winters were also no secret.

The German Army massed a total of 145 divisions between the Baltic Sea and the Carpathians, supported by 45 Finnish and Rumanian divisions. Facing them were 246 Soviet divisions.

Army Group South (von Rundstedt) formed the German right wing, with the 17th Army (von Stülpnagel), Panzer Group 1 (von Kleist) and the 6th Army (von Reichenau), supported by *Luftflotte 4* (Löhr). Then there was Army Group Center (von Bock) with the 4th Army (von Kluge), Panzer Group 2 (Guderian), Panzer Group 3 (Hoth) and the 9th Army (Strauß), supported by *Luftflotte 2* (Kesselring). In East Prussia was Army Group

North (Ritter von Leeb) with the 16th Army (Busch), Panzer Group 4 (von Hoepner) and the 18th Army (Küchler), supported by *Luftflotte 1* (Keller). The Soviet buildup had largely been completed on 1 May 1941.

Luftflotte 4 had its headquarters in Rzeszow (Reichshof) in Army Group South's sector. Attached to the air fleet were:

4. (F)/122 (Ju 88)
KGr.z.b.V. 50 and 104 (Ju 52)
JG 52 (Me 109 F)

V. Fliegerkorps (*Ritter* von Greim)
KG 51 (Ju 88 A-4)
KG 54 (Ju 88 A-4)
KG 55 (He 111 H-4)
JG 3 (Me 109 F)
4. (F)/121 (Ju 88 D)

IV. Fliegerkorps (Pflugbeil)
KG 27 (He 111 H)
JG 77 (Me 109 E)
3. (F)/121 (Ju 88 D)

At the end of May 1941, large advance detachments from the *Staffeln* of KG 51 and the 7th Airfield Operating Company were loaded onto trains. They left Wiener-Neustadt and headed east through Lundenburg (Breclav), Prague, Mährisch-Ostrau and Cracow. After a three-day journey came the order to disembark. The men found themselves standing in a small village station. After about an hour, the units had detrained and resumed their journey by truck. It poured rain. After an uncomfortable night they arrived at their destination, Lezany near Krosno, at 07:30. To use an English phrase, they were "in the middle of nowhere."

There were barracks. Nearby the *Luftwaffe* construction companies were hard at work making a runway. The building of slit trenches and machine-gun posts began the same day. The technical personnel of the flying *Staffeln* began arriving on 4 June as "passengers" in the aircraft of the *I. Gruppe*. No one knew for sure what they were doing there. One "latrine rumor" followed the other.

Everyone knew something new about the reason for our presence. Even though the accommodations were primitive and simple, the men nevertheless lived well during this period. Eggs and geese were cheap, and there was much frying and roasting in the barracks. Water came from a brook that flowed nearby.

"Patrols" discovered that the Polish-Galician city of Krosno (Krossen) was nearby.

In anticipation of the arrival of their airmen, on a lovely mild June evening the men of "the black fraternity" had a probably unforgettable evening in the circle of their company. A three-man band provided music and there was plenty to eat and drink.

The days passed quickly and were consumed by preparations for the arrival of the aircraft. The units arrived by 20 June as planned. Not everything went according to plan, however. One '88' was unable to get its landing gear down and – as usual – landed on its belly and ended up lying at the end of the runway – or more accurately, the grass strip.

On the afternoon of 21 June 1941 the aircraft were loaded with bombs – as a test it was said. Toward evening everyone made their way to their quarters to play cards. At 22:00 the flying personnel were ordered to a higher state of readiness. The drinking stopped but the games went on.

The mission briefing was held at midnight (00:00) on 22 June (Sunday). The men of the airfield operating companies were wakened at 02:20.

At about midnight, *Hauptmann* Bauer, commander of the 7th Airfield Operating Company, had his men gather round him in a semicircle and in the light of a pocket lamp read out Hitler's appeal entitled "Soldiers of the Eastern Front" and called upon them to maintain discipline and do their duty. The weeks of speculation were finally at an end.

Silently and lost in thought, each man walked across the airfield to the dispersals. There wasn't much left to do, as the aircraft were already ready for action.

At the start of the war against Russia, the *Geschwader*'s complement of aircraft (mainly Ju 88 A-4s) was:

Gruppe	**Authorized Strength**	**Serviceable**	**Percentage**
I.	22	22	100%
II.	36	29	79%
III.	32	28	88%
IV.	15	12	80%
Total:	**105**	**91**	**87%**

Of the total of 1,945 aircraft massed against the Soviet Union (61% of all aircraft available to the *Luftwaffe*), 1,400 were reported serviceable on 21 June 1941, equal to 72%. The *Geschwader*'s serviceability level was thus clearly above the average value in the *Luftwaffe* and spoke to the tireless efforts of our men of the maintenance and repair services, who never spared themselves and always displayed a maximum of willingness to serve under difficult conditions in the field.

At about 03:00 the mechanics ran up the engines. The soft pulsating drone grew into an ear-shattering din. The crews, who received last-minute instructions from the *Staffelkapitäne* on the way to the aircraft, arrived, put on their parachutes and checked the bomb bays and weapons.

The sun was fiery red in the eastern sky when, at 03:15 on 22 June 1941, the thump of artillery rumbled from horizon to horizon. The distant guns had initiated the opening barrage against Russian. The inferno began.

Beginning at about 03:30, machine after machine roared down the grass runways at Krosno and Lezany. They lifted off, headed east and soon disappeared from view. On the roads, endless army columns moved towards the nearby front.

The first blow was supposed to strike fully occupied Soviet airfields such as Stryj Stryjski, Buzhov II, Tremblovla, Buczcacz, Khodorov and Lisietztsche. The *Geschwader*'s roughly 80 aircraft destroyed about 100 Russian machines on the ground. On the Russian airfields, reconnaissance aircraft, bombers and fighters were lined up as if on display. Their burnt-out wrecks were later found when the airfields were overrun.

Despite overwhelming German superiority in the air, the *Geschwader* and the entire *Luftwaffe* suffered casualties from flak, fighters and – unfortunately – our own bombs. These included the previously secret SD 2 fragmentation bombs, or "devil's eggs." Looking like tin cans with braking wings, they were dropped in large numbers, but their use turned out to be short-lived.

Developed as an anti-personnel weapon for use by close-support aircraft, on impact or at a preset height they burst into 50 small and 250 tiny fragments that sprayed up to twelve meters and had an effect similar to that of a medium anti-aircraft shell. Dropped in quantity, they almost always made a direct hit.

The 360 small bombs jammed unpredictably in the specially designed dispensers in the bombers (*Vemag*). The slightest jolt (landing or turbulence) was sufficient to set off the fuses, which were live. The exploding bombs tore holes in the belly of the aircraft that were equivalent to a direct flak hit in their effect.

Many fragmentation bombs did not release until the aircraft landed, exploding directly behind it or lying on the ground with treacherous delayed-action fuses.

The armorers and firefighters frequently had to carefully inspect the landing and takeoff areas and carefully remove them, like soap bubbles that might pop at any second.

Despite its success in the opening days of the Russian campaign, the SD 2 was an unsuccessful design, especially after the effective Soviet flak forced our low-flying close-support aircraft to higher altitudes, making use of the SD 2 impossible. Similar difficulties were encountered with the SD 10 bomb. It was too complicated for handling at the front. The objective of achieving air superiority over the battlefield, in order to cover the rapid advance by the army, especially the fast-moving armored spearheads heading towards Lvov and Ternopol, was not made easy by aggressive Russian fighter units.

The *Geschwader* carried out four major attacks on the first day of the war against Russia. All serviceable aircraft took off in the first wave. Seven from the *III. Gruppe* failed to return, including five from the *9. Staffel* alone!

On the evening of the first day, following the last landing at 20:23, in Polanka Castle in Krosno the *Kommodore*, *Oberstleutnant* Schulz-Heyn, drew up the shocking balance:

60 men (15 crews) from the flying personnel were dead or missing. Fourteen aircraft from the *III. Gruppe* alone had been put out of action in crashes or had been written off, equivalent to a loss of 50%. The picture was equally grim in the other *Gruppen*. Among the

dead was *Oberleutnant* von Wenchowski, the "old pig farmer," *Kapitän* of the *5. Staffel*. Everyone missed this popular officer and his earthy humor. The machines were patched up with feverish haste, metal patches were applied over bulletholes, aircraft that had crashlanded were cleared away. The airfield operating companies' workshop platoons got no rest. Bathed in sweat, naked from the waist up, everyone pitched in to make the shot-up, in some cases badly damaged and riddled aircraft serviceable again for the coming day.

Dog-tired, at about midnight the men fell into their bunks in the quarters. At the end of the day, the last thought of those who had come back was: "What has happened to our comrades who didn't make it back? Are they still alive? Hopefully. But what will the coming day bring? How will it all end? What will our families at home think? What is the propaganda likely to tell them?" With these thoughts they fell into a deep sleep and no longer heard the distant rumble of artillery and the closer metallic hammering from the maintenance area, where the aircraft were worked on until early in the morning.

On the first day the Soviets lost 1,811 machines, 332 shot down by German flak and fighters, 1,489 destroyed on the ground by Stukas and close-support aircraft, which included us.

The 23rd of June was a brutally hot day. The unaccustomed heat made life difficult for everyone. The high tempo of operations permitted no rest breaks. The armorers were unable to keep pace filling ammunition belts and drums, as consumption was very high. Everyone who could be spared had to help with the belts. It was only good, comradely cooperation that made it possible for the aircraft to be quickly readied for new operations.

Despite the heavy losses, which made it possible for each man to calculate how long he would last, there was no rest. Those who failed to return included veteran crews with combat experience over France, England and Yugoslavia.

Even then, the *Geschwader*'s successes and heavy losses during the first weeks of the campaign did not stop us from raising the question of whether there was a reasonable balance between our successes and losses. Many asked themselves if the *Luftwaffe* command could allow its modern twin-engined bombers to go on being used as close-support aircraft at the cost of good, well-trained crews.

The technical companies were seriously hampered by inadequate equipment. They lacked cranes and lifting devices for recovering crash-landed machines and making engine changes, as well as many other needed tools and replacement parts.

At the start of the Russian campaign, selected officers and non-commissioned officers often had to fly home to notify the families of crews that failed to return from operations.

By 30 June 1941 the number of available aircraft and crews had sunk to 1/3 of authorized strength. Morale had also reached a low point among the personnel, who had become accustomed to victory.

On 30 June the "devil's eggs" (SD 2) were finally removed from the armory.

As a result of the army's rapid advance, after just a few days Krosno lay far in the rear.

Luck and Wlodzimierz

On 4 July 1941 the unit moved its *I. Gruppe* and *II. Gruppe* to Luck, while the *III. Gruppe* was sent to Wlodzimierz to take part in the fighting at Ternopol, Zhitomir, Kiev and Biala-Tserkov. Enemy armored forces were decisively defeated near Berdichev and the German armored thrust through Vinnitsa towards Uman was close to its successful conclusion.

The first physically- and mentally exhausted crews were sent home to recuperate. Uncertainty as to the fate of missing comrades and heavy losses placed an unbearable strain on their nerves.

On 6 July 1941, *Hauptmann* Serschen, the *Staffelkapitän* of 9./KG 51, failed to return, whereupon *Oberleutnant* Henne took over the *Staffel*.

On 12 July the *Geschwader* destroyed the bridge over the Dniepr near Kanev, preventing Russian troops under Budyonny from interfering with the rapid German advance.

At the beginning of July the first crewmen who had forced-landed behind the front returned to the unit – to the relief of everyone.

The account by *Feldwebel* Scheurich speaks the simple, clear language of the frontline soldier and factually describes his experiences while on the run:

III./KG 51 Luck, 7/7/1941

Report by Fw. Rudolf Scheurich of the crew of 9K+HS (Oberleutnant Bretschneider) concerning the attack on an airfield near Ternopol, forced landing and flight.

Our orders were to attack the Ternopol airfield. About 10 minutes before reaching the actual target, we spotted four or five Martin bombers sitting on an airfield. We attacked with SD 2s and destroyed the machines.

After dropping our bombs, we were attacked by about four Rata fighters. We were hit immediately. The elevators must have been damaged. We touched the ground. The pilot screamed: 'We have to make an emergency landing!' The radio operator jettisoned the roof. The pilot subsequently set up for a forced landing, which went smoothly. We left the aircraft. Obfw. Harenburg activated the self-destruct charge and the aircraft exploded. The crew then crept together from cornfield to cornfield.

After about an hour a farmer came straight towards Oblt. Bretschneider. The farmer mumbled something and went away again. Again we crept from cornfield to cornfield and hid ourselves once more. Shortly before sunset we were discovered by Russian military police. They surrounded our location and escape seemed impossible. Three of us raised our hands to surrender. Oblt. Bretschneider stayed down. The military police fired at the three of us and Fw. Ober collapsed, shot in the head. Obfw. Harenburg and I jumped up and ran out of the cornfield across a potato field. Then Obfw. Harenburg fell, shouting 'Keep going!' I cannot say if he had been hit.

The riflemen then concentrated their fire at me. After 100 meters I also fell and lay on the ground for a moment. They kept shooting at me and I crawled into a gully. A small stream ran through it. I crossed, became stuck in a swamp, and just managed to drag myself across the swampy area. It was about 50 meters wide.

I had a very difficult time getting my bearings, for I had no compass, no watch and no map. I walked towards the setting sun. Suddenly I found myself standing in an artillery position. I silently dropped to the ground and crawled into a cornfield. I lay there until it was dark, Then I rose to my feet and got out of there. The sentries saw nothing.

I had absolutely nothing on me to eat. I must have lost my emergency rations while fleeing. For two days I ate absolutely nothing. On the third day I ate clover flowers, which eased my hunger somewhat. On the fourth day I tried it with clover leaves. I quenched my thirst with water from a puddle, filtering it through my handkerchief. I began experiencing intestinal gas which was so bad that I thought it must blow me apart. After forcing myself to vomit, the gas went away. I then developed a fever and chills. I didn't think I could continue my flight.

On the fifth day I stopped a woman in the field and asked her for a bite of bread, which she gave me. After two or three bits I couldn't eat any more because of thirst. The woman then passed me a bottle of water. I greedily drank it all and immediately threw up again. Seeing that I was very weak, the woman then gave me some milk. This I drank slowly and after each sip ate a piece of bread. I began to feel my strength returning. The woman asked me to leave the field because she was obviously afraid of the Russians.

On the sixth day I thought I would have to give up my flight. I met a Ukrainian farmer on a country road. He was very friendly and shook my hand. He spoke to me in Ukrainian, which I did not understand. When I identified myself as German, however, he was able to converse with me in German, as he had previously served in the Austrian Army. I told him that I was a fleeing airman and that some of my comrades were already dead. He advised me to abandon my flight because there were too many Russians there and thought it impossible that I would get through. He took me to his field and hid me there during the day. He dug a hole and I lay down in it, whereupon he covered me with grass. In the evening we went together to his house.

I had tucked my tunic into a tuft of grass, which the man carried on his back. I pulled on the man's shirt and put on his cap. I also carried the hoe and tote bag. He told me that we now had to pass through an anti-aircraft position. All young Ukrainians had been drafted, so I would have to hobble to avoid standing out. When we reached the house his wife seemed upset, for she was also afraid of the Russians. But when she saw my miserable condition, she came over, stroked my hands and indicated to me that I should sleep in the attic.

I remained there until I was liberated on 5 July 1941. The farmers fed me well. Another poor woman from the village, who spoke good German, helped in this, because my hosts were very poor.

At about 11 o'clock on 5 July I heard machine-gun fire in the distance. It was still Russian. When I thought I heard a German machine-gun, I left my dwelling and recognized German armored cars. Several Ukrainians who saw me immediately gathered round me. Eventually the entire village came out, brought eggs and milk and wanted to help me.

I German motorcyclist then picked me up and took me to the SS Division 'Wiking,' which in turn delivered me to Ternopol. From there the air liaison officer sent me to the command post of Army Reconnaissance Battalion 41 ..."

Such reports became more common and unsettled the crews. From then on each of us had an uncertain feeling when we crossed our lines heading east, as if feeling the sting of a knife thrust into our backs.

Operations were flown in support of the Battle of Kiev, in the course of the advance to the Dniepr, until 19 July 1941. We attacked the Dniepr bridges near Cherkassy, rail junctions near Bakhmach and Kiev, road bridges at Garnostaypol and troop movements near Zwiahel (Novograd), plus airfields at Nezhin, Oster and Chernigov. Although our striking power had been reduced, we suffered no casualties.

Zilistea and Balti

On 15 July the *I. Gruppe* moved to Zilistea near Buçau in Rumania, while the *III. Gruppe* returned to Wiener-Neustadt to rest and reequip – the unit was at an end!

At Tscheschen station the train was besieged by a large crowd of people. It was the first to return to the homeland from the Eastern Front. They were literally showered with gifts. From Wiener-Neustadt crews and ground personnel were first sent on leave. In the meantime the *Gruppen* were issued brand-new aircraft and new young crews arrived. The unit soon reached its operational strength again. Close-support hung on the nail, we finally became a proper bomber unit again.

The elements of the *Geschwader* stationed in Rumania were now attached to the *IV. Fliegerkorps* (Pflugbeil) and took part in the drive by our troops to the Dniepr crossing at Berislav. The second-largest river in European Russia is 700 meters wide at that point. Under covering artillery fire and air cover by units of *Luftflotte 4*, German pioneers threw a bridge across. The pontoon bridge at Berislav demanded a high toll in blood and was probably the most hotly contested pontoon bridge of the last war. It enabled the 11th Army to launch the decisive attack towards the Crimea and the Caucasus.

Hauptmann Willi Stemmler, the *Staffelkapitän* of the *4. Staffel* who had gone missing on the first day of operations in Russia, was alive! This news surprised everyone, especially the men of the *4. Staffel*. He had been discovered deep inside Russia by German mountain troops and brought home. Stemmler visited the *Geschwader* in Balti. He still had burns on his hands and face and looked in poor shape. His account of his wild experiences after the crash of his aircraft in enemy territory and the unexpected help from Ukrainian guerillas captivated all who heard it. It was a miracle that he had survived. Even *Generalfeldmarschall* Milch wanted to hear Stemmler's exciting tale from his own lips and flew to Balti for that sole purpose.

The story of *Obergefreiter* Helmut Bernhardt, observer in the crew of 9K + AM (*Oberleutnant* Höhl, *Unteroffizier* Stelzer and *Unteroffizier* Musiol), is another example of the amazing exploits of individuals in extraordinary circumstances. *General* Pflugbeil, the air corps' commanding general, expressed his wholehearted appreciation, immediately promoted him to *Unteroffizier* and invited the crew to dine with him. The event described in the *General*'s official recognition was one that happened often in war. A good pilot always had a special relationship with his observer and additionally trained him to fly the aircraft in the event of an emergency and even land it:

The Commanding General
of the IV. Fliegerkorps5 August 1941

During an armed reconnaissance mission over Russia in the Ananiev area near Odessa on 30 July 1941, aircraft commander and pilot Oberleutnant Höhl was shot through the head and killed in combat with several Ratas.

Because of the crowded conditions in the Ju 88, the remaining crewmembers could not lift the fallen pilot from his seat. The rudder therefore remained fully deflected by the dead pilot. As well, one of the engines had been damaged and was running irregularly. The autopilot had also been knocked out by enemy fire.

Despite these serious difficulties, observer Obergefreiter Bernhardt of 4./KG 51 immediately took control of the aircraft. Despite having to fly through heavy cloud at times and despite a continuation of the air battle, he safely reached our lines and carried out a smooth belly landing near Racsani.

In doing so he saved the remaining crewmembers and the aircraft.

I express my highest appreciation to Obergefreiter Bernhardt for this outstanding act, which was carried out with the utmost care and fearlessness.

signed Pflugbeil.

The aircraft flown by *Leutnant* Unrau of the *3. Staffel* and his crew of *Feldwebel* Steinbrückner, *Feldwebel* Winter and *Unteroffizier* Polok was rammed by a Rata fighter during an attack on a convoy in the Black Sea. His combat and experience report provides a dry, factual description of the dramatic flight, which fortunately had a happy ending:

Experience Report

Unrau, Leutnant	*location unknown, 16 August 141*
3./Kampfgeschwader 51	*(Zilistea)*

While attacking a convoy off the west coast of the Crimean island [sic] on 15 August 41, I was attacked by four fighters (3 'J 17's and 1 Rata). During the first attack from below by a 'J 17,' the rear gunner, Uffz. Polok, was wounded in the leg. The bullet entered the ventral bath through the gap between the machine-gun mount and the floor armor. The rearwards defense was seriously hampered by the repeated jamming of the MG 81.

After pulling out at 800 meters, we were attacked from behind by a fighter. Accurate fire from the radio operator, Feldwebel Winter, forced its pilot to bale out. The now pilotless fighter, remaining on its attack heading, rammed the tail section of my aircraft, whereupon the entire right half of the horizontal tail broke off and the remaining left part was bent upwards by about 20 degrees.

After initial heavy vibration in the elevator the aircraft became very tail heavy. Despite pushing the control column forward as hard as I could, with the assistance of one leg, the aircraft climbed at 2-3 meters per second at an indicated airspeed of 300 kph. I was able to counter a rolling motion to the left, which began at the same time, by dropping the starboard wing without loading the rudder, which was also twisted.

After about 30 minutes flying time, I was able to maintain an altitude of 3,000 meters by throttling back the engines. About five minutes before reaching the Rumanian coast south of Akkermann, the aft fuselage twisted by another 20 degrees to about 40-50 degrees. As I now had to expect the entire tail to come off at any minute, I gave the order for everyone to prepare to bale out. The crew stuffed maps, bandages and the like into their flight suits.

As there was a light west wing, I tried to fly as far west as possible. When further parts of the tail flew off and heavy swinging and shaking of the control column made it obvious that the tail was about to finally disintegrate, I gave the order to jettison the canopy roof and the escape hatch in the ventral bath. I ordered the crew to remove their radio helmets to avoid the chance of becoming hung up. The crew then left the aircraft through the escape hatch, while I moved to the radio operator's seat, which was easy to do at a speed of 250 kph. I was about to leave the aircraft through the ventral escape hatch when what was left of the tail flew away, making it possible for me to jump out through the canopy roof.

After an estimated free fall of about 20 seconds, I was falling at a constant speed and was able to move freely. As I saw parts of the tail whirling through the air above me, I waited until they had passed before opening my parachute. My life vest cushioned the shock of opening and it was entirely bearable.

I landed very softly, as I pulled myself up in my harness at the moment of touching down. The crew came down after me in an area of 2x2 kilometers.

The farmers who rushed to the scene got there well ahead of the Rumanian soldiers and behaved amicably.

Summary:
If this happens again, I would once again order the canopy hatch jettisoned with the ventral hatch, as this increases the crew's freedom of movement considerably. Unless, as in this case, baling out through the top hatch appears appropriate because of the absence of the tail section, the ventral hatch is the best place for the entire crew to leave the aircraft.

On 29 August the *III. Gruppe* returned to the Eastern Front, arriving in Balti, Bessarabia with new aircraft and rested crews. For a change, the crews were bivouacked in tents. No one is likely to forget the plague of mice we lived with there. We organized contests to see who could catch and kill the most mice in a specified time.

We immediately began operating in support of the army's attacks across the Dniepr. The targets were concentrated in the Khersonyes – Kakhovka – Melitopol area, in the approaches to the Isthmus of Perekop, the entrance to the Crimea.

With few forces – the *Staffeln* often had just three of four aircraft available for operations – our efforts were dispersed and achieved little success. Anyone who sustained minor damage or engine trouble could land in Vosnessensk or Permovaysk.

We flew armed reconnaissance against road intersections, road junctions, railway lines and columns. Only occasionally were airfields and flak positions alternate targets. All our ideas about aerial warfare seemed reversed. Losses, however, remained within bearable limits.

At the beginning of September 1941, the *II. Gruppe* was withdrawn from combat operations to return to the maintenance base in Wiener-Neustadt. It remained in Vienna until about the end of November, reequipping completely on the Ju 88 A-4 and conducting training. It spent a beautiful September and October in the magnificent landscape of the Semmering and Schneeberg, training as if in peacetime. Those who had already taken leave alternated between flying and the classroom.

On 10 September the *9. Staffel* under its '*Kapitän*,' *Oberleutnant* Henne, moved to Vosnessensk to be closer to its targets, the armored trains near Perekop and the Tatar Trench.

Finally, on the afternoon of 13 September, a large force of Ju 88s assembled over Zilistea to attack a proper target for a bomber unit. The port of Odessa. The feared Russian flak rose from ships and the military pier, but it stopped no one from bombing accurately and returning in one piece.

The airfield and tents were frequently under water because of the steady rains in Bessarabia, nevertheless there was as much flying as possible during the day. Armed reconnaissance missions over the Crimea and the gulf lying to the north finally produced results. Regardless of the bad weather, ground personnel and aircrews gave their best in order to keep up the pressure on the enemy.

The men of the *Geschwader* stationed in Bessarabia were shocked by the increasingly frequent confirmations by the RLM that many of those who had gone missing in the opening battles had been found dead, in some cases under pitiful conditions. According to statements by the population, others had been captured by the Russians and died under torture.

As a result of the battle of encirclement at Kiev, the Soviet high command tried to evacuate Odessa, which was under siege by the Rumanian 4th Army, and get as many of its troops as possible to the seriously threatened Crimean Peninsula. The almost regular shipping traffic between Odessa and Sevastopol and Ak-Metsched and Yevpatoria now became the focus of German air attacks.

After the Battle of Kiev, Panzer Group Kleist breached the Russian Dniepr defenses at Zaphorozhye and turned south towards the Sea of Azov, into the rear of two Soviet armies. By 11 October 1941 these had been destroyed between Mariupol and Berdyansk near Chernigovka. The road to the Crimea lay open.

Tiraspol and Nikolayev

Since 10 October the *I. Gruppe* had been in Tiraspol, while the *9. Staffel* had already moved forward to Nikolayev.

On 19 October 1941 there was an incident there that probably made every pilot want to crawl into the deepest hole.

Hauptmann Berger was escorting a battle-damaged Ju 88 of the *I. Gruppe* back to the airfield and passing on instructions to its crew. Concentrating on the task at hand, he forgot to lower his undercarriage and made a perfect belly landing!

This brought to mind an old rule of flying that says that there are only two kinds of pilots: one that has already forgotten to lower his undercarriage before landing and one who is eventually going to! Taganrog fell on 17 October 1941, Stalino on 20 October. German forces finally broke through into the Crimea on 27 Octobcr and captured all of the peninsula except Sevastopol.

Before Moscow the exhausted German troops attacked until exhausted.

From 23 October the *III. Gruppe* was in Nikolayev, where it was joined by the *Kommodore*, *Oberst* Koester, and his headquarters.

Winter arrived. The frustrating muddy period was finally over, and, despite the bitter cold, vehicles could once again move over the broad Russian roads without becoming stuck. The quarters – a spartan facility formerly used by cadets – were more than uncomfortable. No windowpanes, no heating. Lengthy periods of snow and fierce snowstorms transformed the landscape into a desert of snow. Maintenance work had to be carried out with freezing hands. There was no proper winter clothing. Despite the much vaunted "Kärcher heaters," it became difficult to start the aircraft engines. The cold start procedure, described so confidently in theory in the *Luftwaffe* manual, did not always work. The only way the mechanics could ensure that the aircraft would be ready to fly in the morning was to begin warming up the engines at two in the morning.

In places operations by the army were halted completely by the bad weather. The capture of Sevastopol was therefore postponed until 1942, even though the threat to the 11th Army's flank persisted.

In December the Russians landed on the Kerch Peninsula and established a bridgehead near Feodosiya. Their objective was to relieve Sevastopol and, with the troops breaking out of the fortress, retake the Crimea.

Despite bad weather, the units of the *IV. Fliegerkorps* flew against Sevastopol, Kerch, Feodosiya and Yevpatoria without pause. *Generalleutnant* Count Sponeck, commanding general of the XXXXII Corps, acted independently and evacuated the Crimea to avoid the destruction of his corps.

This was the first case of military disobedience in the eastern campaign. This upright, cool-headed man was subsequently brought before a court martial and senselessly executed shortly before the end of the war.

Beginning in November 1941, our attacks targeted the Don bridges near Rostov and Bataysk.

Zaphorozhye

On 4 December 1941 the *II. Gruppe* left Wiener-Neustadt and moved to Zaphorozhye, from where it took part in operations during the battles for Taganrog and Rostov and the Donets Basin. It was not uncommon for attacks to be made beneath a ceiling of barely 30 meters. The Russian flak made things hot for us. Ratas frequently made harassing attacks against our airfields by day and night.

We spent the third Christmas of the war with Italian airmen. There was no mail. Don Cossacks sang for us. Despite this, our spirits remained low.

In their aviation medicine reports, medical officers Dr. Denkhaus (I./51) and Dr. Ott (III./51) described symptoms of serious nervous exhaustion among the crews (crying fits, irritability, even epileptic seizures). A shortage of coal made the situation worse and made the winter even more unbearable. Most crews had received no proper leave since the start of the campaign, no days off from flying. A report by one of our crews dated 9 December 1941 illustrates the stress faced by our flying personnel. A Ju 88 of the *III. Gruppe*, part of a formation of seven aircraft, was attacked and seriously damaged by one of our Me 109s over Taganrog. It was probably a typical event for overworked, overly nervous men who were long overdue for a period of rest in the Reich. *Generaloberst* Löhr, the commander of *Luftflotte 4*, praised KG 51 several times for its actions during the Battle of Rostov. With at least two *Gruppe* in continuous frontline action at all times, by 11 December 1941 the *Geschwader* had already dropped 5,000,000 kilograms of bombs on the enemy.

At the beginning of 1942 the fighting at Feodosiya made it necessary to move the *II. Gruppe* and 9./KG 51 forward to Zaphorozhye.

Finally, at the beginning of February 1942 the *I. Gruppe* and the *9. Staffel* were given a rest from operations until the spring. In Odessa they took on replacements and received new aircraft. The units' aircraft were handed over to the *II. Gruppe* and 7. and 8./KG 51, which on 24 March were then able to take a break from operations.

This was surely a gratifying, insightful result of the reports submitted by the medical officers, who stressed that the personnel were in need of time to regain their strength. This is all the more understandable when one considers that the *Gruppen* were often only able to put one or two machines into the air daily. Use of the *IV. Gruppe* received special mention. It was recommended that it become more involved, in order to ensure a more regular relief and exchange of personnel and the "thorough recuperation" of personnel through home leave. Poor rations (only 'bread and onions') weakened the strongest fighting spirit. The *Geschwader* had to overcome a low in morale.

In the north, the Russian winter offensive resulted in the German army's withdrawal behind the Volkhov, in the central sector towards the line Orel – Rzhev, to a penetration into the Vyazma – Smolensk – Vitebsk area and the encirclement of German troops at Demyansk. And in the south, following the loss of Kerch, the Russians broke into the German front at Izyum, Kupyansk and Valuiki, where our *Geschwader* saw action in January 1942.

Meanwhile, after sacking *Generalfeldmarschall* von Brauchitsch, commander-in-chief of the army, Hitler assumed command of the army.

The *I. Gruppe* and elements of the *III. Gruppe* (*7.* and *8. Staffel*) flew repeatedly against Valuiki and Kupyansk, where the Russians, experienced winter fighters, were attempting to take Kharkov in a pincer movement.

When aircraft landed away from home base, mission orders were received directly from *Generaloberst* von Richthofen, the close-support leader, so that as many as four missions per day could be flown.

Not until March 1942 was there better weather, but it was about to get worse. The spring thaw began, placing everything under water and creating literal seas of mud. The runway looked like one big swamp. Called "sewing machines" because of the unusual noise made by their engines, Russian aircraft appeared over out bases every night, robbing personnel of their sleep. These nuisance raids regularly inflicted casualties upon our ground personnel.

The guiding principle of the German 1942 offensive was to strike a decisive blow against the Russian economy by capturing the oil regions of the Caucasus and severing the Volga at a vital point (Stalingrad) to limit deliveries of American aid via Iran.

The immediate goal of the spring offensive of 1942 in the south was the capture of Kerch and Sevastopol. Since February, targets for attack had included other sites near Sevastopol (Yuzhnaya Bay), Balaclava, Kerch, Anapa, Novorossisk and other Caucasian ports.

On 14 March 1942 the *Kommandeur* of the *III. Gruppe*, *Hauptmann* Baron Ernst von Bibra, welcomed the famous bomber pilot *Hauptmann* Baumbach of KG 30, the "Eagle *Geschwader*," who arrived in Nikolayev in his aircraft 4D + KM to assist in anti-shipping operations around the Crimea. Baumbach was supposed to pass on his wealth of experience in the field on to the crews of KG 51. He had been ordered to the theater by *Oberst* Peltz.

Baumbach flew his first sortie on 5 March 1942, taking off at 13:13 and heading for the waters south of the Crimea in order to familiarize himself with the local conditions. At the same time, the first crews returned to their previously decimated *Staffeln* after a period of rest in the Reich.

On 18 March Baumbach, who came from a *Geschwader* considered the *Luftwaffe*'s most effective anti-shipping unit, led a mission against the port of Novorossisk, which enjoyed natural protection provided by steep cliffs. Baumbach led a seven-aircraft formation that consisted of the *III. Gruppe*'s reconnaissance/command *Kette* under *Hauptmann* von Bibra, the *7. Staffel* under *Hauptmann* Heilmann and one aircraft from the *8. Staffel* (*Leutnant* Roßberg).

Heavy anti-aircraft fire forced the attackers to take evasive action during the approach to the target, making their bombsights useless. In order not to go home empty handed, the bombers attacked targets of opportunity in the harbor, aiming their heavy PC 1000 bombs as best they could.

The formation continued to receive murderous anti-aircraft fire from the hills and ships in the harbor and from the city itself, fortunately no aircraft were hit.

The next major attack, on 20 March, was aimed at ships in the port of Sevastopol and the bombers were escorted by fighters of JG 77.

In his combat report, *Hauptmann* Baumbach noted that the success of dive-bombing attacks against shipping targets depended on good weather.

Had this finding been made by a veteran unit leader solely to confirm to the air force command that the men of KG 51 had not previously lacked the necessary daring, that the weather had not been taken into consideration as a deciding factor?

Hauptmann Baumbach flew his last mission with us on 24 March 1942 against Tuapse. He surely flew back to the Reich from Nikolayev with the feeling that everyone in the unit was giving his best in skill and courage in order to fly successful missions every time there was good weather.

After these difficult missions, *Major* von Bibra reported that surprise attacks by day simply were no longer possible or worthwhile. These flights were not only wearing on the individual, they also struck at the very substance of a *Geschwader*.

The Kerch Peninsula had been retaken on 15 May. 150,000 prisoners were taken. The Battle of Kharkov subsequently became the focal point. The Russian penetration at Izyum was pinched off and eliminated. The Donets had thus been retaken as a jumping off point.

The *Geschwader* played a major role in "Operation Fridericus" in the areas east of Kharkov. The Izyum – Kupyansk – Volchansk area was so difficult to take, because the troops fought closely interlocked. On 29 May 1942 the *Geschwader* moved to Kharkov-Voychenko.

Ternovaya Wood

The wood near Ternovaya and Varvarowka, where a German infantry unit with unserviceable armored vehicles had been bogged down and encircled for days, was one of the main focal points.

On 20 May alone, between the early morning hours and sunset, a single *Gruppe* flew twelve missions totaling 46 Ju 88 sorties, while on 21 May it flew thirteen missions totaling 63 sorties! The total for the *Geschwader* was 294 sorties by Ju 88s in two days.

Two letters, written by one of the soldiers in the pocket, describes the operations from the infantryman's point of view. They reveal that it was always easier to hold a position when there was support from German bombers:

To my comrades of the 9. Staffel of office L. 37922

Near Ternovaya one of your comrades dropped a cooking pot containing smoking material and a short greeting from you. This inspired me to write to you and at the same time thank you for your valiant and brave support. You were undoubtedly well aware of our situation. The Russians wanted to crush us, but they failed. Ultimately your bombs wore them down. Some fell very close to our holes, making the earth tremble. You gave us courage, and we are proud of you, for this was an example of true comradeship. We were amazed by how tireless you were!

We are happy to be out of that witch's cauldron, as we wouldn't have had the strength to hold out much longer. For ten days we got almost nothing to eat. Now we are getting some rest, which we desperately need in order to recover.

We thank you once again for the support that was so vital to us and wish the 9. Staffel the best of luck in the future.

Dear Comrade!
Your bomb in the form of pleasant surprises was found by an Obergefreiter of my platoon. I personally offer my sincerest thanks and also do not want to neglect to answer your most kind letter. As you know, we were encircled for ten days and had to defend ourselves against a vastly superior foe (approx. 30,000 men). We, on the other hand, were about 1,000 men, without any heavy weapons. The Russians attacked constantly, including with masses of tanks. As well our positions were bombarded fearfully all day long by every kind of weapon. We also had little ammunition and almost no food for ten days.

Now, dear comrade, you can figure out for yourself in what a complicated position we found ourselves. We fought as hard as we could and happily were relieved after ten days.

Now to you, dear comrade. German aircraft and German tanks gave us effective support during our liberation. But what you accomplished, I cannot put down on this piece of paper. I express my highest appreciation and can assure you that you are very, very popular among all our soldiers. I, for example, had to defend a dangerous sector. 150 meters away about 1,500 Russians were preparing to attack. They would undoubtedly have broken through if you hadn't come with your bombs at the last minute. You really had a great 'nose,' for the entire bomb load fell into the wood, where I wanted it to go. Your waves of attacks also smashed a number of the enemy's concentration areas. Now I must tell you modestly that it was you who saved our lives or prevented us from certain capture. The effect of your bombs was simply frightful and the Russians soon lost their lust for attacking. Now you may book another major accolade for yourself; in the truest sense of the word you did precision work, precision work not to be outdone by any professional.

You dropped bombs 50 meters in front of our noses, which was where they had to go. We felt sure that our final hour had come, but your bomb aimers hit their targets. The most dangerous moment, however, was when a large bomb landed four meters from my hole but, thank God, failed to explode. All in all, you did your job extraordinarily well and we will always remember this experience.

Once again I say to all of you who took part that we have you to thank for our lives and offer:

"Three cheers to our airmen!"

If, dear comrade, you have the time, then please write to me again. I wish you and all of your comrades all the best and good luck.

The Russian strength had been broken, Timoshenko beaten. Near Barvenkovo he lost twenty-two rifle and seven cavalry divisions. Fourteen tank and motorized brigades were totally destroyed.

240,000 Red Army troops were taken prisoner, 1,205 tanks and 2,026 artillery pieces had been destroyed or captured. It was the end of the Battle of Kharkov, where the Soviets had intended to encircle the Germans and were themselves encircled.

The road to Stalingrad was now open.

Kerch and Kharkov had fallen in two weeks and six Soviet armies had been destroyed. The terrible winter was forgotten.

Sevastopol and the Black Sea Ports

The next objective was to crack Sevastopol, the most powerful fortress in the world. The assault, which was supposed to take five days, was to last five weeks.

Obergefreiter Friedrich Schulz of the *4. Staffel* described his unit's operations in a letter to his parents dated 21 June 1942. Not long after he wrote it, on 8 August, he and his crew were posted missing over the Black Sea:

Dear parents! *Russia, 21 June 1942*

I flew several more successful missions today. I would like to tell you the story of one of them.

03:00, I step out of our tent on the small forward airfield in the east. The sun is already up and blinds my eyes, accustomed to the inside of the tent. The observers from the other crews emerge from the other tents and rush with me to the command post. We mark the new target, the industrial installations in Sevastopol, on our maps. Brief orders about the location and timing of the attack, and the flight briefing is over. We make our way quickly to the breakfast table to reawaken our spirits with butter and coffee. Then we slip into our flight suits and walk to the aircraft, where the mechanics are waiting for us. The pilot checks the aircraft's flight controls. I busy myself with the bombs, while Hans and Alfred smoke another cigarette. Right on schedule, the engines are started.

03:45, the engines howl, the Ju 88 picks up speed, a short hop and we were airborne. The undercarriage comes up and we turn on course. Flying ahead of us is the Staffelkapitän in '9K + Ida Marie.' We are flying '9K + Ludwig Marie,' as the right 'Kette dog.' On our left is the new Unteroffizier in 'Berta Marie.' I look at today's target on the ordnance map. There is the north fort of Sevastopol, then the dry dock, workshop halls, magazine and factories. We will drop our 250-kg bombs on the north fort, the 50-kg bombs on the workshop halls.

Ahead the coast and the Black Sea appear below us. We alter course towards Sevastopol. The voice of the Staffelkapitän rings out over the intercom: 'Ida Marie to Kette. Go to line abreast right, attack south of Balaclava, reassemble at an altitude of 2500 meters.'

Sevastopol appears before us. The first smoke clouds from anti-aircraft shells appear to our right. I open the bomb doors and preselect the bombs. Then I point out the target, the north fort, to Walter – our pilot. We will make a diving attack. 'Pullout at 2000 meters,' Walter says to me. The radiator flaps are closed, the propeller pitch adjusted. I turn on the bomb fusing panel.

Walter's voice sounds over the intercom: 'Ready to dive!' Three voices echo 'ready!' in return. The machine gives a jerk and we dive steeply towards the earth. The fort beneath us grows larger, the slipstream whistles past the canopy. I look at the altimeter – 2,500, 2,200, 2,100, 2,000 meters! I tap Walter on the knee, pull out! I am pressed into my seat as if seized by a giant fist. The aircraft climbs steeply. 'Bombs gone!' reports our gunner. I switch off the bomb fusing panel and preselect the next bombs. In a steep turn, we see our bombs explode in the north fort. We regain altitude in a right turn. The anti-aircraft guns fire furiously. We are over the target again. Headlong we dive towards the enemy. The pilot presses a button on his control yoke and the bombs fall onto the target and explode. The aircraft pulls out of its dive and climbs, anti-aircraft guns blazing away at us the whole time. The next bombs will be dropped on the workshop halls from level flight. I set up my bombsight for level bombing, preselect the bombs and once again switch on the bomb fusing panel. Then my eye is glued to the eyepiece. I bring the target into the vertical crosshair, the workshop halls move into the center of the reticle, turn the bombsight's star switch, set the slant view to the end mark. The target again moves into the center of the reticle, I rotate the star switch again, align the recessed marks and now the target slides into the center of the reticle again. I press the button and the bombs fall towards the target at intervals of 50 meters. I turn the slant view back in order to see the bombs strike – 4, 5, 6, 7, 8, 9 bombs. I hear Hans' voice over the intercom, 'Great, it's burning!' In the eyepiece I see the bombs exploding in the workshop halls. Heavy smoke suggests that fires have broken out. We enter a steep turn and I can no longer see the target. I close the bomb doors. The anti-aircraft guns blaze away as we fly towards the sea. Bang! Something hits me in the head. Amazed, I turn my head and see a hole in the glazing beside me. The others also look in astonishment. We have been lucky again.

We dive toward the assembly point, where the other two machines are already circling. We join formation and head for home. We see busy traffic on the roads to

Sevastopol. Scattered clouds are forming. I get some music on the DF. Soon afterwards we land at our airfield. After leaving the aircraft we discover a hit in one of the radiators. The crew chief is already working on the damage. We fly the second mission in another aircraft. We fly against the enemy six or seven times a day."

The *I. Gruppe* of KG 51 was attached to *Generaloberst* Wolfram Baron von Richthofen's *VIII. Fliegerkorps*, which flew more than 2,000 sorties daily.

A special occurrence during this battle is worthy of note, because it was witnessed by thousands of German soldiers on the hills around Severnaya Bay.

For weeks, a floating anti-aircraft barge in Severnaya Bay, near the big Sevastopol lighthouse on Cape Khersonyes, armed with 164 anti-aircraft guns, had prevented German land, sea and air forces from launching effective attacks on the fort. Whether one took off from Tiraspol, Kitay or Sarabus, this anti-aircraft platform was a thorn in the eye of the bomber crews and a dangerous obstacle.

2./KG 51 under *Hauptmann* Fuhrhop had already attacked this target three times, and the *Staffelkapitän* intended to carry out another attack on 25 June 1942. *Oberstleutnant* Ernst Hinrichs was to fly with him. His aircraft was initially unserviceable, but then it was made operational again and was loaded with SC 250 bombs for the next day. Late in the afternoon the *Staffelkapitän* summoned *Oberleutnant* Hinrichs to a briefing, informing him that he was to accompany him. Hinrichs was to drop his bombs to suppress the anticipated anti-aircraft fire, so that he – Fuhrhop – could finally strike the anti-aircraft platform and put it out of action.

The sun was already low on the horizon when the *Oberleutnant* and his *Kapitän* took off from Sarabus. Soon afterwards they flew over the old Tatar castle of Bakhchisary, from where they would dive into the hell of Sevastopol. Contrary to the old tactical rule of attacking from "out of the sun," because of the prevailing west wind Hinrichs came in from the east in his aircraft 9K + FK, flying low along Severnaya Bay to attack the platform, which was bathed in sunset light. The Russian anti-aircraft guns blazed away at the pair of bombers. *Hauptmann* Fuhrhop circled, waiting for his turn to attack.

Oberleutnant Hinrichs dove on his target. The crew was so concentrated on the task at hand that it had no time to notice the projectiles – called "flat-irons." Hinrichs' first bombs were direct hits. The anti-aircraft platform sank and its guns were silenced. The ammunition stored on board ensured that it was completely destroyed.

Hauptmann Fuhrhop began his dive, but seeing the effect of Hinrichs' bombs he broke off the attack. There was nothing left to bomb. It is said that *Generaloberst* von Richthofen, who happened to be airborne in his Fieseler *Storch*, witnessed the attack. After landing, he immediately telephoned the unit and inquired as to the identity of the pilot so that he could personally decorate him with the Knight's Cross. Several weeks later, on 27 July 1942, *Oberleutnant* was awarded the coveted decoration. Because of this, he was not awarded the German Cross in Gold, which had already been on its way to the unit.

This decisive action, which was accompanied by a certain element of luck, had a decisive impact on the taking of Sevastopol. Because of a bomb shortage, each bomb had to be dropped individually. For each crew this meant 25-30 dives per day from 3500 meters to 800 meters – a tremendous physical strain in the summer heat in the Crimea.

Sevastopol fell on 4 July 1942. The 11th Army under von Manstein had taken the Crimea. Russian partisans still held out in the Jayla Mountains, tying up German security forces and inflicting casualties on them.

The *Geschwader* took part in "Operation Wilhelm" from 10 to 13 June 1942, flying a total of 300 Ju 88 sorties, mainly against railway lines and road targets in the area of Kupyansk – Volchansk. On 28 June 1942, Army Group South (*Generalfeldmarschall* von Bock) attacked from the area east of Kharkov – Kursk, following Directive No.41, "Case Blue" (capture of the Volga Bend near Stalingrad), its ultimate objective being the oil fields of the Caucasus.

The offensive began with a drive on Voronezh. The 6th Army (Paulus) turned south down the Don and reached the river west of Stalingrad. Supply problems hampered operations significantly.

Major von Friedeburg, *Kommandeur* of the *III. Gruppe*, took over command of the *Geschwader* from *Oberst* Koester in Zaporozhye on 4 July 1942. On 10 July the *Geschwader* moved to Stalino (present day Donetsk). From there it mainly attacked bridges over the Don and Donets in support of our forces. Rostov, which had been turned into a fortress, was at the point of being retaken. Russian troops accumulated around Shakhty and Konstantinov. Beyond Rostov towards the Kalmuck Steppe, I. and II./KG 51 attacked railway targets.

Despite accurate anti-aircraft fire, there was just one loss to report. The aircraft flown by the crew of *Leutnant* Focke from Essen was hit by heavy flak; out of control, it dove vertically to the ground, where it crashed and exploded. Just two parachutes were seen. A third took the form of a banana and fell to earth. The fate of the crew remains uncertain. They were posted missing. The remaining crews flew confidently and concentrated their subsequent missions. The *Kommandeur* of the *III. Gruppe*, *Major* von Bibra, regularly flew combat missions.

Rostov and Bataysk fell into German hands on 25 July. German troops crossed the Manych and advanced towards the Caucasus.

Stalingrad became a target for the *Geschwader* for the first time on 27 July.

On 29 July the *Geschwader* completed its 15,000th combat mission in the east, during which had dropped 1,805,000 kg of bombs.

Before long the drive towards the Caucasus had to be supported again. Armavir and Maykop were the targets, and both were reached on 6 August.

A battle of encirclement raged near Kalach. There, too, the *Geschwader* intervened effectively. It had become used to always being inserted at the focal point of operations.

The 1st Mountain Division under *General* Lanz drove into the Caucasus. Its sector included Mount Elbrus. This giant, with a height of 5,633 meters, was a secondary objective. On 21 August German flags flew atop the highest mountain in the Caucasus. The standard of the 1st Mountain Division bearing the edelweiss and that of the 4th Mountain Division with the gentian were stuck side by side in the ice.

Since 5 August the *Geschwader* had been in Kerch, in order to shorten the long transit flights to the Caucasus. Only the *I. Gruppe* continued flying four- to five-hour missions into the northern combat sector.

The *IV. Gruppe* in Bobruisk on the Beresina regularly sent fresh, well-trained crews to the *Staffeln. Hauptmann* Stemmler, *Kommandeur* of the *Gruppe*, provided realistic training to his "young hares," aided by capable instructors like Häberlen and Capesius. For familiarization, anti-partisan missions were flown in the Kholm – Glinka – Yelnya area. Since 8 August the operational *Gruppen* had been striking Black Sea ports in the Caucasus. These well-defended natural ports of Novorossisk, Tuapse, Sochi, Sukhumi, Poti and Batumi all claimed victims.

The C-6, a *Zerstörer* version of the Ju 88, was used, especially against shipping between Kerch and Temryuk. To confuse enemy fighters, the noses of these aircraft were painted silver-bronze to simulate the glazed nose of the standard Ju 88. Increasing losses revealed how difficult such missions were. A number of command errors, for example the absence of air-sea rescue aircraft, non-standardized marking of the aircraft and the use of the same frequencies within two different units unsettled our flyers more than a little.

On 15 August the crew of Ingo Seel failed to return from a sortie over the Black Sea. Two aircraft (*Leutnant* Damm and *Leutnant* Schwenk) were sent to search for the missing crew, however both failed to return.

A tragic mishap occurred during one of these missions. A formation of five aircraft from the *I. Gruppe* attacked Tuapse. Fully loaded, the aircraft were heavy and sluggish. *Leutnant* Meyer lagged behind the rest. Suddenly Russian fighters appeared. *Leutnant* Meyer put his aircraft's nose down in order to gain speed and catch up to the others. When he arrived over the target, he was several hundred meters below the other aircraft, and his machine was struck by the bombs dropped by the other aircraft and literally torn apart. Albin Gernert and Ernst Pinkerneil were a killed in addition to the gunner. In appreciation of the excellent support the *Geschwader* had provided the 1st Mountain Division, the latter's commanding officer, *General* Lanz, authorized all of its members to wear the mountain troops' edelweiss emblem as a cap badge in future. Of course, this did not appear in any service manual.

From Tatsinskaya towards Stalingrad

On 16 August there was a move via Taganrog to Tatsinskaya, an airfield in the steppe, from where the first sustained sorties against Stalingrad began on 20 August. The *II. Gruppe* assumed responsibility for servicing and maintaining the aircraft of the *I.* and *III. Gruppe* and sent them rested aircrews, until on 7 September it was sent to Stalino to reequip and then briefly saw action in *Luftflotte 1*'s sector. In the beginning, Stalingrad was not a primary objective of the summer offensive. As a port on the Volga and an armaments center, the city was supposed to be eliminated, but as it was of secondary importance it would be left as a target for aircraft and long-range artillery.

After the Soviet 62nd Army had been encircled near Kalach in mid-August 1942, the 6th Army from the west and the 4th Panzer Army from the southwest advanced towards the bend in the Volga near Stalingrad. Hitler wanted to see the city bearing Stalin's name fall.

As the battle began, the *Geschwader* provided air support for the 4th Panzer Army. The aerial offensive began on 23 August 1942. During one of these attacks, aircraft 9K + AA, flown by *Major* von Bibra and his crew of *Obergefreiter* Heyse, *Unteroffizier* Moser and *Obergefreiter* Repinski, was hit by anti-aircraft fire and forced down next to the Chir River. *Oberleutnant* Poppenburg of the *7. Staffel* saw this and without hesitation landed nearby to pick up the crew. Before the Russians could intervene, 9K + AD's engines roared and the aircraft took off again from the rough stretch of steppe.

Von Bibra had made his forced landing at about 11:00. At 16.27 he took to the air again with a partially new crew. The crews flew as many as five sorties per day. By evening the battered city was in flames from north to south.

On 30 August the 4th Panzer Army breached the city's outer defense ring from the south. The Russians were prepared for this eventuality and withdrew to the city limits to avoid encirclement.

In the words of Soviet General Chuikov, "the German airmen nailed everything to the ground." Operations were aided by good weather and relatively weak and inaccurate anti-aircraft fire. The principal targets were artillery positions, armor concentrations and troop concentration areas. Targets in the Gumrak, Pitomnik, Gorodishche and Leninsk areas were repeatedly struck. Despite the loss of the crew consisting of *Hauptmann* Walter Heilmann, *Gefreiter* Albert Huber, *Flieger* Horst Rehling and *Unteroffizier* Heinz Haase on 12 September, losses were surprisingly low.

At the end of September the units were able to leave the hot and dusty steppe airfield in Tatsinskaya. The continuous dive-bombing sorties negatively affected the motivation and operational readiness of the crews.

Gastric influenza and dysentery were common health problems, brought on by poor rations and unhygienic living conditions.

A rest position was established in Sarabus in the Crimea, where the weather was milder. Despite a ban on home leave, if a crewmember came down with jaundice or some other serious illness, the rest of the crew was sent home.

The *II. Gruppe* reequipped in Stalino and on 5 October it moved to Bobruisk, from where, like the *IV. Gruppe* also based there, it was to operate in *Luftflotte 1*'s sector.

It is unlikely that anyone will forget the days in the Crimea.

Whether it was the pleasant "joyrides" around the beautiful peninsula with no enemy contact, the day trips to the Tatar Castle in Bakhchisary and to Sevastopol, or a long, brisk hike in the mountains past the vineyards, it did the airmen good and allowed them to unwind, even though they were very far away from their families and the problems in the homeland. The spirit and unity in a unit had always been something special and supporting. The men were brought together not just by the war but by having to rely on one another day in day out. Who in a military unit solves political problems? Only someone who has experienced it under special circumstances can judge true military life without pathos.

These special conditions indirectly force men into behaviors often declared dead by highly-developed civilizations and which alone enable a community to survive in exceptional circumstances, as in war: comradeship, loyalty, and the acceptance of strict command, which daily proves its effectiveness.

In the period from 25 October to 5 November 1942, the *II. Gruppe*, less its ground units, moved to Armavir, accompanied only by its maintenance crew chiefs. From there it raided Ordzhonikidze, Chegem I and II, Naltchik and Tuapse.

At about 22:00 on the night of 4 November, a Russian nuisance raider scored a lucky hit on a huge fuel dump at the end of Armavir airfield. Such a target was the dream of every airman. The fire spread quickly to aircraft loaded with fuel and bombs. As the airfield was home to several units, with more than 100 Ju 88s and He 111s present, there was plenty of fuel for the fires.

Just one of the *II. Gruppe*'s aircraft escaped damage. The unit quickly moved back to Bagerovo on the Kerch Peninsula and began trying to find new aircraft. The crews were eager to fly and there were plenty of targets.

The quiet was short-lived. On 3 November the unit returned to Tatsinskaya. Cold, snow and icy winds made life difficult in the earth bunkers. Outside temperatures of minus 18 to 32 degrees Celsius were not uncommon. The conditions made life especially difficult for the ground personnel, who before dawn had to begin shoveling out and warming up aircraft stuck in the snow. Cases of frostbite were especially common among the specialists who had to check radio equipment, bomb mounts and engines for serviceability. They could not work wearing heavy wool gloves. Machine-guns and cannon froze. Oil congealed. It was enough to drive the technical personnel to desperation. But the aircraft had to fly, that was the impetus. And this despite the Russian illness, called "quick release," and the fact that mail only came from Sarabus every fourteen days. That was the location of the *Geschwaderstab* with *Kommodore Major* von Friedeburg, who also occasionally flew combat sorties.

The unit's actions in the Battle of Stalingrad were mentioned daily in the *Wehrmacht* communiqué. Each night Russian nuisance raiders appeared overhead, straining the nerves of the overtired men and inflicting casualties on the ground personnel.

Major "Fritze" Dierich led the *I. Gruppe* in Tatsinskaya and elements of the *III. Gruppe* were also placed under his command. After the loss of *Oberst* Conrady he assumed command of the *Geschwader* until *Major* von Frankenberg-Proschlitz arrived on

5 February 1943. When flying was suspended due to fog and snow, there was a literal orgy of paperwork, unavoidable even during war.

One procedure did a great deal to improve morale. By using coordinated transmission times, the *Geschwader* and several "specialists" maintained radio communications with a German station inside the Reich. Occasionally, somewhere in Russia, a Ju 88 would climb to altitude, extend its trailing antenna and make contact with the OKW or the *Luftwaffe* communications center in Berlin, in order to exchange messages to and from the front, including some of a coded private nature. The *Staffelkapitän* of 2./KG 51, *Hauptmann* Häberlen, had a hand in many of these communications. On one occasion the *Geschwader* meteorologist RegRat Rumbaum was informed about the birth of a daughter thusly: "Secret Command Matter, R.R. Rumbaum: new tailless aircraft ready for takeoff, maintenance hangar remains receptive."

The Soviet Army Groups Southwest (Vatutin), Don (Rokossovski) and Stalingrad (Yeremenko) attacked the front held by the Rumanian 3rd and 4th Armies, which were deployed on the left and right of the German 6th Army, and broke through. They linked up at the Don Bend near Kalach at 16:00 hours on 22 November, completing the encirclement of the 6th Army. 284,000 men of the 6th Army and elements of the 4th Panzer Army were trapped.

Hitler rejected a proposed breakout attempt, because Göring, wrongly assessing the situation, promised to supply the pocket from the air.

When about 1,000 transport gliders were sitting near Zaporozhye and the military told itself that they were near Leningrad, it is not surprising that rumors of intentional sabotage began to circulate.

Rostov

The Caucasus front was frozen.

The *Geschwader* with headquarters had finally been in permanent quarters again, in Rostov, since 7 December. The cold holes in the ground in Tatsinskaya had sapped everyone's strength. Although airmen could also be tough, the accommodations and airfield conditions in "Tazi" were no longer bearable. Operational effectiveness suffered as a result. As well, the airfield was needed by the bomber and transport units earmarked for the Stalingrad airlift.

Despite the Christmas season there was no holiday spirit. Many soldiers spent the fourth Christmas of the war in the field.

From Tatsinskaya came news that the airfield, where *General* Fiebig and his air corps staff were still present, had been attacked and overrun by Soviet armor in the early morning hours of Christmas Eve. Despite adverse weather, most of the aircraft managed to fly out to Rostov-West and Taganrog. And that despite visibility of just 500 meters and a ceiling of 30 meters! Our unit had been lucky once again. Several days later German troops retook Tatsinskaya.

In this emergency situation, on the spur of the moment *General der Flieger* Alfred Mahncke, the first *Kommodore* of KG 1 *"Hindenburg,"* formed *"Flieger Division Donez"* (Air Division Donets) made up of close-support units of the *VIII. Fliegerkorps*, Battle Unit Carganico and elements of a flak division, in order to support Army Detachments Hollidt and Fretter-Pico during the winter battle between the Don and the Donets

Battle Group Stahel, a colorful mixture of air force and army alarm units, scattered flak units, troops returning from leave and separated from their units, convalescents from a hospital, an armored train, members of the Organisation Todt and the military postal service, all of whom had been caught up in the maelstrom of the collapsing Chir front, fought its way back from the Chir towards the airfields of Oblivskaya, Morozovskaya and Tatsinskaya, which were still held by the *Luftwaffe*.

Out of this almost hopeless situation, with ammunition running low and food almost non-existent, it reached its objective. Foggy weather prevented our air units from providing air support, which would have been decisive.

In a three-day overland journey, the *Geschwader* headquarters brought the Christmas mail by truck from Sarabus to Rostov. That was all that the *Geschwader* command could do for the morale of the troops.

One day was like another. No holidays, no Christmas. War! Despite the foggy weather, the *Geschwader* flew relief sorties into the Don Bend. On Christmas Eve the airmen gathered in the mess in Rostov and celebrated the issuing of goods: 1 cake, 50 cigarettes, razorblades, red wine and tooth powder. Everyone was satisfied with this and somehow happy.

Much Christmas mail was still missing, because transport was needed for other important things everywhere on the front. The crews fraternally shared with each other their marzipan bread and stale gingerbread from home.

The crew of *Oberleutnant* Ernst Hinrichs of the *2. Staffel* was in an especially high spirits that evening. They had been shot down beyond the German lines and reported missing: German radio reported this news on 23 December 1942, by which time the crew was already back with its unit! With the help of higher offices, the returned men were able to speak with parents, wives or fiancés before Christmas. It was not uncommon for newspapers to report aircrew missing or killed, only to have them return to their units after privation-filled marches through enemy lines.

Army Group Don (von Manstein) attempted to relieve Stalingrad from the southwest with the 4th Panzer Army. It got to within 48 kilometers of the city. When the Soviet offensive on the Don shattered the front of the Italian 8th Army, the relief effort had to be abandoned. Fuel shortages were also a contributing factor.

The *Geschwader* flew missions in which it dropped leaflets in the Rumanian language, a sad, depressing undertaking. It was part of an effort to get the Rumanian units fleeing in panic to stop and hold their ground. It failed.

The Stalingrad airlift faced insurmountable difficulties caused by the cold, the bad weather and serious interruptions in the supply system.

The Russians, whose troops were used to fighting in winter conditions, drove energetically to the lower Chir and the Donets. Relief for the southern front was not available, as the German troops in the northern and central sectors were also involved in heavy fighting.

On 3 January 1943, *Oberst* Conrady arrived in Rostov. He was the new *Kommodore*, taking the place of the fallen *Major* von Friedeburg. He quickly earned the trust of his men, who thought highly of him both as an airman and a superior. Just five days later he failed to return from a sortie against the rail junction in Baskunchak, on the main supply line to Stalingrad. After dropping his bombs, against all rules he flew over the target a second time to assess the results. His aircraft, 9K + AP, was hit by anti-aircraft fire and went down in flames, killing all aboard. That day marked the beginning of a run of bad luck for the *Geschwader*. In the space of just three days, the *I. Gruppe* alone lost 13 crews! When the weather cleared again, fresh fighting erupted in the vast, sunlit, snow-covered landscape of the Kalmuck Steppe for possession of Elista.

Unteroffizier Schwachenfeld, radio operator in the crew of *Hauptmann* Winkel, who later became *Staffelkapitän* of 3./KG 51, wrote:

> *"Beneath us an endless tapeworm of retreating Rumanians. Our missions were crowned by success but altogether useless, as most were merely isolated actions. Vehicles, flak positions and retreating Russian ground troops. Here in front of Rostov we experienced the conduct of warfare with opposing portents. Everything went wrong, nothing worked any more. We were short of bombs, equipment, spare parts and fuel for the aircraft. Our quarters went unheated, it was terribly cold. Anything we could lay our hands on, whether door frames, tables or chairs, was burned as heating material to keep from freezing."*

In the Battle of Rostov the *Geschwader* again intervened decisively in the fighting despite the worst weather (ceiling 30 meters, visibility 400 meters) and was several times praised by *Generaloberst* von Richthofen in orders of the day.

While, in January 1943, the fighting withdrawal from the Maykop – Krasnodar area toward the Taman Peninsula was supported mainly by the "*Edelweiß-Geschwader*," at Stalingrad the fighting was nearing its end. Terrible casualties, deep cold and hunger sapped the strength of the defenders day by day in house-to-house fighting. Many of the desperately needed supply canisters dropped into the pocket were lost and fell into Russian hands.

Generalfeldmarschall Paulus surrendered on 31 January. The last units laid down their arms on 2 February. Stalingrad had become the symbol of an unparalleled defeat, indeed a military disaster. It was the Cannae of the German Army.

An attempted landing in Novorossisk failed on 4 February 1943. The last technical personnel of the airfield operating companies, with the technical equipment of the "*Edelweiß-Geschwader*," evacuated Rostov on 5 February 1943, with Russian tanks already threatening the airfield perimeter. Saving valuable technical equipment under these conditions was one of the great achievements by the *Geschwader*'s "black men." A German pioneer unit was supposed to blow up the Sapadny railway station west of Rostov, even though the train – albeit without a locomotive – was standing ready. They had barely an hour. The bulk of the technical personnel reached an army train and got away. Only *Oberleutnant* Feldmann and twenty volunteers refused to give up. Two wagons filled with post exchange goods were quickly opened and emptied; the alcoholic effect, on the railway men in particular, was considerable. By chance Feldmann was able to establish contact with Taganrog by telephone and request an additional locomotive. It arrived at the last minute and pulled out of the station with the fully loaded train. The railway station was blown up moments after it left. The pioneers had had to follow a precise schedule. Valuable specialists and technical equipment had been saved thanks to the persistence of a few members of the *Geschwader*. The results had justified the means. Their actions were a matter of course, recognition was not usual. Only success counted!

In the confusion between the abandonment of Rostov and the move to Zaporozhye, on 27 February 1943 the *I. Gruppe* lost the well-liked and daring *Kapitän* of the *3. Staffel*, Knight's Cross wearer *Hauptmann* Georg Holle, during a weather reconnaissance sortie over the front. He was probably shot down by anti-aircraft fire.

Because of recent events at the front, on 5 February 1943 the *Geschwader* moved to Zaporozhye again. The *II. Gruppe* handed its aircraft over to the *I.* and *III. Gruppe* and was withdrawn from operations to rest and reequip.

During this phase of the eastern campaign, in which massed Russian anti-aircraft defenses at key points became the rule, many crews ended sorties in their shot-up aircraft in the deep snow of the vast Russian landscape. Some reached the German lines or were recued by German troops after parachuting to safety or making forced- or crashlandings. Many were lost forever.

It was not uncommon for element leaders to land next to a shot-up wingman, pick up him and his crew and, with great daring, rescue them from a truly desperate situation.

War reporter Jochen Schulze reported on the 201st combat mission by the crew of *Leutnant* Winkel. In a daring operation he rescued *Leutnant* Geruschke, *Unteroffizier* Flögel, *Unteroffizier* Silberhauer and *Unteroffizier* Bröggelwirt from enemy territory in this way.

With hits in both engines, *Leutnant* Geruschke was forced to crashland. The fate of him and his men was uncertain. Would they make it through? The crew was forced to flee. Russian soldiers were already after them. They tried to reach a railway embankment to find cover. From above *Leutnant* Winkel saw that the downed crew was heading straight towards a village occupied by Russian tanks. With the calm he always displayed, the *Leutnant* acted. He dropped his bombs on the village, landed on an open, snow-covered field, surrounded by the enemy, and taxied, trailing a long plume of snow, after his fleeing comrades. The radio operator, *Unteroffizier* Schwachenfeld, immediately pinned down the Russians with machine-gun fire, assisted by the observer, *Unteroffizier* Siecker. Finally the fleeing crew noticed the aircraft and stopped running. That was enough to allow *Leutnant* Winkel to reach them. The gunner, *Unteroffizier* Ziemann, quickly opened the "Bola" (ventral gondola) and helped the exhausted *Leutnant* Geruschke aboard. The others hastily squeezed themselves into the bomb bay, knowing that there were only springs holding the bomb doors shut. Engines roaring, Winkel's Ju 88 took off. It zoomed over the heads of the astonished Russian tank crews, who, shooting wildly, had at first thought that they were going to be able to kill two birds with one stone. The aircraft and the two crews nevertheless made it home safely. Four comrades, a valuable and well-respected crew, had been saved. Incidentally, one month earlier *Leutnant* Geruschke had performed a similar feat, landing in no-man's-land south of Rostov/Bataysk on 27 January 1943 to rescue *Oberleutnant* Berger (killed) and his crew (*Unteroffizier* Puls was seriously wounded).

Leutnant Geruschke from Essen was an outstanding bomber pilot and undoubtedly had the highest success rate during the anti-tank operation at Alexandrovka (21 February 1943). He hit almost every moving tank, knocking them out with 50-kg bombs.

On that day Russian armored spearheads of the Popov armored group had advanced to Alexandrovka, just a few kilometers north of Kirovograd and had encircled a German armored train. Crews from KG 51 recognized the situation and immediately reported it.

In Zaporozhye, the *Kommandeur* of the *I. Gruppe*, *Hauptmann* Klaus Häberlen, responded immediately and, without first informing and involving his superiors, ordered his forces against this target. This daring, inspiring officer was later awarded the Knight's Cross for his actions. In the air constantly, the crews flew as many as seven sorties per day, and the Russian armored force, which had advanced undetected, was completely wiped out. The air corps' official attack order did not arrive until after the *Gruppe* had transmitted its report on the successful operation. At first, senior officers were skeptical. The next day (22 February 1943), the *Gruppe* attacked Russian tanks east of Zaporozhye. They were only 15 km from the airfield.

This threat, too, was eliminated. On 17 February Hitler arrived at von Manstein's command post in Zaporozhye in order to investigate for himself the "disobedience" of SS Panzer Corps Hausser, which, contrary to a "Führer order," had given up Kharkov on 15 February. Manstein briefed Hitler on the situation. Because of the proximity of Russian tanks, Hitler quickly left Zaporozhye in his Fw 200 Condor, leaving von Manstein a free hand to deal with the dangerous situation. He directed skillful battles of movement between the Dniepr and Donets, destroying the Russian 6th Army and the Popov armored group. Manstein's corps then formed up for the attack on Kharkov.

The *I. Gruppe* saw constant action in support of the army until the recapture of Kharkov (by Panzer Group Hausser) on 15 March 1943. Numbered among its targets were Balakleya, Izyum and Kupyansk – areas familiar to the crews from the days of the rapid German advance.

Leutnant Geruschke and his crew were grounded for eight days to recover from their ordeal. Ultimately they could barely wait for the forced rest to end.

A Russian unit had been encircled near Izyum. Despite poor weather, orders were issued for an aircraft to fly a reconnaissance sortie to determine the exact location of the front. Geruschke flew it. Over the small pocket he and his crew fell victim to massed Soviet anti-aircraft fire. Their bodies were found and identified somewhere between the lines.

Meanwhile the crews of the *III. Gruppe* were operating on the Manych in the Caucasus, where Stalin was determined to crush the southern wing of the German Army. His objective was a super Stalingrad. He wanted to close Rostov, the gateway to the Caucasus. Badanov's armored units ambushed Tatsinskaya – but it turned out to be a trap and they were destroyed.

A Russian bridgehead near Manychskaya was eliminated, leaving Rostov open for the retreat of German troops from the Caucasus. The 1st Panzer Army was able to secure the Don crossings at Rostov, while the 17th Army was able to withstand intense Russian pressure behind the Goth Position on the Kuban Peninsula. Stalin wanted to cut off this army with a land and sea operation from the Taman Peninsula.

The *Gruppe* attacked troops, artillery and railway targets at Mineralny Vody, Armavir, Kropotkin and Krasnodar. These were the focal points, where so often before, the *Geschwader* saw action. By then it was familiar with its "fire brigade" role.

A special train-busting unit, 7. (Eis.)/KG 51 was equipped with the Ju 88 C-6, a heavy fighter version of the Junkers bomber.

Bagerovo

As of 27 February 1943, the *Geschwader* was stationed in Bagerovo on the Kerch Peninsula in the eastern Crimea. *Major* Egbert von Frankenberg und Proschlitz – who after the war became a defense expert in East Germany – was *Kommodore*. Under *Major* Häberlen, the *I. Gruppe* was located in Zaporozhye, while the *III. Gruppe* under *Major* Rath was also in Bagerovo.

Thanks to technical modifications, the famous-infamous SD 2 could now be dropped more effectively from higher altitudes using the AB 23 bomb dispenser.

The following is part of a performance given by the *Kommodore* of a Stuka *Geschwader*, *Major* Dr. Kupfer, in the mess in Kerch in July 1943. Though intentionally exaggerated, the parody reflects the feelings and thoughts of the bomber crews about their command

and the distribution of decorations. It shows that even in the midst of the war, one could speak an open and critical word in an officers' mess without disciplinary or even political consequences:

March through the Brandenburg Gate 1961

Drums beating, 175 Luftwaffe bands march past, then for a long time nothing. With measured pace, clothed in simple gold, the world marshal marches past. Then follows the half-world marshal, and two more kilometers behind him the underworld marshal. Then the people break into jubilation: star-studded, the fighter pilots, the darlings of the German people, march past, led by the Knight's Cross of the Iron Cross with Giant Cross on a prime mover with built-in music box and Bengali illumination.

Then, again, for a long time there is nothing. Then come 25 Reichsmarschalls under 30 years of age in plain white.

Then a small boy with a sign: "I am the advance detachment of the cleanup party that was forgotten in Greece."

Then comes a grief-stricken old woman, supported by the responsible party authorities, the widow of the last strategic reconnaissance pilot. Then a man with white hair and haggard face, a file under his arm and in it a secret command matter telex: "My acknowledgement of the bomber crews!"

Then the crowd freezes: pulled by four black horses, a wagon approaches, on it a cage, inside a man forging iron, surrounded by eight guards with signs: "Caution! Do not provoke! Dangerous to public safety!" It is the last dive-bomber pilot, who saw action on every front.

Then the people begin to cheer, the sun breaks through the clouds:

Tanned and accustomed to victory, the members of the staffs march through the Brandenburg Gate.

As always, the technical personnel could not take part in the parade because they were informed too late!

It should be noted that when it came to the awarding of honors and decorations, the bomber men in no way came off badly.

On 19 April 1943 the *I. Gruppe* moved via Zaporozhye to Poltava, in preparation for assuming new responsibilities in the Reich.

In April 1943, despite enormous losses, a German front was reestablished in the east and stabilized during the relative quiet of the spring muddy period. An almost rectangular salient in the Kursk area gave rise to fears that the Soviets might exploit it for an offensive. Hitler rejected the idea of pulling back the German line farther north to eliminate the German salient east of Oral and later decided to launch an attack codenamed "Citadel."

The *III. Gruppe* continued flying in support of the *Luftwaffe* Staff Crimea (*Oberst* Bormann) until the end of May 1943 and was mentioned in the *Wehrmacht* communiqué several times for its actions in the northern Caucasus. *Gruppenkommandeur Major* Rath moved his *Gruppe* to join the *Geschwaderstab* in Briansk, as did *Major* Voß with his *II. Gruppe*. The transfer flight was routed over Konotop to avoid overflying the front west of Kursk.

Kommodore Major Egbert von Frankenberg und Proschlitz and his crew (observer Fischbacker, radio operator Miehe, gunner Hain) failed to arrive on 8 May 1943. He, his crew and the *Geschwader* operations officer with all his documents ended up over the Russian lines and were shot down or forced to make a crash-landing – no one knows for sure. To our dismay, the very next evening von Frankenberg was heard on Russian radio! In Krasnograd, Zone 1, he then became part of the "initiative group" during the founding of the "League of German Officers." His speeches, which heretofore had been very much in tune with Goebbels' propaganda speeches, suddenly began towing the line of his handlers in Moscow.

Briansk – Sechinskaya – Kirovograd

Oberstleutnant Hans Heise assumed command of the *Geschwader* in Briansk. On 10 May 1943, the *II.* and *III. Gruppe* began operations against railway stations and supply centers in the Kursk area. Losses were relatively light. On 2 June several *Kampfgeschwader* joined forces to carry out concentrated night attacks against the tank works and foundries in Gorki, far to the east of Moscow.

During these night missions, the crews spent as many as five hours over enemy territory. The operation was organized by the *1. Fliegerdivision* under the command of *Generalmajor* Bülowius. Five such night raids, each involving about 180 bombers, significantly affected tank production in Gorki for several months. On the night of 20 June, the chemical combine in Yaroslavl, north of Moscow, was also bombed.

The day before this, the *Kommodore* was shot down during a night raid on Yelets. He just managed to nurse his aircraft back to the German lines before he and his crew baled out. The next day he was back in the air. That was nothing special for an airmen in those days, under these circumstances.

Beginning the end of June, the *Geschwader* turned its efforts to daily army support missions in the Kursk – Orel area in preparation for the big "Operation Citadel." This huge double battle, the largest and most decisive of the war in Russia, began at 03:30 on 5 July 1943 with strikes against airfields, trenches and artillery positions by 1,700 bombers, Stukas, fighters and close-support aircraft. Despite many individual successes – such as the destruction of an entire Soviet armored brigade from the air – the offensive failed to achieve its operational objective. The enemy was too powerful. The attack had to be called off on 17 July. Soviet military history justifiably calls it "the battle of world-historical importance." It was this battle that turned the tide of the war, not Stalingrad.

The German Army exhausted its reserves in this battle and German offensive power was broken forever.

On 12 July in Briansk, the *III. Gruppe* flew its 10,000th combat mission. On 26 July 1943, because of events at the front, the *Geschwaderstab* and the *II.* and *III. Gruppe* moved to Sechinskaya near Roslavl. From there dusk and daylight missions in the Belev area became their daily bread.

During operations there the *Gruppen* lost many crews to actions by partisans. They mixed in with the "Hiwis," Russian auxiliaries working for the Germans, and under cover of darkness attached barometrically controlled explosive devices to the rear 900-liter fuel tanks of the Ju 88s. When there was a sudden loss of altitude, as during a diving attack, the devices exploded, destroying the aircraft in the air. At first everyone was at a loss to explain what had happened, until, during a comprehensive search of the entire airfield, an explosive device with magnetic plate was found in the egg basket of a seemingly harmless Russian peasant woman.

After the collapse of the German front in the central sector, on 10 August 1943 the *Geschwader* moved to Kirovograd on the southern sector, where the front had become destabilized. Novorossisk fell. Only the Crimea was still held by the 17th Army (*Generaloberst* Jaenecke). A Russian salient formed near Kremenchug, pointing towards Kirovograd and Krivoy Rog.

The units flew constantly in support of the army. This made it necessary for them to move temporarily to Poltava and Kiev. On 7 September the *Geschwaderstab* and the *III. Gruppe* were transferred to Illesheim in Germany to reequip on the Me 410.

Meanwhile the *II. Gruppe* was given a special assignment in the southeast of Europe.

The Aegean and the Last Operations in Russia

On 19 September *Major* Voß and his *Gruppe* moved to Salonika at short notice. What had happened?

On 8 September Marshall Badoglio, the new Italian prime minister, had concluded an official ceasefire with the Allies, who had landed on Sicily. Since 1941 the Italians had been responsible for Greece. Small contingents of British troops had landed on the islands of Leros, Kios, Samos and Kos. It was vital that these islands be retaken, and the *Luftwaffe* was directed to support German landings. In addition to attacks on the islands, it attacked shipping near Cyprus and south of Crete. British Beaufighter long-range fighters made life extremely difficult for the German bombers.

The *II. Gruppe* recorded its 13,000th combat mission in Salonika on 14 November 1943. By then it had dropped 20,000,000 kg of bombs.

Armed reconnaissance sorties were flown into the waters of the Dodecanese in search of enemy warships, especially British cruisers and destroyers, which were delivering troops and supplies to the islands under cover of darkness. They were nowhere to be found. Long and strenuous overwater sorties were flown in search of the enemy vessels. The airmen of the *II. Gruppe* of the "Edelweiss *Geschwader*" had to look into hundreds of hidden island bays, until finally the enemy was found.

Sunday, the 22nd of November 1943, was "air force travel day." At 15:00 two *Ketten* of Ju 88s of the *II. Gruppe* took off from Salonika on the "island trip."

The two formations were forced to part ways soon after takeoff due to poor visibility. The crews of Moser, Schaper and Winkler stayed together. They felt their way over Rhodes in the direction of Castellrosso, the last offshoot of the Dodecanese before the shores of Asia Minor, near the island of Cyprus. Finding nothing, the crews continued their search, crisscrossing the waters between Africa and Crete.

Suddenly, near Leros, the ships for which they had searched so long in vain appeared below them. Two cruisers and three destroyers. The ships were sailing in a straight line at top speed, their screws leaving long white wakes.

Hans Moser's aircraft was slightly ahead of the others and was in the best position from which to attack. He picked out the biggest ship and dropped his bombs from low altitude after a diving approach. As the other aircraft dove toward the armored vessels, the ships' anti-aircraft guns opened fire. All of the aircraft were hit by fragments, but they concentrated their attacks on one of the cruisers. The bombs fell. Two jets of flame rose from the warship. The Moser crew had scored a direct hit! Two 1000-kg bombs ad struck the cruiser. In seconds the vessel turned almost 90 degrees. Shrouded in smoke, it began leaving a heavy oil trail. The bombers quickly left the scene. During the return flight three Beaufighters attacked the flight but were able to achieve nothing. One enemy fighter was shot down in flames by the Schaper crew. The rest of the flight was uneventful, and at 17:30 all of the bombers landed safely in Salonika. On 28 November the *Gruppe* retuned to Russia.

Major Barth replaced *Major* Voß as *Kommandeur*. After operating from Kalinovka (in support of the Cherkassy Pocket), Vinnitsa (Russian advance near Fastov/Zhitomir) and Lublin, in the spring of 1944 this *Gruppe* also moved to Hildesheim to convert onto the Me 410. Part of the *Gruppe* became a special *Staffel* in KG 3, which flew the He 111 on operations against England using the V 1 flying bomb.

According to available records, the *Geschwader* lost a total of 703 personnel in Russia, consisting of:

146 officers
416 non-commissioned officers
141 enlisted men.

Chapter 6

With the Me 410 in the Fighter Role over Germany and as a Zerstörer against England

Transfer back to the Reich

By 1943 the German armies were on the retreat on every front. Hitler coined the phrase "Fortress Europe," but he forgot to give it a roof. The air defenses of the Reich had been criminally neglected. The catastrophic air raids on Hamburg in July 1943 finally provided the impetus to strengthen the fighter force. As part of this effort, KG 51 was ordered to back to Germany to retrain on the new Me 410 *Hornisse* (Hornet) twin-engined fighter, which could carry 210-mm air-to-air rockets. The *Gruppen* assembled in Illesheim and Hildesheim.

Adolf Schwachenwald described the transfer flight to the Reich in his diary, which miraculously survived the war:

> *"With great tension and anticipation, which had gripped all of the crews of the I. Gruppe, we looked forward excitedly to the transfer to the Reich. After two years of war in Russia and continuous action on almost every front, this excitement was easily understandable. The aircraft were crammed with our baggage and equipment and we were inwardly prepared to bid Russia adieu forever.*
>
> *The moment came at 07:02 on 6 May 1943. In fine May weather we took off into the Russian sky and headed west. In Germany we would begin new, as yet unknown tasks. It was a precise, exemplary formation flight by veteran airmen. And the mood on board was simply indescribable. No wonder; we were heading home!*
>
> *In two formations of six to eight aircraft each, we flew towards our border at an altitude of about 3,000 meters. We looked forward eagerly to the border crossing, which we intended to carry out close up and in a visually impressive way. And so just before we reached the frontier between Poland and Germany, we dropped down into a loose low-level formation. Our return home was indescribably beautiful. Firing a*

salute of joy into the air from all our machineguns, we flew over the border landscape. The sudden danger of our outbreak of joy caused frightened people to throw themselves to the ground and take cover. After a few minutes of flying low, our flight regained altitude and closed up in an effort to conduct the remaining flight to our destination airfields with some semblance of discipline.

We all landed safely at Illesheim near Nuremberg at about 14:08. With the stopover in Warsaw, the flight had lasted over 343 minutes. It was a flight that gave us time enough to develop thoughts, get an impression of the landscape and awaken memories.

After our quarters had been inspected and accepted, the entire Gruppe went on leave and then on a health cure. After this most pleasant leave for us run-down airmen was over, in July 1943 we were informed about our new functions and assigned to the Zerstörer school in Memmingen for training on the Me 110."

Not without the pain of parting, unfortunately. The new machines with their smaller crews made the observers and dorsal gunners redundant. Friendships and comradeships forged during the course of many operational flights came to a sudden and officially mandated end.

The veteran airmen found positions in the parachute troops, the military police, the flying schools and many other units. In some cases it was not possible to keep track of their subsequent fate.

The popular Knight's Cross wearer *Oberfeldwebel* Albert Spieth was supposed to fly the *Geschwader*'s liaison aircraft, a He 111, to Bobruisk on 4 October 1943 to collect the *Geschwader*'s cleanup detachment, however he was killed in the unit's quarters, the lone victim of a Russian night bombing raid.

The Flight into Happiness

Dialogue and thoughts of a meteorologist with an airman's heart: my "bird" floats gently in the sky … One last farewell circuit and the figures down on the airfield below grow ever smaller … my proud successor, my delighted Herr inspectors, the female auxiliaries again sensing a change of fortune – and a short girl with curly blonde hair …

"We don't have much time, and anyway it's better if we remain on course, as Ivan doesn't like making flights to the west to aid his digestion at this time," observed my pilot drily. "Therefore we'll climb straight through the clouds and head southwest. According to your forecast we'll be between layers all the way to Berlin …"

Will my forecast prove correct, I thought to myself.

My pilot interrupted my musings: "But this damned rain isn't in your forecast, *Herr Regierungsrat*."

"No, but I did advise you to climb through every break in the cloud."

"Soft as rubber, but not for chewing, that was always the meteorologists' success system!"

"That's why you were given meteorology lectures. Or did you only make high-altitude flights when a warm front was forecast?," I shouted to my aerial coachman over the roar of the engines.

"But science is something noble; it can be twisted and turned as it seems opportune, like a hat with three corners – but in the end it remains what it is."

"Some learn that, others forget before they are born," I replied, "the scientist is still always alone, especially in present-day Germany. Inventors and scientists at the front – yes, they call for them when things stop moving along."

"You may be right!" remarked my pilot reflectively, "one thing is sure," I think, "if only those in command realized that."

Hour after hour passed, my eyes almost closed …

The radio operator woke me from my twilight state: "Here is the Königsberg weather: 7/10 at 200 to 500 meters." I quickly passed it on …

"We're going to go lower," my pilot called to me, "and get some East Prussian country air."

Below us lay Königsberg, lit in places by isolated sunbeams. And my heart opened itself wide …

What had happened back then? It could just as well have been yesterday! … Joy and summer holidays, a time of becoming and maturing in the first overflowing delight of youth. A time of idealism. Max Hölz once spoke about the World War at a party meeting in my hometown in 1927, the only one I ever attended. His words involuntarily come to mind: "Yes, we will find a solution, take the difficult but sure path to a better, peaceful future with our eastern neighbor. I believed that was my wish on the first threshold of my life, it always had to be! And today? Millions face each other in the field, fighting. Men who never saw each other in their lives, who had nothing against each other. When I saw that I had to say to myself: if there is a god, this god is the biggest robber and murderer the earth has ever seen and I would be the first to shoot him." And already these images escape my thoughts again.

Life in the past, when all the present can offer is emptiness. To be able to be happy as in the May of one's life. But what was it that gave this place the mysterious charm that elevated it above everywhere else, with the exception of my home on distant Lake Constance?

Where are all those who lived and joked with me here "like a free boy does"? Where are they?

But no one answered me, in vain my heart sought fulfillment … the engines hummed their monotonous song and finally shrouded me in the dim, cool sleep of salvation when, shortly before flying over fortress of Marienburg, earth and sky melted away into pleasant nothing …

Finally we reached Berlin. Able to forget, wanting to forget in the noise of the big city – or not, I'm not sure myself ..."

Conversion into the Me 410

Bomber pilots were now supposed to become fighter or close-support pilots. The tenor of our new mission was: "Defense of the Reich."

The new Me 410 aircraft, initially equipped with four underwing rocket-launching tubes, called "*Dödel*" (slang term for the male sex organ), and with considerable firepower provided by cannon and heavy machine-guns, was supposed to attack the Allied bomber fleets and thin out the formations with rocket fire. Conversion training began. The new aircraft were maneuverable, fast and had a tremendous rate of climb, and they were also capable of carrying a special 1,000 kg parachute-retarded high-explosive bomb in an internal bomb bay. We soon realized that the Me 410 was a real improvement over the older, slower Ju 88.

The first three Me 410s reached the *Geschwader* in Illesheim in mid-June 1943. The initial confrontation with the enemy was supposed to come after the *Gruppe*n had been equipped with the new machines, deliveries of which were slow, and training had been completed. The crews waited for this day with anticipation and pounding hearts. It came on 6 September 1943: the *I. Gruppe*, with about ten to twelve Me 410s armed with rockets, headed towards bomber formations that had come in over the Channel, Holland, Belgium and France and intercepted them abeam the Black Forest. There were 200 American heavy bombers flying in close formation. They directed their massed defensive fire at the attackers. As the heavy fighters closed in, a huge volume of tracer passed uncomfortably close. Evading the fire, they attacked the second formation from slightly above at an altitude of 5,000 meters. The rockets were fired and they raced away from the machines in a slightly arced ballistic curve. A fireball in the formation signaled the first success. One bomber rolled onto its side and went down burning. Nearby bombers were rocked by the blast but regained position and continued their flight. By then the fighters were in the midst of the bomber stream. The bombers blazed away with everything they had. Some of our machines were hit; Hptm. Winkel lost an engine. He dove away to look for a place to land. Unable to find a suitable strip, he ordered the aircraft lightened. First the fuel was drained from the reserve tank, then ammunition and armor plate was thrown out. In this way he was able to compensate for the loss of altitude and fly directly to home base in Illesheim, where he made a single-engine landing.

The resume: all of the crews had similar experiences! The success ratio was pitifully lopsided. Victories balanced out with our own losses and the *Gruppe* was no longer operational after its first mission. The *Gruppe* was brought up to strength again. New crews arrived. Deliveries of replacement aircraft were much slower. Production bottlenecks were already making themselves felt.

Before September ended the unit was moved to Hörsching near Linz for tactical reasons, and the crews tensely awaited a return to action. They took off on the next mission on 2 October 1943 and assembled over the Alps at 7,000 meters over Zeltweg. Unfortunately the bombers, which were coming from Italy, turned back, and the disappointed eager warriors landed again in Hörsching.

Schweinfurt

Mission orders were issued again on 14 October 1943. The men raced to their machines. The massed takeoff began: caught in the wake turbulence produced by the machines taking off, just before becoming airborne one of the trailing aircraft veered, and its port propeller sawed about one meter off the tail of the aircraft next to it. The aircraft that had been "shortened" veered off, rolled across the field and, like the one that had caused the collision, turned on its axis and came to rest somewhere. For both crews the mission was over before it started. An unusual spectacle and good luck: two machines stayed on the ground, destroyed, their crews fortunate to have survived with nothing worse than a bad scare.

The crews were initially vectored west as they gained altitude. The *Gruppe* was flying in loose formation, every man for himself, towards the bomber force from the American 8th Air Force, 291 aircraft, now reported over the Frankfurt area. Finally, in the Schweinfurt area, visual contact was made with the bombers, which had already attacked and destroyed the ball bearing factories. The aircraft pursued the bombers, fired their *Nebelwerfer* rockets and then attacked again. Once again they found themselves in the midst of the firestorm of return fire from the tight bomber formations.

It was a successful day for the German defenses. Flak, fighters and our own aircraft shot down 50 to 60 bombers. A good day was reported by the radio, but it was another black day for the *Gruppen*. Almost all their aircraft had battle damage and were no longer serviceable. In the end, 77 American aircraft were shot down, another 121 damaged. It was a big success for the *Luftwaffe*, but was it perhaps the last?

Obviously the ratio of sorties and losses compared to the expected success was giving the high command headaches. The *Reichsmarschall* himself set out to give the commanders a "rocket." There were rumors of fat cigars, but Hermann Göring missed the boat. There were also Göring's statements, like "cowardice in the face of the enemy" and the usual unconvincing, pithy words. The result was the general removal from the theater and "punitive transfers" to operations against England. One couldn't turn bomber pilots into fighter pilots so quickly.

With their new fuses, because of the cold temperatures at high altitude the "*Ködel*" had the habit of flying but not exploding on hitting the target. The fusing mechanism froze up! If, during the flight home, the pilot pressed the release button, this curious weapon sometimes launched and caused only aggravation. It was difficult for the German people to understand such "miracle weapons."

The Reichsmarschall in Fels am Wagram

The Commander-in-Chief of the *Luftwaffe*, *Reichsmarschall* Hermann Göring, had announced that he was coming to Fels am Wagram on Monday, the 11th of October 1943, to inspect the fighter units stationed there.

Major Klaus Häberlen, *Kommodore* of I./KG 51, had been ordered there with his adjutant, *Oberleutnant* Werner Pape, to represent the *Geschwader*. They took off from Hörsching in an Me 108 Taifun at 09:10. The trip to Fels was a 70-minute "joyride" over the beautiful Wachau region. This still left sufficient time before the parade.

Two *Jagdgruppen* formed up for inspection. As the senior officer present, Häberlen presented the assembled units to the *Reichsmarschall* for inspection. The usual conversation about successes and missions developed between the two.

When the topic of problems came up, Häberlen related factually and with personal commitment that the Me 410 with two engines and single-stage superchargers was inferior in performance to the American heavy bombers with two-stage superchargers at heights of 4,000-6,000 meters, much to the displeasure of the commander-in-chief and his aides! In the course of the dispute, Göring accused this dashing Knight's Cross wearer of cowardice in front of the assembled personnel.

On Göring's order, *General der Kampfflieger* General Staff *Oberst* Dieter Peltz was forced to relieve Häberlen as *Kommandeur*.

In a fair fashion, on 15 October – one day after the air battle near Schweinfurt – Peltz and Häberlen together flew in a Ju 88 from Ainring to Hörsching, where Peltz formally transferred command to *Major* Meister.

Häberlen was one of the many brave frontline officers whose openness, long since unwanted in the highest circles, was rewarded by the loss of their positions. He satisfactorily served as operations officer under *General der Flieger* Alfred Mahncke with *Feldluftgaukommando XVII* in Italy.

Unsuitable as a Fighter

Schweinfurt was the unit's last mission in the Defense of the Reich. On 6 November 1943 the *Gruppe* moved to Lager Lechfeld and began training in instrument and night flying on the very likeable Me 410 in preparation for operations against England. Actually the machine hadn't been conceived for that, but after the installation of some additional equipment and the removal of the rocket-launching tubes from under the wings, we flew our first night circuits as well as night cross-country flights and simulated missions over southern Germany.

The necessary higher landings speed compared to the Ju 88 and the various automatic controls for the landing flaps and undercarriage caused the young replacement pilots then joining the *Geschwader* major problems. For example, in one week three aircraft made belly landings on the paved runway during night flying, although the pilots believed they had made normal wheeled landings.

Each belly landing meant a loss for our already meager airpark – and each incident was investigated to determine if there might be a possibility of sabotage. The guilty parties were then punished for the careless handling and destruction of *Wehrmacht* property. Many pilots, very capable young people, were sent to the "hole" for eight days.

Given the military situation, such punishments were laughable. In those days there were more combat-proven, intelligent pilots in the detention cells in Lager Lechfeld than real scapegoats and crooks.

Return to Operations against England

On 6 December 1943 the first part of the *I. Gruppe* moved to Evreux, France. From there it began flying missions over England carrying special 1,000-kg parachute-stabilized bombs.

1./KG 51 was stationed in St. André, 2./KG 51 in Dreux and 3./KG 51 and the *Gruppenstab* in Evreux. Once again the unit faced new difficulties that had to be overcome.

The English anti-aircraft guns and night-fighters, with their excellent airborne radar, soon located even high-flying aircraft and placed them under heavy fire. The enemy's searchlight batteries accompanied the raiders all the way to their assigned targets. Even at altitudes of 7,000 meters it was bright as day in the cockpit. There was no need for the flashlights we carried for map reading. New defensive methods and tricks had to be devised, in order to survive in that technically well-organized witch's cauldron.

Meanwhile the *III. Gruppe* was disbanded. *Gruppenkommandeur Major* Rath became *Kommodore* of KG 2, while most of the *Gruppe*'s personnel joined the other three *Gruppe*n. Some, however, were sent to *Luftwaffe* field divisions where, untrained in the infantry role, they suffered heavy casualties. Another account by Adolf Schwachenfeld sheds light on the *Geschwader*'s life and daily bread at that time:

> *"On 20 February 1944, we, my pilot Hauptmann Winkel and I, also flew to St. André as the advance party for our Staffel, 1./51. When the forecast permitted a night mission over England on the 23rd, we voluntarily joined the other Staffeln and flew our first sortie over the Channel as part of a big raid on the city of London. The night takeoff by the aircraft was done at two-minute intervals. The airfield and runway lights were switched on briefly, then the dark night swallowed us up. We followed a precise*

zigzag course en route to the target London. Waiting there, at the precise attack time, was a target illumination aircraft at high altitude, about 10,000 meters, guided by radio beams. From start to finish, the entire operation ran like a precise clockwork mechanism. Over the Channel we began taking anti-aircraft fire from English ships and were welcomed by a tremendous display of fireworks. Then came the searchlights, reaching into the night sky for us like ghost hands. Then the coastal batteries fired their salvoes. In most cases the direction was correct, but the height was usually off. Shells burst above and below us, and it took nerves of steel to maintain our prescribed course and arrive over the illuminated target on time in those murderous conditions. The attack time and the target illumination were issued for a time difference of a few minutes. Our 'over man' at 10,000 meters constantly dropped new illumination bombs. On this, our first mission over England, we arrived over the target rather early, and we made a 360-degree turn over the northern city with our bombs. Then, precisely following the red marker, we dropped our load on the city below us, which was already burning in many places. Relieved, we gained altitude and then crossed the Channel towards the French coast in a shallow dive at high-speed (600 to 700 kph), again under constant fire.

Over the Channel the rough waters were reflected in the fire's glow. Streams of tracer moved through the sky like strings of pearls, as warships and motor torpedo boats exchanged fire.

On the way home, a slower-flying German aircraft was shot down by a night-fighter less than 100 meters from us and crashed in flames into the Channel. Goose flesh came over us as we heard the last emergency transmission by our comrades: 'Ju 88 ... call sign ... SOS ... we're going down in flames! ...'

After a few more minutes in our shallow dive, the mainland was again beneath us and by radio we made preparations to land. As during takeoff, the airfield lights were switched on only briefly, and we made our landing. When we felt the earth beneath us again, we heaved a sigh – excited, trembling, sweat-soaked, but relieved. At 23:28, after 118 minutes in the air and a flight such as we had never before experienced, we climbed out of our aircraft.

Our judgment: anyone who survived further combat missions over England at this time had unbelievable luck and the dear Lord on his side!"

The next day this crew flew back to Lechfeld and reported its experiences and impressions from its first flight over England. Then, on 29 February 1944, the entire *1. Staffel* moved to prepared quarters in Evreux, near St. André, where the *Kommodore* of I./KG 51, *Hauptmann* Unrau, and the *Gruppenstab* had arrived. Unrau had previously handed his *1. Staffel* over to *Oberleutnant* Werner Pape. Meanwhile the newly promoted *Oberstleutnant* Wolf Meister had become the new *Geschwaderkommodore*.

Together with V./KG 2, which subsequently became II./KG 51, the *I. Gruppe* of the *"Edelweiss Geschwader"* flew regular night missions over the British island kingdom.

The weather was poor, and consequently missions over England did not begin until 13 March 1944. In the face of the massed British defenses, which steadily grew stronger, each was essentially a suicide mission. There followed about ten more raids on Brighton, London, Bristol and Portsmouth – and each time two or three crews, good friends and comrades, fell to the British defenses. There were few survivors. Those who failed to return were dead and their aircraft written off.

To confuse the British radar, throughout the flights the aircraft dropped bundles of chaff – meter-long strips of tinfoil. Attack and landing times were based on the phase of the moon, and most were scheduled between 23:00 and 03:00. Apart from the flak, crews needed a great deal of luck and flying skill to avoid being shot down by lurking night-fighters.

The *Fernnachtjägerstaffel/KG 51* was formed under Knight's Cross wearer *Major* Dietrich Puttfarken. The men of this special *Staffel* had the task of locating and shooting down English night-fighters as they were returning to their airfields. Puttfarken was killed near Cambridge during one such mission on 23 April 1944.

London was attacked again on 24 March. The aircraft took off at 23:15. During the return flight, the crews were advised of bad weather and developing fog. *Hauptmann* Winkel in aircraft 9K + CL diverted east over Holland to avoid the bad weather. Approaching an unidentified airfield, he fired flares to request that the lights be turned on. A set of runway lights came on briefly. Passing beneath high-tension wires, he landed at Mönchen-Gladbach, an airfield much too small for the Me 410, and, braking harshly, came to a stop just short of the airfield perimeter. Fire trucks and rescue personnel were already on the scene. It turned out that several minutes earlier a German aircraft had been shot down by a British night-fighter while attempting to land. Even in Germany the airmen were no longer safe from Allied aircraft, even at night.

The *Gruppe* was almost wiped out in these operations and shortly before the invasion it returned to the Reich. On 3 June 1944 *Kommodore Oberst* Wolf-Dietrich Meister greeted his people with the words that they would now be converting onto the Me 262 jet fighter.

At Hildesheim the *II. Gruppe* carried out an orderly conversion onto the Me 410 with the *IV. Gruppe* under *Major* Josef Schölß. The training *Gruppe* later moved to Munich-Riem. According to Wolfgang Baetz, losses during conversion training were about 50%. Some of the *II. Gruppe* crews went to Chartres, France and Gilze-Rijen in Holland to take part in long-range night-fighter missions against Allied bombers returning from attacks on the Ruhr. *Feldwebel* Beier and *Oberfeldwebel* Trenke, in particular, achieved success in this new role, shooting down several four-engined bombers as they attempted to land at their bases in England.

Because of certain disputes over jurisdiction between the *General der Kampfflieger* and the *General der Nachtjäger*, the *Gruppe* was again withdrawn from action and released from Me 410 conversion training. Then, in October 1944, it began retraining on the Me 262 A-2a.

On 30 June 1944, I./SKG 10, equipped with Fw 190s, was briefly incorporated as the *Geschwader*'s third *Gruppe*, and on 20 October it received the official designation III./KG 51 in the night close-support role. On 31 October 1944 it left the *Geschwader* again to become *Nachtschlachtgruppe 20*, an independent night close-support unit. Most members of the *Geschwader* knew nothing about this strengthening of the *"Edelweiss Geschwader,"* as it was too brief and was probably only the result of global planning and shifting of units by the RLM.

During the approximately nine months that the *Geschwader* flew the Me 410, KG 51 lost 138 personnel, specifically:

45 officers
72 non-commissioned officers
21 enlisted men.

Chapter 7
In Action with the Me 262 "Sturmvogel" Jet Aircraft

Retraining on the Me 262

Much has been written about the Me 262. On Hitler's order, this epoch-making, high-performance aircraft was forced into a role for which it had not been conceived, as the so-called "Blitz bomber." The first operational jet fighter in the world, this Messerschmitt design with two Jumo 004 turbojet engines was to join the air war as a superior aircraft and begin a new chapter in aviation history, only not for Germany.

Flugkapitän Wendel, holder of the world speed record for powered aircraft, subsequently technical adviser with KG 51, briefed Adolf Galland, the *General der Jagdflieger*, on how to handle the aircraft in May 1943.

After the flight, Galland declared drily, factually and yet enthusiastically: "It is as if an angel is pushing."

In fact this new design could not be described more aptly. The Me 262 was an aircraft with pleasant handling characteristics. It was necessary, however, to follow precisely the checklists and the directives and notes from the manufacturer's flight test reports.

The pilot of this machine had to handle it with precision and technical sensitivity. If he met these conditions, his reward was a flying experience the like of which one could only dream in those days.

Even in the climb after takeoff, the airspeed indicator quickly reached values that could previously not be achieved even in a headlong dive. And then the pilot was surrounded by quiet in the cockpit, as if he was flying an unpowered glider.

The aircraft's aerodynamic characteristics were outstanding. The broad leading edge slats improved safety during takeoff and landing. Failure to pay attention to weight distribution could prove fatal, however.

The Me 262 was originally conceived as a fighter aircraft. It had two fuel tanks, each with a capacity of 900 liters, and four 30-mm automatic cannon. When Hitler ordered its use as a bomb carrier, several major modifications were required that reduced its original performance.

To augment the two 900-liter tanks fore and aft of the cockpit, two additional tanks were fitted for increased range. One held 250 liters and was located right beneath the pilot's seat. The only space for the other 600-liter tank was in the fuselage behind the rearmost main tank, far from the aircraft's center of gravity.

In operational use this was counterbalanced by two 250-kg bombs, although two of the aircraft's 30-mm cannon had to be removed. Without bombs, with a full 600-liter tank the aircraft was so tail-heavy that it was dangerous to fly. Without bombs, therefore, the rearmost tank had to be left empty. As well, during initial operations with bombs it had to be emptied before the bombs were dropped. It is likely that several crashes were caused by the pilot incorrectly selecting tanks in the heat of the moment. If the forward main tank was mistakenly emptied first and the bombs were then dropped in a shallow dive, the aircraft – now tail-heavy – pitched up. This could result in the loss of the leading edge slats, and the elevator was not effective enough to bring the aircraft back into level flight.

There were also limits in the upper speed range. Control effectiveness was unaffected at speeds up to 900 kph. Between 930 and 1000 kph, however, the aircraft could no longer be controlled. It is also likely that a number of crashes resulted from exceeding the aerodynamically permissible airspeed. More problematic than aerodynamic handling was the operation of the power plants. Most pilots of KG 51 who retrained on the aircraft had a great deal of flying experience. Turbojet engines, however, were new ground and forced even veterans to fundamentally relearn.

At the front of the engine in the air intake was a small Riedel two-stroke engine. Its purpose was to spin the turbine up to 2,000 rpm, at which point it could run on its own power. This Riedel was unpredictable and capricious. It had to be started with an electric motor or pull cord. Often, however, this required much persuasion combined with technical tricks. Sometimes even that was not enough.

Once the Riedel's "assistance" was assured, it was coupled with the turbine. At 800 rpm the turbine was ignited and at 2,000 rpm the Riedel was disengaged. Then the turbine could slowly be run up to its maximum speed of 8,300 rpm.

The engine start and run-up, but especially acceleration during takeoff, demanded skill and patience. Applying power too quickly inevitably killed the engine; if this happened on takeoff, it was fatal to the aircraft and pilot. The turbine wheel at the rear of the power plant, made of an alloy because of a raw materials shortage, was only equal to the gentlest handling and melted if the fuel injection was even slightly mishandled. This was the undoing of many pilots used to pushing the throttle all the way forward and pulling it all the way back.

Looking back, it can be said that, in terms of aerodynamics and airframe, the Me 262 was an inspired design. It was ahead of its time. A landing speed of 180 kph and a maximum speed of 820 kph with an endurance of more than an hour represented a phenomenal performance at that time. It is a pity that no reliable power plants were available.

Me 262 training was carried out centrally in Lechfeld. Messerschmitt, with its experts, especially *Flugkapitän* Fritz Wendel as aviation-technical advisor, tirelessly instructed a stream of pilots and technical personnel in the fine points of the "miracle bird." *Oberst* Meister, along with the *Geschwaderstab*, moved into quarters there on 2 June 1944 and then waited for his "men," who were in the process of turning in their Me 410s and slowly making their way to the airfield. Once again KG 51 had been selected as one of the first units in the *Luftwaffe* to reequip on the most modern aircraft. Unlike the Ju 88, for example, the Me 262 was not equipped with a dive-bombing sight. Instead it had just a reflector gunsight. Practiced pilots were able to achieve good results with this makeshift arrangement, however.

The enemy's anti-aircraft defenses never really adjusted to the aircraft's speed range. In most cases, tracer showed that they usually fired behind the aircraft.

On the other hand enemy fighters, especially the Hawker Tempest, could on occasion close with a Me 262 in a dive from above if it still had its bombs on board. The best chance for enemy fighters, however, was to attack the Me 262 when it was on approach to land at its base with little fuel in reserve. In this respect the enemy's air superiority during the final months of the war had its full effect.

Before several tragic losses, the aircraft lacked armor to protect the pilot's head. This was first installed in March 1945.

One surprise was the appearance in November-December 1944 of serious poisoning symptoms among pilots who had sustained burns in combat. *Oberfeldwebel* Kohler (?), buried in Bremen, died of such poisoning after suffering seemingly minor burns to his hands. The cause was the fuel used by the jet engines. All pilots were subsequently issued high-grade leather flight gear and thick leather gloves.

New pilots made their first practice flights after brief technical familiarization. There was still no two-seater. The instructor gave his instructions prior to takeoff, observed the critical engine start and, with the help of a radio operator from one of our crews, stood by to offer assistance by radio in the event of problems. Pilots were often amazed by the aircraft's performance.

Meanwhile, on 6 June 1944 the Allies had landed in France between Cherbourg and Caen; it was the start of the expected invasion. The "Blitz bombers" were not yet quite operational, however.

In the first days of the invasion the Allied air forces flew 8,149 sorties, compared to just 350 by the Germans, a ratio of 23:1!

Elements of the *3. Staffel* were renamed *E-Kdo Schenck* (also *Sonderkommando E-51*). This operational trials unit was commanded by *Major* Wolfgang Schenck, a highly regarded pilot and holder of the Oak Leaves who had come from ZG 26. He was ordered to proceed immediately to the invasion front and support the German forces grappling with the invaders. It was during retraining that Count Schenck von Stauffenberg, an *Oberst* in the army general staff, attempted to assassinate Hitler on 20 July 1944. What went through the minds of the men at the front and motivated them varied and can only be understood against the background of the times in which they lived. Their motivations are sufficiently well known.

Lechfeld soon became a thorn in the side of the Allies. Their efficient network of spies had revealed that a new weapon was being tested there and they were determined to prevent it from becoming operational. Galland wrote about an attack on the airfield in which 60 Me 262s of the trials unit and KG 51 were destroyed or damaged on the ground.

The first aircraft did not wear unit codes on their fuselages, instead only large letters from A to Z.

Various problems were encountered in converting the aircraft for use as a bomber. The undercarriage and tires were beefed up in Schwäbisch-Hall, and additional tanks had to be installed. If insufficient care was exercised in transferring fuel between tanks, the result could be a "hopeless" shift in the center of gravity, tail-heaviness and instability. There were shortages of bomb racks and sights. It was impossible to dive-bomb accurately. A *Führer* Order (!) forbade exceeding 850 kph in a dive or flying over enemy territory at heights lower than 4000 meters, in order to reduce the chances of being shot down by anti-aircraft fire and prevent any aircraft from falling into enemy hands. The *Geschwader* was thus doomed to failure from the beginning; poor bombing results were inevitable and depressing. The restrictive orders were lifted in December 1944. And even if the expression "crop damage *Geschwader*" was added to the airmen's slang, it did absolutely nothing to improve morale. Many aircraft that flew to Swäbisch Hall for conversion never returned because they were destroyed in Allied bombing raids. The "*Sturmvögel*" (Petrels) – codenamed "Silver" – were hunted at every turn. Every takeoff, flight and every landing was a minor suicide mission and wore at already frayed nerves.

E-Kdo. Schenck Moves to France

Training began on 20 June 1944, two weeks after the Allies landed in France. By the 20th of June about twelve of the *3. Staffel*'s pilots were somewhat acquainted with the new aircraft after just four familiarization flights; under the conditions that existed, they were considered operational. The 20th of July 1944 left no time to reflect on the events of the day. The unit moved to Châteaudun with nine aircraft. Missions to England had to be flown immediately. The abandonment of the Caen bridgehead (10 July) marked the beginning of the German withdrawal from France. The weak German front could not withstand the pressure. On 12 August the unit was forced to move to the Étampes airfield.

The technical personnel performed magnificently. As the Me 262's Jumo power plants had an average life of just eight hours, there was always a small escorted convoy under way somewhere in France carrying engines and spare parts for special detachment E-51. They were always accompanied by special plenipotentiaries with travel passes. Former radio operators from the Ju 88 and Me 410 times, experienced but now "unemployed," found ways to reach their objective, their unit. On 15 August the detachment moved to Creil, but it, too, was under threat and on the 22nd the unit moved to Juvincourt near Reims. One of the convoys transporting power plants learned of this too late, and while on its way to Creil it was captured by Allied troops.

The British and Canadians had broken through near Falaise, and Fontainebleau had to be abandoned. French troops under De Gaulle were on the verge of entering Paris.

On 23 August, elements of the *3. Staffel* were despatched to bring *Kommando Schenck* up to strength. Of nine aircraft just five arrived. Two crashed on takeoff due to pilot error, the third crashed at Schwäbisch-Hall, and the pilot of the fourth failed to locate Juvincourt and made a crashlanding not far from his destination airfield.

From Juvincourt the small detachment flew several sorties daily against targets on the Seine northwest of Paris and around Melun.

The enemy then broke through at Soissons, Chalons-sur-Marne and Vitry-le-François and street fighting broke out in nearby Juvincourt, and on 28 August orders were issued for the unit to hurriedly move to Ath-Chièvres in Belgium. *Feldwebel* "Ronny" Lauer was chased by four Spitfires and forced to make a crash-landing at Haltert near Brussels. Fortunately the Me 262 was relatively easy to belly-land and did not catch fire quickly. The unit was constantly on the run from enemy fighters and bombers. It remained in Chièvres for just two days and on 30 August moved to Volkel and Eindhoven in Holland. In the now familiar rush, missions were flown against targets near Löwen and Antwerp and against the defense line on the Albert Canal. After Volkel was attacked by Lancaster and Halifax bombers in daylight on the night of 4-5 September, the *Kommando* had to be hastily withdrawn to the Reich. It safely crossed the Rhine near Wesel at two in the morning. The *I. Gruppe*, into which "*Kdo. Schenck*" had since been merged, established itself in and around Rhine/Westfalen, with quarters in Rheine-Bentlage, Dreierwalde and Hopsten. The *Gruppe* was slowly brought up to strength as aircraft arrived from Lechfeld. The familiar *Geschwader* code 9K reappeared on the fuselages of the unit's aircraft, while the edelweiss emblem was applied beneath the cockpit. *Oberstleutnant* Schenck took over as *Geschwaderkommodore*. By then, the formation of the *II. Gruppe* under *Major* Grundmann in Schwäbisch-Hall had reached the stage that it could begin high-speed bomber operations from Hesepe near Achmer air base.

Rheine, Hopsten and Hesepe

Since autumn 1944 Hitler had been pondering a new and decisive offensive in the west, but the attack date was repeatedly postponed. Then, at 05:30 on 16 December 1944, German forces launched "Operation Watch on the Rhine" or "Autumn Mist," as the Ardennes offensive was to go down in the history of the war.

Bad weather initially prevented the *Luftwaffe* from taking part, but then it cleared on the 22nd of December. Bitter fighting developed at Bastogne and west of Rochefort. Allied air superiority was crushing. The few German bombers proved ineffective and suffered heavy losses. The only way they could avoid enemy fighters was to strike their targets at treetop height. The Me 262's high speed was often its only salvation against the Tempest fighters that lurked in the Hopsten-Achmer and Rheine areas, waiting to shoot down the "blitz bombers" when they were most vulnerable, on approach to land.

Our airfields were defended by as many as 160 quad 20-mm anti-aircraft guns, as for example along Rheine's east-west runway. This significantly reduced the chances of being shot down by enemy fighters. As well, fighter units were based nearby to protect the "turbo" units. The Allies quickly adapted their tactics to meet this new situation.

The Ardennes offensive became bogged down in the mud. There were shortages of fuel and ammunition, which even the courage and bravery of the German army could not overcome. The Allied drive into the Reich would not be long coming.

The *Geschwader* was regularly committed at the many crisis points. The men were used to this from Russia. In Munich-Riem and Erding, the *IV. Gruppe* trained the volunteers streaming in from every bomber unit. Many experienced Ju 88 and Me 410 pilots had problems adapting to the new aircraft and found employment elsewhere. They found it hard to trust the new "screaming" power plants and in some cases had considerable difficulty adapting to the new type. The constant shortage of fuel hampered training considerably. Sixty-five tons of fuel was needed to train just one new pilot. Like the aircraft factories, the synthetic fuel plants had been under regular and effective attack by the Allies for some time. Raw materials bottlenecks grew more serious.

The *II. Gruppe* operated – not particularly successfully – from Hesepe and Achmer with KG 76, which operated the Ar 234 "Blitz" jet bomber, mainly in the Holland-Belgium area.

On 13 November 1944 Rheine was carpet-bombed and several heavy bombs struck the RAD camp, which was partly destroyed. Many *Geschwader* personnel were killed and many more were injured to varying degrees. *Oberleutnant* Merlau and *Feldwebel* Hoffmann of the flying personnel were killed. The badly injured included the *I. Gruppe*'s medical officer, *Stabsarzt* Dr. Denkhaus.

In Hesepe, many members of the *5. Staffel* also fell victim to enemy bombs. The members of the jet units were always on the run. They were hunted wherever they went. The *Gruppestab* subsequently moved near to Hopsten and in turns occupied quarters in Hörstel, Dreierwalde and Esch.

The jet bombers concentrated their efforts mainly against targets in the Liege, Antwerp, Nijmwegen, Volkel and Eindhoven area and troop concentrations following the unsuccessful airborne landing near Arnhem. From the base at Essen-Mühlheim – with its relatively short runway – the *II. Gruppe* operated against enemy positions near Euskirchen, Düren and Jülich, where there was heavy fighting for possession of the Reichswald and the

Hürtgen Forest. The Me 262s could only take off from the Essen-Mühlheim airfield with the use of takeoff-assist rockets.

On New Year' Eve 1944 all German air force units had a 19:00 curfew. Something special and very secret was being planned. Even the unit commanders did not know what the targets would be. No one could sleep well. So it was at the *I. Gruppe*, where the *3. Staffel*'s technical officer in Rheine, *Leutnant* Maser, stayed with the technicians in the hangar until late into the night to ensure that the maximum number of aircraft was available. In any event, 21 of 30 aircraft were reported serviceable. The men were roused at three in the morning. In the flight briefing rooms the *Kommandeure* and *Kapitäne* had mysterious envelopes waiting for the crews – target maps for a large-scale low-level attack on airfields in Belgium and Holland.

Each pilot was issued a well-prepared map, on which were marked bases, airfields and flak batteries in the Allied rear were already marked, along with return routes. Takeoff time was 07:45. Ju 88 pathfinders led the units to the front. One large formation set course for Brussels, a second headed for Arnhem-Eindhoven, and the third Venlo. On that cold winter morning I./KG 51 attacked the Eindhoven and Hertogenbusch airfields in Holland. The British and Americans were still asleep when the sun rose on the horizon, probably still feeling the effects of the New Year's celebrations. No one could have expected such a blow from the *Luftwaffe*, which was thought to be on its last legs. The attackers found the airfields quiet and covered with aircraft of all types.

Soon aircraft, fuel dumps, hangars and buildings were in flames. The element of surprise had been achieved. Dark smoke clouds signaled the success.

By the time the aircraft headed for home the anti-aircraft defense were wide awake. Aerial combats began and smoldering spots in the snow showed where aircraft had crashed. The enemy's material losses were great, 810 aircraft destroyed by the 800 *Luftwaffe* aircraft that took part in the operation. 293 German aircraft were lost, including 18 flown by experienced unit commanders. These were losses that could not be made good.

Enemy anti-aircraft guns alone shot down 200 aircraft. These aircraft had flown down a "flak road" that the Allies had created to shoot down V 1 flying bombs. The operation also cost the life of *Oberfeldwebel* Erich Kaiser, one of the most experienced pilots in the *Geschwader*.

The effects of the attack on the Allied air forces lasted just one week. On the afternoon of 1 January the *Gruppe*'s air elements moved to Giebelstadt. Frankfurt-Rheine/Main was also prepared to receive aircraft. Because of the rapidly changing situation at the front, however, nothing came of this move. At the end of February the unit moved back to Hopsten. The British had reached the Rhine in the area north of Kalkar, while the Americans had already launched a major assault on the Ruhr. After the Americans captured the lightly-damaged bridge at Remagen on 7 March and established a bridgehead, I./KG 51's duty officer in Hopsten received a personal call from *Reichsmarschall* Göring at two in the morning with orders for the unit to immediately supply volunteers for suicide attacks on the bridge, much like the Japanese kamikazes. Only two daredevils volunteered. Fortunately the mission was not carried out.

It was too late!

Final Operations in the South of Germany

On 13 March the *I. Gruppe* moved to Leipheim, where its aircraft took off from the autobahn and landed on the airfield's runways. After landing they were hidden beneath the trees. The jet bomber unit established its command post in the autobahn rest stop in Leipheim/Günzburg.

Elements of the unit were also in Giebelstadt. The focal point of operations was the Lower Alsace in the area of the Hagenau Forest. It was there that *Leutnant* Ritter von Rittersheim was killed. During one of these sorties, *Leutnant* Batel shot down an American Thunderbolt, something the "bombers" were capable of when required.

There was a tragic incident in Leipheim. As a result of the growing disorganization within the *Luftwaffe*–the right hand did not know what the left was doing – the *Geschwader* had two commanding officers. *Major* Barth had an official paper designating him *Kommodore*, as did *Oberstleutnant* Hallensleben. While driving to the command post in his staff car, Hallensleben and three of his men were killed by American fighter-bombers while crossing the road bridge near Leipheim. They were buried in Leipheim.

Barth led the *Geschwader* from that time until the bitter end. From Leipheim, targets were attacked in the Würzburg, Tauberbischofsheim, Crailsheim area, in effect in all of Swabia – Franconia, while from Schwäbisch-Hall the *II. Gruppe* struck targets on the Rhine near Speyer and in the Pfalz Region around Kaiserslautern. On 21 March the popular and successful *Staffelkapitän* of 3./KG 51, *Hauptmann* Winkel was killed by a stray bullet from an American Thunderbolt. Winkel, who had just taken off on his 300th operational sortie, was shot through the head. In response to this, a thick armor plate was immediately installed in the cockpit of all the unit's Me 262s to protect the pilot's head and neck.

Soon the thunder of Allied guns could be heard again. The unit moved with the now familiar haste. Events were moving quickly and the jet fighter airfields were bombed constantly by the Allies. The end was approaching. On 21 April the *I. Gruppe* moved to Memmingen. The *II. Gruppe* flew via Nuremberg-Fürth to Linz/Hörsching. The Americans were at the gates of Ulm and Munich. The signs of disintegration of a once proud army were depressing to watch. Press gangs, dubbed "hero snatchers," were everywhere, securing men for local defense units. Despite special passes that identified the holder as "... a member of a jet unit and by order of the *Führer* not to be pressed into service in a ground role! ..." the airmen were often fortunate to escape the clutches of the *Volkssturm*.

At Straßkirchen, near Landau/Isar, 80% of the *II. Gruppe* under *Major* Grundmann was captured by the Americans. In Kammern near Landau, *Oberleutnant* Baetz sent the rest of the *Gruppe* home.

Only the *I. Gruppe* succeeded in escaping at the last minute to Memmingen with its aircraft and ground personnel. In a final show of defiance, sorties were flown against the Danube bridges near Dillingen. On the afternoon of 23 April the cry "the French are approaching Memmingen" rang out at the base in Memmingen. The pilots rushed from the mess and flew their aircraft to Munich-Riem, where the Me 262s were handed over to *Jagdverband Galland.* As soon as they landed, they were towed off the runway and camouflaged. One air raid alarm followed the other.

Unused to physical labor, digging foxholes in the stony ground in Riem cost the airmen plenty of sweat and nervous strain. It was not unusual for two airmen to jump simultaneously into a one-man hole and, with bombs exploding left and right, wonder why it was so crowded.

While the bulk of the *I. Gruppe* withdrew towards the Schönegg-Nordhof estate in Dietramszell near Holzkirchen, a few others had to undertake a special assignment. With a heavy heart, the technical officer of IV./KG 51, Dr. Woernle, had to blow up about fifty Me 262s in Neuburg/Donau when the airfield came under American artillery fire.

Detachment in Prague-Ruzyne

It was 30 April and Munich was trembling under American artillery fire. In Czechoslovakia, troops under General Vlasov, who had previously fought on the German side, joined an uprising that had broken out. The *Wehrmacht* had to intervene to enable and protect a retreat by German troops and German civilians. Terrible scenes were played out, much described and hard to comprehend in posterity. In the smoke from bursting artillery shells, in Munich-Riem seven upstanding volunteers under *Hauptmann* Abrahamczik stepped forward and flew their aircraft via Hörsching to Prague-Ruzyne. With great difficulty and much improvisation, a small team of dedicated mechanics followed in a few workshop trucks to look after the aircraft. Galland's jet fighter unit withdrew to Salzburg.

In Prague this small group of men was attached to "Battle Unit Hogeback." It intervened in the fighting in and around Prague and became familiar with the difficult street and house fighting from the air. *Leutnant* Schimmel was killed in action on 6 May, *Oberleutnant* Strothmann and *Uffz*. Poling on 7 May 1945.

The situation became untenable. Prague-Ruzyne was evacuated on 6 May. The new base was Saaz (Zatec). There was nothing left there to attack, and the unit established an all-round defense as best it could. There were shortages of fuel and spare parts. The men of the ground personnel were unable to get through. They surrendered to the Americans in Prague, Saaz and Pilsen to avoid being captured by the Russians or Czechs. Many were later handed over to the Soviets and never saw their homes again.

On 8 May in Saaz, after it was learned that German troops on the British front had already signed the surrender, *Hauptmann* Abrahamczik ordered his airmen only to land in areas held by the western allies.

The German military had surrendered unconditionally in Reims at 02:41 on 7 May. Hostilities would officially end at 00:01 on 9 May 1945.

It was the end of the world. All that mattered now was survival.

Completely on their own, the four pilots considered how to make the best of this hopeless situation. They were about to make the last flight of their lives as military airmen.

The brilliant blue sky did not inspire sadness in these men, who had never resorted to alternative solutions. Despite everything they were somehow confident. They had to carry on under these difficult circumstances – just not in the direction of the east, which they knew all too well.

The Last Flight

On 8 May 1945, the day of the surrender, the question facing the German soldier was not "what to do?," rather it was "where to?" For *Leutnant* Wilhelm Batel there could only be one answer: "Home, if possible, if not then to a British airfield." This is the story of his last flight.

At 14:30 on 8 May 1945, he took off from Saaz in aircraft 9K + FB and set course for Lüneburg. The weather was excellent with unrestricted visibility. His average cruising height was 3,000 meters. He remembers this flight very well, and with good reason. Unthinkably, conditions for him had changed completely overnight. In particular the dangers of war were absent. His aircraft was fully armed, but for what? The landscape was completely unfamiliar, no anti-aircraft fire, no fires from air raids, no moving locomotives, to give just a few examples. On the airfields near Dresden, Leipzig (he had learned instrument flying in Machern) and Magdeburg, the Allied aircraft were lined up as if on parade. He arrived over Lüneburg airfield, which was obviously occupied by the British, shortly after 15:00. His parents lived on an agricultural estate 30 kilometers away. His plan, to at least signal that he was alive by flying over, was initially frustrated by navigation problems. He had hiked all over his home but had never flown over it, and in the Me 262 he had difficulty getting his bearings. He soon made the necessary adjustments, however. When he flew over the small agricultural estate he saw that there was heavy Jeep and truck traffic on the adjacent roads. Landing in the immediate vicinity made no sense. He therefore selected a field next to a wood about 3 kilometers away, near which he could not see any concentrations of troops or civilians. He began the approach for his last landing at 15:28. The belly landing in the grain field worked very well. The aircraft stopped about eight meters from the edge of the wood. Carrying his briefcase and parachute, he was able to reach cover quickly. Prior to this, he had tried to set the aircraft on fire. He ignited the fuel in the engines but the resulting fire did little damage and he left it at that.

Batel then began walking in the direction of his parents' house, but while crossing a forest road not far from where he had come down, he met a farmer who didn't recognize him. He subsequently asked about a town that was in the opposite direction from where he had landed. This proved beneficial when the English subsequently launched an intensive search effort. The information the farmer gave him later spared him from this search. At about 16:30 he arrived at the so-called "White Mountain," from where he had a view of his parents' community but not the part of town where they lived. He then took a sunbath and observed the activity in the town and on the roads. When darkness came, he crept across the field, making use of the cover offered by trees, hedges and fences, to the district about one kilometer away and reached his parents' house without being seen. His arrival was announced by his parents' German shepherd dogs.

It was a cheerful but not very quiet reunion, for there were numerous refugees living in the house. After a few days Wilhelm Batel left his hiding place and declared that he had been officially discharged.

In his Me 262, *Staffelkapitän* Abrahamczik accompanied *Oberleutnant* Haeffner, who could not retract his machine's undercarriage due to a technical malfunction. Their destination was Munich-Riem, from where they had once come at the start of their adventurous operation in Czechoslovakia. The Americans happily took charge of the two jet fighters and the pilots became POWs.

The fourth member of the group, *Oberleutnant* Fröhlich, selected Fassberg as a landing place. He also landed undisturbed. The British stationed there were more than a little surprised by his unannounced arrival. They were already celebrating the ceasefire noisily and wetly, and they took the bemused German into their circle. It was almost two days before their heads cleared and realized that it was time to relieve the "enemy airman" of his pistol and hand him over to the army. He was unable to avoid the fate of so many German soldiers, becoming a prisoner of war.

The war was over, Germany was beaten. For Germans, flying was probably over for good.

During the *Geschwader*'s relatively brief period of operations on the Me 262, 172 members of the unit lost their lives, specifically:

52 officers
91 non-commissioned officers
28 enlisted men.

Chapter 8
The Bitter End

For most members of the *Geschwader*, the war ended in the last days of April 1945. Their official discharge was by a *Geschwader* order dated 24 April 1945. The order required each man to report to the mayor in his new place of residence for assignment of work. There was no compensation and it was left to the soldiers to provide themselves with clothes and shoes. There had long since ceased to be official seals for confirmation.

The *III. Gruppe* had already been disbanded, the remnants of the *II. Gruppe* were captured during the defense of the Isar position near Landau. Only elements of the *2. Staffel* under *Staffelkapitän Hauptmann* Abrahamczik fought to the last in Prague-Ruzyne and Saaz.

On 30 April the bulk of the *I. Gruppe* moved to the Schönegg-Nordhof farm in Dietramszell near Holzkirchen and the surrounding towns. There its personnel were incorporated into "*Feldjagdkommando Schomann*" of *Luftwaffen-Feldjagdabteilung 103 (mot.)*. From then on the airmen and technicians formed an order group for the maintenance of discipline among German troops streaming back into the "Alpine redoubt." The men were issued *panzerfaust* anti-tank weapons and given instructions in their use. Though lavishly equipped with these weapons, vehicles, numerous important-looking papers with numerous official stamps, and supplied with plenty of food, this duty was no bed of roses for the individual soldiers.

From Dietramszell, the remnants of the former flying units, armed, and equipped with *Kettenkräder* (previously used to tow our Me 262s), moved noisily through Bad Tölz to Winkel, south of Lenggries, as if the war had just begun. By order of the local SS commander (a highly-decorated officer with the rank of major), we were supposed arrest and disarm any officers and men caught fleeing to the south. We were then supposed to hand them over to a unit that was supposed to make a last stand in Bad Tölz. What a miserable job with the end so near!

Another order directed the "dashing crew" to proceed through the Achen Pass on the Tratzburg near Jenbach, Tyrol. There Professor Heinkel and several of his directors received the former bomber airmen in the canteen of the Heinkel factory. The conversations revealed the despondency, fear and helplessness felt by these men. We learned many previously unknown details of why so much had gone wrong in the aircraft development technical organization. Why Heinkel, Focke-Wulf or Messerschmitt enjoyed or failed to enjoy the *Reichsmarschall*'s favor at various times, why conversions and modifications to the aircraft had to be carried out to intentionally disadvantage one aircraft against another. Fear of Hitler's Gestapo, power struggles in the procurement system, personal greed, perhaps a little corruption and sabotage created unfair manipulation in the competitions to win a production contract.

On 3 May the men moved on to Seegatterl near Reit im Winkl, where the *3. Staffel* was partially disbanded. Some members fell back towards the Scheibelbergalm after they were sniped at by former Austrian comrades in arms. There was obviously a certain amount of opportunism at play there. Only by sending patrols in to the valley daily was it possible to protect the stragglers. Cut off and alone, the unit retained its cohesion because none of its officers left prematurely without permission.

The remainder of the unit split up. Part remained in Reit im Winkl. Another, under *Oberleutnant* Stephan and *Leutnant* Maser, was supposed to assist an SS unit. This did not happen, however. On 9 May it was captured by the Americans and sent to the camp in Blindau near Reit. The men of the *2. Staffel* had a similar experience in Heutal near Unken, Tyrol.

Before they were taken prisoner, most of the detachments held one last military formation in a field somewhere. The senior soldiers spoke a few brief, sometimes moving words, ending a long and eventful period of service that had often been filled with hardships. The last of the *Gruppe*'s food was handed out, the well-guarded military service books given back. And so, in an alpine pasture with few observers – mainly cows – and mixed feelings, there came to an end for many an almost won war, an idea, an illusion.

When food among the members of the *Geschwader* living on the mountain began running low, representatives were sent to make contact with the occupation forces in the valley, in this case an American airborne division. It had had very bad experiences with *Waffen-SS* troops at Bastogne, but any of those who had been briefly held in a *Luftwaffe* camp appreciated the proper handling they had received.

In the Blindau camp, a farm with large fields, the men lived as prisoners of war for about three weeks. Officers were permitted to retain their weapons.

Of course the Me 262 pilots were interrogated at length. The Americans were skeptical about their accounts of combat and frontline operations. For example, when *Oberfeldwebel* Werschnik stated under interrogation that he had flown about 330 sorties on the Me 262 alone, the German-speaking American officers made incredulous faces. They refused to believe him and arranged for a psychological test with the aid of a lie detector, a recent invention. After his statements were found to be the truth, the Americans began treating him like a demigod. The idea of a pilot flying more than 100 combat missions was unheard of in the American military.

A larger element of I./KG 51 stayed between Hallein and Bischofshofen, near Werfen in the Blühnbach Valley. For a time they lived well in the Krupps hunting lodge. After the surrender *Major* Unrau reported to Colonel Edson, commander of the American 15th Infantry Division, in Werfen. The latter greeted him with a handshake and gave the elements of the *I. Gruppe* in the area the task of maintaining order and directing former German troops from all branches of the service arriving in the area to the designated reception areas.

Another part of the *Gruppe* looked after the numerous enemy aircraft, especially Fieseler Storch liaison machines, captured by the American unit.

At the end of May its area of responsibility was moved to Feldkirchen in Bavaria. *General* Korte, one of the first *Gruppenkommandeure* in KG 255, deployed his *Luftwaffe* order unit to direct German troops returning from the Alps into the occupying powers' discharge camps. They hoped to complete the discharge action as smoothly and quickly as possible.

The comradely intrigues of the veteran frontline soldiers should not go unmentioned. The Bad Aibling camp was well known for bad treatment of prisoners. The discharge process there took about eight days and involved every sort of harassment. Conditions in the camp in Rosenheim were much more humane. There it only took about three hours to receive discharge papers. It is not surprising, therefore, that most of our men made their way to Rosenheim and were processed quickly.

One day the famous trans-Atlantic flyer, Charles Lindbergh, a colonel in the USAAF, greeted almost all of the known Me 262 pilots in the St. Peter and Paul Monastery by the Mangfall Bridge near Weyarn. The friendly manner in which he greeted each man with a handshake and personally asked him about his experiences with this modern, trend-setting aircraft was unusual and far from the norm at that time. His manner was a pleasant change from that usually encountered by the German airmen. Everyone who met this individual was surely impressed by the attitude and conduct of the American air force. It should be noted that the captured pilots had previously discussed the matter and decided to hide nothing from this fine officer.

Airmen of all eras, nations and political persuasions always communicate with each other on a very different "frequency." The third dimension always spans worlds and short horizons.

By about the end of July – beginning of August 1945, the bulk of the *Geschwader*'s personnel had been released by the Americans. A few languished in prison or even in Russian prison camps for several years longer.

The former airmen now had to turn their efforts to building a new world, a new existence.

By the end of the war. The *Luftwaffe* had lost about 140,000 men, about 155,000 were missing, 40,000 had been wounded or injured.

Of a total of 94,435 aircraft, the bomber units alone had lost 21,807.

A world collapsed. Somehow life had to go on. Germany lay in ruins. The war was over. The soldiers had to rebuild Germany, a new and hopefully forever purified Germany.

Afterword

The KG 51 Veterans Association

A handful of comrades who met by chance in Penzing and Landsberg in 1951 decided that it would be a good idea to meet again. At first they thought only of the comrades living in the Landsberg area. That is how it remained at first, as everyone was reluctant to take on the task of organizing a larger reunion.

During a chance meeting of comrades Delles and Graffenberger in the spring of 1955, old memories were exchanged and a decision was made to get in touch with the veterans. Hermann Schneider immediately agreed to help out. To prevent it from once again remaining nothing more than an idea, they agreed on the following Sunday. It was 6 March 1955.

Together they composed a circular that would be sent to all those with known addresses. The summons received an enthusiastic response and the number of replies quickly rose. The first reunion was scheduled for Saturday, 30 July 1955, at 19:30 in the Gasthaus Frank in Penzing.

The organizers were doubtful as the day approached. While some individuals began trickling in in the early afternoon, by 19:15 everyone was discouraged to see less than twenty people in the room. Despite everything, at 19:45 the planned service for the fallen was held at the war memorial in Penzing. Helmut Rammig gave the memorial address. No one could believe his eyes when the square around the memorial filled, almost blocking traffic.

After the laying of wreaths the veterans returned to the room and – much to their surprise – found it full. More than 100 former comrades had come from far and near. Cheerful reunions soon reawakened the old spirit. When a film of *Geschwader* life was shown, the barometer rose even higher.

During the evening, Henry Barsch made the suggestion that they should form a veterans association. The proposal was immediately accepted. The question of who should lead the organization was settled quickly and Rammig, Delles and Graffenberger, the men who had organized the first meeting, were immediately given the job. Rammig's suggestion that the old chapel near Höschl-Hof be rebuilt as a memorial, was given enthusiastic approval.

At the same time that the formation of a veteran's association was being approved in Penzing, former members living in the Munich area also decided to form closer ties. The tried and true word of mouth method brought people together, and it was decided to hold a small meeting in Landsberg on 26 November 1955. On that day Unrau, a member of the Munich group, joined Rammig, Greffenberger and Delles as a provisional board member. The Munich group sent the Landsberg group a small amount of cash, symbolically merging the two groups.

The still-young veterans association demanded a great deal of work, which was at first underestimated. Its goal, after all, was to prepare a *Geschwader* reunion for 1956 and, in particular, create a memorial to our fallen and missing comrades. In mind was the chapel of the former Höschl-Hof. The former commander of I./KG 255, *Oberstleutnant* Kurt Mälzer, and the local management of works had been able to prevent the demolition of the chapel and turn it into a memorial to our comrades who had lost their lives in the course of their duties. The site was subsequently cared for and maintained mainly by the commanders stationed at the airfield. The chapel was dedicated to this purpose until after the war. In 1946 or 1947, with no one to look after the chapel, the American unit stationed on the airfield "repurposed" it for the storage of ammunition.

A chance visit in the winter of 1955-56 caused the observer, who knew the chapel from earlier times, to somewhat sadly think of better days. It was a ruin in the truest sense of the word. It was grated and armored, surrounded by tall barbed wire fences, making an approach impossible. More daunting than the fences were the difficulties encountered in procuring the chapel for the planned purpose. How should this be achieved? All negotiations proved fruitless. No one seriously believed that the objective could be achieved in 1956.

Inspired by never ending hope, Delles spared no effort in obtaining approval. The first cold rejections could not deter him. When amicable negotiations had failed, he successfully he successfully used subterfuge, at least succeeding in having the goods stored in the chapel removed. But he had not yet obtained its release. He therefore contacted personalities and former members of the *Geschwader* with influence. They were secretly let in on the plan and asked for support, which was forthcoming. Then, in February, the chapel was released. The fence was torn down.

Motivated by the concept, who says A must also say B, action was taken without delay. No one wished to proceed without architectural advice. Architect Peter Zorzi from Regensburg was brought in as an advisor. Without much discussion, he completed plans based on his ideas, which received broad acceptance.

While architect Zorzi was developing his plans over his drawing board, the veterans association experienced another important day in its existence. A workshop was held in Landsberg on 10 March 1956, which was attended by a considerable number of comrades from as far away as the Rhineland. After a brief financial statement, much time was dedicated to the work on the chapel and the planned reunion. Until then the opinion prevailed that the number of comrades to be memorialized had to be estimated at at least 600. Perpetuating all these names in the chapel where they could be seen was the most serious problem faced by the group.

It was Rammig who suggested having a parchment book made and entering all the names in it. The way ahead was indicated to the board and there was full confidence that what was being done would find approval.

Extensive work now began, strengthened by the knowledge that the comrades stood by their word. Circulars were sent out. Replies came and they in turn had to be answered. The architect presented his designs and an estimate of the costs. The latter was enough to weaken the knees of the strongest man. Well begun is half done was the motto and negotiations were immediately started with tradesmen, cost proposals were obtained and contracts issued. The question of who was going to pay was raised by all of the contractors. He who places the order pays the bill, was the short answer and that was good enough for everyone. Work on the chapel began at a feverish pace. But how were they to raise the necessary funds? The board knew that it could depend on every comrade, just as everyone was depended on in earlier days. The estimate of at least 10,000 Deutschmarks made by the architect sent the mood barometer plunging. The resolution made by the workshop was realized and the pledge forms went to print. The mailing to the membership was meant to impress upon everyone the extent of the work and costs. The close and truly comradely cooperation with the men of the Munich circle must be praised. Visits and return visits, at which films of *Geschwader* life were shown, provided fresh impetus. Complaints that it was irresponsible to begin such an expensive project without funds did nothing to lift spirits and ease concerns. Nevertheless, they did not allow themselves to be discouraged. The idea that we will succeed or go down with flags waving, spurred us to work harder. Our comrade Wittmann from Munich deserves special thanks. He offered to have his company make and deliver the double lattice doors free of charge. This offer immediately improved spirits. Schölß and Wieczoreck subsequently succeeded masterfully in rousing the circle of comrades in Munich and finally having them assume the cost of the copper tablet at the altar. The Penzing municipal council under Mayor Steichele made a generous donation, which gave courage. Similar appeals to the city council and the rural district of Landsberg were also successful. The bills came in faster than the money, however. Each time the necessary funds were found, either from personal donations or loans. The municipal council of Memmingerberg under Mayor Kratzert also made a contribution. The appeal to comrades and families in the province, to honor their pledges was largely successful. Donations for this good cause flowed in. As a result there were no serious delays in work on the chapel.

While most of the work on the walls and the carpentry work was completed satisfactorily by the Lutz Company of Landsberg, the oak door at the entrance, the roof, the alter and the pews in the chapel were made by master carpenter Baumann in Landsberg. The freelance artist and carver Albert Prochaska of Landsberg did the necessary wood carving on the altar. Special thanks are due to Col. R.O. Mosher and Lt.Col. Marcel Lind of the American airfield administration, who provided a great deal of support, and the training department of the German air force. The workshops and craftsmen and their superiors from Penzing air base also did really good work. It was only through their assistance that total costs were kept as low as possible.

On Monday, the 24th of September 1956, we received the news that Alfred Krupp of Bohlen and Halbach had donated a bell for the memorial chapel.

It was only possible to overcome all of the difficulties standing in the way thanks to the donations from our comrades of all classes, the families of our fallen and missing, and supporters of this good cause.

We were dismayed to discover that the number of fallen and missing comrades from our *Geschwader* exceeded 1,500. All of these names were entered in a parchment book made in the monastery bookbindery in St. Ottilien. We have the enthusiastic support of our members, their families and in particular the information center for fallen and missing in Berlin-Wittenau and the Red Cross to thank for completeness of our information.

Along with this work, we also had the task of preparing the *Geschwader* reunion. A few figures will give some idea of the work involved: more tan 200 personal letters and over 5,000 pieces of printed matter were sent, about 1,000 file cards of living and 1,400 file cards of fallen and missing were made and constantly updated or corrected. The details had to be compiled from many individual letters and from lists. Creation of the commemorative publication made it necessary to compile a list of all available names. The same went for a list of addresses, which each member received.

All of the work was of course voluntary. At last the promises made to preserve comradeship and loyalty even after death and to never forget comrades who gave their lives, could be seen as kept. May everyone reverently enter the memorial chapel of the Kampfgeschwader 51 veterans association in this spirit. May the many names in the book of remembrance inspire remembrance and reflection. The chapel itself is entrusted to the special care of the population and our comrades of the new German air force.

The annual Remembrance Day reunion at our chapel will always be a solemn obligation for us, as long as it is possible for us to get to the airbase in Landsberg/Lech – a modest and grateful gesture of fidelity to our fallen airmen comrades.

The edelweiss of the *III. Gruppe* of the Alpine *Geschwader* is now the emblem of the 2. *Staffel* of *Jagdbombergeschwader 34* in Memmingerberg. The names of the airmen of this unit who gave their young lives while serving in the *Bundeswehr* have been entered in our book of remembrance and tie the knot between young and old in keeping with military tradition.

Appendices

"And we, who remain behind in the cozy, peaceful warmth, we lower our heads ..."
— Antoine de Saint-Exupéry (from Flight to Arras)

Appendix 1
KG 51 *Edelweiss* Losses

The *Kampfgeschwader "Edelweiss"* lost approximately 1,500 men in the Second World War, consisting of approximately:

330 officers
800 non-commissioned officers
300 enlisted men
70 unknown ranks

We have attempted to document as completely as possible the fates of the fallen and missing, with assistance from the German Red Cross missing persons tracing service, the *Wehrmacht* Inquiries Office (WASt) Berlin, the German War Graves Commission and numerous submissions by former members of the *Geschwader*.

A reading of the list of names will undoubtedly result in the discovery of errors that can only be corrected with the assistance of the readers.

Where exact dates could not be determined, only the year or month is given. We consciously decided not to present the names in alphabetical order, so as to more clearly illustrate periods of busier activity and heavier losses.

Suggestions and information for the clarification of the fates of killed or missing personnel may be sent at any time to:

Traditionsgemeinschaft
Kampfgeschwader 51
891 Landsberg/Lech
Postfach 247

1937/38

25/4	Kretschmer		Uffz.	†	crashed Neu-Ulm	
25/5	Stüsser	Klemens	Flg.	†	Penzing	

1938

?	Willer		Oblt.	†	Spain	
?	Pawelcik	Hans	Oblt.	†	Spain	

1938/39

?	Schmidt	Joachim	Ltn.	†	crashed Memmingen	
?	Grunwald	Gerhard	Uffz.	†	Neubiberg	9.
13/1	Popp	Albrecht	Gefr.	†		
20/1	Dönig	Hugo	Obfw.	†	Innsbruck	
26/1	Weichenberger	Ernst	Uffz.	†		
28/4	Peters		Uffz.	†	Aalen, training flight in Do 17	
28/4	Hunger	Paul	Uffz.	†	Aalen	
28/4	Heinrich		Uffz.	†	Aalen	
3/5	Schirmer	Erwin	Gefr.	†		
3/5	Stahlforth	Friedrich	Ltn.	†		
3/5	Grosche	Heinz	Uffz.	†		
8/5	Wölfing	Willi	Uffz.	†	crashed Unterschlauersbach	
8/5	Wicke		Lt.	†	crashed Unterschlauersbach	
8/5	Kretschmer		Uffz.	†	crashed Unterschlauersbach	
17/6	Halter	Siegmund	Lt.	†	Gunzenhausen	
17/6	Beilharz	Gottlob	Fw.	†	Gunzenhausen	
17/6	Ficher	Erwin	Fw.	†	Gunzenhausen	
1/8	Grote	Rudolf	Lt.	†	Landsberg	
11/8	Stockinger	Willibald	Obgefr.	†		
12/11	Häder	Herbert	Uffz.	†		
12/11	Kampa	Ernst	Uffz.	†		
13/12	Galle	Hans	Fw.	†		

1939

20/2	Sewalda	Johann	Tech.Insp.	†	Austria	
20/2	Mazeth	Andreas	Uffz.	†	Austria	
20/2	Urban	Fritz	Uffz.	†	Austria	
8/3	Stritzel	Kurt	Obgefr.	†	Austria	
11/3	Redenbacher	Walter	Lt.	†		
17/5	Sippel		Uffz.	†	Swabian Alps	9.
17/5	Libor		Uffz.	†	Swabian Alps	9.
17/5	Ebert		Uffz.	†	Swabian Alps	9.
17/5	Fleig		Uffz.	†	Swabian Alps	9.
12/6	Beulig	Erich	Uffz.	†		
15/8	Pawlizek	Josef	Uffz.	†	Königgrätz	
15/8	Karo	Hans	Uffz.	†	Königgrätz	
15/9	Wagner	Johann	Uffz.	†	Poland	
27/9	Wittmer	Helmut	Uffz.	†	Neuhausen o.E.	
27/9	Schwitz	Heinrich	Flg.	†	Neuhausen o.E.	
27/9	Albrecht	Georg	Uffz.	†	Neuhausen o.E.	
27/9	Bergmann	Franz	Flg.	†	Neuhausen o.E.	
27/9	Fischer	Kurt	Gefr.	†	Neuhausen o.E.	all 7. FBK
27/9	Graser	Hermann	Flg.	†	Neuhausen o.E.	

1939/40

27/9	Grünsch	Alfred	Flg.	†	Neuhausen o.E.	
27/9	Reichel	Richard	Gefr.	†	Neuhausen o.E.	
27/9	Hauk	Paulus	Flg.	†	Neuhausen o.E.	
27/9	Hering	Otto	Uffz.	†	Neuhausen o.E.	
27/9	Schaale	Waldemar	Obfw.	†	Neuhausen o.E.	
7/11	Neuenfeld	Otto	Major	†	France, Staffelkapitän	3.
17/11	Altmann	Wilhelm	Uffz.	†	Salzburg (on combat mission to France)	
17/11	Trautner	Wilhelm	Fw.	†	Salzburg (on combat mission to France)	
17/11	Tesch	Erhard	Uffz.	†	Salzburg (on combat mission to France)	
17/11	Domke	Helmut	Lt.	†	Salzburg (on combat mission to France)	
17/11	Hössl	Karl	Uffz.	†	Italy (on combat mission to France)	
17/11	Pfordte	Klaus	Oblt.	†	Italy (on combat mission to France)	
17/11	Reschke	Heinz	Uffz.	†	Salzburg (on combat mission to France)	
17/11	Plischke	Gerhard	Hptm.	†	Salzburg (on combat mission to France)	

1940

?	Dürr		Gefr.	†	England	
?	Stölze		Obfw.	†	Echterdingen	
?	Happert	Max	Gefr.	†	England	
?	Richter		Gefr.	†	England	
?	Peukert		Uffz.	†	France	
?	Troh		Gefr.	†	England	
January:						
16/1	Torenz	Gustav	Uffz.	†	Affing	2.
16/1	Borrmann	Alfred	Uffz.	†	Affing	2.
16/1	Eschenbach	Günther	Lt.	†	Affing	2.
16/1	Ochs	Heinrich	Uffz.	†	Affing	2.
16/1	Wagner		Flg.	†	Affing	2.
February:						
17/2	Gönner	Hans	Obfw.	†	Memmingen	7.
17/2	Müller	Joachim	Uffz.	†	Memmingen	7.
17/2	Knobelspieß	Bernhard	Obfw.	†	Memmingen	7.
17/2	Klinke	Rudolf	Obfw.	†	Memmingen	7.
March:						
10/3	Threiner		Obfw.	†	France	
19/3	Karl Dr.	Erich	Uffz.	†	Landsberg	7.
19/3	Draheim	Artur	Uffz.	†	Landsberg	7.
May:						
?/5	Labermeier	Konrad	Uffz.	†	France	
1/5	Wolf	Artur	Lt.	†	Oberpfaffenhofen	3.
1/5	Haberl	Lorenz	Gefr.	†	Oberpfaffenhofen	3.
1/5	Plotteg von	Arthur Wolff	Lt.	†	Oberpfaffenhofen	3.
10/5	Müller	Ludwig	Fw.	†	France	9.
10/5	Groche	Gerhard		†	France	9.
10/5	Grocke		Uffz.	†	Munich-Riem	6.
10/5	Kramer		Obfw.	†	Munich-Riem	6.
10/5	Treutle	Max	Uffz.	†	France	2.
10/5	Spengler	Valentin	Uffz.	†	France	Stab I.
11/5	Niedermayer	Franz	Uffz.	†	France	7.
14/5	Schildt	Gerhardt	Uffz.	†	France	Stab
14/5	Schäkel	Wilhelm	Uffz.	†	France	8.
14/5	Eckrich	Willi	Gefr.	†	France	8.
14/5	Schneider II		Uffz.	†	Ehingen	

14/5	Kroll	Franz	Uffz.	†	Zwiefalten	3.
14/5	Holtfurth	Paul	Gefr.	†	Zwiefalten	3.
15/5	Dimpfl	Eugen	Fw.	†	France	9.
15/5	Fläming	Heinz	Fw.	†	France	9.
15/5	Glufke	Günther	Fw.	†	France	9.
15/5	Lamm	Toni	Fw.	†	France	9.
15/5	Landmann	Karl	Gefr.	†	France	9.
15/5	Richter	Alfred.	Uffz.	†	France	9.
15/5	Straub	Josef	Fw.	†	France	9.
15/5	Hauff	Kurt		†	France	
15/5	Stufke	Günther	Fw.	†	EEE	
15/5	Schwarz	Walter	Flg.	†		
19/5	Putzbach	Joachim	Uffz.	†	Bobingen	2.
19/5	Böttcher	Alfred	Uffz.	†	Bobingen	2.
19/5	Stretz	Sebastian	Uffz.	†	Bobingen	2.
19/5	Sturzbach		Fw.	†	Bobingen	2.
19/5	De Maas	Ernst	Uffz.	†	France	III.
19/5	Baake	Edmund	Gefr.	†	France	III.
19/5	Heil	Walter	Uffz.	†	France	III.
19/5	Lang	Karl	Fw.	†	France	3.
19/5	Graml	Richard	Flg.	†	France	
19/5	Thelen	Franz	Lt.	†	France	6.
19/5	Badura	Heinrich	Fw.	†	France	6.
19/5	Pfeiffer	Maximilian	Fw.	†	France	3.
19/5	Schallenberg	Walter	Oblt.	†	France	3.
19/5	Lomi	Fritz	Flg.	†	France	
19/5	Lang	Fritz	Flg.	†	France	
27/5	Kassegger	Alfred	Gefr.	†	France	7.
27/5	Bartelt	Paul	Gefr.	†	France	7.
27/5	Gild	Rudolf	Lt.	†	France	7.
27/5	Göttlicher	Alfred	Fw.	†	France	7.
27/5	Kannenwurf	Heinz	Uffz.	M	England	
25/5	Lackinger	Gustav	Uffz.	†	Erding	II.
25/5	Stein	Gustav	Uffz.	†	Erding	II.
29/5	Ruthmann	Heinrich	Obfw.	†	Norway	1.
June:						
2/6	Kiebele	Paul	Oblt.	†	France	3.
2/6	Köppel	Georg	Fw.	†	France	3.
2/6	Schultzki	Max	Obfw.	†	France	3.
5/6	Hepp	Rudolf	Lt.	†	France	4.
5/6	Hohenstein	Fritz	Lt.	†	France	4.
5/6	Geiger	Kurt	Gefr.	M	France	6.
9/6	Wühle	Otto	Gefr.	†	Lechfeld	2.
9/6	Frey	Alois	Gefr.	†	Lechfeld	2.
9/6	Müller	Georg	Uffz.	†	Lechfeld	2.
9/6	Kaun	Heinrich	Lt.	†	Lechfeld	2.
9/6	Hauptmeier	Günther	Uffz.	†	Lechfeld	2.
11/6	Meier	Rudolf	Uffz.	†	Gilching	Stab
14/6	Ziger	Johannes	Flg.	†	France	2.
18/6	Vitt	Erich	Obfw.	†	Bad Nauheim	
19/6	Swoboda	Kurt	Fw.	†	Weilheim/Teck	1.
23/6	Groß	Eduard	Fw.	†	Birkenfeld	II.
23/6	Schmidt	Anton	Uffz.	†	Birkenfeld	II.
July:						
4/7	Bischoff	Gerhard	Uffz.	†	England	7.
9/7	Heinrich		Lt.	†	England	7.
9/7	Becher	Josef	Uffz.	†	England	4.

12/7	Rattel	Joscf	Obfw.	†	France	3.
13/7	Kesper	Fritz	Oblt.	†	Channel	6.
17/7	Rechenberg	Dieter	Oblt.	†	Channel	3.
20/7	Steszyn	Roman	Hptm.	†	England	1.
22/7	Pagel	Wolfgang	Oblt.	†	England	1.
25/7	Theiner	Walter		†	England	
30/7	Böhmisch		Gefr.	†	France	7.
30/7	Kurzweg	Emil	Fw.	†	France	7.
30/7	Jörg	Wilhelm	Fw.	†	France	7.
30/7	Oschließ	Ewald	Fw.	†	France	7.
***August*:**						
8/8	Berghammer	Josef	Uffz.	M	Barth	
8/8	Schifferings	Ernst	Oblt.	†	France	9.
12/8	Rösch	Konrad	Uffz.	†	England	8.
12/8	Nölken	Wilhelm	Oblt.	†	England	7.
12/8	Lokuschuß		Fw.	†	England	8.
12/8	Gundlach	Otto	Fw.	†	England	8.
12/8	Graf	Hans	Oblt.	†	England	3.
12/8	Floeter	Walter	Uffz.	†	England	8.
12/8	Czepik	Horst	Gefr.	†	England	8.
12/8	Hochstätter	Heinrich	Lt..	†	England	III.
12/8	Keffel	Karl	Obfw.	†	England	8.
12/8	Dr. Fisser	Johann	Oberst.	†	England	Kommodore
12/8	Flegel		Oblt.	†	England	6.
12/8	Storeck	Herbert	Obgefr.	†	England	4.
12/8	Kessel		Obfw.	†	England	4.
12/8	Merker		Gefr.	M	England	4.
12/8	Stahr	Alfred	Uffz.	†	England	4.
12/8	Schuß		Fw.	†	England	4.
12/8	Noetel	Siebo	Gefr.	†	England	
12/8	Nowak	Gottfried	Uffz.	†	England	
12/8	Fischer		Uffz.	†	England	8.
12/8	Bigalke		S.Fhr.	†	England	8.
12/8	Velten		Fw.	†	England	8.
12/8	Seidel	Paul	Lt.	†	England	8.
12/8	Hausen	Georg	Uffz.	†	England	
12/8	Lange	Hans	Oblt.	†	England	8.
12/8	Reiser	Heinrich	Uffz.	†	England	
14/8	Stoeckl	Alois	Oberst	†	England	as Kommodore of KG 55
16/8	Schwärzler	Josef	Fw.	†	England	
16/8	Stangel	Sebastian	Fw.	†	England	
18/8	Kirchhoff	Hans-Jürgen	Oblt.	†	England	9.
19/8	Schachtner	Max	Fw.	†	England	7.
19/8	Bachauer		Fw.	†	England	7.
19/8	Moser	Johann	Fw.	†	England	7.
19/8	Haag		Fw.	†	England	7.
21/8	Haak	Wilhelm	Uffz.	†	England	
24/8	Schulze		Uffz.	†	England	
25/8	Maurer		Uffz.	†	England	7.
25/8	Schulz		Uffz.	†	England	7.
25/8	Pfaff		Gefr.	†	England	7.
26/8	Roy	Walter	Lt.	†	England	5.
26/8	Rückert	Emil	Flg.	†	England	5.
***September*:**						
12/9	Rueba		Obgefr.	†	England	9.
12/9	Gutberlet		Uffz.	†	England	9.
12/9	Hölzner	Wilhelm	Uffz.	†	England	2.

12/9	Kirch	Helmut	Uffz.	†	England	2.
12/9	Köhler		Gefr.	†	England	2.
12/9	Wöhler	Fritz	Uffz.	†	England	2.
12/9	Hennike	Karl	Uffz.	†	England	2.
15/9	Richter	Wilhelm	Lt.	†	England	I.
15/9	Schubert	Konrad	Uffz.	†	England	I.
15/9	de Vivanco		Oblt.	†	England	II.
15/9	Stelzner		Gefr.	†	England	II.
15/9	Vogel	Kurt	Fw.	†	England	II.
15/9	Breuker	Heinz	Fw.	†	England	1.
15/9	Hirschfeld		Uffz.	†	England	I.
18/9	Friedel	Erhard	Fw.	†	England	
19/9	Luckhardt	Heinrich	Obfw.	†	England	3.
19/9	Walter	Wilhelm	Fw.	†	England	3.
19/9	Henker	Woldemar	Uffz.	†	England	3.
19/9	Röder		Uffz.	†	England	I.
25/9	Eimers		Fw.	†	England	7.
25/9	Altmann		Gefr.	†	England	7.
25/9	Maier	Gustav	Lt..	†	England	7.
25/9	Herich		Gefr.	†	England	7.
25/9	Meiser		Lt.	†	France	
25/9	Andree		Gefr.	†	France	
27/9	Hartmann		Uffz.	†	England	
27/9	Maier		Uffz.	†	France	7.
27/9	Conrad		Fw.	†	France	7.
27/9	Brünningsen		Fw.	†	France	7.
27/9	Israel	Kurt	Gefr.	†	France	7.
27/9	Jung		Gefr.	†	France	7.
27/9	Kienbauer	Erwin	Gefr.	†	France	7.
27/9	Bender	Emil	Uffz.	†	France	7.
27/9	Gravenreuth v.	Ullrich	Oblt.	†	England	1.
30/9	Geyer	Willy	Obgefr.	†	England	
30/9	Roppert		Gefr.	†	England	I.
30/9	Dürrschmidt	Eduard	Gefr.	†	England	I.
30/9	Peuka		Gefr.	†	England	I.
30/9	Paczinski	Fritz	Fw.	†	England	I.

October:

1/10	Kaltenhauser	Alois		†	England	I.
1/10	Heinig	Günther	Oblt.	†	England	I.
1/10	Muche	Helmut	Fw.	†	England	I.
1/10	Kussin	Hans	Fw.	†	England	I.
6/10	Kurzer	Albert		†	England	
6/10	Stadlbauer	Franz	Gefr.	†	England	
6/10	Vogel	Kurt	Fw.	†	England	
6/10	Rieder		Oblt.	†	England	
7/10	Heye	Sigmund	Oblt.	†	England	II.
7/10	König		Obfw.	†	England	II.
7/10	Krell		Obfw.	†	England	II.
8/10	Sepmer	Gerhard	Uffz.	†	England	4.
8/10	Bittner		Gefr.	†	England	4.
8/10	Döttlinger	Gottfried	Lt..	†	England	4.
8/10	Kühne	Siegfried	Gefr.	†	England	4.
9/10	Wagner	Johann	Fw.	†	England	3.
10/10	Metschulat		Uffz.	M	England	
10/10	Wolff		Fw.	†	England	
10/10	Schragel		Uffz.	M	England	
10/10	Kafka		Uffz.	†	England	

12/10	Torpzisseck	Bruno	Fw.	†	England	7.
18/10	Stegmüller	Anton	Obfw.	†	England	4.
18/10	Sonntag	Siegfried	Lt.	†	England	4.
18/10	Clear von	Helmut	Oblt.	†	England	4.
20/10	Reisach	Hermann		†	Lechfeld	
20/10	Apfelbeck	Johannes	Fw.	†	Lechfeld	
21/10	Scholz	Max	Uffz.	†	England	1.
21/10	Wilhelm	Ernst	Uffz.	†	England	1.
21/10	Fabian	Maximilian	Oblt.	†	England	1.
21/10	Stadelbauer		Gefr.	†	England	I.
28/10	Hauff	Arnold	Gefr.	†	England	
28/10	König	Erich	Gefr.	†	England	
28/10	Krämer	Ernst	Uffz.	†	England	
28/10	Zimmermann		Gefr.	†	England	
November:						
6/11	Geilenkirchen	Hans	Lt.	†	England	8.
6/11	Schulze		Uffz.	†	England	8.
6/11	Mathias		Oblt.	†	England	8.
6/11	Mader	Eusebius	Gefr.	†	England	8.
9/11	Hinterlang	Gustav	Uffz.	†	England	6.
9/11	Knoll	Leonhard	Gefr.	†	England	6.
9/11	Laube	Erich	Fw.	†	England	6.
9/11	Lemke	Fritz	Fw.	†	England	6.
10/11	Besenbeck			†	England	
17/11	Freundl	Hans	Uffz.	†	England	
18/11	Rothhäußer	Friedrich	Gefr.	†	France	7.
18/11	Wolf		Gefr.	†	France	7.
18/11	Effler		Gefr.	†	France	7.
18/11	Meißner	Helmut	Uffz.	†	France	7.
20/11	Burmeister	Herbert	Gefr.	†	Kaufering	
20/11	Gosch	Hans-Jürgen	Gefr.	†	Kaufering	
20/11	Kahlmann	Heinz	Uffz.	†	Kaufering	
26/11	Vogel	Josef		†	France	
December:						
1/12	Jedicke	Rudi	Gefr.	†	England	4.
7/12	Baussart	Armin	Obfw.	†	England	4.
7/12	Helms	Hugo	Obfw.	†	England	4.
20/12	Zimmermann	Willi		†	England	
21/12	Rieber	Ludwig	Oblt.	†	France	2.
21/12	Pahl	Karl-Heinz	Fhr.	†	France	9.
21/12	Dorn		Uffz.	†	France	9.
21/12	Reibel		Gefr.	†	France	9.
21/12	Bier		Gefr.	†	France	9.

1941

?/41	Blusch		Fw.	†	France	6.
?/41	Dürrschmidt	Walter	Gefr.	†	England	
?/41	Uhlig		Obfw.	†	Crete	
?/41	Weigel		Uffz.	†	Crete	
January:						
17/1	Gülzow	Friedrich	Fw.	†	Channel	2.
February:						
20/2	Berger	Johann	Uffz.	†	France	4.
21/2	Keiler	Heinrich	Uffz.	†	France	4.
March:						
4/3	Rödiger	Kurt	Uffz.	†	France	I.

10/3	Giersch	Harry	Hptm.	†	Silesia	III.
15/3	Hoffmann		Uffz.	†	France	8.
16/3	Lindemeier	Karl	Uffz.	†	France	III.
16/3	Ettig	Fritz	Gefr.	†	France	3.
20/3	Meyer	Johannes	Hptm.	†	France	5.
20/3	Mehl	Eberhard	StFw.	†	France	5.
20/3	Karlhofer	Franz	Obfw..	†	France	5.
20/3	Natusch	Ernst	Fw.	†	France	5.
21/3	Unruh	Gustav	Uffz.	†	France	7.
21/3	Murra		Obgefr.	†	France	7.
21/3	Niestädt	Hinrich	Gefr.	†	France	7.
21/3	Neikes	Josef	Uffz.	†	France	7.
23/3	Behnke	Hermann	Uffz.	†	Rumania	special duties
24/3	Selbert		Uffz.	†	France	9.
24/3	Glier		Gefr.	†	France	9.
24/3	Jenkel		Uffz.	†	France	9.
24/3	Knoth		Uffz.	†	France	9.
28/3	Müller		Obgefr.	†	England	6.
28/3	Müller		Obgefr.	†	Rastatt	8.
28/3	Hinzpeter		Obgefr.	†	Rastatt	8.
28/3	Emmert		Uffz.	†	Rastatt	8.
30/3	Gerhardt		Uffz.	†	Black Forest	5.
30/3	Erdmann	Reinhold	Uffz.	†	Black Forest	5.
30/3	Klappert	Walter	Fw.	†	France	
30/3	Döring		Uffz.	†	Black Forest	5.
April:						
?/4	Hannig		Uffz.	†	Yugoslavia	5.
?/4	Harles	Erwin	Fw.	†	Yugoslavia	5.
1/4	Weigl	Johann	Uffz.	†	Black Forest	1st AOC
1/4	Linke	Fritz	Fw.	†	Black Forest	1st AOC
1/4	Leutert	Hans	Fw.	†	Black Forest	1st AOC
7/4	Richtsteiger	Erich	Fw.	†	Rumania	6.
7/4	Böhme	John-Harry	Gefr.	†	Yugoslavia	2.
7/4	Voigtländer	Werner	Lt.	†	France	NK
7/4	Krüger	Hans-Jürgen	Lt.	†	Hungary	1.
7/4	Kierig	Heinz	Fw.	†	Hungary	1.
7/4	Ohme		Fw.	†	Belgrade	1.
7/4	Lehmann	Georg	Uffz.	†	Hungary	1.
11/4	Vossen		Uffz.	†	Yugoslavia	6.
11/4	Zur Westen	Helmut	Oblt.	†	Yugoslavia	6.
11/4	Langlotz	Heinrich	Fw.	†	Yugoslavia	6.
11/4	Berlin	Hans	Hptm.	†	Yugoslavia	6.
13/4	Schneider	Wilhelm	Fw.	†	Hungary	2.
16/4	Rohrmann	Heinrich	Gefr.	†	Bulgaria	1.
16/4	Fuchs	Gerhard	Uffz.	†	Bulgaria	1.
16/4	Fredebeul	Wilhelm	Uffz.	†	Bulgaria	1.
19/4	Martin	Karl	Fw.	†	Greece	4.
21/4	Sachweh		Lt.	†	Africa	4.
May:						
3/5	Conre	Hans	Uffz.	†	Crete	1.
3/5	Illgner	Dietrich	Hptm.	†	Crete	1.
3/5	Konze	Hans	Uffz.	†	Crete	
3/5	Beckmann	Ernst	Uffz.	†	Crete	1.
10/5	Kretschmann	Reinhold	Uffz.	†	North Sea	5.
10/5	Ante	Eduard	Uffz.	M	North Sea	
15/5	Rose	Robert		†	France	
21/5	Wuthenau von	Hilmar	Oblt.	†	Crete	8.

23/5	Balzer	Alfred	Uffz.	†	Hungary	8.
23/5	Flach	Johannes	Uffz.	†	Hungary	8.
23/5	Maletz	Gerhard	Oblt.	†	Hungary	8.
23/5	Reutzel	Heinrich	Fw.	†	Hungary	8.
June:						
?/6	Müller	Friedrich-Wil.	Lt.	M	Galicia	5.
16/6	Hamburger	Franz	Flg.	†		
22/6	Wagner	Ludwig	Gefr.	†	Crimea	
22/6	Pohle		Lt.	†	Russia	
22/6	Ludwig	Helmut	Obfw.	†	Russia	4.
22/6	Steglich	Hermann	Obfw.	†	Russia	4.
22/6	Salzberger			†	Russia	1.
22/6	Els		Uffz.	M	Russia	2.
22/6	Berz	Ludwig	Uffz.	M	Russia	2.
22/6	König	Willibald	Uffz.	M	Russia	2.
22/6	Küster		Uffz.	†	Russia	9.
22/6	Ungericht		Fw.	†	Russia	9.
22/6	Dorr	Sepp	Fw.	†	Russia	9.
22/6	Maier	Georg	Fw.	†	Russia	9.
22/6	Lyker	Franz	Uffz.	†	Russia	9.
22/6	Lobinger		Gefr.	†	Russia	9.
22/6	Kutalek		Gefr.	†	Russia	9.
22/6	Krauss		Gefr.	†	Russia	9.
22/6	Holm	Heinrich	Uffz.	†	Russia	9.
22/6	Evers		Uffz.	†	Russia	9.
22/6	Böhm		Oblt.	†	Russia	9.
22/6	Bobinger		Gefr.	†	Russia	9.
22/6	Arens		Gefr.	†	Russia	9.
22/6	Wagner		Fw.	†	Russia	9.
22/6	Dittmer	Hermann	Uffz.	†	Russia	8.
22/6	Kärner	Willi	Fw.	†	Russia	8.
22/6	Lehmann	Werner	Uffz.	†	Russia	8.
22/6	Schote		Gefr.	†	Russia	8.
22/6	Knoch	Fritz	Fw.	†	Russia	8.
22/6	Smolka		Gefr.	†	Russia	8.
22/6	Herrmann		Lt.	†	Russia	8.
22/6	Plücker		Uffz.	†	Russia	8.
22/6	Müller	Ludwig	Obfw.	M	Russia	4.
22/6	Maier		Fw.	M	Russia	4.
22/6	Kürner	Wilhelm	Fw.	†	Russia	4.
22/6	Stadlmeier	Max	Hptm.	†	Russia	II. Kdr.
22/6	Müller	Gerhard	Lt.	†	Russia	5.
22/6	Wulf		Gefr.	†	Russia	5.
22/6	Waske	Walter	Gefr.	†	Russia	5.
22/6	Schwerdt		Obfw.	†	Russia	5.
22/6	Sorgenfrei	Johann	Uffz.	†	Russia	5.
22/6	Kinagel		Gefr.	†	Russia	5.
22/6	Gries		Uffz.	†	Russia	5.
22/6	Fritze	Arno	Uffz.	†	Russia	5.
22/6	Eschle		Lt.	†	Russia	5.
22/6	Döring		Fw.	†	Russia	5.
22/6	Thobias		Oblt.	†	Russia	7.
22/6	Buckenmayer		Uffz.	†	Russia	7.
22/6	Körner		Uffz.	†	Russia	III.
22/6	Steinmetz	Herbert	Oblt.	†	Russia	III.
22/6	Deisinger	Reimund	Obfw.	†	Russia	7.
22/6	Hark	Franz	Uffz.	M	Russia	4.

22/6	Kruse	Günther	Uffz.	M	Russia	4.
22/6	Weidele	Karl	Uffz.	M	Russia	4.
22/6	Schneider	Hans	Gefr.	M	Russia	4.
25/6	Harenburg	Karl	Obfw.	†	Russia	8.
25/6	Ober	Fritz	Obfw.	†	Russia	8.
25/6	Wellnitz		Uffz.	†	Russia	4.
25/6	Brandt	Willi	Hptm.	M	Russia	6.
25/6	Kümper	Herbert	Obfw.	†	Russia	6.
25/6	Schwarz		Uffz.	†	Russia	4.
25/6	Müller	Karl	Obfw.	†	Russia	
25/6	Bauschulte	Paul	Fw.	M	Russia	4.
25/6	Teischmann	Willy	Lt.	†	Russia	8.
25/6	Wallnitz		Uffz.	†	Russia	8.
25/6	Pfaff	Karl	Fw.	†	Russia	8.
25/6	Brauneder	Franz	Obfw.	†	Russia	8.
25/6	Bußmann		Fw.	†	Russia	7.
25/6	Scholz	Alfred	Obfw.	†	Russia	7.
25/6	Müller	Karl	Obfw.	†	Russia	7.
25/6	Lohnes	Adam	Fw.	†	Russia	7.
27/6	Rading	Kurt	Uffz.	†	Russia	4.
27/6	Grodeck			†	Russia	4.
27/6	Rottbacher		Uffz.	†	Russia	8.
27/6	Bullrich		Uffz.	†	Russia	9.
27/6	Günther	Heinrich	Fw.	†	Russia	III.
27/6	Käding		Uffz.	†	Russia	9.
27/6	Küchle	Fritz	Oblt.	†	Russia	9.
30/6	Schneider		Uffz.	†	Russia	4.
30/6	Habermann	Heino	Fw.	†	Russia	4.
30/6	Dickhut	Paul	Fw.	†	Russia	4.
30/6	Priebsch		Lt.	†	Russia	4.
30/6	Bonn		Uffz.	†	Russia	
July:						
?/7	Herrmann	Otto	Obfw.	M	Russia	8.
?/7	Dohr	Theodor	Flg.	M	Russia	1st AOC
6/7	Serschen		Major	†	Russian	4.
6/7	Rintelen	Werner	Lt.	†	Russia	8.
7/7	Werthner	Leonhard	Obfw.	†	Russia	8.
7/7	Kress	Alfred	StFw.	†	Russia	8.
7/7	Wolf		Uffz.	M	Russia	4.
7/7	Helm		Uffz.	M	Russia	4.
7/7	Spannheimer	Rudolf	Obfw.	†	Russia	4.
7/7	Haug	Karl-Wilhelm	Uffz.	M	Russia	4.
7/7	Schwerdt	Paul	Obfw.	†	North Sea	1.
8/7	Ehrenstein	Ernst	Fw.	†	North Sea	1.
8/7	Krieg	Wilhelm	Uffz.	†	Russia	
13/7	Gerhard	Franz	Uffz.	†	Russia	8.
15/7	Mayer	Gerg	Uffz.	†	Russia	4.
15/7	Mayer	Wilhelm	Prüfmster	†	Russia	2.
15/7	Albrecht	Reinhold	Uffz.	†	Russia	1.
15/7	Otto	Herbert	Fw.	†	Russia	3.
18/7	Sliwka		Fw.	†	Russia	3.
18/7	Scholand	Egon	Gefr.	†	Russia	3.
18/7	Caessar	Siegfried	Oblt.	†	Russia	3.
20/7	Wauer	Gerhard	Obfw.	†	England	4.
23/7	Gilg	Josef	Uffz.	†	Channel	3.
23/7	Öchsle	Simon	Oblt.	†	Russia	4.
26/7	Kutschbach	Kurt	Obgefr.	†	Russia	1.

26/7	Krause	Walter	Uffz.	†	Russia	4.
26/7	Bertera	Rudolf	Gefr.	†	Russia	4.
26/7	Berger	Gerhard	Gefr.	†	Russia	4.
***August*:**						
?/8	Ortmann	Bruno	Obfw.	M	Russia	4.
9/8	Knothe	Josef	Flg.	†	Russia	4th AOC
9/8	Pfefferer	Karl	Oblt.	†	North Africa	4. (courier *Staffel*)
9/8	Thormann	Siegfried	Lt.	†	North Africa	4. (courier *Staffel*)
10/8	Flohrmann	Eduard	Uffz.	†	Vilnius	Stab
***September*:**						
2/9	Roth		Fw.	†	Russia	III.
2/9	Hoestermann	Wilhelm	Uffz.	†	Russia	III.
2/9	Dorn	Willi	Uffz.	†	Russia	
2/9	Klodt		Uffz.	†	France	4. (courier flight)
2/9	Moosblech		Obfw.	†	France	4. (courier flight)
8/9	Andree	Heinz	Gefr.	†	Russia	8.
14/9	Schmid		Lt.	†	Russia	4.
14/9	Bargenda	Heinz	Lt.	M	Russia	4.
14/9	Zehrt		Gefr.	†	Russia	8.
14/9	Woraczek		Uffz.	†	Russia	8.
15/9	Hoffmann	Heinz	Lt.	†	Russia	4.
17/9	Schmied	Hans	Lt.	†	Russia	8.
18/9	Kühnast	Arthur	Fw.	†	Russia	5.
19/9	Hennig		Gefr.	†	Russia	
19/9	Ebers	Hermann	Uffz.	†	Russia	
23/9	Janser	Josef	Obfw.	†	Russia	
***October*:**						
?/10	Bersch	Walter	Fw.	M	Russia	5.
?/10	Garbe	Rudi	Fw.	†	Russia	4.
?/10	Weiß		Lt.	†	Russia	4.
8/10	Ebensing	Otto	Uffz.	†	Russia	
12/10	Eibig		Gefr.	†	Russia	7.
***November*:**						
?/11	Essig	Erwin	Fw.	M	Russia	I.
?/11	Heipp	H. Gustav	Fw.	M	Vienn	
?/11	Lasch	Hans	Uffz.	M		I.
2/11	Hellberg	Karl-Hans	Obfw.	M	Russia	7.
2/11	Koch		Uffz.	†	Russia	7.
2/11	Leibinger	Hans	Uffz.	M	Russia	7.
2/11	Seifert		Obfw.	†	Russia	7.
6/11	Daubach	Franz	Uffz.	†	Russia	
15/11	Geuß	Theodor	Uffz.	†	Russia	8.
15/11	Beckert	Siegfried	Uffz.	†	Russia	8.
18/11	Antesberger	Franz	Uffz.	†	Seligenstadt	
25/11	Zeep	Gerhard	Hptm.	M	Russia	7.
25/11	Mayerhoefer	Hans	Fw.	M	Russia	7.
25/11	Bischof	Karl	Lt.	M	Russia	7.
25/11	Eberlein		Obfw.	†	Russia	7.
***December*:**						
5/12	Schieferdecker	Kurt	Gefr.	M	Russia	2.
5/12	Zuellich	Karl	Lt.	M	Russia	2.
5/12	Fillmann	Erwin	Gefr.	M	Russia	2.
5/12	Griebke	August	Gefr.	M	Russia	2.
8/12	Vogt		Uffz.	†	Russia	
8/12	Lange		Uffz.	†	Russia	
10/12	Wildies	Karl	Lt.	†	Austria	
12/12	Vüllers	Franz	Oblt.	†	France	4.

13/12	Hochreuther	Fritz	Gefr.	†	Russia	
25/12	Bischoff	Paul	Lt.	M	Russia	III.
26/12	Danigel		Fw.	†	Russia	9.
26/12	Eichhorn	Franz	Uffz.	†	Russia	9.
26/12	Plumhoff		Gefr.	†	Russia	9.
26/12	Hille		Obfw.	†	Russia	9.

1942

?/42	Bauer		Uffz.	†		3.
?/42	Meier		Fw.	†	Russia	II.
?/42	Mergelsberger	Rolf	Lt.	†	Russia	10.
?/42	Reimann		Obgefr.	†	Russia	signals
?/42	Raguse		Obfw.	†	England	
?/42	Schulte	Fritz	Uffz.	M	England	
?/42	Seyfert		Obfw.	†	Russia	7.
?/42	Sommer		Oblt.	†	Russia	II.
?/42	Völkl	Hans	Obfw.	†	Russia	
?/42	Wangelin von	Joachim	Oblt.	†	England	6.
January:						
?/1	Hohmann	Leopold	Fw.	M		5.
?/1	Kühner	Karl	Obgefr.	M	Russia	
1/1	Wolf		Uffz.	†	Russia	Stab
1/1	Knäb		Uffz.	†	Russia	Stab
1/1	Kosel		Gefr.	†	Russia	Stab
1/1	Häseling	Pit	Lt.	†	Russia	5.
4/1	Brase	Alex	Lt.	†	Russia	
10/1	Stöffler	Ernst	Fw.	†	Russia	5.
10/1	Lutz	Karl	Fw.	†	Russia	5.
10/1	Herzau		Fw.	†	Russia	5.
10/1	Born		Fw.	†	Russia	5.
12/1	Schweiger	Karl	Uffz.	†	Russia	
13/1	Hug	Xaver	Obfw.	†	Russia	
16/1	Dietrich		Obgefr.	†	Russia	7.
16/1	Sälzle		Obgefr.	†	Russia	7.
16/1	Mattes		Obgefr.	†	Russia	7.
16/1	Haller		Fw.	†	Russia	7.
20/1	Girrbach	Friedrich	Fw.	†	Russia	
21/1	Ventrop		Obgefr.	†	Russia	5.
30/1	Zeitler		Gefr.	†	Russia	5.
30/1	Spundflasche		Obgefr.	†	Russia	5.
30/1	Schaaf		Obgefr.	†	Russia	5.
30/1	Pipereit		Obgefr.	†	Russia	5.
31/1	Tillheim		Uffz.	†	Penzing	
31/1	Rückert	Otto	Obfw.	†	Penzing	
February:						
?/2	Lischka	Ferdinand	Uffz.	M	Russia	5.
3/2	Hahn	Heinrich	Hptm.	†	Russia	2.
3/2	Graichen	Reinhard	Fw.	†	Russia	2.
10/2	Schneider	Artur	Gefr.	†	Russia	10.
13/2	Venjakob	Bernhard	Uffz.	M	Russia	9.
13/2	Homfeld		Fw.	†	Russia	9.
13/2	Herr	Peter	Oblt.	†	Russia	9.
13/2	Reichfeld		Gefr.	†	Russia	9.
21/2	Wolf	Roman	Uffz.	†	Russia	5.
21/2	Sterken	Jupp	Obgefr.	†	Russia	5.
21/2	Frentrop	Heinz	Obgefr.	†	Russia	5.

21/2	Wendt	Hans	Lt.	†	Russia	5.
21/2	Jellen	Hans	Uffz.	†	Russia	5.
25/2	Schnabel		Obgefr.	†	Russia	5.
25/2	Krügel		Obgefr.	†	Russia	5.
25/2	Hüter		Obgefr.	†	Russia	5.
28/2	Püst		Obfw.	†	Russia	4.
March:						
?/3	Apel	Robert	Uffz.	M	Russia	I.
?/3	Brückner	Erich	Obgefr.	M	Russia	III.
1/3	Seifert	Rudolf	Oblt.	M	Russia	8.
1/3	Garms	Werner	Oblt.	M	Russia	10.
1/3	Hofmann		Gefr.	†	Russia	8.
1/3	Groher	Manfred	Obfw.	†	Russia	8.
1/3	Graher	Siegfried	Obfw.	†	Russia	
3/3	Winhard	Fritz	Gefr.	M	Russia	4.
8/3	Haberger	Josef	Gefr.	†	Russia	
15/3	Meierhofer		Oblt.	†	Russia	III.
18/3	Meck	Heinz	Fw.	†	Russia	1.
20/3	Bühl	Richard	Obgefr.	†	Russia	
26/3	Lind	Wolfgang	Gefr.	M	Russia	7.
26/3	Lampsch	Friedrich	Uffz.	M	Russia	7.
26/3	Effmann		Uffz.	†	Russia	7.
26/3	Delf		Obgefr.	†	Russia	7.
April:						
?/4	Dockborn	Hans	Obfw.	M	Russia	II.
?/4	Friedrich	Heinz	Uffz.	M	Russia	II.
?/4	Gürtler	Manfred	Uffz.	M	Russia	II.
?/4	Hilgarth	Franz	Uffz.	M	Russia	II.
?/4	Koeser	Ernst	Obfw.	M	Russia	I.
?/4	Prell	Karl	Uffz.	M	Russia	1.
?/4	Schneidbauer	Edgar	Lt.	M	Russia	II.
8/4	Schlippenbach Baron von	Wendt	Hptm.	†	North Sea	4.
8/4	Thiele		Obfw.	†	North Sea	4.
8/4	Schulz	Paul	Obfw.	†	North Sea	4.
8/4	Schmidt	Konrad	Obfw.	†	North Sea	4.
19/4	Plesse	Rolf	Uffz.	†	Russia	2.
21/4	Schmidmeister		Obfw.	†	Russia	5.
21/4	Rambacher	Alois	Uffz.	†	Russia	5.
21/4	Kaufner	Friedrich Wil.	Major	†	Russia	5.
21/4	Heimann		Fw.	†	Russia	5.
22/4	Kaufmann		Major	†	Russia	II.
23/4	Lorbach	Franz	Gefr.	†	Russia	4.
25/4	Huber	Max	Uffz.	†	Russia	
28/4	Köser	Ernst	Obfw.	M	Russia	2.
28/4	Klingenbiehl	Friedrich	Fw.	M	Russia	2.
28/4	Preiser	Walter	Fw.	M	Russia	2.
28/4	Geusen	Josef	Gefr.	M	Russia	2.
28/4	Pfneisl	Ernst	Oblt.	†	Russia	1.
29/4	Sommer	Erwin	Obfw.	†	Finland	6.
May:						
2/5	Miekina	Rudolf	Fw.	†	Russia	2.
2/5	Prorok	Odilo	Uffz.	†	Russia	2.
2/5	Ahrens	Josef	Oblt.	†	Russia	2.
2/5	Brockmann		Uffz.	†	Russia	2.
3/5	Baumgärtner	Ernst	Reg.Insp.	†	Vienna died in hospital	
7/5	Schmidt	Rudi	Flg.	†	Russia	

8/5	Witte	Günther	Obgefr.	†	Russia	1.
8/5	Rück	Thomas	Uffz.	†	Russia	1st AOC
10/5	Katzmann	Horst	Uffz.	†	Russia	
10/5	Herrmann	Martin	Uffz.	†	Russia	
10/5	Hecht	Hubert	Obgefr.	†	Russia	
10/5	Richter	Armin	Hptm.	†	Russia	5.
10/5	Fuchsluger	Stefan	Uffz.	†	Russia	
10/5	Bertele von		Fw.	†	Russia	5.
10/5	Bos		Uffz.	†	Russia	
11/5	Herrling	Josef	Fw.	†	Russia	4.
13/5	Schmikaly	Peter	Lt.	†	Russia	4.
13/5	Schick	Gerhard	Gefr.	†	Russia	4.
13/5	Lechermaier	Josef	Gefr.	†	Russia	4.
13/5	Riedel	Heinz	Obgefr.	†	Russia	4.
16/5	Schreiber	Gustav	Obfw.	†	Russia	1.
17/5	Lippek	Wilhelm	Uffz.	†	Russia	4.
23/5	Müller	Christoph	Obfw.	†	Russia	2.
23/5	Blume	Gerd	Oblt.	†	Russia	1.
23/5	Deussen	Heinrich	Fw.	†	Russia	2.
23/5	Drage von	Werner	Uffz.	†	Russia	1.
26/5	Kühn	Hubert	Obfw.	M	Russia	2.
26/5	Rüther	Hermann	Fw.	M	Russia	2.
26/5	Christossek	Franz	Uffz.	M	Russia	2.
26/5	Geritzer	Johann	Obfw.	M	Russia	2.
27/5	Zollhöfer	Hans	Fw.	†	Russia	signals
June:						
?/6	John	Alfred	Uffz.	M	Russia	2nd AOC
?/6	Prepens	Horst	Fw.	M	Russia	
2/6	Lachenmaier	Fritz	Fw.	†	Russia	7.
2/6	Kühn	Herbert	Obfw.	†	Russia	7.
2/6	Flieger	Sebastian	Uffz.	†	Russia	7.
2/6	Drechsler	Siegfried	Lt.	†	Russia	7.
2/6	Drechsler	Artur	Fw.	†	Russia	9.
3/6	Selter	Erwin	Fw.	†	Russia	4.
3/6	Wagner	Ludwig	Uffz.	†	Russia	4.
3/6	Rudzinski	Franz	Gefr.	†	Russia	4.
3/6	Jubba	Josef	Gefr.	†	Russia	4.
11/6	Heimayer	Albert	Oblt.	†	Russia	4.
13/6	Philipek		Uffz.	†	Russia	10.
13/6	Härtl		Uffz.	†	Russia	10.
13/6	Ziegler		Gefr.	†	Russia	10.
18/6	Lange	Hans	Hptm.	†	Russia	2.
22/6	Branneder	Franz	Obfw.	M	Russia	9.
23/6	Zoglmann	Karl	Obfw.	†	Russia	
July:						
?/7	Albrecht	Georg	Uffz.	M	Russia	5.
?/7	Drasdo	Paul	Uffz.	M	Russia	
?/7	Gotsche	Heinz	Flg.	M	Russia	4th AOC
?/7	Haase	Karl	Gefr.	†	Russia	9.
?/7	Kuber	Hans	Oblt.	M	Russia	5.
?/7	Nadler	Anton	Uffz.	M	Russia	
?/7	Oswald	Josef	Obgefr.	M	Russia	IV.
?/7	Otto	Erwin	Gefr.	M	Russia	
?/7	Petzold	Kurt	Fw.	M	Russia	
?/7	Pokorny	Adolf	Gefr.	M	Russia	IV.
2/7	Wistuba	Erich	Gefr.	†	Russia	7.
2/7	Poetscher	Wilhelm	Obgefr.	†	Russia	7.

2/7	Gburek	Kurt	Uffz.	†	Russia	7.
2/7	Becker	Edwin	Gefr.	†	Russia	7.
10/7	Schramm	Karl	Obfw.	†	Russia	4.
10/7	Höcke	Martin	Oblt.	†	Russia	4.
10/7	Windstruth		Uffz.	†	Russia	4.
11/7	Scholterer	Wilhelm	Uffz.	†	Africa	4.
12/7	Klischat	Helmut	Oblt.	†	Russia	2.
12/7	Pinne	Gert	Uffz.	†	Russia	2.
14/7	Winter	Helmut	Obfw.	†	Russia	
15/7	Josupeit		Uffz.	†	Russia	8.
15/7	Haseneder	Max	Oblt.	†	Russia	
15/7	Petersen		Obgefr.	†	Russia	8.
15/7	Berg		Gefr.	†	Russia	8.
21/7	Sixl		Uffz.	†	Russia	7.
21/7	Welpers	Heinz	Obfw.	M	England	5.
21/7	Schmidt		Fw.	M	England	5.
21/7	Frank		Hptm.	M	England	5.
21/7	Eyrich		Obfw.	M	England	5.
21/7	Wildemann		Uffz.	†	Russia	7.
21/7	Wanke		Fw.	†	Russia	7.
21/7	Kielhorn	Gerhard	Oblt.	†	Russia	7.
22/7	Otto	Günther	Obgefr.	M	Russia	2.
22/7	Ditmann		Obgefr.	M	Russia	2.
22/7	Eckardt	Herbert	Uffz.	M	Russia	2.
23/7	Ochs	Helmut	Uffz.	†	Russia	7.
26/7	Jahn		Lt.	†	Russia	5.
27/7	Focke		Lt.	†	Russia	
29/7	Dobler	Ernst	Uffz.	†	Russia	
29/7	Koops	Heinrich	Oberstlt.	†	Russia	Stab
August:						
?/8	Farwich	Theodor	Uffz.	M	Russia	5.
?/8	Fürstenberg	Kurt	Uffz.	M	Russia	
?/8	Hubert	Johann	Obgefr.	M	Russia	
?/8	Lippe	Alfred	Uffz.	M	Russia	III.
?/8	Mainke	Alfred	Obgefr.	M	Russia	III.
?/8	Pallaschke	Emil	Fw.	M	Russia	5.
?/8	Schneider	Karl	Obfw.	M	Russia	5.
?/8	Wemann	Hans	Gefr.	M	Russia	III.
?/8	Wisser	Heinz	Fw.	M	Russia	II.
2/8	Kreuter		Fw.	M	Russia	Stab
2/8	Klamroth	Ekehard	Oblt.	M	Russia	Stab
2/8	Rühlmann		Uffz.	M	Russia	Stab
8/8	Schulz	Friedrich	Obgefr.	M	Russia	2.
8/8	Schenk	Hans	Lt.	M	Russia	2.
8/8	Leder	Heinz	Obgefr.	M	Russia	2.
8/8	Krist	Bruno	Obgefr.	M	Russia	2.
8/8	Emminger	Herbert	Obgefr.	M	Russia	2.
8/8	Damm	Werner	Lt.	M	Russia	2.
8/8	Borchert	Hans	Obgefr.	M	Russia	2.
8/8	Geither	Florian	Obgefr.	M	Russia	2.
13/8	Pinkerneil	Ernst	Uffz.	†	Russia	6.
13/8	Gernert	Albin	Obgefr.	†	Russia	2.
13/8	Meyer		Lt.	†	Russia	3.
13/8	Kellner	Heinz	Uffz.	†	Russia	
13/8	Sahl	Josef	Gefr.	†	Russia	10.
13/8	Krebs	Alfred	Lt.	M	Russia	7.
13/8	Müller	Detlef	Obgefr.	†	Russia	10.

13/8	Kühnath	Helmut	Gefr.	†	Russia	10.
13/8	Ksienzyk	Georg	Uffz.	†	Russia	7.
13/8	Kettner	Heinz	Uffz.	†	Russia	7.
13/8	Radau	Willi	Uffz.	†	Russia	7.
13/8	Brönimann	Heinz	Lt.	†	Russia	10.
15/8	Seel	Ingo	Uffz.	†	Russia	
15/8	Schwenk		Lt.	†	Russia	
15/8	Damm		Lt.	†	Russia	2.
19/8	Schodl	Mathias	Obgefr.	†	Russia	6.
28/8	Kolodzie	Paul	Obfw.	†	England	4.
29/8	Schwarz	Karl	Obfw.	†	Russia	
***September**:*						
?/9	Albers	Alfons	Obgefr.	M		III.
?/9	Jahn		Fw.	†	Russia	
?/9	Nadler	Franz	Flg.	M	Russia	I.
?/9	Schaefer	Erich	Uffz.	M	Russia	I.
?/9	Wengel	Fritz	Fw.	M	Russia	5.
3/9	Keppler	Hans	Major	†	Russia	Stab
5/9	Köppel	Richard	Obfw.	†	Rechlin	1.
7/9	Stader	Alfons	Obfw.	M	Russia	2.
7/9	Plaumann	Eitel	Obfw.	†	Russia	2.
7/9	Benz	Alfons	Obfw.	M	Russia	2.
7/9	Buhmann	Georg	Obfw.	M	Russia	2.
12/9	Huber	Albert	Gefr.	†	Russia	7.
12/9	Heilmann	Walter	Hptm.	†	Russia	7.
12/9	Haase	Heinz	Uffz.	†	Russia	7.
12/9	Rehling	Horst	Flg..	†	Russia	7.
17/9	Richter	Johannes	Oblt.	†	Russia	III.
24/9	Hillebrandt	Jakob		†	Baden-Baden	
30/9	Johannsen		Lt.	†	Caucasus	II.
***October**:*						
?/10	Frank	Theodor		†	Sicily	
?/10	Höcker	Karl	Uffz.	M	Russia	
?/10	Jenner	Georg	Uffz.	M	Russia	
?/10	Kästel	Lothar	Gefr.	M	Russia	
?/10	Mierzowski	Albert	Gefr.	M	Russia	
9/10	Würschinger	Hans	Obfw.	†	Mediterranean	6.
12/10	Roy	Walter	Oblt.	†	Russia	
24/10	Weber	Hans	Oblt.	†	Russia	
***November**:*						
?/11	Dietsche	Rudolf	Uffz.	M	Russia	
?/11	Grosch	Richard	Obgefr.	M	Russia	
?/11	Kall	Fritz	Uffz.	M	Russia	I.
?/11	Kolmanitsch	Bruno	Lt.	M	Russia	3.
?/11	Pape	Wilhelm	Uffz.	M	Russia	III.
?/11	Voges	Fritz	Uffz.	M	Russia	
?/11	Wittig	Gerhard	Obgefr.	M	Russia	I.
3/11	Korthals	Gerd	Hptm.	M	Russia	III.
6/11	Warcescha	Franz	Obfw.	†	Russia	4.
17/11	Siedler	Heinz	Uffz.	†	Russia	2.
17/11	Nebelung	Harald	Oblt.	†	Russia	2.
17/11	Buge	Werner	Uffz.	†	Russia	2.
17/11	Fahrner	Richard	Obfw.	†	Russia	2.
22/11	Wegmann	Willi	Uffz.	M	Russia	2.
22/11	Jahn	Joachim	Lt.	M	Russia	2.
22/11	Herwig	Reinhard	Uffz.	M	Russia	2.
22/11	Nadler	Franz	Gefr.	M	Russia	2.

23/11	Tautz	Erich	Uffz.	†	Russia	
23/11	Mitzelfeld		Uffz.	M	Russia	2.
23/11	Hirneise	Josef	Obfw.	†	Russia	2.
23/11	Rautz		Uffz.	†	Russia	2.
28/11	Brandt	Kurt	Major	†	Mediterranean	9.
December:						
?/12	Brinkmann	Harry	Uffz.	M		IV.
?/12	Dingel	Jakob	Uffz.	M		III.
?/12	Galgon	Josef	Uffz.	M		III.
?/12	Jaeckel	Gerhard	Gefr.	M		I.
?/12	Krabbenhoeft	Heinz	Lt.	M		II.
?/12	Kunert	Rudolf	Obgefr.	M		I.
?/12	Schmidt	Hermann	Uffz.	M	Russia	
?/12	Schneider	Karl-Heinz	Oblt.	†	Russia	
?/12	Woche	Fritz	Obgefr.	M		I.
?/12	Zöttl	Josef	Uffz.	M	Russia	
2/12	Borutta	Wilhelm	Fw.	†	Africa	II.
7/12	Walter	Anton	Fw.	†	Sicily	II.
7/12	Waller	Alois	Uffz.	†	Sicily	II.
7/12	Freitag	Oskar	Lt.	†	Sicily	II.
17/12	Lessle		Obfw.	†	Russia	5.
31/12	Schweter	Rudolf	Uffz.	†	Russia	
31/12	Lorenz	Rudolf	Uffz.	†	Sicily	II.

1943

?/43	Roßmaier		Fw.	†	Russia	4.
?/43	Kolb		Lt.	†	England	II.
?/43	Slozik		Fw.	†	England	6.
?/43	Andresen		Uffz.	†	Russia	
?/43	Winkler		Major	†	Paris	
January:						
?/1	Sturm	Willi	Obfw.	M	Russia	I.
?/1	Dickert	Kurt	Obfw.	M	Russia	I.
?/1	Blass	Fritz	Uffz.	M		I.
?/1	Homann	Anton	Obgefr.	M		I.
?/1	Gebauer	Werner	Obgefr.	M	Russia	
?/1	Ussart	Bernhard	Flg.	M		1st AOC
?/1	Ochner	Wilhelm	Fw.	M		III.
?/1	Weber	Heinrich	Uffz.	M		III.
?/1	Schulz	Erich	Fw.	M		III.
?/1	Gedauer	Werner	Fw.	M		III.
?/1	Bordan	Heinz	Obgefr.	M		III.
?/1	Braig	Karl	Uffz.	M		III.
?/1	Delf	Alfred	Uffz.	M		III.
?/1	Wilmers	Karl-Heinz	Fw.	M		III.
?/1	Sturen	Wilhelm	Obfw.	M		IV.
?/1	Bauer	Friedrich	Uffz.	M	Russia	
?/1	Dühring	Adolf	Obfw.	M	Russia	
?/1	Wannemacher	Josef	Uffz.	M	Russia	
?/1	Winkler	Josef	Obgefr.	M	Russia	
?/1	Lesert	Franz	Uffz.	M	Russia	
?/1	Helbing	Fritz	Obfw.	M		IV.
2/1	Wandel	Siegfried	artificer	†	Crete	4.
5/1	Vilsmeier		Lt.	†	Burgbernheim	9.
6/1	Haustein		ObFhr.	†	Burgbernheim	9.
8/1	Schröter	Hermann	Uffz.	†	Russia	

8/1	Helm	Joachim	Lt.	M		III.
8/1	Conrady	Heinrich	Oberst	†	Russia	Kommodore
8/1	Stöhr	Edwin	Oblt.	†	Russia	6.
8/1	Schröter	Wilhelm	Uffz.	†	Russia	6.
8/1	Voigt	Rudi	Fw.	†	Russia	6.
11/1	Howald	Bruno	Obfw.	†	Mediterranean	
11/1	Müller	Hugo	Obgefr.	†	Russia	
11/1	Ising	Wilhelm	Uffz.	†	Russia	2.
11/1	Peuker	Friedrich	Lt.	†	Russia	2.
11/1	Paschke	Heinz	Fw.	†	Russia	2.
11/1	Bräck	Hermann	Oblt.	M	Russia	III.
13/1	Finkenzeller	Wilhelm	Uffz.	†	Russia	2.
13/1	Hönnicke	Kurt	Lt.	†	Russia	2.
16/1	Wistuba	Günther	Lt.	†		
19/1	Knapp	Willi	Uffz.	M	Russia	
20/1	Lawatscheck	Gerhard	Oblt.	†	Russia	2.
27/1	Sachs	Hans	Uffz.	†	Russia	2.
27/1	Berger	Alfons	Hptm.	†	Russia	1.
27/1	Weiss	Erich	Gefr.	†	Russia	
28/1	Sprandel	Theodor	Obgefr.	†	Russia	2.
28/1	Irmscher	Heinz	Uffz.	†	Russia	2.
28/1	Bangel	Gerhard	Obgefr.	†	Russia	2.
28/1	Balls		Uffz.	†	Russia	2.
February:						
?/2	Alleborn	Philipp Heinrich	Uffz.	M		III.
?/2	Borantzky	Gnther	Uffz.	M		
?/2	Borsutzky	Gustav	Uffz.	M		I.
?/2	Gröning		Uffz.	†		
?/2	Krocker		Uffz.	†		
?/2	Römer	Dieter	Lt.	†	Russia	
?/2	Schleth	Kurt	Uffz.	M		I.
?/2	Schmitt	Franz	Obfw.	M		I.
?/2	Welling	Wilhelm	Fw.	M		I.
?/2	Wildner	Werner	Uffz.	M		5.
15/2	Woinke	Kurt	Uffz.	M		I.
15/2	Bibra Baron von	Ernst	Major	M	Russia	III.Kdr.
15/2	Mayerhofer	Karl	Oblt.	M	Russia	III.
16/2	Peukert	Martin	Obfw.	†	Sardinia	7th AOC
16/2	Dold	Nikolaus	Lt.	†	Russia	
19/2	Honrich	Oscar	Uffz.	†	Russia	7.
19/2	Brehm		Uffz.	†	Russia	7.
19/2	Flachskamp	Karl	Obgefr.	†	Russia	2.
24/2	Bönig		Obfw.	†	Yalta	7.
24/2	Meyer		Fw.	†	Yalta	7.
24/2	Michaelis		Obgefr.	†	Yalta	7.
24/2	Wolf		Fw.	†	Yalta	7.
24/2	Giebelmann		Obgefr.	†	Russia	8.
24/2	Rössner		Uffz.	†	Russia	8.
24/2	Müller	Bruno	Oblt.	†	Russia	8.
24/2	Würstle	Anton	Uffz.	M	Russia	8.
26/2	Becker	Julius	Fw.	†	Tuapse	4.
26/2	Baier	Emil	Fw.	†	Tuapse	4.
26/2	Ellmerich	Josef	Uffz.	†	Tuapse	4.
26/2	Frohnert	Helmut	Uffz.	†	Tuapse	9.
26/2	Jordan	Willi	Obgefr.	†	Tuapse	4.
26/2	Krger	Karl-Heinz	Lt.	M	Tuapse	9.
26/2	Wallmeyer	Theodor	Uffz.	M	Tuapse	9.

26/2	Walther	Otto	Uffz.	M	Tuapse	4.
27/2	Holle	Georg	Hptm.	†	Russia	3.
27/2	Binder	Johann	Fw.	†	Russia	3.
28/2	Schlegel		Obgefr.	†	Russia	4.
28/2	Sonnenschein	Rüdiger	Fw.	M	Russia	4.
28/2	Noehoff	Paul	Uffz.	M	Russia	4.
March :						
?/3	Andersen	Aristides	Uffz.	M		I.
?/3	Arentz	Helmut	Obgefr.	M		I.
?/3	Bormann	Willy	Gefr.	M		I.
?/3	Fischbacher	Karl	Lt.	M		I.
?/3	Jans	Kurt	Uffz.	M		I.
?/3	Küfner	Martin	Fw.	M		II.
?/3	Rauche	Fritz	Uffz.	M		I.
1/3	Hagedorn		Fw.	†	Russia	8.
1/3	Kluck		Obgefr.	†	Russia	8.
1/3	Richter		Uffz.	†	Russia	8.
1/3	Brosius		Uffz.	†	Russia	8.
3/3	Silberbauer	Herbert	Uffz.	†	Russia	2.
3/3	Geruschke	Karl-Heinz	Lt.	†	Russia	2.
3/3	Flögel	Gotthard	Uffz.	†	Russia	2.
3/3	Borrmann	Günther	Oblt.	†	Russia	III.
3/3	Bröggelwirt	Josef	Uffz.	†	Russia	2.
10/3	Boelcke		Fw.	†	Russia	
10/3	Bormann		Lt.	†	Russia	
10/3	Wagner		Uffz.	†	Russia	
10/3	Walther		Uffz.	†	Russia	
10/3	Weindl		Obfw.	†	Russia	
10/3	Noack	Otto	Uffz.	M		III.
10/3	Behm	Werner	Uffz.	M	Russia	9.
10/3	Nonck	Friedrich	Uffz.	†	Russia	9.
10/3	Hosse	Wilhelm	Gefr.	M	Russia	9.
10/3	Schweizer		Fw.	†	Russia	9.
10/3	Schuh	Helmut	Lt.	M	Russia	9.
10/3	Suchland		Uffz.	†	Russia	9.
11/3	Seipp	Karl	Hptm.	M	Russia	8.
19/3	Andriani	Heinz	Uffz.	†	Russia	7.
24/2	Lang	Fritz	Obfw.	†	England	
24/3	Kleih	Karl	Obfw.	†	England	4.
26/3	Heckel	Friedrich	Uffz.	†	Russia	
28/3	Thorley	Gottfried	Oblt.	†	England	8.
April:						
?/4	Ruhland		Uffz.	†	Russia	4.
?/4	Brandt	Peter	Hptm.	†	Russia	I.
?/4	Hein	Erich	Obfw.	M	Russia	
?/4	Schönauer	Walter	Obgefr.	M		5.
?/4	Stein	Erich	Obfw.	M		Stab
2/4	Breuer		Obgefr.	†	Russia	
2/4	Kubitscheck		Uffz.	†	Russia	7.
2/4	Horny		Uffz.	†	Russia	7.
2/4	Dormann		Gefr.	†	Russia	7.
2/4	Brauer		Obgefr.	†	Russia	7.
4/4	Sommer	Joachim	Major	†	Russia	7.
4/4	Vogt	Herbert	Fw.	†	Russia	7.
4/4	Maier		Fw.	†	Russia	7.
4/4	Lampe		Fw.	†	Russia	7.
9/4	Lange		Fw.	†	Russia	II.

15/4	Smettana	Erich	Tech.Insp.	†	Sicily	II.
26/4	Kase		Obfw.	†	Caucasus	7.
26/4	Ponzew		Obfw.	†	Caucasus	7.
26/4	Faßbender		Uffz.	†	Caucasus	7.
27/4	Schmitz	Heinz	Fw.	†	sea off North Africa	5.
28/4	Schilling	August	Uffz.	M	Caucasus	7.
28/4	Hofmeister	Leopold	Uffz.	M	Caucasus	7.
28/4	Enders	Franz	Fw.	M	Caucasus	7.
30/4	Reichelt	Rudolf	Oblt.	†	Russia	
***May*:**						
?/5	Dannegger	Ernst	Gefr.	M	Russia	5.
?/5	Harth	Karl	Uffz.	M	Russia	II.
?/5	Koch	Heinrich	Uffz.	M	Russia	III.
?/5	Martin	Heinrich	Fw.	M	Russia	
?/5	Pospiech	Herbert	Uffz.	M	Russia	II.
?/5	Preugschat	Arno	Gefr.	M	Russia	5.
?/5	Schwitanski	Erich	Uffz.	M	Russia	5.
4/5	Schweter		Fw.	†	Russia	7.
4/5	Zelsacher	Adolf	Lt.	†	Russia	7.
4/5	Kunkel	Fritz	Fw.	†	Russia	7.
4/5	Bandl		Uffz.	†	Russia	7.
9/5	Zuischke		Obgefr.	†	Russia	8.
9/5	Xoch		Uffz.	†	Russia	8.
9/5	Lindemann		Uffz.	†	Russia	8.
9/5	Gossing		Uffz.	†	Russia	8.
22/5	Wagner	Karl	Hptm.	†	Russia	IV.
26/5	Reinfelder	Franz	Fw.	†	Italy	4.
27/5	Schmidt		Lt.	†	Russia	9.
27/5	Steinrück	Helmut	Uffz.	M	Russia	9.
27/5	Neimcke	Rudolf	Uffz.	M	Russia	9.
27/5	Sixl	Franz	Uffz.	†	Russia	9.
29/5	Ficher	Hans	Lt.	†	Russia	9.
***June*:**						
?/5	Meggenhofer	Kurt	Uffz.	M	Russia	III.
4/6	Hille	Walter	Lt.	†	Russia	
21/6	Drzewicke	Willi	Obgefr.	†	Russia	
28/6	Henningsen	Helmut	Uffz.	†	France	
***July*:**						
?/7	Echtle	Karl	Uffz.	M		III.
?/7	Grube	Hubert	Uffz.	M	Russia	II.
?/7	Heggenhofen	Kurt	Uffz.	M	Russia	IV.
?/7	Helsberg	Josef	Oblt.	M	Russia	Stab
?/7	König	Helmut	Fw.	M	Russia	
?/7	Kowollik	Friedrich	Uffz.	M	Russia	
?/7	Kratzer	Karl	Fw.	M	Russia	III.
?/7	Krisch	Heinrich	Obfw.	M	Russia	III.
?/7	Kröger	Willi	Uffz.	M	Russia	II.
?/7	Leitner	Alois	Obgefr.	M	Russia	III.
?/7	Pause	Hans	Uffz.	M	Russia	II.
?/7	Rien	Hans	Gefr.	M	Russia	III.
?/7	Schreiber	Helmut	Uffz.	M	Russia	
?/7	Schulz	Erich	Oblt.	M	Russia	III.
?/7	Schweitzer	Waldemar	Lt.	M	Russia	IV.
?/7	Thaler	Georg	Fw.	M	Russia	
?/7	Walbroel	Willi	Obgefr.	M	Russia	III.
?/7	Wittmann	Helmut	Obgefr.	M	Russia	III.
6/7	Schleicher	Viktor	Fw.	†	Russia	5.

7/7	Schmidt	Erwin	Lt.	M	Russia	III.
7/7	Richter	Udo	Oberstlt.	M	Russia	III.
8/7	Protz	Kurt	Lt.	†	Russia	
9/7	Winter	Helmuth	Hptm.	†	Croatia	4.
13/7	Uelsberg	Josef	Oblt.	M	Russia	Signals Company
25/7	Maess	Ernst	Major	†	Sicily	9.
27/7	Finke	Gustav	Uffz.	†	Russia	4.
27/7	Chorus	Hans	Lt.	†	Russia	4.
28/7	Lansky			†	Russia	
29/7	Jahl	Josef	Uffz.	†	Vienna	
August:						
?/8	Bachmann	Fritz	Uffz.	M	Russia	
?/8	Frisch	Karl-Heinz	ObFhr.	M	Russia	IV.
?/8	Gerke	Heinrich	Lt.	M	Russia	
?/8	Krieg	Hans	Uffz.	M	Russia	II.
?/8	Oertel	Johann	Uffz.	M	Russia	II.
?/8	Pieper	Erich	Uffz.	M	Russia	II.
?/8	Reimers	Hermann	Uffz.	M	Russia	6.
?/8	Starke	Alfred	Obgefr.	M	Russia	III.
?/8	Stoffels	Karl	Obgefr.	M	Russia	III.
?/8	Theiss	Otto	Obgefr.	M	Russia	
?/8	Wegener	Heinz	Fw.	M	Russia	III.
6/8	Gruber	Wilhelm	Fw.	†	Bergheim	
7/8	Siegel	Werner		†	Russia	IV.
7/8	Eberwein		Lt.	†	Russia	IV.
8/8	Ilg	Robert	Lt.	†	Russia	9.
10/8	Kahnenbley		Lt.	†	Russia	9.
12/8	Hille	Wilhelm	Lt.	†	Russia	9.
16/8	Hepp	Rudolf	Oberstlt.	†	France	4.
18/8	Nösslböck	Gerhard	Uffz.	†	Penzing	1.
25/8	Hippler	Ekkard	Lt.	†	Russia	
September:						
?/9	Kruse	Heinrich	Obgefr.	M	Russia	
6/9	Ebert	Heinz	Uffz.	†	shot down Freudenstadt	
17/9	Strube		Fw.	†	Russia	
20/9	Schultheis	Johannes	Obfw.	†	Illesheim	2.
October:						
?/10	Brogmus	Hans	Uffz.	M	Russia	5.
?/10	Stodczyk	Georg	Obfw.	M	Russia	5.
4/10	Spieth	Albert	Obfw.	†	Russia	10.
8/10	Simon	Erich	Major	†	North Sea	7.
12/10	Wolpert	Hans	Hptm.	†	Russia	
15/10	Kappel	Hans	Fw.	†	Regensburg	
15/10	Hartwig		Lt.	†	Regensburg	
20/10	Horker	Alfons		†	Lechfeld	
20/10	Türpisch	Gustav	Lt.	†	Salonika	II.
25/10	Penner	Horst	Uffz.	†	Lechfeld	1.
26/10	Kleinfeld		Obgefr.	†	Sudetenland	
26/10	Hurka	Heiner	Lt.	†	Sudetenland	
November:						
?/11	Blachse	Franz	Uffz.	M	France	4th AOC
?/11	Fischer	Wilfried	Uffz.	M		II.
?/11	Haack	Werner		†	Wiener-Neustadt	
?/11	Heinzinger	Felix	Uffz.	M	Russia	5.
?/11	Leinweber	Fritz	Uffz.	M	Russia	
?/11	Schmitter	Wilhelm	Major	M	Russia	5.
1/11	Pfeiler	Arthur	Obfw.	†	Serbia	4.

4/11	Götz	Werner	Uffz.	†	Crimea	4.
13/11	Venske	Gerhard	Uffz.	†	Fürstenfeldbruck	4.
13/11	Stefka	Gerhard	Lt.	†	Fürstenfeldbruck	4.
16/11	Franke	Martin	Lt.	†	Leros	
22/11	Thomann	Klaus	Lt.	†	Wiener-Neustadt	
22/11	Bräth		Uffz.	†	Wiener-Neustadt	
22/11	Caak		Uffz.	†	Wiener-Neustadt	
***December**:*						
?/12	Jansen	Karl	Uffz.	M	Russia	II.
?/12	Steigleder	Hellmuth	Obgefr.	M	Russia	
1/12	Teuber	Gnther	Uffz.	†	Russia	6.
1/12	Blechschmid	Adalbert	Fw.	†	Russia	6.
1/12	Schulz	Friedrich	Fw.	†	Russia	6.
3/12	Helbig	Heinrich	Hptm.	†	Vinnitsa	4.
18/12	Tobias	Hans	Hptm.	†	Wiener-Neustadt	IV.
19/12	Eidel	Heinrich	Stfw.	†	Eisenburg	
29/12	Schobert	Georg-Heinrich	Hptm.	†	Atlantic	
31/12	Linau	Günter	Fw.	†	Russia	
31/12	Große	Günther	Fw.	†	Russia	
31/12	Jakobs		Gefr.	†	Russia	9.
31/12	Hßlbich	Wilhelm	Hptm.	†	Russia	4.

1944

?/44	Dörfer	Gerhard	Lt.	†	Crimea	
?/44	Hampe	Paul	Obgefr.	†		II.
?/44	Klein	Johann	Uffz.	†	England	6.
?/44	Lapschies	Erich	Obgefr.	†	Munich-Riem	IV.
?/44	Müller		Uffz.	†	England	6.
?/44	Pahl	Karl	Lt.	†	England	
?/44	Quatfasel		Uffz.	†	England	6.
?/44	Runge		Obfw.	†	England	II.
?/44	Schönberger		Uffz.	†	England	6.
?/44	Kimba			†	France	6.
***January**:*						
?/1	Becher	Hans	Gefr.	M		5.
?/1	Forster	Ludwig	Obgefr.	M		II.
?/1	Gabelt	Franz	Uffz.	M	Russia	
?/1	Hess	Friedel	Fw.	M		6.
?/1	Rosenau	Heinz	Uffz.	M	Russia	
?/1	Uecker	Hans	Lt.	M	Russia	6.
3/1	Rox	Rudolf	Obfw.	†	Holland	6.
7/1	Ikrath		Uffz.	†	Schweinfurt	12.
7/1	Heymann		Uffz.	†	Schweinfurt	12.
22/1	Heintz	Kurt	Hptm.	†	England	Stab
***February**:*						
?/2	Zimmer	Erich	Uffz.	†	Memmingen	
3/2	Treml	Alois	Obfw.	†	Cisterna/Africa	4.
8/2	Rattke	Heinz	Fw.	†	Italy	
12/2	Rieder	Walter	Major	†	Atlantic	4.
16/2	Pfarius		Obgefr.	†	Kitzingen	
22/2	Muschler	Günther	Uffz.	†	Lechfeld	2.
22/2	Drescher	Georg	Uffz.	†	Lechfeld	2.
22/2	Milbrad		Oblt.	†	Lechfeld	10.
22/2	Vornberger		Gefr.	†	Lechfeld	
22/2	Buschmann		Lt.	†	Lechfeld	
23/2	Delp	Gustav	Fw.	†	England	6.

23/2	Keilholz	Kurt	Obgefr.	†	England	3.
29/2	Fuhrhop	Helmut	Major	†	northern France	2.
29/2	Schachtschabel	Wilhelm	Oblt.	†	northern France	3.
29/2	Rehfeld	Walter	StFw.	†	Belgium	
March:						
?/3	Kwiatkowski	Rudolf	Uffz.	M		IV.
?/3	Ritter	Adam	Obfw.	M	Brodny	
?/3	Thönes	Werner	Obgefr.	M	Lvov	
2/3	Abel	Fritz	Hptm.	†	Rheine	
3/3	Strobel	Hubert	Fhj.Uffz.	†	Mering	
3/3	Kalmar	Ludwig	Gefr.	†	Mering	
3/3	Heinrich	Helmut	Gefr.	†	Mering	
3/3	Döring	Ernst	Gefr.	†	Mering	
4/3	Jürka		Fw.	†	Illesheim	III.
4/3	Naser		Uffz.	†	Illesheim	III.
14/3	Eppendorf von	Horst	Lt.	†	France	2.
15/3	Zabrodsky	Günther	Uffz.	†	France	2.
15/3	Pape von	Werner	Oblt.	†	France	1.
16/3	Scott	Walter	Lt.	†	Zainingen	
23/3	Krause	Willi	Uffz.	†		2.
24/3	Hübner	Joachim	Fw.	†	St. André	1.
24/3	Bitzer	Hermann	Uffz.	†	Evreux	2.
26/3	Feldner		Lt.	†	Hildesheim	IV.
28/3	Schneider	Leopold		†	Ingolstadt	4.
28/3	Brillmann	Detlef	Uffz.	†	Ingolstadt	4.
28/3	Heinze	Otmar	Oblt.	†	Ingolstadt	4.
April:						
5/4	Zickler	Helmut	Gefr.	†	Lengenfeld (shot down)	
5/4	Renatus	Walter	Lt.	†	France	3.
6/4	Briel	Johann	Prüfmster	†	Rennes	
9/4	Schäfer	Eberhard	Oblt.	†	Russia	II.
14/4	Zähmisch	Heinz	Uffz.	†	England	3.
14/4	Kierstein	Heinz	Uffz.	†	England	3.
18/4	Trunsperger	Alban	Stfw.	†	France	
19/4	Leidel	Siegfried	Oblt.	†	Hohenstein	II.
19/4	Wenk		Obfw.	†	Hohenstein	
19/4	Schuberth	Wilhelm	Fw.	†	England	
19/4	Seeland		Obgefr.	†	England	3.
19/4	Witt		Lt.	†	England	2.
19/4	Märte	Heinrich	Obfw.	†	Greifswald	
19/4	Pahl	Richard	Oblt.	†	England	2.
23/4	Lux	Willi	Obfw.	†	England	
23/4	Puttfarken	Dietrich	Major	†	England	
24/4	Rischke	Rudolf	Uffz.	†	Erding	
27/4	Wenning	Wolfgang	Lt.	†	England	6.
May:						
?/5	Friedel	Anton	Obgefr.	M		8th AOC
?/5	Künzig	Paul	Uffz.	M		8th AOC
?/5	Nießler	Gerhard	Lt.	†		II.
13/5	Hungershausen	Helmut		†	Reppen	
13/5	Roß	Karl-Heinz	Fhj.Uffz.	†	Reppen	
20/5	Dietrich	Karl-Heinz	Lt.	†	Dietmannsried	
22/5	Rath	Wilhelm	Major	†	England	Kommodore KG 2
22/5	Trauth	Sepp	Obfw.	†	England	
24/5	Hörner	Nikolaus	Uffz.	†	Königsberg	
28/5	Reil	Franz	Oblt.	†	Hohenstein	
28/5	Appel	Karl	Obfw.	†	Wangerode	

29/5	Schwenk	Adolf	Uffz.	†	Russia	
30/5	Kratel	Erwin	Lt.	†		
***June*:**						
?/6	Brügel	Walter	Uffz.	M		II.
?/6	Duero	Werner	Hptm.	M		II.
?/6	Eidenmüller	Karl-Friedrich	Obgefr.	M		8th AOC
?/6	Heinemann	Walter	Fw.	†	France	II.
?/6	Schlötzer	Alois	Uffz.	M		8th AOC
?/6	Weiss	Wilhelm	Obfw.	M		8th AOC
7/6	Koller	Josef	Fw.	†	Caseaux, France	
7/6	Mono	Karl-Heinz	Uffz.	†	Juist Island	3.
7/6	Hagel	Hugo	Uffz.	†	Juist Island	3.
8/6	Marizy	Walter	Lt.	†	Caen	
10/6	Pradzynski von	Alex	Obfw.	†	Isny, died in hospital	
20/6	Peter		Fw.	†	Lingen	
21/6	Borkert	Günther	Lt.	†		
28/6	Sehrbrock	Karl	Uffz.	†		2.
***July*:**						
?/7	Barth	Helmut	Obgefr.	M		I.
?/7	Bock	Karl	Obgefr.	†	Sicily	
?/7	Büchner	Eugen	Uffz.	†	Invasion Front	II.
?/7	Denk	Karl	Lt.	†	Invasion Front	5.
?/7	Markau		Lt.	†	Invasion Front	5.
?/7	Pieper	Heinz	Lt.	†	Invasion Front	II.
?/7	Schmidt	Heinz	Uffz.	M	Russia	II.
?/7	Schorer	Alban	Uffz.	M		II.
?/7	Seufert	Kurt	Uffz.	M		II.
?/7	Sperlich	Rudolf	Uffz.	M	Belgium	II.
?/7	Wekwart		Lt.	†	Munich-Riem	IV.
5/7	Mayer	Rudolf	Uffz.	†	Holland	
6/7	Ziegler	Hans-Joachim	Uffz.	†	aerial combat over France	4.
8/7	Kroth	Albert	Uffz.	†	aerial combat over France	4.
16/7	Richter	Winfried	ObFhr.	†	Kohlgrub	
18/7	Ellerbrock	Heinz		†	Memmingen	
18/7	Schreithofer	Ferdinand		†	Bordeaux	
20/7	Horn	Martin	Uffz.	†	Allexon, France	
21/7	Winkler	Herbert	Uffz.	†	Lechfeld	2.
21/7	Borkert	Günther	Lt.	†	Prenzlau	5.
23/7	Dingfelder	Ferdinand	ObFhr.	M		
31/7	Schultz	Werner	Lt.	†	Russia	
***August*:**						
?/8	Chrobak	Anton	Uffz.	M		I.
?/8	Fink		ObFhr.	†	Invasion Front	II.
1/8	Laas	Uwe	Lt.	†	France	
10/8	Berger	Johann		†	Baltic Sea	
29/8	Uebach	Heinrich	Obgefr.	†	Russia	
30/8	Bidoli	Herbert	Hfw.	†	Athens	
***September*:**						
?/9	Bonnet	Günther	Oblt.	M		II.
?/9	Denig	Helmut	Lt.	M		II.
?/9	Kern	Franz	Fw.	M		II.
?/9	Regnet	Karl	Gefr.	M		II.
?/9	Rupp	Karl	Gefr.	M		II.
?/9	Sieber	Artur	Fw.	M		II.
8/9	Weidemann	Rolf	Lt.	†	Liege	3.
9/9	Gärtner		Oblt.	†	Soesterberg	3.
11/9	Mündelein	Ernst	Fw.	†	Erz Mountains	4.

17/9	Bertelsbeck		Fw.	†	Leipheim	I.
20/9	Winter	Karl	Hptm.	†	Cadore, Italy	
20/9	Baumann	Peter	Major	†	Stargard	
27/9	Erk	Wilhelm	Uffz.	†	Lechfeld	
October:						
?/10	Junghans	Edgar	Fw.	†	Rheine	I.
?/10	Krüger	Edith	Fmle Aux.	M	Limburg	
5/10	Buttmann		Hptm.	†	Nijmwegen	3.
5/10	Franke		Uffz.	†	Nijmwegen	3.
16/10	Gravenreuth Baron von	Siegesmund	Oberst	†	Breslau	
23/10	Marienfeld	Walter	Oberstlt.	†	Giebelstadt	General der Kampfflieger
November:						
?/11	Lutz	Josef	Flg.	M		8th AOC
?/11	Sander	Hans	Obfw.	†	Göppingen	
?/11	Zimmermann		Uffz.	†	Schwäbisch-Hall	
2/11	Herterich	Emil	Obfw.	†	Aachen	
13/11	Merlau	Heinz	Oblt.	†	Rheine	I.
13/11	Hoffmann		Fw.	†	Rheine	II.
26/11	Lehmann	Heinz-Artur	Oblt.	†	Helmond	2.
28/11	Rösch	Rudolf	Hptm.	†	Helmond	2.
30/11	Sanio	Horst	Uffz.	†	Helmond	2.
December:						
?/12	Hampel	Erhard	Hfw.	M	North Sea	
?/12	Lübke		Lt.	†		II.
?/12	Maass	Karl-Heinz	Obgefr.	M		
?/12	Schneider	Gustav	Uffz.	†	Posen	
?/12	Thoma	Johannes	Fw.	†	Stalingrad	
2/12	Freistedt		Hptm.	†	Schwäbisch-Hall	5.
3/12	Valet	Hans-Joachim	Oblt.	†	Rheine	1.
5/12	Petersen	Karl-Heinz	Obfw.	†	Burgsteinfurt	
7/12	Brocke	Helmut	Hptm.	†	Schwäbisch-Hall	4.
7/12	Mecklenburg		Uffz.	†	Schwäbisch-Hall	
8/12	Peters	Ernst	Obfw.	†		2.
10/12	Lenk	Herbert	Fw.	†	Rheine	I.
12/12	Kohler	Hans	Obfw.	†	Rheine	I.
13/12	Niedermeier	Werner	Obgefr.	†	Landsberg	
13/12	Berckes	Wilhelm	Uffz.	†	Landsberg	
25/12	Meyer	Hans	Fw.	†	Liege	2.
26/12	Lamle	Hans-Georg	Oblt.	†	Rheine	II.
29/12	Raith	Max	Hptm.	†	Neuburg	II.
29/12	Bock	Emil	Obfw.	†	Bregenz, died in hospital	

1945

?/45	Krautner	Gustav	Uffz.	†	Eastern Front	
?/45	Neußer	Ludwig	Uffz.	†	Aachen	
?/45	Poppenburg	Werner	Oblt.	†	Berlin	7.
?/45	Willmann	Ottmar	Hptm.	†	near Aachen	III.
January:						
?/1	Nedele	Kurt	Fw.	†	Breslau	
?/1	Abel	Herbert	Sold.	M		3rd AOC
?/1	Adam	Peter	Uffz.	M	Russia	
?/1	Bier	Ernst	Lt.	†	Munich-Riem	
?/1	Hoge	Walter	Obgefr.	M		4th AOC
?/1	Hoffmann	Rudi	Fw.	†		
?/1	Koch	Walter	Obgefr.	M		3rd AOC

?/1	Müller	Otto	Flg.	†	Leipheim	
?/1	Niedworok	Alfred	Gefr.	M		1st AOC
?/1	Schulz	Willi	Sold.	M	Hertegen	
?/1	Schulz		Fw.	†	Rheine	I.
?/1	Steger	Heinrich	Uffz.	†	Breslau	
?/1	Schwaiger	Martin		M	Breslau	
1/1	Kaiser	Erich	Obfw.	†	Rheine	2.
1/1	Hettlich	Josef	Lt.	†	Holland	
3/1	Schoch	Albert	St.Gefr.	M	Munich	IV.
5/1	Steinbrückner	Wilhelm	Obfw.	†	Vahrenwald	
14/1	Baron Ritter von	Rittersheim	Lt.	†	Rittershofen	2.
23/1	Holzwarth	Hans	Oblt.	†	Hopsten	12.
29/1	Brenner	Karl	Obfw.	†	Eastern Front	
30/1	Geiger	Konrad	Obgefr.	†	Würringen	
***February*:**						
?/2	Benkert	Helmut		†	Bad Aibling	
?/2	Chermin	Stefan	Fw.	M		IV.
?/2	Gatys	Gerhard	Obgefr.	†	Memmingen	
?/2	Greitsch	Max	Uffz.	M		4th AOC
?/2	Hinz	Aloisiua	Uffz.	M		1st AOC
?/2	Neuenfeld	Rudolf	Schütze	†	Landsberg	
?/2	Seidel	Helmut	Uffz.	M		I.
?/2	Wilke	Paul	Flg.	M		4th AOC
2/2	Bührich		Hptm.	†	Mergentheim	3.
11/2	Sauter	Kurt	Fw.	†	Gütersloh	III.
16/2	Spiess	Robert	Obfw.	†	Cosel	
16/2	Schütz	Adolf	Lt.	†	Kitzingen	
22/2	Piel	Kurt	Lt.	†	Hopsten	2.
23/2	Stölzle	Karl	Obfw.	†	Belgium	I.
27/2	Mayrl	Michael	Fw.	†	Zobten	
***March*:**						
?/3	Abel	Fritz	Hptm.	M		5.
?/3	Brückner	Karl	Obgefr.	M		4th AOC
?/3	Hoehne	Jürgen	ObFhr.	M		I.
?/3	Kowal	Paul	Obgefr.	M		4th AOC
?/3	Pöhling	Eberhard	Uffz.	†	Wimborn	
?/3	Pollak	Armund	Uffz.	†	Göttingen	
?/3	Wilde	Mathias	Obgefr.	M		4th AOC
?/3	Woestenbrück	Bernhard	Fw.	M		4th AOC
?/3	Würrge	Helmut	Fw.	M		4th AOC
9/3	Benninger	Alfred	Uffz.	†	Remagen	
21/3	Winkel	Eberhard	Hptm.	†	Giebelstadt	3.
21/3	Erben	Heinz	Uffz.	†	Wertheim	2.
21/3	Gietmann		Lt.	†	Giebelstadt	3.
***April*:**						
?/4	Bloteck	Karl	Fw.	M	Russia	
?/4	Geisler	Horst	Uffz.	M		4th AOC
?/4	Heiligtag	Walter	Uffz.	M		II.
?/4	Keilbach	Friedrich	Fw.	†	Landsberg	
?/4	Mühlbacher	Lorenz	Gefr.	M		4th AOC
?/4	Müller	Fritz	Uffz.	M		4th AOC
?/4	Reichardt	Horst	Uffz.	M		4th AOC
?/4	Ruf		Obfw.	†	Lagerlechfeld	
?/4	Woithe	Gerhard	Obgefr.	M		4th AOC
?/4	Geisler	Horst	Uffz.	M		I.
4/4	Dannhoff	Robert	Uffz.	†	Oberkirchen	
4/4	Filser	Mathias	Obfw.	M		2nd AOC

15/4	Schenk	Johann		†		
17/4	Lampert	August	Oblt.	†	Hoyerswerda	
18/4	Lubrich	Hans	Lt.	†	Africa	
18/4	Schwegler	Mathias	Major	†	Neuses/Ansbach	III.
23/4	Hauner	Horst	Obfw.	†	Italy	
20/4	Müller	Gottlob	General	†	Berlin	
24/4	Amelung		Lt.	†	Neuburg	IV.
25/4	Werntgen	Heinz	Uffz.	†	Leipheim	2.
28/4	Haller	Hans	Uffz.	†	Penzing	3rd AOC
May:						
?/5	Preuss	Herbert	Obgefr.	M		4th AOC
?/5	Ortlepp	Ernst	Fw.	M		I.
6/5	Schimmel		Lt.	†	Prague	2.
7/5	Strothmann	Heinz	Oblt.	†	Saaz	2.
7/5	Pöling		Uffz.	†	Prague	2.
8/5	Herberger	Ernst	Uffz.	†	Berlin	
13/5	Guggenberg	Michael	Obfw.	†	Belgium	

After the war:

5/6	Schubert	Herbert	Obfw.	†	died in English POW camp
15/9	Volger	Karl	Hfw.	†	died as prisoner in Landsberg
?/45	Starnschied	Walter	Obfw.	†	died as prisoner in Neu-Ulm

1946

12/9	Bock	Ludwig	Fw.	†	Russia
?/1947	Ebermann	Erich	Stfw.	†	Russia

1952

24/3	Mälzer	Kurt	Gen.Lt.	†	Werl

Killed or missing, about whom specific details are not known:

Bark		Lt.	†		
Becker	Julius	Gefr.	†		
Beckmann von			†		
Böttcher	Heinz	Fw.	†		III. Gruppe, Gallermann crew
Bargstädt	Karl-Heinz	Uffz.	†	France	
Bereiter		Uffz.	†	Russia, Nikolayev	
Brandenburg		Uffz.	†		
Brücke		Hptm.	†		
Dumke		Lt.	†	France	
Dotzer			†	Russia	
Dippel	Heinz	Obgefr.	†	Russia	
Fernberg			†		
Garus		Oblt.	†	Russia, Kerch	
Gress		Obfw.	†		
Höll		Oblt.	†	Balti	
Hellinger	Hans	Oberzmstr	†	France	II
Helbig		Oblt.	†	Russia	4.
Heinze	Otmar	Oblt.	†		
Hohendahl	Hans	Lt.	†		
Holz	Wolfgang	Lt.			
Holzmann		Fw.	†		
Jung	Herbert	Gefr.	†	France	

Katte	Joachim	Obfw.	†		
Kleinschmidt		Fw.	†		
Kaak			†		
Kutschmann		Fw.			
Kunze	Helmut	Lt.	†	England	III.
Köhler	Egon	Gefr.	†	Russia, executed by shooting	IV.
Kärkel	Lothar		†	Russia	
Lahs		ObFhr.	†		
Lehmann		Gefr.	†		
Lütke van Daltrop		Gefr.	†		
Lutz	Paul		†		
Lenkheit		Lt.	†		
Lönecker	Heinz		†		
Moser	Jakob	Uffz.	†		7.
Mühlenberg		Fw.	†		
Meumeier	Rudolf	Obgefr.	†	England	
Ochsenbauer	Fritz		†		
Ramm	Heinrich	Uffz.	†	England	
Redchen	Felix	Fw.	†	Russia	Stab
Ratl	Wilhelm	Oberstlt.	†		
Seibold	Wilhelm		†	Southern France	maintenance
Sorg		Oblt.	†		
Sieber		Oblt.	†		
Sippe	Alfred	Uffz.	†		
Schneez	Albert	Hptm.	†		
Schoen	Gerhard	Major	†		
Schneider		Lt.	†	Russia, Don Bend	
Schöppe		Uffz.	†	Russia, Nikolayev	
Schenk Baron zu	Schweinsberg	Major	†		
Thoma	Klaus	Lt.	†		
Tilli	Hubert	Obgefr.	†		
Weichselberger			†	Russia	
Westerhoff	Josef		†		
Wittig	Hermann	Obfw.	†	Russia, Yalta	
Zingraff	Emil		M	Russia	4th AOC
Saborowski		Uffz.	†		

The following died airmen's deaths while serving with Jabo G 34:

Czechowsky	Joachim	Oblt.	† 31/8/1959	Steinheim	2./34
Häse	Klaus	Stuffz.	† 19/10/1961	Memmingen	2./34
Tetzner	Michael	Oblt.	† 23/4/1963	Siegenburg	1./34
Klatt	Günter	Hptm.	† 14/10/1964	Bad Wurzbach	1./34
Thormeyer	Dieter	Hptm.	† 5/11/1965	Sontheim	1./34
Klenk	Karl-Oskar	Oblt.	† 11/6/1968	Hochgrat	2./34
Vaterrodt	Gustav	Hfw.	† 21/9/68	Bernbach	1./34
Kunz	Georg	Oberstlt.	† 19/4/1970	Karlsruhe	Kommodore
Drescher	Werner	Hfw.	† 19/4/1970	Karlsruhe	2./34
Dr. Bachlehner	Oskar	Oblt.(Rtd.)	† 19/4/1970	Karlsruhe	
Augustin	Wolf-Dietrich	Oblt.	† 23/3/1971	Jever	2./34
Müller	Klaus	Major	† 1/12/1972	Luke AFB	Stab
Schiller	Johannes	Oblt.	† 1/2/1973	U.Kammlach	2./34
Doepke	Klaus-Peter	Hptm.	† 29/8/1973	Luke AFB	2./34
Hübner	Hans-Joachim	Hptm.	† 18/2/1975	Luke AFB	1./34
Schumann	Klaus	Oberstlt.	† 24/4/1975	Wielen	Stab
Kepp	Bernd	Oblt.	† 6/8/1975	Capo Frasca	2./34

Appendix 2

The Knight's Cross Winners of KG 51

The Knight's Cross of the Iron Cross was the most coveted decoration in the German armed forces during the Second World War. Created on 1 September 1939 for "conspicuous bravery in the face of the enemy," this decoration was an extension of the Order of the Iron Cross of 10 March 1838; additional grades, such as the Oak Leaves, Swords and Diamonds were added later in the war.

Of the 7,500 Knight's Crosses that were awarded, approximately 1,730 went to members of the Luftwaffe, with aircrew of all ranks accounting for about 1,320.

The Knight's Cross was awarded to 538 members of day or night-fighter and *Zerstörer* units, while 640 were won by members of bomber, Stuka and close-support units.

The award requirements changed over the course of the war and were based mainly on the number of operational missions flown. In March 1943, for example, the required number of missions for various decorations were:

15 combat missions	Iron Cross, Second Class
20 combat missions	Operational Flying Clasp in Bronze
25-40 combat missions	Iron Cross, First Class
60 combat missions	Operational Flying Clasp in Silver
80 combat missions	Honor Goblet
110 combat missions	Operational Flying Clasp in Gold
140 combat missions	German Cross in Gold
200-400 combat missions	Knight's Cross of the Iron Cross

An examination of the awarding of decorations to bomber crewmen reveals that in 1940 almost all were *Geschwaderkommodore* or *Gruppenkommandeure*, who were given the decoration in the name of their units for their overall accomplishments in various campaigns. (First Knight's Cross awarded to a member of a bomber unit was to *Oberst* Robert Fuchs, *Kommodore* of KG 26.) All other pilots required approximately 100 day and/or night missions, especially against England.

In 1941 the "interesting" number of combat missions rose to 200.

In the later war years the required figure was 200 to 400, with the majority receiving the Knight's Cross after about 300 missions. Crews operating in Russia, in particular, often had this many and even more missions when they were decorated. Observers, radio operators, flight engineers and gunners almost all had more than 300 combat missions and were often part of the crew of a very successful pilot or unit commander who already had the Knight's Cross.

The higher levels of the Knight's Cross (4 Swords, 27 Oak Leaves) were only awarded to extraordinarily successful pilots, who as a rule were also unit commanders (*Staffelkapitän*, *Gruppenkommandeur*, *Kommodore*) who had survived many combat missions or whose units had achieved outstanding results.

The Knight's Cross was also awarded posthumously.

Knight's Cross Winners of KG 51 "Edelweiss"

Rank	*Name*	*Award Date*	*Unit*	*Killed/Died*
Awarded while a member of the *Geschwader*				
Oblt.	Matthias Schwegler	18/12/1941	Kpt. 1./51	18/4/1945
Fw.	Georg Fanderl	24/1/1942	pilot 1./51	4/1/1953
Hptm.	Rudolf Henne	12/4/1942	Kpt. 9./51	13/4/1962
Oblt.	Ernst Hinricks	25/7/1942	pilot 2./51	25/01/2009
Hptm.	Siegfried Barth	2/10/1942	Kpt. 4./51	19/12/1997
Hptm.	Gerd Korthals	2/10/1942	Kpt. 8./51	3/11/1942
Oblt.	Dietrich Puttfarken	7/10/1942	pilot 1./51	23/4/1944
Major	Ernst Baron von Bibra	23/12/1942	Gr.Kdr. III./51	15/2/1943
Hptm.	Hellmuth Hauser	23/12/1942	Kpt. in I./51	05/09/2004
Obfw.	Alberth Spieth	24/3/1943	pilot 3./51	4/10/1943
Oblt.	Georg Holle	3/4/1943	St.Fhr. 2./51	27/2/1943
Hptm.	Klaus Häberlen	20/6/1943	Gr.Kdr. I./51	07/04/2002
Hptm.	Josef Schölß	25/5/1943	St.Kpt. 3./51	22/09/2009
Oblt.	Günther Löffelbein	19/9/1943	Kpt. 3./51	29/01/2011
Major	Herbert Voß	5/2/1944	Gr.Kdr. II./51	05/07/1976
Hptm.	Hans Gutzmer	29/2/1944	Kpt. 3./51	04/06/2004
Oblt.	Rudolf Roesch	26/3/1944	Kpt. 9./51	28/11/1944
Oblt.	Bernhard Sartor	20/7/1944	observer Stab KG 51	09/02/1975
Obfw.	Hans Frach	29/10/1944	pilot 6./51	05/11/2004
Awarded after leaving the *Geschwader*:				
Major	Martin Vetter	16/5/1940	Gr.Kdr. II./KG 26	
Oberst	Alois Stoeckl	4/7/1940	Kommodore KG 55	14/8/1940
GenMaj.	Wolf con Stutterheim	4/7/1940	*Kommodore* KG 77	3/12/1940
	Pour le Mérite	29/8/1918		
Fw.	Otto Eichloff	16/8/1940	pilot 4./KG 30	03/06/1987
Major	Edgar Petersen	21/10/1940	Gr.Kdr. I./KG 40	10/06/1986
Oblt.	Sigmar Baron von Gravenreuth	24/11/1940	pilot 1./KG 30	
	Awarded 692nd Oak Leaves posthumously as Oberstlt.	9/1/1945	Kommodore KG 30	16/10/1944
GenMaj.	Josef Kammhuber	9/7/1941	commander 1, Nachtjagddivision	
Oblt.	Wolfgang Schenck	14/8/1941	Kpt. 1./SKG 210	
	Awarded 139th Oak Leaves as Hptm.	30/10/1942	Kdr. I./ZG 1	
Obfw.	Wilhelm Bender	8/9/1941	pilot 5./KG 3	20/01/1992
Oberstlt.	Dr. Ernst Bormann	5/10/1941	*Kommodore* KG 76	1/8/1960
	Awarded 119th Oak Leaves as *Oberst* (reinforced KG 76)	3/9/1942	C.O. "Gefechtsverband Bormann"	
Oberstlt.	Walter Marienfeld	27/11/1941	*Kommodore* KG 54	23/10/1944
Hptm.	Joachim Poetter	16/4/1942	Kdr. I./KG 77	17/11/1992
Major	Hans Keppler	20/8/1942	Gr.Kdr. III./KG 1	3/9/1942
Hptm.	Hanns Heise	3/9/1942	Gr.Kdr. I./KG 76	18/05/1992
Hptm.	Heinrich Prinz zu Sayn-Wittgenstein	2/10/1942	St.Kpt. 9./NJG 2	
	Oak Leaves No. 290 as Hptm.	31/8/1943	Gr.Kdr. I./NJG 100	
	Swords No. 44 posthumously as Major	23/1/1944	*Kommodore* NJG 2	21/1/1944

Major	Paul Darjes	14/10/1942	Gr.Kdr. II./Sch.G. 1	
Major	Friedolin Fath	23/12/1942	Gr.Kdr. IV./KGz.b.V. 1	
GenMaj.	Gottlob Müller	8/6/1943	Commander Tunis	20/4/1945
Major	Rudolf Hallensleben	29/10/1943	*Kommodore* KG 76	19/4/1945
Major	Helmut Fuhrhop	22/11/1943	Gr.Kdr. I./KG 76	29/2/1944
Hptm.	Rudolf Abrahamczik	29/2/1944	Kpt. 14./KG 2	04/12/1995
Oblt.	Eberhard Schaefer	7/4/1944	pilot II./KG 51	9/4/1944
Oblt.	Hans-Joachim Valet	28/4/1944	pilot I./TG 2	
			with I./KG(J) 51	31/12/1944
Hptm.	Kurt Dahlmann	11/6/1944	Gr.Kdr. I./SKG 10	
	Oak Leaves No. 711			
	as Major	24//1945	Kdr. NSGr. 20	
Fahnenjunker-Feldwebel				
	Hanns Trenke	5/9/1944	pilot 6./KG 1	29/4/1957
GenMaj.	Hans Korte	30/9/1944	C.O. 2. (Torpedo-) Flieger-Div.	08/04/1990
Major	Wilhelm Stemmler	6/10/1944	*Kommodore* KG 77	12/5/1967
Hptm.	Kurt Capesius	21/12/1944	Kdr. III./KG 66	died October 1958
Hptm.	Helmut Eberspächer	24/1/1945	St.Kap. 3./NSGr. 20	

List generously provided by *Herr* Ernst Obermaier.

Appendix 3
Command Personnel of the "Edelweiss" *Geschwader*

Unfortunately, not all of the *Luftwaffe* Personnel Office's personnel change reports have survived, consequently it is impossible to completely reconstruct the staffing of the *Staffenl*, *Gruppen* and the *Geschwaderstab* from these records. The documents were probably lost as a result of the war. The following lists were compiled as accurately as possible, like a mosaic, thanks to the tireless efforts of the *Bundesarchiv*'s Central Verification Office in Kornelimünster and inquiries made of those members of the *Geschwader* still living. It had been impossible to provide exact dates for the *Staffelkapitänen*. The crosses (†) that appear after the dates mean that the person in question was killed in action on that day, while crosses after the names mean that the person in question was killed or died at a later date.

Geschwader Kommodore

15/3/1937 – 1/11/1938	*Oberst* Willibald Spang
1/11/1938 – 1/2/1939	*Oberst* Ritter von Lex †
1/2/1939 – 26/3/1940	*Oberst* Dr. Johann-Volkmar Fisser
26/3/1940 – 3/6/1940	*Oberst* Josef Kammhuber
3/6/1940 – 12/8/1940 †	*Oberst* Dr. Johann-Volkmar Fisser
12/8/1940 – 31/8/1941	*Major* Hans Bruno Schulz-Heyn
1/9/1941 – 4/7/1942	*Oberst* Paul Koester
4/7/1942 – 30/11/1942	*Major* Wilhelm von Friedeburg
1/12/1942 – 8/1/1943 †	*Oberst* Heinrich Conrady
8/1/1943 – 9/5/1943	*Major* Egbert von Frankenburg und Proschlitz
9/5/1943 – 25/2/1944	*Major* Hanns Heise
25/2/1944 – 4/12/1944	*Oberstleutnant* Wolf Dieter Meister
5/12/1944 – 31/1/1945	*Major* Wolfgang Schenck
1/2/1945 – 19/4/1945 †	*Oberstleutnant* Rudolf Hallensleben
19/4/1945 – 28/4/1945	*Oberstleutnant* Siegfried Barth

Gruppenkommandeur* and *Staffelkapitäne

I. Gruppe

Kommandeure

15/3/1937 – 31/3/1938	*Oberstleutnant* Kurt Mälzer †
31/3/1938 – 18/12/1939	*Oberstleutnant* Hans Korte
19/12/1939 – 12/8/1940	*Major* Hans Bruno Schulz-Heyn
12/8/1940 – 14/2/1941	*Hauptmann* Kurt von Greiff
14/2/1941 – 3/2/1942 †	*Hauptmann* Heinrich Hahn
3/2/1942 – 6/10/1942	*Major* Hans-Joachim Ritter
6/10/1942 – 5/2/1943	*Major* Fritzherbert Dierich
5/2/1943 – 11/10/1943	*Major* Klaus Häberlen
11/10/1943 – 25/2/1944	*Major* Wolf Dietrich Meister
25/2/1944 – 8/5/1944	*Major* Heinrich Unrau

Staffelkapitäne

1. Staffel	*2. Staffel*	*3. Staffel*
Hptm. Schlüter	Hptm. Pfister	*Major* Neuenfeld †
Hptm. Petersen	Hptm. Keppler	Hptm. Pflüger
Hptm. Muggenthaler	Hptm. von Groddeck	Oblt. Lange †
Hptm. von Greiff	Hptm. von Sichart	Hptm. Schölß
Hptm. Panitzki	Hptm. Hahn †	Oblt. Löffelbein

Oblt. Illgner †	Hptm. Fuhrhop †	Oblt. Holle
Hptm. Schwegler †	Oblt. Hinrichs	Oblt. Berger †
Major Ebert †	Hptm. Häberlen	Hptm. Winkel †
Oblt. Puttfarken †	Hptm. Müller	Oblt. Stephan
Oblt. Berger †	Hptm. Abrahamczik	
Hptm. Unrau		
Oblt. Pape †		
Oblt. Pahl†		
Hptm. Csurusky		

II. Gruppe

Kommandeure

1/3/1937 – 1/2/1939	*Oberstleutnant* Dr. Johann Fisser †
1/2/1939 – 1/5/1939	*Oberst* Wolf von Stutterheim †
15/4/1940 – 31/3/1941	*Major* Winkler
31/1/1941 – 22/6/1941	*Hauptmann* Max Stadelmeier †
22/6/1941 – 1/4/1942	*Major* Wilhelm von Friedeburg
1/4/1942 - 21/5/1942 †	*Major* Friedrich Wilhelm Kaufner
21/5/1942 – 26/2/1943	*Hauptmann* Rudolf Henne †
26/2/1943 – 31/12/1944	*Major* Herbert Voß
1/1/1945 – 6/2/1945	*Major* Martin Vetter
21/3/1945 – 8/5/1945	*Hauptmann* Hans-Joachim Grundmann

4. Staffel	*5. Staffel*	*6. Staffel*
Hptm. Pilger	Oblt. Maier †	Hptm. Berlin †
Oblt. von Greiff	Oblt. von Wenchowsky †	Hptm. Grundmann
Oblt. Bretschneider	Oblt. Bülow	Oblt. Vetter
Oblt. Stemmler †	Oblt. Henne †	Oblt. Guth
Hptm. Schölß	Hptm. Kaufner †	Oblt. Baetz
Hptm. Keppler †	Oblt. Nebelung †	
Hptm. Barth	Oblt. Henning †	
Oblt. Hälbich	Oblt. Baetz	
Lt. Türpisch †	Hptm. Abel †	
Oblt. Csurusky		

III. Gruppe (disbanded on 31/12/1943)

Kommandeure

1/3/1937 – 1/4/1937	*Oberst* Gottlob Müller †
1/4/1937 – 7/3/1940	*Oberst* Alois Stoeckl †
7/3/1940 – 24/6/1940	*Major* Johann-Wilhelm Kind
24/6/1940 – 23/11/1941	*Major* Walter Marienfeld †
23/11/1941 – 15/2/1943 †	*Major* Ernst Baron von Bibra
15/2/1943 – 31/12/1943	*Hauptmann* Wilhelm Rath †

Staffelkapitäne

7. Staffel	*8. Staffel*	*9. Staffel*
Major Schroeder	Hptm. Plischke †	Hptm. Möst
Hptm. Poetter	Hptm. Schenk von Schweinsburg †	Hptm. Brandt †
Hptm. Zeep	Hptm. Meyert	Hptm. Serschen †
Hptm. von Bibra †	Hptm. Bretschneider	Hptm. Henne †
Hptm. Rath †		Oblt. Raith

Hptm. Heilmann †	Hptm. Korthals †	Oblt. Roesch †
Hptm. Gutzmer	Oblt. Bräck	
	Lt. Wistuba †	
	Oblt. Seipp †	

IV. Gruppe

Kommandeure

1940 – 6/4/1941	*Hauptmann* Martin Vetter
6/4/1941 – 25/2/1942	*Hauptmann* Hans-Joachim Ritter
25/2/1942 – 13/12/1942	*Hauptmann* Wilhelm Stemmler †
13/12/1942 – 31/1/1944	*Hauptmann* Josef Schölß
1/2/1944 – 21/3/1945	*Major* Siegfried Barth
22/3/1945 – 8/5/1945	*Major* "Mile" Bender

Staffelkapitäne

10. Staffel	*11. Staffel*	*12. Staffel*
Oblt. Capesius †	Oblt. Berger †	Oblt. Schwegler †
Oblt. Häberlen	Hptm. Puttfarken †	Hptm. Vetter
Hptm. Rath †	Hptm. Träuptmann	Oblt. Löffelbein
Hptm. Hinrichs		
Oblt. Löffelbein		

Appendix 4

***Geschwader* Locations**

(from 1 April 1937)

Geschwaderstab	*I. Gruppe*	*II. Gruppe*	*III. Gruppe*	*IV. Gruppe*
Landsberg/Lech (1/4/1937 – 20/6/1940)	Landsberg (1/4/1937 – 20/8/1939) Memmingen (20/8/1939 – 6/5/1940) Lechfeld (6/5/1940 – 20/6/1940)	disbanded (to KG 77) Munich-Riem (1/4/1940 – 14/6/1940) Stuttgart-Echterdingen (14/6/1940 – 18/6/1940)	Memmingen (1/4/1937 – 6/11/1939) Landsberg (6/11/1939 – 20/6/1940)	–
Paris-Orly (20/6/1940 – 30/3/1941)	Paris-Orly (20/6/1940 – 1/8/1940) Villaroche (1/8/1940 – 30/3/1941)	Étampes-Mondésir (20/6/1940 – 24/8/1940) Paris-Orly (24/8/1940 – 12/4/1941)	Étampes-Mondésir (20/6/1940 – 3/11/1940) Brétigny (3/11/1940 – 30/3/1941)	– – Lechfeld (10/1/1941 – 22/4/1941)
Wiener-Neustadt (30/3/1941 – 16/4/1941)	Wiener-Neustadt (30/3/1941 – 16/4/1941) Krumovo (16/4/1941 – 14/5/1941) Wiener-Neustadt (14/5/1941 – 4/6/1941)	Wiener-Neustadt (12/4/1941 – 20/6/1941)	Wiener-Neustadt (30/3/1941 – 18/6/1941)	Wiener-Neustadt (22/4/1941 – 24/12/1941)
Krosno (4/6/1941 – 15/7/1941)	Krosno (4/6/1941 – 4/7/1941) Luck (4/7/1941 – 15/7/1941)	Krosno (20/6/1941 – 27/6/1941) Balti (27/6/1941 – 8/9/1941)	Lezany (18/6/1941 – 5/7/1941) Wlodzimierz (5/7/1941 – 18/7/1941) Wiener-Neustadt (rest and refit until 30/8/1941)	Wiener-Neustadt
Zilistea/Balti (15/7/1941 – 17/10/1941)	Zilistea (15/7/1941 – 10/10/1941)	Wiener-Neustadt rest and refit until 4/12/1941	Balti (30/8/1941 – 23/10/1941)	Wiener-Neustadt
Nikolayev (17/10/1941 – 3/4/1942)	Tiraspol (10/10/1941 – 24/1/1942) rest and refit until 3/4/1942 (Odessa)	Nikolayev, Kitay (4/12/1941 – 12/12/1941)	Nikolayev (23/10/1941 -24/3/1942) rest and refit until 15/5/1942 (Odessa)	Wiener-Neustadt

Zaporozhye (3/4/1942 – 10/7/1942)	Zaporozhye (3/4/1942 – 30/5/1942) Kharkov-West (30/5/1942 – 10/7/1942)	Zaporozhye (12/12/1941 – 7/9/1942)	Zaporozhye (15/5/1942 – 29/5/1942) Kharkov-West (29/5/1942 – 10/7/1942)	Bobruisk (24/2/1941 – 11/8/1943)
Stalino (10/7/1942 – 12/9/1942)	Stalino (10/7/1942 – 5/8/1942) Kerch (5/8/1942 – 19/8/1942) Tatsinskaya (19/8/1942 – 23/9/1942)	Stalino (7/9/1942 – 20/9/1942)	Stalino (10/7/1942 – 5/8/1942) Kerch (5/8/1942 – 20/8/1942) Tatsinskaya (20/8/1942 – 28/9/1942)	Bobruisk
Bagerovo (12/9/1942 – 8/10/1942)	Tatsinskaya	Bagerovo (20/9/1942 – 25/10/1942)	Tatsinskaya	Bobruisk
Sarabus (8/10/1942 – 5/2/1943)	Sarabus (6/10/1942 – 3/11/1942) Tatsinskaya (3/11/1942 – 7/12/1942)	Armavir (25/10/1942 – 6/11/1942)	Sarabus (28/9/1942 – 20/12/1942) – without aircraft –	Bobruisk
Rostov (7/12/1942 – 27/2/1943)	Rostov (7/12/1942 – 5/2/1943)	Bagerovo – without aircraft –	Rostov (20/12/1942 – 6/2/1943)	Bobruisk
Zaporozhye (5/2/1943 – 27/2/1943)	Zaporozhye (5/2/1943 – 2/4/1943)	Zaporozhye (6/2/1943 – 8/5/1943)	Zaporozhye (6/2/1943 – 27/2/1943)	Bobruisk
Bagerovo (27/2/1943 – 8/5/1943)	Bagerovo (2/4/1943 – 8/5/1943)	Briansk (8/5/1943 – 26/7/1943)	Bagerovo (27/2/1943 – 10/5/1943)	Bobruisk
Briansk (8/5/1943 – 26/7/1943)	Illesheim (8/5/1943 – 6/8/1943)	Briansk	Briansk (10/5/1943 – 21/7/1943)	Bobruisk
Sechinskaya (26/7/1943 – 16/8/1943)	Memmingen/Lechfeld (6/8/1943 – 30/8/1943)	Sechinskaya (26/7/1943 – 1/8/1943) Bobruisk (1/8/1943 – 1/9/1943)	Sechinskaya (21/7/1943 – 9/8/1943)	Hildesheim (11/8/1943 – 1/4/1944)
Kirovograd (16/8/1943 – 7/9/1943)	Illesheim (30/8/1943 – 29/9/1943)	Kirovograd, Kharkov, Zhitomir (1/9/1943 – 18/9/1943)	Kirovograd (9/8/1943 – 31/8/1943)	Hildesheim
Illesheim (7/9/1943 – 6/12/1943)	Hörsching (29/9/1943 – 6/12/1943)	Salonika (18/9/1943 – 28/11/1943)	Illesheim 31/8/1943 – 31/12/1943) disbanded 31/12/1943	Hildesheim Munich-Riem (1/4/1944 – 29/12/1944) renamed IV.(Erg.) KG 1 also stationed in Neuburg, Erding
Evreux (6/12/1943 – 15/2/1944)	Evreux (6/12/1943 – 25/5/1944)	Kalinovka (28/11/1943 – 4/1/1944) Vinnitsa (4/1/1944 – 8/1/1944) Lublin (8/1/1944 – April 1944)		
St. Georges-Môtel (15/2/1944 – 23/5/1944)	Dreux/St. André (25/4/1944 – 23/5/1944)	Gilze Rijen (April 1944 – August 1944)		

Lechfeld (23/5/1944 – 5/9/1944)	Lechfeld/Leipheim (23/5/1944 – 20/7/1944)	Schwäbisch-Hall (August 1944 – Sept. 1944)		
	Châteaudun (20/7/1944 – 12/8/1944)	Schwäbisch-Hall		
	Étampes (12/8/1944 – 15/8/1944)			
	Creil (15/8/1944 – 27/8/1944)	Achmer/Hesepe		
	Corbeny Juvincourt (27/8/1944 – 28/8/1944)			
	Ath-Chièvres (28/8/1944 – 30/8/1944)			
	Volkel (30/8/1944 – 5/9/1944)			
Rheine/Hörstel/Hopsten (5/9/1944 – 20/3/1945)	Rheine/Hörstel/Hopsten (5/9/1944 – 20/3/1945)	Essen-Mühlheim		
Giebelstadt (20/3/1945 – 30/3/1945)	Giebelstadt (20/3/1945 – 30/3/1945)	Schwäbisch-Hall Fürth Linz-Hörsching	disbanded	Munich-Riem, Neuburg 30/3/1945 – *Gruppe* hands aircraft over to JV 44
Leipheim (30/3/1945 – 21/4/1945)	Leipheim (30/3/1945 – 21/4/1945)			
Memmingen (21/4/1945 – 30/4/1945)	Memmingen (21/4/1945 – 30/4/1945)			
Holzkirchen (24/4/1945 – 30/4/1945)	Munich-Riem (24/4/1945 – 30/4/1945) subsequently with	Landau/Isar Gruppe disbanded on 24/4/1945 and attached to a grenadier regiment		
Luftwaffen-Feldjagdabteilung 103 (mot.)	for ground action			
	Prague-Ruzyne (30/4/1945 – 6/5/1945)			
	Saaz (6/5/1945 – 8/5/1945) Partial detachment disbanded Since 30/4/1945 elements of the *Gruppe* attached to *Luftwaffe* Feldjagdkommando “*Luftwaffe* Order Unit” in the “Alpine Redoubt”			

Appendix 5
Organization of a Kampfgeschwader

During the war, operational events dominated everything. Only a few bomber crewmen had the time and opportunity to concern themselves with the organization of a bomber *Geschwader*. Those who ever worked in a staff or headquarters unit (*Stab*) are familiar with the terms "Table of Organization" and "Wartime Table of Organization." For a *Stab*, a *Gruppe*, a *Staffel* or other unit, they precisely prescribed their entitlement with respect to number and type of officers, non-commissioned officers, enlisted men and officials, and their equipment and armament. In many cases, because of wartime conditions the reality was much different than the table of organization.

A *Kampfgeschwader* consisted of three *Kampfgruppen* and a fourth (IV.) Replacement Training *Gruppe* for operational training purposes. Each *Gruppe* was assigned an airfield operating company (FBK) and a headquarters company.

The *Gruppe* was organized into three *Kampfstaffeln* each with nine to twelve aircraft, with aircrews plus technical and non-technical ground personnel. Including the *Gruppe* and *Geschwader* reconnaissance flights, the *Geschwader* had available a maximum of 200 bomber aircraft. On average, 110-120 aircraft were serviceable or available for operations, while the remainder were in general overhaul or undergoing repairs. A *Kampfgeschwader* had a personnel strength of about 2,500 men.

The following list describes the duties of various staff positions with abbreviations:

Major beim Stabe	–	non-flying officer for routines matters ("calming influence")
(Special Duties Officer)		
I a	–	operations officer
I c	–	enemy intelligence (e.g. enemy aircraft types, weapons, strengths etc.), but no intelligence gathering or espionage responsibilities
II a	–	adjutant, matters relating to officers
II b	–	adjutant, matters relating to NCOs and enlisted men
I N/NVW	–	navigation and signals
I TO	–	technical officer (aircrew)
IV a	–	official responsible for administration of the *Gruppe* (responsible for rations, administration, merchandise)
IV b	–	medical officer
LnO	–	air signals officer (signal communications)

(This list makes no claim to completeness due to the lack of relevant documents.)

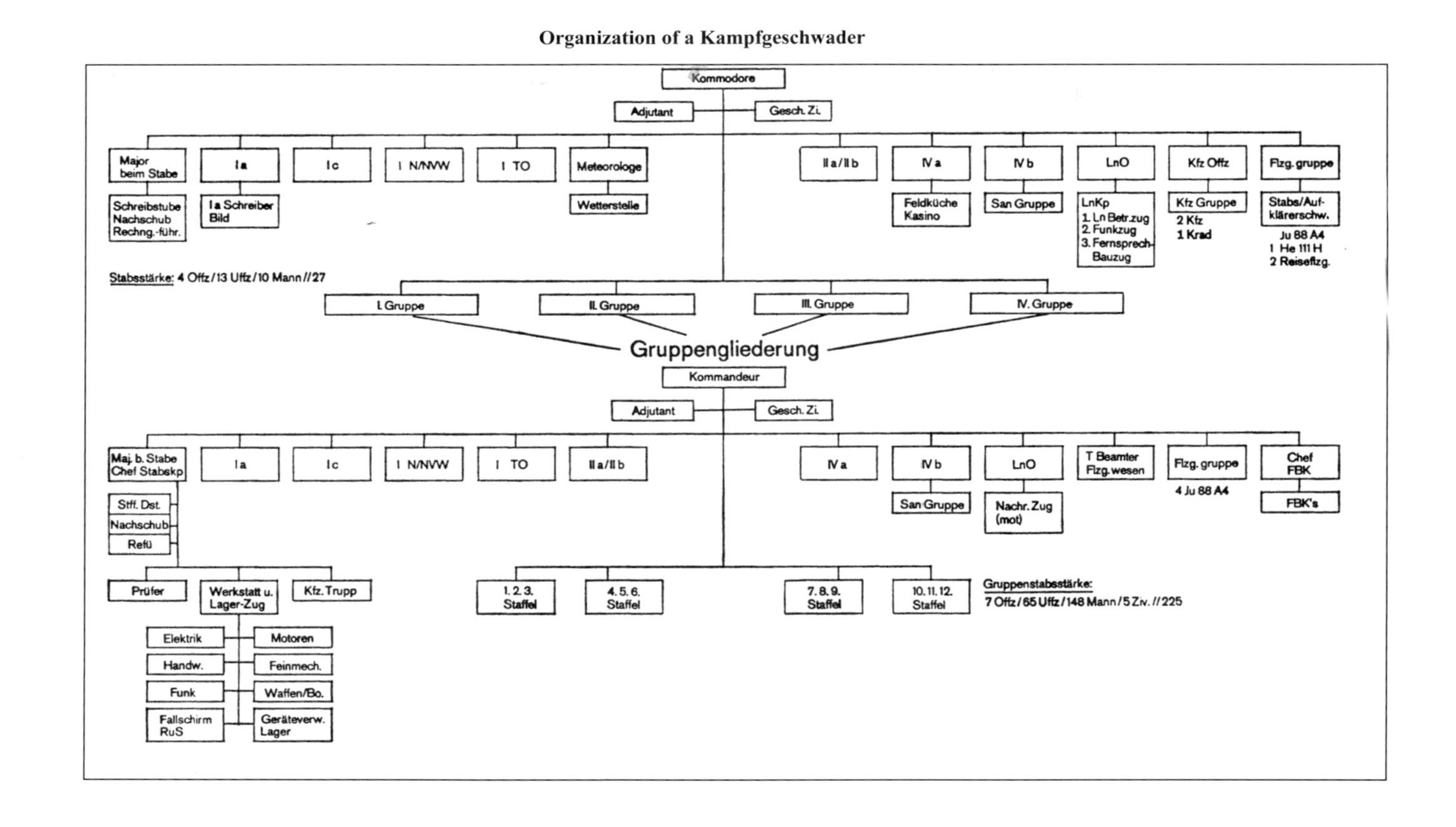
Organization of a Kampfgeschwader
Kommodore
Adjutant
Gesch. Zi.
Major beim Stabe
Schreibstube Nachschub Rechng.-führ.
I a
I a Schreiber Bild
I c
I N/NVW
I TO
Meteorologe
Wetterstelle
II a/II b
IV a
Feldküche Kasino
IV b
San Gruppe
LnO
LnKp 1. Ln Betr.zug 2. Funkzug 3. Fernsprech-Bauzug
Kfz Offz
Kfz Gruppe 2 Kfz 1 Krad
Flzg. gruppe
Stabs/Aufklärerschw.
Ju 88 A4
1 He 111 H
2 Reiseflzg.
Stabsstärke: 4 Offz/13 Uffz/10 Mann//27
I. Gruppe
II. Gruppe
III. Gruppe
IV. Gruppe
Gruppengliederung
Kommandeur
Adjutant
Gesch. Zi.
Maj. b. Stabe Chef Stabskp
Stff. Dst.
Nachschub
Refü
Prüfer
Werkstatt u. Lager-Zug
Kfz. Trupp
Elektrik
Motoren
Handw.
Feinmech.
Funk
Waffen/Bo.
Fallschirm RuS
Geräteverw. Lager
I a
I c
I N/NVW
I TO
II a/II b
1. 2. 3. Staffel
4. 5. 6. Staffel
7. 8. 9. Staffel
10. 11. 12. Staffel
IV a
IV b
San Gruppe
LnO
Nachr. Zug (mot)
T Beamter Flzg. wesen
Flzg. gruppe
4 Ju 88 A4
Chef FBK
FBK's
Gruppenstabsstärke: 7 Offz/65 Uffz/148 Mann/5 Ziv.//225

Staffel Organization

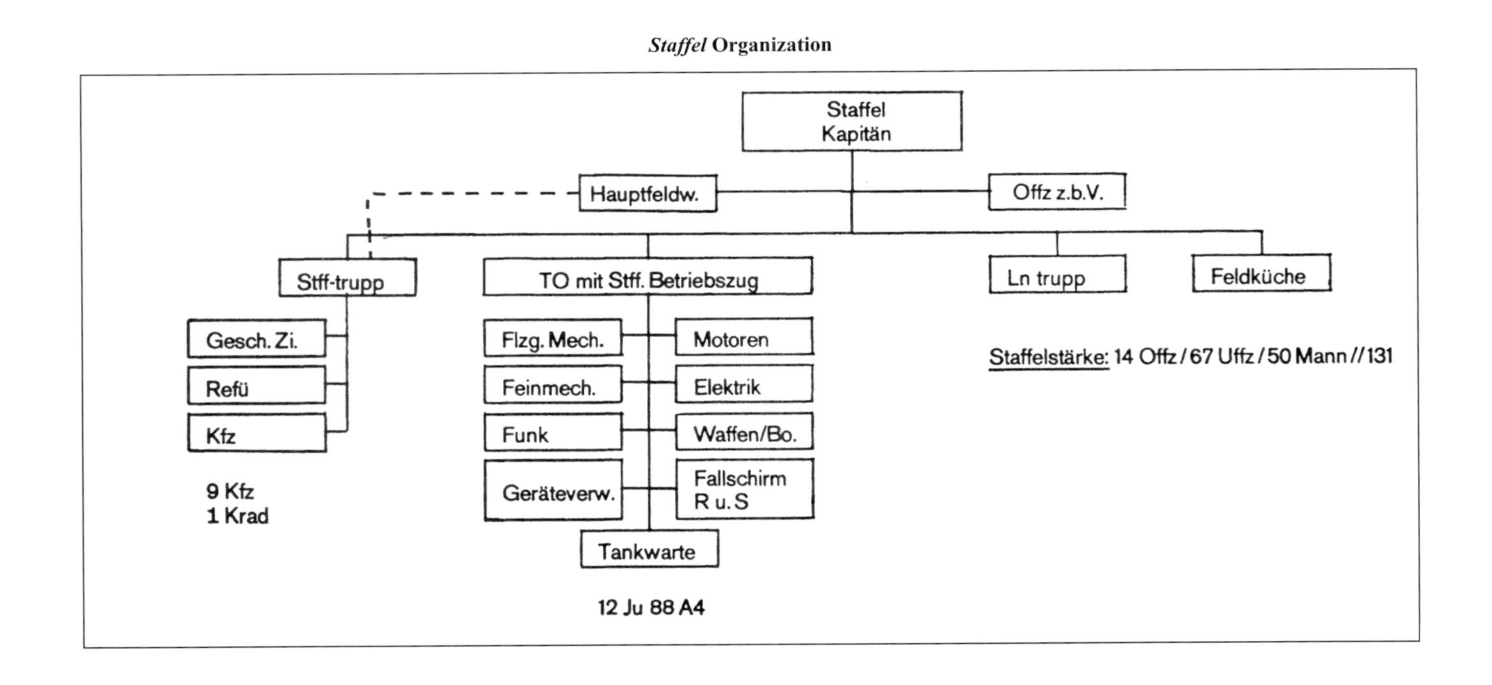

Appendix 6

The Airfield Operating Company

The airfield operating companies ensured that the *Kampfgruppen* and *Kampfstaffeln* got into the air and into action. They were formed in 1938 from the personnel of the old airbase and headquarters companies and specialist personnel of the flying *Staffeln*, so that, as an entire body of technical specialists, they could achieve an optimum level of performance, providing functional and effective support for flight operations. The airfield operating companies of KG 51 did not always just support "their" unit or *Gruppe*, also providing technical support to fighter and *Zerstörer* units. Toward the end of 1938 these units were redesignated: the 1. FBK 51 became the 143. FBK (Qu.) and the 8. FBK 51 was renamed 112. FBK (Qu.). For the airfield operating companies, movements were the order of the day.

With a strength of 150 men, the airfield operating company was led by a company commander, usually an experienced technician and engineering officer. He was assisted by a capable *Hauptfeldwebel* ("Top") with a company headquarters squad of eight to ten men (orderly office, bookkeeper, cooks, fourier).

Three 30-man operating companies looked after the operational *Staffeln*. They consisted of:

> 1 platoon leader (*Oberwerkmeister*), 12 aircraft mechanics, 2 engine fitters, 1 precision mechanic (flight instruments), 6 bomb technicians, 2 radio technicians and 1 parachute technician (rescue and safety equipment).

A workshop platoon with specialist personnel capable of performing all small and medium repairs supported operations with:

> 1 platoon leader, 12 aircraft engine fitters, 4 aircraft metal workers, 2 aircraft painters, 1 aircraft upholsterer, 2 aircraft "carpenters" and a few other specialists.

These personnel received their military training from the aircrew training regiments. Aviation technical training was received at the technical schools.
The average age of the company members was between 20 and 26 years. All were reenlisted soldiers.
Among the units that earned "solid" reputations were:

> 1. FBK 51 at Landsberg   7. FBK 51 Memmingen
> 4. FBK 51 Leipheim   8. FBK 51 Memmingen
> 2. FBK 51, later 142. FBK (Qu., ultimately stationed in Rheine, Wahn and Hangelar.

Appendix 7
The Motorized Signals Company *Kampfgeschwader* 51 (LnKp(mot)/KG 51)

During peacetime, with the exception of the radio operators that formed part of the crews, signals communications were the responsibility of the airbase commanders' permanent radio stations. After war broke out, it became apparent that the *Kampfgeschwader* needed its own signals companies. As a result, motorized signals platoons were formed from radio stations in Saxony and southern Germany and these were then combined to form the Motorized Signals Company/KG 51. The company was responsible to the *Geschwaderkommodore* in every respect and only received technical directives from the air division or air corps signals officer. In contrast to the signals platoons attached to the flak artillery or parachute troops, after being incorporated into the flying unit, the Motorized signals platoons became part of the Luftwaffe signals corps and wore its brown service color. In addition to the headquarters signals platoon attached to the *Geschwaderstab*, the company consisted of three platoons that were attached to the *Gruppen* and were only subordinate to the *Gruppenkommandeur* in operational matters.

The company's table of organization envisaged that the headquarters signals platoon, in addition to the signals squad, would be responsible for maintaining signals communications between the *Geschwaderstab* and superior offices and the *Gruppen* by means of radio, beacon and radio direction finder squads. In KG 51, however, these navigation aids were in fact always assigned to the platoons attached to the *Gruppen* and fully incorporated there. Until at least 1943, however, unit strengths far surpassed what was authorized. In some cases the platoons were 120 men strong and had extensive signals equipment. Additional equipment was provided during operations against England from permanent bases, as were captured French, British and Russian vehicles.

Thanks to this abundance of equipment, the platoons were able to look after the signals requirements of the *Gruppen* at forward operational airfields. As a rule, however, during wartime the signals platoons were also capable of supporting airbase commanders at existing radio stations.

Because of the threat of interception, commands to the units were transmitted by telephone or telex whenever possible. In any event, the signals platoons maintained their own telephone exchanges for the *Gruppe*, where, depending on the duration of its stay at an airfield, there were numerous extensions to headquarters and the *Staffeln*. Sometimes it also made sense to have separate exchanges for the dispersals and quarters. In addition, depending on local conditions, direct lines to the meteorologist, direction finder or local flak units were also installed or activated.

In addition to telephone, there were also telex connections. As a rule, however, during the eastern campaign the signals company's teletype squad was only used to support the air base telex centers during mobile operations.

If these lines did not exist, were disrupted or overloaded, the units had to rely on ground radio communications. As a rule, a *Geschwader* net was maintained. Frequently, however, the *Gruppen* also formed part of the air corps or air fleet communications net.

Shortwave key communications were maintained with aircraft in the air. The ground station was a heavy shortwave transmitter, the well-proven FuG III or the more modern FuG X, which members of the signals platoon removed from crashed machines and installed in homemade panels as a ground station. At first these were only used to monitor radio communications within the flying units. The range was so good, however, that it was also possible to establish contact with the formation leaders, who could use this simple means to transmit initial success reports and other information to the command post.

The III. *Gruppe* also experimented with the use of the FuG XVI to provide "bomber control." In the summer of 1942, an experienced bomber observer—the *Gruppe* operations officer (*Oblt.* Fritsch)—and a Luftwaffe signals officer (*Lt.* Bömer)—leader of the 4th Platoon—were detached to the 23rd Panzer Division with a small radio squad to transmit requests for air support, reports on the status of the front, etc., to the unit in the air and, when possible, direct attacks. Unfortunately the *Gruppe* was not committed against frontline targets at that time, and this command and control capacity was not exploited.

The platoons' navigation aids were used to support and augment the systems at airbases and forward airfields.

The frequent moves by the units tested the operational will and inventiveness of the signals troops. The installations at the old airfields had to be maintained until the last aircraft was airborne, while at the new base dispersals and a command post had to be prepared for the arrival of the *Gruppen*. This was only possible because the signals platoons carried far more than their authorized signals equipment.

Success, however, depended on the signals platoon dispatching an adequate advance party with equipment by air. It was found that, in most cases, two of the first transport aircraft (Ju 52s) could be loaded with the telephone and radio operators. These two Junkers loads were sufficient to prepare the new command post for initial operations. The rest of the platoon followed in often boring overland marches over clogged, dusty but also frequently muddy or ice-covered roads or by rail.

The company commander was also the *Geschwader* signals officer. In the beginning, the *Gruppe* headquarters included radio and navigation officers who were aircrew. They were responsible for radio and navigation documents, supplying maps and instructing the radio operators. Later in the war, signals officers with radio and direction-finding training were only transferred to *Geschwader* signals companies, and consequently the *Gruppenkommandeure* frequently assigned this task to the signals platoon commander as a secondary responsibility. It was also not unusual for the signals officer, of the N.O. as he was usually called, to have to assist in other headquarters functions, such as standing in for the *Gruppe* operations officer in the command post.

As most crews were reluctant to fly operational sorties with an unfamiliar radio operator, most signals officers were able to fly few combat missions. Despite this, they always pushed to fly, and a number of officers of KG 51's motorized signals company failed to return from combat missions over France, England, the Balkans, the Mediterranean and Russia.

During operations on every war front, the *Geschwader* signals company and the signals platoons attached to the *Gruppen* became permanent parts of the units. Their tireless efforts in establishing and maintaining communications links in heat and bitter cold, in snow and mud, in operating in relief round the clock, sometimes under enemy fire, were acknowledged and appreciated by the command and aircrews, who knew that they could depend on their comrades with the brown service patches.

Extract from Luftwaffe Table of Organization No. 3383 (L) dated 01 June 1943:

1. *Strength allocations*

The table of organization (Lw) dated 01 June 1943 designates strengths as follows:

Gruppe Officer	2 officers	12 NCOs	14 men	6 vehicles	2 trailers	1 motorcycle
1st HQ Signals Platoon	1	25	87	25	–	3
2nd HQ Signals Platoon	1 16	46	14	1	1	
3rd HQ Signals Platoon	1 16	46	14	1	1	
4th HQ Signals Platoon	1 16	46	14	1	1	
Total strength without medical	6	85	239	73	5	7

2. *Establishments of the squads in the platoons*

Gruppe Officer	1 battery charging squad (motorized) 1 vehicle repair squad
1st Platoon (HQ Motorized Signals Platoon)	1 telephone exchange squad 2 teletype connection squads (motorized) 1 teletype connection squad (G) 3 telephone installation squads (FFK) (motorized) 1 light radio squad (shortwave/long wave) (motorized) 2 light beacon squads (motorized) 1 radio receiver squad (motorized) 1 DF navigation squad (long wave) (motorized)
2nd Platoon (Motorized Signals Platoon)	1 heavy radio squad (shortwave) (motorized) 1 light radio squad (shortwave) (motorized) 1 telephone exchange squad 1 light radio squad (long wave) (motorized) 1 field cable-laying squad (motorized) 1 radio blind landing calibration squad
3rd and 4th Platoons	as 2nd Platoon

Appendix 8
The Bomber Crew

... a flying team for better or for worse ...

The crew of a bomber aircraft consisted of a pilot ("coachman"), an observer ("Franz"), a radio operator, a gunner ("gunwoman"), and in some aircraft a flight engineer ("mixer").

In a division of work accepted in a spirit of unity, the pilot had to fly his aircraft day and night in icing conditions, fog and clouds, and master navigation and operation of the radio; the observer, with and without a view of the ground, had to guide his aircraft or the entire formation to the correct target and accurately drop the bombs; and the radio operator had to be able to maintain contact with other aircraft and the various ground radio and direction finding stations. Responsibility for the safety of the crew and the technical viability of the mission rested on the flight engineer, the gunner and the crew chief left behind on the ground. As well, everyone had to function as effective gunners, operating the various machine-guns and cannon in the aircraft.

The Luftwaffe soldier began his service with a half year of basic training at one of the aircrew replacement battalions. Successful completion of a non-commissioned officer's course was followed by promotion to the rank of *Unteroffizier*.

The officer and reserve officer candidates attended an officer's school.

The E flight training schools at the aircrew replacement training battalions provided basic and intermediate aircrew training and trained air gunners. Prospective pilots trained on single-engined aircraft at the A and B flight training schools and multiengine aircraft up to instrument flying at the C schools. Additional training followed at the armament schools – for example the bomber schools in Faßberg, Jüterbog, Lechfeld, Prenzlau and Tutow. Obtaining the Luftwaffe pilot rating or even the Luftwaffe advanced pilot rating was a condition for the transfer of every officer, non-commissioned officer or enlisted men to a flying unit.

The observer or assistant observer gave the pilot instructions for the bomb run, prepared the navigation documents, determined the flight heading, served as bomb aimer and was responsible for visually and photographically reconnoitering the target. Observer training took about six months.

The radio operator was trained and employed both as an important assistant to the pilot and observer/navigator and as a gunner. He was responsible for communicating with air traffic control, aircraft-to-aircraft and aircraft-to-ground radio communications, as well as radio navigation and direction finding. Training took approximately one whole year (air signals school, instrument flying school, air gunnery training).

Technical maintenance of the aircraft was the responsibility of the flight engineer, who was also supposed to possess a knowledge of terrestrial navigation. They were recruited from the ranks of the members of the aviation-technical personnel fit for flight duty and all received air gunnery training.

Not until combat and unit training at the bomber schools and in the *Geschwader*, with day and night navigation flights in all weathers combined with intensive bomb dropping and gunnery training flights at all altitudes, did the crews come together. All members of the crew had to work closely together get to know one another intimately in order to be able to carry out the tasks demanded of them.

The amount of time required for a bomber crew to achieve full operational status varied, and to a large extent it depended on the abilities and interactions of the individual crewmembers.

Appendix 9
"About the Bomber Pilot"
by Werner Baumbach

"The bomber pilot had a different approach than the fighter pilot. The nature of his missions over great distances in the enemy rear, over water, in bad weather and at night, the closed attack in formation, even the characteristics of the slower bomber aircraft, all these things characterized the face of the bomber pilot, who appeared outwardly calmer and steadier ("stolid" in fighter pilot parlance). As the war went on, greater flexibility was demanded of bomber pilots in handling their aircraft, especially in attack and defense.

The fighter pilot came to know our hardships during close-support aircraft and long-range missions. Thus, towards the end of the war, more and more there developed a single type of combat pilot. However, a good fighter pilot rarely made a good bomber pilot, and vice versa. The bomber pilot always had to be on the go, to avoid being shot down. Constantly seeking help and ways to avoid danger, he could not forget his actual objective, to put his bombs on the target. The dichotomy between fighters and bombers, to which the Stukas also belonged, was bridged by an unspoken comradeship that proved itself.

In contrast to the fighter arm, the bomber arm did not present a unified picture in the first years of the war. Until 1941, most *Kampfgeschwader* flew few missions that broke new ground compared to those they had flown in training. The He 111 and Do 217 bombers usually bombed while in level flight, in formation during daylight and individually at night. This type of mission encouraged senior staff officers, even generals, to complete their "Knight's Cross course." In fact, a younger *Oberleutnant* or *Hauptmann* frequently took command of the airborne *Geschwader* after takeoff. Of course there were exceptions.

One can rightly claim that the bomber arm achieved its initial successes in the Blitz campaigns without operational or strategic command. In the tactical sphere, lieutenants and captains led as aircraft commanders and *Staffelkapitäne*. Their mentality, their lifestyle, their military forms, their youthful way of expressing themselves, and their personal drive, which inspired others, was in such stark contrast to the military tone, the heel clicking, the drill of the reactivated and "ironed" veterans who commanded them that, as the war went on, the bomber arm was divided into two by an unbridgeable gulf. Standing in the camp of the young were the "Staff Majors." They were World War veterans who even in peacetime had remained true to flying out of idealism and had kept a youthful heart. What would we have been without them, these men who, as reserve officers, served the flying units as "maids of all work."

Technology eagerly helped deepen the chasm between the generations. In the Ju 88 the pilot was the aircraft commander. He led as pilot and tactician. In a dive-bombing attack he dropped the bombs himself. The role of the observer was limited to the functions of bomb aimer for horizontal attacks and assistant navigator. Unbelievably high demands were placed on the aircraft commanders, however this created among us similar conditions to those faced by the fighter pilots. As well, space in the Ju 88 was so limited that it was impossible to carry any additional crewmembers, or "sandbags," as was possible in the He 111 or Do 217. The time of the older *Geschwaderkommodore* appeared to have arrived.

As well, representatives of the younger generation of prewar staff officers, who embodied the ideal type of flying commander, were transferred to the front. Unfortunately there were too few of them – and they soon taken away by flyer's fate. Among them – to name but two – were the *Kommodore* of the first Ju 88 *Geschwader*, *Oberstleutnant* Loebel, and his *Gruppenkommandeur Major* Dönch. They typified the new face of the German bomber arm. They led with their heads and by personal example. A new soldierly style and a strong, sincere comradeship enabled the *Geschwader* to achieve outstanding results. A tête-à-tête among the leading airmen soon developed there.

Additional *Geschwader* were equipped with the Ju 88 as the year went on, but in some cases the "old ones" held on grimly. Their greatest supporter was a personally very honorable, but excessively formal and senile general who, as head of the personnel office, was to the new Luftwaffe as Methuselah was to Cleopatra. Suggestions for rejuvenation won us no bouquets there. I decided there and then to turn to the head of the general staff, who at forty years of age had retained his youthful heart and always favored youth. He presented my views to Göring.

The direct result of this intervention, which coincided with a similar report by Hauptmann Peltz, was the formation of a unit leader's school for bomber pilots, command of which was given to Peltz, one of the most capable junior bomber pilots. Göring gave Peltz unprecedented authority. In future, no one could become commander of a bomber unit without having successfully attended this school. Even the "old ones" had to undergo a review there. The chaff was soon separated from the wheat. These courses soon became the reservoir of a young leadership class, but also a strong opposition to anything that was not the front: against the Luftwaffe operations staff, against the staffs of the air fleets, against the State Aviation Ministry (RLM), against the "party bigwigs." But they remained loyal to their Führer and their Commander-in-Chief. Göring, who had done everything for his airmen in the good times, and whose human side often demonstrated a captivating comradeship, solicitude and generosity, could also have found his staunchest support among this circle of young combat officers.

With the rejuvenation cure of the fighters and bombers at the front, there also came a reorganization in the inspectorates of fighters and bombers. After Mölders' death in a crash, Galland became Inspector of Fighters. Together with Peltz, at the end of 1942 I was transferred from the Mediterranean to Berlin as the Inspector of Bombers. Our responsibilities now also extended to training, the tactical and technical evaluation of frontline experiences, technical requirements and the staffing of command positions. As well, the commander-in-chief had given us a certain right of veto over the general staff.

But the deep differences between the front and command could not be settled. The difference in their activity in war is probably always so great that only the highest human and professional qualities are capable of building a lasting bridge. As the war went on, with the constant expansion of the areas of operations and the growing enemy superiority, the demands made of the units at the front became ever harder. Only through superior command and the teamwork of every crew was it possible to conduct a successful mission. The "star performance" became increasingly rare in the bomber arm. And who wanted to ascertain which crew had bombed most accurately during a night attack in bad weather? The overall performance of the unit was most important. Success depended on a determined and functional command.

So the concepts and ideas of the First World War had changed completely. Back then, for example, the combat aircraft had been the fighter, now it was the bomber. This change was not entirely meaningless, such as a changed technical definition. Instead it characterized the basic change in focus of the air war. In 1914-1918 the fighter pilots had borne the brunt of the war in the air and were therefore called combat pilots, but now they had been forced to relinquish their role with its associated name to the bombers. The bomber arm was simply to be the backbone of aerial warfare. Influenced by the theories of Douhet and Rougerons, the German command paid homage to this concept during the building of the Luftwaffe and the war. Designers and technicians created the German combat aircraft in these terms and were convinced that they were almost invulnerable, indeed that they were superior to all foreign fighter aircraft. From the very outset, however, the front had to experience the exact opposite of this concept. Nevertheless, the command and the majority of the technical officials clung to their beliefs and thought that the war could be won with these once proven bombers."

Appendix 10
Aircraft Types and Performances

Kampfgeschwader 51 "Edelweiss" holds a special place in the history of the German air force with respect to the aircraft it operated.

It began the war with the most modern, fastest bomber of its day, the Dornier Do 17, and its developments, and ended the war flying the epoch-making Messerschmitt Me 262, a turbojet powered fighter and bomber.

The following brief overview will illustrate to the reader what aircraft in many variations were flown by KG 51 from the time of its establishment in Merseburg.

To be found in the *Geschwader*'s aircraft park were training, communications and bomber aircraft, which are presented in the order in which they were employed or entered service.

The silhouettes are supplemented by photographs in the preceding chapters taken during the *Geschwader*'s development phase and during the war.

The complete "Type Sheet of the Technical Office of the State Ministry of Aviation for the Aircraft Types Junkers Ju 52" and extracts from that for the "Do 11A" from the years 1933 and 1935 may serve as an example of the detailed information available to the *Geschwader* and command about aircraft types and introduce the survey of types with some development dates and key information.

Bomber Aircraft

Junkers Ju 52

The first aircraft of the Ju 52 series were powered by just a single engine (Ju 51/1m) and was nothing more than a larger version of the Junkers W 33, which Hermann Köhl made famous in his east-west crossing of the Atlantic. Like the W 33, the Ju 52 employed Junkers' typical corrugated metal construction.

Dipl.-Ing. Ernst Zindel, the father of this world-famous creation, redesigned the Ju 52 for three engines, and with it *Flugkapitän* Willi Polte won the transport aircraft competition in the International Alpine Air Meet in 1932, capturing the Chavez-Bider Cup. For decades the "old auntie Ju" was the symbol of absolute safety and reliability; the type was flown by 30 airlines in 25 countries and is still flying today—although most of these are French copies.

During the war the *Luftwaffe* employed the Ju 52 mainly as a transport aircraft. In the *Reichswehr* days, German mobilization plans included a modified version of the Junkers airliner as a long-range "makeshift bomber."

The type sheet provided the working basis for all required technical modifications and installations (including conversion of the passenger compartment for the carriage of bombs, installation of an open dorsal gun position with MG 15 on the fuselage spine, and the installation of a ventral position—a retractable "dustbin" turret accommodating another MG 15).

KG 153 operated the Ju 52/3mg3 before the arrival of the Dornier Do 11A/13/23, after which it was used primarily for crew training.

Type Sheet of the Technical Office of the State Ministry of Aviation for the Aircraft Type Junkers Ju 52

1933
Secret Command Matter!
L.C.
B.B.Nr. 2763/33 0 1 Secret Command Matter

Interim Type Sheet for the Aircraft Type Ju 52

1. Purpose:	Interim bomber (land)
2. Crew:	1 pilot 1 commander (observer) also bomb aimer and ventral gunner 1 radio operator 1 fuselage gunner

3. Power Plants: Engine type: BMW-Hornet A (525 hp)
or S 3 D 1 (650 hp)
Number of engines: 3
Tank capacities: Fuel 2500 l | for flight of
Lubricants 200 l | 1,500 km

4. Armament: In the fuselage:
1 flexibly-mounted MG 15 in Type 30 ring mount with
13 double drums for a total of 975 rounds of ammunition
In the ventral turret:
1 flexibly-mounted MG 15 in a Junkers ring mount with
10 double drums for a total of 750 rounds

5. Bomb Equipment: Bomb-dropping mechanism for:
a) 6 C-250-kg bombs in double vertical cells in the cockpit
b) 24 C-50-kg bombs in the same device as a), but with 4 C 50 shaft plates
c) 96 C-10-kg bombs in the same device and shaft plates as b),
but with 4 C 10 harness
d) 864 1-kg El incendiary bombs in the device and shaft plates as b), but with 36 EL 1 bomb dispensers
Bomb loads:

a) for 1,500 km flight distance	450 kg
b) for 1,200 km flight distance	900 kg
c) for 1,000 km flight distance	1,200 kg
d) for 750 flight distance	1,500 kg (max. load)

Mixed loads:
in each desired load, quantity and caliber
limited by a)-d)
Bomb sight: Goerz Fl 219 b

6. Gross Weight: 9,200 kg

7. Performance
(only partially verified):
Maximum speed at low level:
230 kph with Hornet A
250 kph with Hornet S 3 D 1
Service ceiling: 4.2 km with Hornet A
5.2 km/h with Hornet S 3 D 1
Time to climb from 0 to 3 km:
20 minutes with Hornet A
18 min. with Hornet S 3 D 1
Maximum flight distances:
1,500 km (at altitude of 3-4 km including climb and descent)
Takeoff distance to height of 20 meters: 600 m
Landing distance from 20 meters to complete stop (braked): 600 m
Landing speed:
(at touchdown) approx. 100 kph

Dornier 11A

The Do 11 was a product of the secret Reichswehr armaments program of 1929-1933 and was derived from the Dornier Do F, which was built in Japan and Switzerland in 1925.

There are plenty of "airmen's tales" about its manually retracted undercarriage. If the aircraft's speed was too great (!!), it was impossible to extend or lower and lock the undercarriage against the slipstream using the large, bulky crank wheel. For this reason the undercarriage was later fixed and provided with fairings.

The Do 13 offered a slight improvement in performance, with two 750-hp BMW-VI engines, reduced wingspan with large ailerons and landing flaps, which resulted in better landing characteristics.

The second version of the Do 13 was given the designation Do 23 and was equipped with revolving machine-gun mounts, stabilizing fins on the vertical tail, BMW-V-I engines, fixed-pitch four-blade wooden propellers and increased fuel and oil capacities (1860 l/152 l).

Several hundred Dornier Do 23s were built for the *Luftwaffe* between 1934 and 1935. Later, during the war, they were employed as "minesweepers" with an electrically charged mine ring beneath the wings.

KG 153 struggled – in comparison to the types that followed – through training with these "flying coffins" in Saxony and Thuringia.

– extracts –

Type Sheet of the Technical Office of the State Ministry of Aviation for the Aircraft Type Do 11 A, 1935

L.C. — 100 copies
B.B. Nr. 1850/350 1 Secret Command Matter — 36th copy
Type Sheet for the Aircraft Type Do 11 A

1. Purpose: Night bomber (land-based)
2. Designation: Do 11 A
3. Crew: 1 pilot
   1 commander (observer), also bomb aimer and cockpit gunner
   1 fuselage gunner (2nd pilot)
   1 radio operator, also fuselage gunner

5. Dimensions:
   Aircraft length: 18.5 m
   Aircraft height: 4.3 m
   Wingspan: 28.0 m

6. Power Plants:
   Engine type: Siemens Jupiter VI and 6.3 Z air-cooled radial engine Maximum output approx. 600 hp
   Number of engines: 2
   Propellers: four-blade
   Starter: compressed air starter with external Connection
   Tank contents: 2 fuel tanks each with a capacity of 770 l = 1,540 l = 1,230 kg
   2 oil tanks each with a capacity of 73 l = 146 l = 240 kg

7. d) Radio Equipment:
   Type C aircraft radio with transmitter and receiver for key traffic, range 600 km, wave band 500-950 m, trailing antenna, direction finder for position determination
   Wind-powered generator 73 kg

7. g) Armament: In the cockpit:
   1 flexibly-mounted MG 15 in Type 30 rotating mount with 10 double drums for a total of 750 rounds
   In the fuselage:
   1 MG 15 in a ventral position with 7 double drums for a total of 525 rounds 172 kg

7. h) Bomb Equipment: Bomb dropping mechanism for:
   a) 5 250-kg bombs on individual racks beneath the fuselage
   b) 30 50-kg bombs in 6 vertical cells in the fuselage
   c) 120 10-kg bombs in the same vertical cells as b), but with special mounting harness
   d) 1,080 1-kg El incendiary bombs in the same vertical cells as in b), but with bomb dispensers
   Normal load: 1,000 kg for maximum range (1100 km)
   1,500 kg for range of 690 km,
   in each selected mixture

Bomb Sight:	Goerz Fl. 219 b	215 kg
Weight breakdown:		
Empty weight (aircraft, power plants, fixed equipment):		4,660 kg
Gross weight:		8,000 kg
Service ceiling:		3.65 km

Range:
1,200 km (at altitude of 3.65 km including climb and descent).
This is equivalent to a total flying time of about 6 hours (maximum speed in level flight at combat altitude 212 kph)

Takeoff and landing:	
Takeoff distance:	280 m
to height of 20 m:	590 m
Landing distance:	240 m (braked)
from height to 20 m to complete stop:	610 m (braked)
Approx. landing speed: (at touchdown)	100 kph

Dornier Do 17
The Dornier Do 17 can trace its origins to an order by Deutsche Lufthansa for a high-speed mail and passenger aircraft in late 1933. The first prototypes flew in 1934, powered by BMW-VI engines. Because the fuselage was too cramped and uncomfortable for non-athletic passengers, DLH understandably rejected the aircraft. Thanks to the urging of *Flugkapitän* Untucht and advocates of the Rougeron concept of the fast, unarmed bomber, Dornier built the Do 17 V9, a prototype of a military version, in response to a contract from the RLM. It had twin fins and rudders for an improved field of fire to the rear. The design was a success, and in July 1937 the Do 17 M V1 proved faster than the participating production fighters in the Alpine Circuit for Military Aircraft at the 4th International Air Meet in Dubendorf near Zurich. The addition of heavy weapons installations turned the intended "high-speed bomber" into a normal medium bomber. By 1940 Dornier would deliver 500 examples in various versions to the *Luftwaffe* (475 bombers, 16 reconnaissance aircraft and 9 night-fighters).

Because of its slender, streamlined fuselage, in flying circles the promising bomber aircraft was dubbed the "flying pencil."

KG 255, the "Alpine *Geschwader*," was the first unit of the *Luftwaffe* to be equipped with this aircraft and until 8 August 1939 flew the Do 17E (later M-1). The unit flew its first missions over Sudetenland and Austria with the type.

A subsequent development was the improved and refined Do 217, which was built in several versions.

The hydraulically operated undercarriage and landing flaps of the Do 17E-1 were replaced with electrical systems in the M-1.

Other differences:

E-1	*M-1*
2x750-hp BMW-VI 12-cyl.	2x840-hp Bramo Fafnir 323 A 19-cyl.
liquid-cooled V engines	air-cooled radial engines with supercharger
fixed-pitch three-blade wooden propellers	VDM variable-pitch propellers
open dorsal gun position	enclosed dorsal gun position
maximum bomb load of 500 kg	
maximum bomb load of 1000 kg	
	Siemens K 4 ü autopilot
	Lotfe C 7 bomb sight

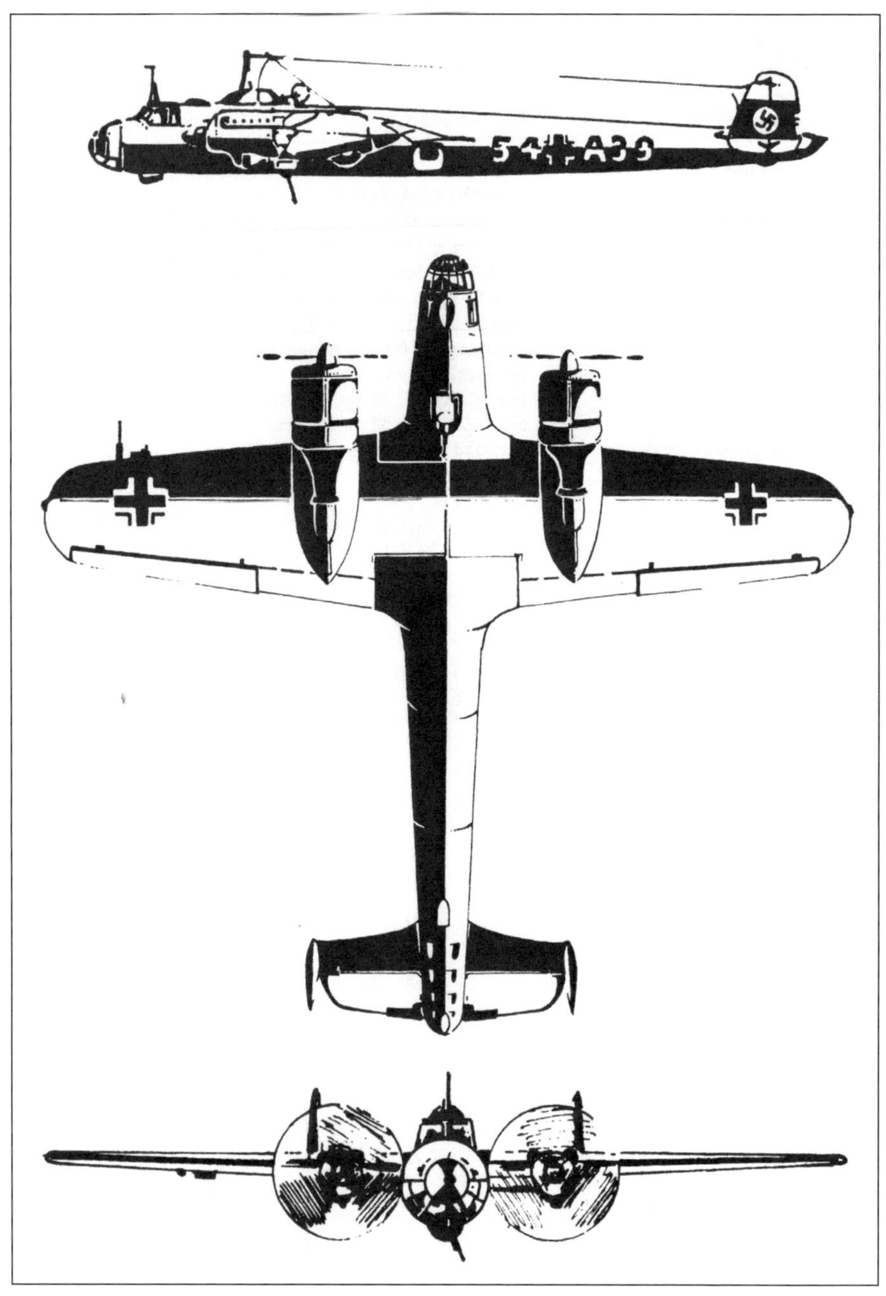

Do 17

Do 17		
Wingspan:	18 m	
Length:	16.24 m	
Height:	4.59 m	
Takeoff weight:	E-1	8,840 kg
	M-1	10,000 kg
Crew:	3 (pilot, radio operator/observer, bomb aimer)	
Armament:	1 x 7.9-mm MG 15, semi-rigid mount in windscreen 1 x 7.9-mm MG 15 in dorsal position, in some cases 1 x 7.9-mm MG 15 in fuselage nose	
Bomb load:	10 x 50-kg in two magazines 5 x 50-kg or 1 x 250-kg or 20 x 50 kg Elvemag C 10 for low-level attacks with 10-kg fragmentation bombs	
Range:	E-1: 1,590 km; M-1: 2830 km	
Service ceiling:	E-1: 5,500 m; M-1: 6,900 m	
Maximum speed:	E-1: 354 kph; M-1 484 kph	

Heinkel He 111

Once again it was DLH which, in 1934, issued a development contract for a high-speed airliner that would become the *Luftwaffe*'s standard horizontal bomber.

In the He 111, Heinkel created a true successor to the He 70 Blitz with its streamlined teardrop fuselage and characteristic elliptically shaped wing and horizontal tail.

The first He 111 a (V1) made its maiden flight on 24 February 1935. The V3 was a bomber version powered by BMW-VI engines, however the proving center at Rechlin found it to be underpowered.

It was not until the advent of the Jumo 211 F twelve-cylinder liquid-cooled engine producing 1,340 hp and the Junkers metal variable-pitch propeller that the Heinkel bomber achieved its desired performance. Later versions were simplified for mass production and the elliptical wing was replaced. The four new self-sealing tanks made it less vulnerable to enemy fire.

The He 111 remained in production until 1944 and 5,656 examples of the various versions were completed. These included torpedo bombers, glide bomb carriers (Hs 293, V 1), balloon cable cutters, long-range bomber versions and last but not least the He 111Z series. The latter was created by joining two He 111H-6s by means of a wing center section with three engines. The result was a powerful, long-range glider tug capable of towing up to three gliders.

The aircraft was popular with its crews because it handled well, was easy to fly and was solidly equipped.

The "Edelweiss" *Geschwader* flew the He 111H-6 from 6 August 1939 until early 1941 in missions against France and England.

He 111H-6

Wingspan:	22.6 m
Length:	16.6 m
Height:	4.18 m
Takeoff weight:	14,200 kg
Crew:	5 (pilot left, observer right on folding seat, bomb aimer/nose gunner prone in nose, radio operator/gunner in dorsal position, gunner in ventral position)
Armament:	1 x 20-mm MG FF in cupola position 1 x 7.9-mm MG 15 in dorsal position, 2 x 7.9-mm MG 15 in ventral position one machine-gun in lens mount fore and aft in ventral gondola

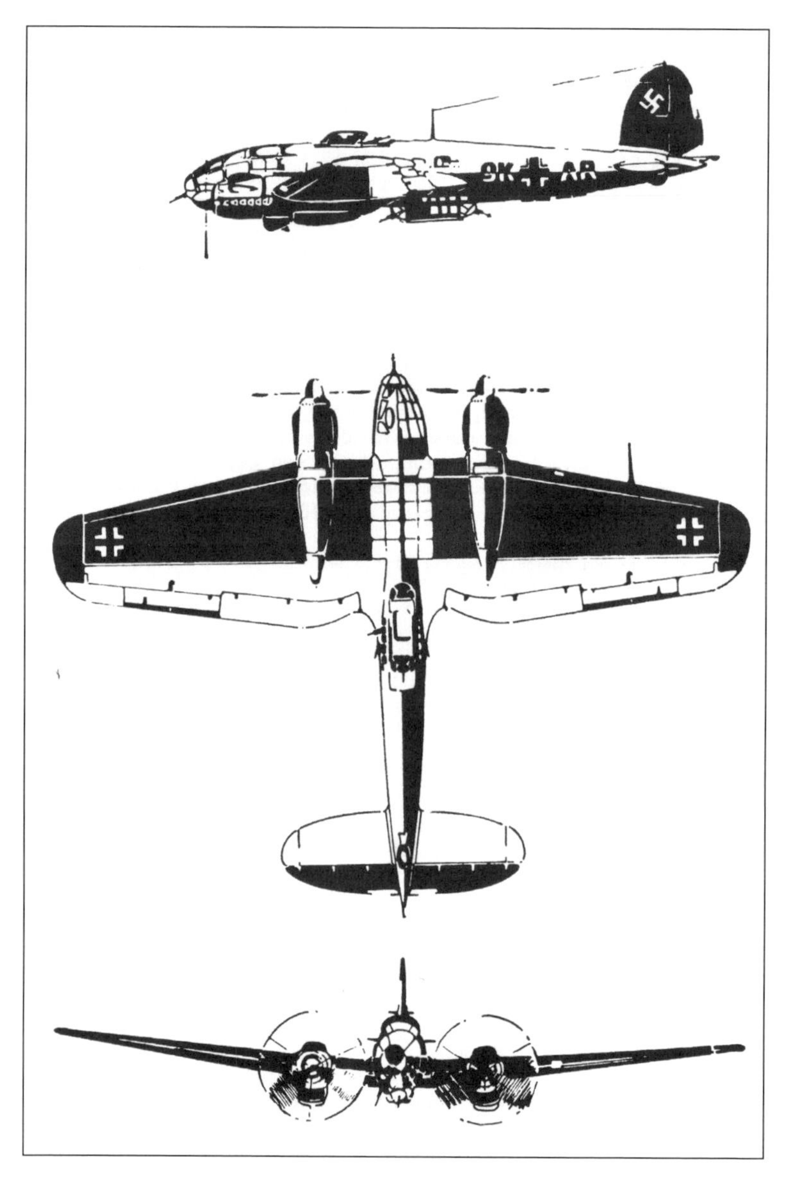

He 111

Bomb load:	8 x 250-kg internal load 2 external racks for 1 x 1,000-kg and 1 x 500-kg or 1 x 1,400 kg and 1 x 1,000-kg or 1 x 1,800 kg or 1 x 2,000 kg
Range:	2,800 km (1,250 km with max bomb load of 2,000 kg)
Service ceiling:	7,800 m
Maximum speed:	415 kph at altitude of 5200 m

Junkers Ju 88

When, on 15 January 1936, the Junkers works in Dessau began design work on a new twin-engined high-speed bomber, the type was given the RLM designation Ju 88. The magical Ju 88 became synonymous with the bomber aircraft in Germany, just as the Flying Fortress was in the USA or the Sturmovik in Russia.

Work proceeded quickly, and the Ju 88 V1 was ready for its maiden flight by 21 December 1936. The Ju 88 V2, with the already typical annular radiators, followed on 10 April 1937 and achieved speeds in excess of 500 kph. It is not surprising, therefore, that in 1939 a specially prepared aircraft broke two FAI speed records with payload (517.004 kph with 1,000 kg over 2,000 km on 19 March, and 500.786 kph with 2,000 kg over 2,000 km on 30 June).

Unfortunately the *Luftwaffe* clung to the requirement for dive-bombing capability. The aircraft's structure was beefed up, it became heavier and performance suffered.

The Ju 88 was an excellent medium bomber and proved to be a workhorse as a tactical combat aircraft on every front, but it was no strategic bomber.

Altogether 15,000 examples of this versatile machine were built (including 9,122 bomber versions) in a bewildering number of variants, including night-fighters, reconnaissance aircraft and close-support aircraft. The *Geschwader* flew mainly the A-series. The aircraft demanded capable and often cool-headed crews, who remained faithful to their "Ju" on account of its whims and idiosyncrasies and today still speak of it with pride and respect.

The first major production variant was the Ju 88 A-5 powered by two Jumo 211 B/G twelve cylinder engines each producing 1,200 hp at 2,600 rpm. Its wingspan of 20.08 meters was greater than that of its predecessor the A-1 (18.38 meters). It had the familiar hydraulically-operated single-leg undercarriage, which rotated through 90 degrees when it retracted, three-blade VDM metal variable-pitch propellers, four ETC bomb racks beneath the wing center section in place of the forward bomb cells, the proven self-sealing fuel tanks and an automatic pull-out device which used Flettner tabs.

The A-3 was a training aircraft with dual controls and instrumentation.

II./KG 51 was reformed on 1 April 1940 with the Ju 88 A-1, while I./KG 51 converted onto the type in Greifswald and Lechfeld from 9 April to 10 May 1940. III./KG 51 did not reequip until after the campaign in France, training on the new type in Regensburg in June 1940. 7. (Eis.)/KG 51 received the Ju 88 C-6 while resting and reequipping in Krosno from 7 June to 19 July 1943.

The *Geschwader* operated the Ju 88 in the French, Balkan, Greek and Russian campaigns and in the Battle of Britain. The A-4 series, which followed the A-5, had a considerably improved performance.

Ju 88 A-4

Power Plants:	2 x 1,340 – 1,420 hp Jumo 211 F/J engines
Propellers:	VS 11 three-blade (wood) variable-pitch propellers
Wingspan:	20.08 m
Length:	14.36 m
Height:	4.85 m
Takeoff weight:	up to 13,590 kg, with RATO 17,600 kg
Crew:	4 (pilot, observer/bomb aimer, radio operator, gunner in ventral bath)
Armament:	1 x 7.9-mm MG 81 in windscreen for pilot or observer 1 x 13-mm MG 131 in nose for the observer, 2 x 7.9-mm MG 81 in lens mounts in rear cockpit glazing as dorsal position for the radio operator,

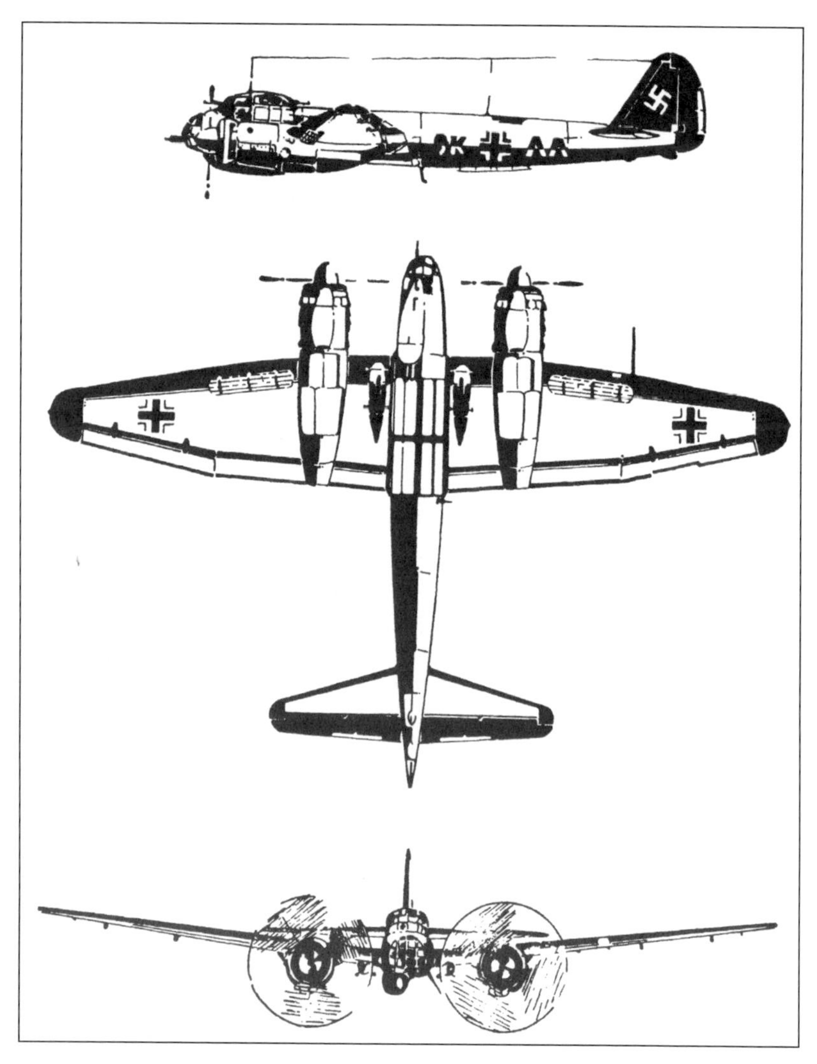

Ju 88

	1 x MG 81 Z (2 x 7.9-mm) in the gondola (Bola 39 or Bola 81 Z) as ventral position
Bomb load:	max. bomb load 3,600 kg; ETC on center section 2 x 1,000-kg or 4 x 500-kg or 2 x 1,000-kg and 2 x 250/500-kg, plus 10 x 50 kg in fuselage bomb bay. Normal load from grass runway: 1,000 kg; takeoff from paved runway: 1,400 kg

The first Jumo 211 J engines were delivered without the large supercharger air cooler. Externally, the A-4 differed from the earlier A-5 only in its massive-looking wooden propellers and the fairings for the supercharger air coolers beneath the engine nacelles.

Dive brakes and the automatic pull out device were not installed in most A-4s, as operational tactics changed as the war progressed.

Range:	2,730 km (1,400 km with max bomb load)
Service ceiling:	max. 8,500 m (without bombs), loaded 6,000 m
Maximum speed:	472 kph at altitude of 5,300 m (560 kph in a dive)

Messerschmitt Me 410 Hornisse

The Geschwader flew this type, which was derived from the unsuccessful Me 210, for just under a year.

In autumn 1942 Messerschmitt rebuilt Me 210 A-0 machines coming back from the units, creating the "new" Me 410 by extending the fuselage, redesigning the outer wings and installing DB 603 A (later G) liquid-cooled engines each producing 1,740 hp with VDM variable-pitch propellers. The A-1 (high-speed bomber and fighter-bomber) and A-2 (heavy fighter and night-fighter) series entered production before the year ended.

In none of these roles did the Me 410 meet the expectations and requirements of the operational units. The men of KG 51 and ZG 26 were enthusiastic about the type's speed and climb rate, but they could not understand the areas of operations assigned by the OKL – high-speed bomber on the Western Front, heavy fighter on the Eastern Front. Operations were further hampered by troublesome armament packages – there were rumors of sabotage.

1,013 examples of this aircraft were delivered from 1943 to 1944, of which 900 were bombers of heavy fighters.

Some aircraft were fitted with the BK 5 heavy cannon, but this armament never lived up to expectations.

The *Geschwader* converted onto the Me 410 in Illesheim by the end of 1943 and flew missions in the Defense of the Reich as well as over England. It achieved little at a time when the only thing that mattered was victories and destroying enemy capacity.

The Me 410 was no more than an interlude in the grim events of wartime, its sting was not fatal! The Me 262 caused it to soon be forgotten.

Me 410B-1 *(high-speed bomber)*

Wingspan:	16.36 m; length: 12.48 m; height: 4.28 m. Takeoff weight: 11,237 kg
Crew:	2 (pilot sitting back-to-back with observer/radio operator)
Armament:	2 x 20-mm MG 151/20 (250 rounds per gun) 2 x 7.9-mm MG 17 (1,000 rounds per gun) in fixed mounts in fuselage nose and 2 x 7.9-mm MG 131 (500 rounds per gun) in two remotely-controlled barbettes (FDL 131) in the fuselage sides operated by the observer. Launching tubes for 210-mm Nebelwerfer rockets could be carried beneath the wings.
Bomb Load:	Up to 1,000 kg in forward fuselage beneath cockpit (8 x 50-kg or 2 x 250-kg or 1 x 500-kg or 1 x 1,000-kg Special), plus 4 x 50 kg on external bomb racks.
Range:	1,500 km
Service Ceiling:	9,500 m
Maximum Speed:	606 kph at altitude of 6,000 m (582 kph with max. bomb load)

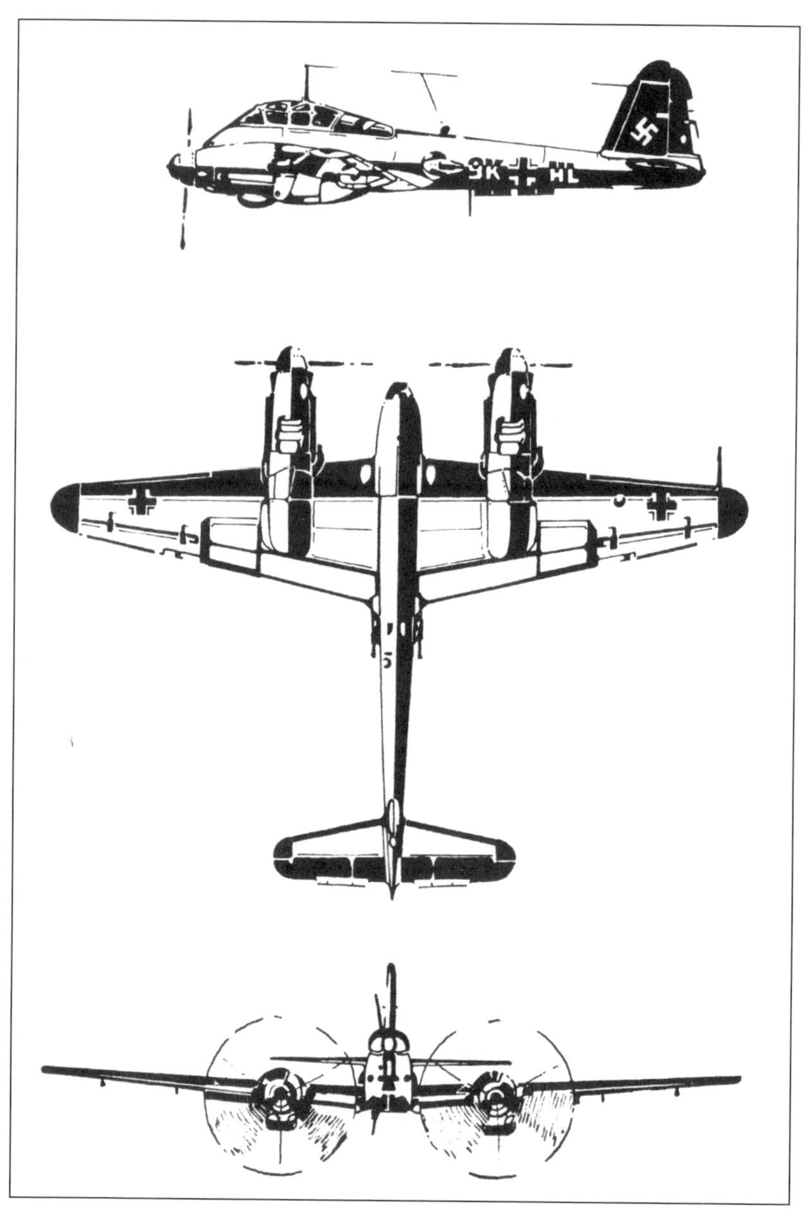

Me 410

Messerschmitt Me 262
"Too late" – surely an apt expression in describing the sometimes tortured development history of the epoch-making Me 262, the first effective jet aircraft in the world.

On 26 November 1943, during a demonstration at Insterburg, Hitler asked Professor Messerschmitt the fateful question, whether the Me 262, originally conceived as a fighter aircraft – with two Jumo 004 B-1 turbojets each producing 900 kg of thrust – could be equipped to carry bombs. The naïve affirmative to the question led Hitler to declare: "At last this is the *Blitzbomber*!" With this, any further discussion about a different context and incorrect use of the aircraft was forbidden.

Of the 1,433 examples of the Me 262 completed by war's end, 569 were built by the end of 1944. The overwhelming majority of these were assigned to the bomber wings KG 51, KG 6, KG 27 and KG 54 for use as blitz bombers (*Sturmvogel*, or petrel). Only a few examples of the fighter version (*Schwalbe*, or swallow) were allocated to *Kommando Nowotny*. Operating from Achmer and Hesepe near Osnabrück, they shot down a considerable number of enemy bombers.

The prototype of the blitz bomber/fighter bomber version was the Me 262 V10. To shorten the aircraft's takeoff run (about 1,100 m), two jettisonable RI-502 takeoff-assist rockets, each producing 1,000 kg of thrust for 6 seconds, could be fitted. Landing speed was 175 kph.

KG 51 was the first *Geschwader* to receive the Me 262A-2 *Sturmvogel*, and its *3. Staffel* (*Kommando Schenck*) began operating from airfields in France in July 1944.

Despite its temperamental power plants, which tended to overheat, and thanks to its excellent aerodynamic shape and its leading edge slats and system of flaps, the Me 262 was pleasant to fly. Hydraulic brakes and a steerable nosewheel made the aircraft easy to handle on the ground. IV. (Erg.)/KG 51, a training unit that was later used several examples of the two-seat Me 262 B-1a trainer, converted pilots onto the new aircraft.

Some bombers were fitted with the TSA (low-level and dive-bombing system), which integrated speed, altitude and attitude and displayed the information in the sight.

At the end of April 1945, KG 51 "*Edelweiss*" gave its remaining serviceable aircraft to JV 44, commanded by *Oberst* Steinhoff, at Munich-Riem.

Me 262A-2 *("Blitzbomber")*

Wingspan:	12.51 m; length: 10.6 m; height: 3.83 m. Takeoff weight: 6,400 kg
Crew:	1
Armament*):	2 x 30-mm MK 108 cannon in upper nose (100 rounds per gun) 2 x 30-mm MK 108 cannon beneath the upper pair of cannon (80 rounds per gun) 2 x 12 R4M "*Orkan*" (Hurricane) 55-mm rockets on racks beneath the wings
Bomb Load:	2 x 250-kg on ETC 504 "*Schiffchen*" (boat) bomb racks beneath the fuselage
Range:	1,020 km at altitude of 9,000 m
Service Ceiling:	11,400 m
Maximum Speed:	870 kph at altitude of 6,000 m (750 kph with max. bomb load) 920 kph at 9,000 m without bombs

* If range-increasing drop tanks were fitted under the fuselage, two of the 30-mm cannon had to be removed in order to keep maximum gross weight within acceptable limits.

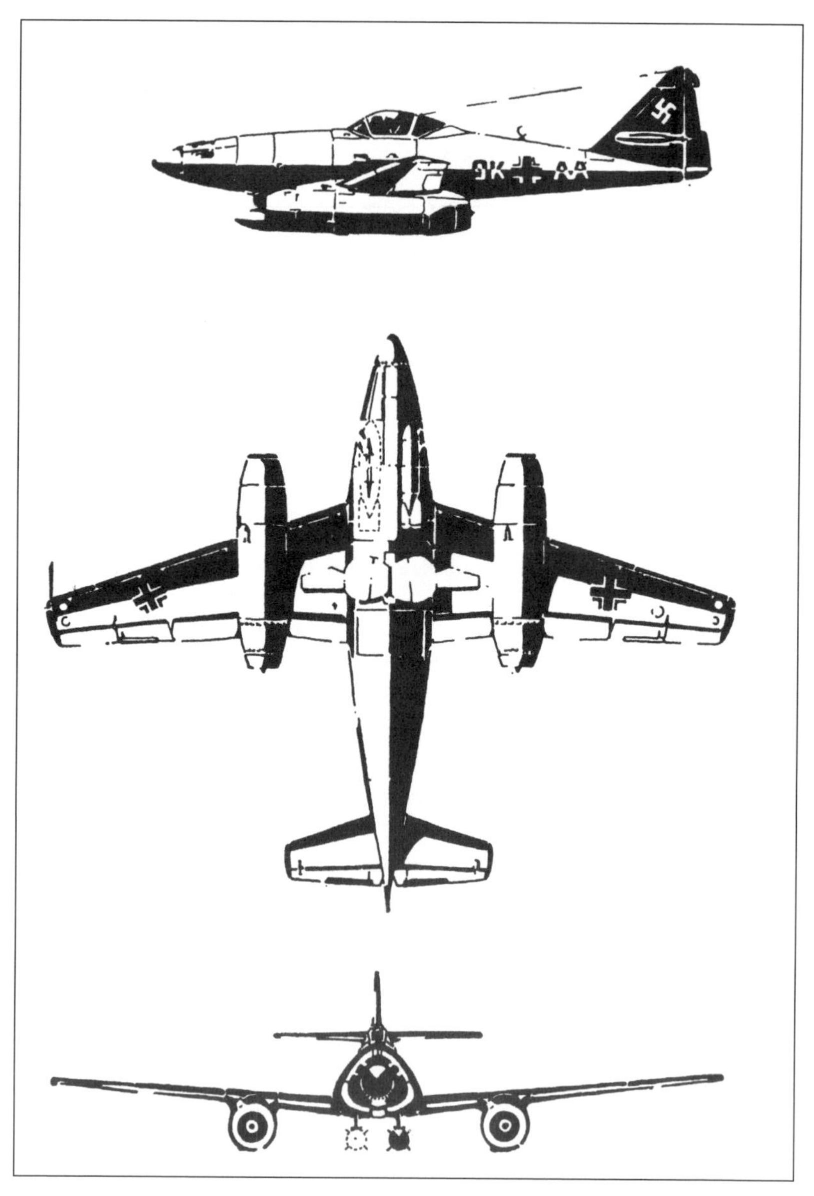

Me 262

Training Aircraft

Focke-Wulf Fw 58 Weihe *(Harrier)*
Also called the "*Leukoplastbomber*" (band-aid bomber), this versatile aircraft was built in large numbers until the end of the war. It was used to convert pilots to multiengine types, radio training, instrument and night training, the training of machine-gunners and bomb aimers and, not last, as a popular communications aircraft.

A strut-braced, low-wing monoplane, the aircraft had a good performance and handling characteristics thanks to its two Argus As 10 C eight-cylinder, air-cooled inverted-vee engines, each producing 240 hp, and two-blade, fixed-pitch propellers.

Crew:	4 (pilot, two students, 1 instructor)
Military Equipment:	1 x 7.9-mm MG 15 in cupola position in the nose
	1 x 7.9-mm MG 15 on ring mount in open dorsal position
	bombsight and radio equipment

Arado Ar 66 C
This single-bay biplane with excellent handling characteristics was used for basic and advanced pilot training. It was powered by the same Argus engine as the *Weihe*.

Crew:	2 in open cockpit
Military Equipment:	instrument and night-flying equipment, radio
	Camera

Junkers Ju (W) 34
The W 34 was a development of the ground breaking F 13 and W 33 and entered service in 1928 as an aircraft capable of carrying cargo and passengers. In *Luftwaffe* service it was used as a navigation, photography and instrument flight trainer until the end of the war.

1 BMW 132 A nine-cylinder radial engine producing 660 hp powered the *hi* version, 1 BMW Bramo 322 the *hau* version.

Crew:	2 side-by-side (dual controls) in enclosed cockpit, cabin for 6 Passengers

Junkers Ju 86
Developed in parallel with the He 111, the good field of fire offered by the type's twin tails prompted the RLM to issue a contract for a bomber version.

The Ju 86A, which was operated by *Deutsche Lufthansa*, was powered by two Jumo 205 six-cylinder, liquid-cooled diesel engines each producing 600 hp.

The Ju 86E had a partially glazed nose and three gun positions and replaced the Ju 52 "interim bomber." The diesel engines were prone to overheating at combat power and were therefore replaced by two BMW 132 DC nine-cylinder radial engines each producing 845 hp and driving three-blade metal variable-pitch propellers in the Ju 86 E-2.

After the outbreak of war the type was used as a training aircraft. Some crews of KG 153 trained on the Ju 86.

Crew:	4 (pilot, bomb-aimer in nose position, radio operator in dorsal position and ventral gunner in crew compartment aft of the bomb bay).
Military Equipment:	1 x 7.9-mm MG 15 in cupola position in the nose
	1 x 7.9-mm MG 15 mounted flexibly in partly-open dorsal position
	1 x 7.9-mm MG 15 in retractable ventral position beneath the fuselage, bomb bay for maximum of 1,000 kg of bombs

Communications Aircraft

While all of the unit's bombers and training aircraft were also used as communications aircraft, the Messerschmitt Bf 109 Taifun and even a Messerschmitt Me 110 were probably the most popular, as they were handy, comfortable, fast and easily maintained. They were reliable and could be landed on any firm field.

Appendix 11
Tactical Numbers and Markings

During the concealment period, aircraft of the bomber *Geschwader* and *Gruppen*, like all military aircraft, flew with the usual civilian registration (the letter D plus four letters or numbers) and a pale grey finish on the upper and lower surfaces.
The letter combination also identified the aircraft's weight class and the type of pilot rating required to fly it.

The three-digit unit designation, such as KG 153 or KG 255, identified the unit's role and in which air district (*Luftkreis*) it had been established.

1st number:	number of the unit in the air district		
2nd number:	role:	1.	Tactical reconnaissance unit
		2.	Strategic reconnaissance unit
		3.	Fighter unit
		4.	heavy fighter unit (kept open)
		5.	Bomber unit
		6.	dive-bomber unit
		7.	Auxiliary *Geschwader*
		8.	Multi-purpose unit
3rd number:	number of the air district		

KG 153 was thus the 1st (bomber) *Geschwader* in *Luftkreis III* (Dresden), while KG 255 was the 2nd (bomber) *Geschwader* in *Luftkreis IV* (Munich).

On 28 May 1936 it was decreed that all militarily-equipped aircraft, meaning those with permanently-installed weapons or bomb-carrying equipment, were to wear the military nationality marking (swastika), the white-outlined *Balkenkreuz* (bar cross) plus a code made up of numbers and letters on the fuselage and wings to identify to which unit it belonged.

The two numbers forward of the *Balkenkreuz* indicated to which Luftkreis the *Geschwader* belonged, the letters and numbers aft of the cross which *Staffel* the particular aircraft belonged to. The letter of the alphabet was a simple code for the running aircraft numbering.

The code 32 + A 25 meant: *Luftkreis III*, 2nd *Geschwader*, 1st aircraft, *II. Gruppe*, *5. Staffel* from Finsterwalde, where the *5. Staffel* of KG 153 was based.

The reconnaissance *Staffeln* (K) of a bomber *Geschwader* were given the number) as *Gruppe* number and the letter K instead of a *Staffel* number.

54 + DOK thus meant: *Luftkreis V*, 4th *Geschwader*, 4th aircraft of the reconnaissance *Staffel* in a *Kampfgeschwader*, here an aircraft of KG 255 "Alpine *Geschwader*" from Landsberg/Lech.

On 4 July 1939 the codes of frontline military aircraft – apart from fighter aircraft – were changed to a format that would be retained for the entire duration of the war.

Once again, the code identified to which *Geschwader*, *Gruppe* and *Staffel* an aircraft belonged.

Looking at the Balkenkreuz, the letters/numbers were applied as follows:

- unit code for a senior headquarters, a *Geschwader* or an independent *Gruppe*, consisting of a combination of letters and numbers
- black Balkenkreuz outlined in white
- aircraft letter within the headquarters or *Staffel*
- identity letter within the *Geschwader* or independent *Gruppe*

The *Kampfgeschwader* were assigned the following unit codes:

KG 1	*"Hindenburg"*	V4 +
KG 2	(Wooden Mallet *Geschwader**)	U5 +
KG 3	(Blitz *Geschwader*)	5K +
KG 4	*"General Wever"*	5J +
KG 6		K6 +
KG 26	(Lion *Geschwader*)	1H +

KG 27	*"Boelcke"*	1G +
KG 28		1T +
KG 30	(Eagle *Geschwader*)	4D +
KG 51	*"Edelweiss"*	9K +
KG 53	*"Legion Condor"*	A1 +
KG 54	(Death's Head *Geschwader*)	B3 +
KG 55	(Gryphon *Geschwader*)	G1 +
KG 66		Z6 +
KG 76		F1 +
KG 77		3Z +
KGr 100		6N +
KG 200		A3 +
LG 1		L1 +
LG 2		L2 +

*In brackets are unofficial designations, based on *Geschwader* emblems, in contrast to officially-bestowed traditional names.

The letters after the *Balkenkreuz* indicated the consecutive numbering of the aircraft within the headquarters or *Staffel* in alphabetical order and were color-coded for:

Geschwaderstab	blue
Gruppenstäbe	green
I. Gruppe	white
II. Gruppe	red
III. Gruppe	yellow
IV. Gruppe	blue
first *Staffeln* of the *Gruppen* (*1./4./7./10. Staffel*)	white
second *Staffeln* of the *Gruppen* (*2./5./8./11. Staffel*)	red
third *Staffeln* of the *Gruppen* (*3./6./9./12. Staffel*)	yellow

The second letter (less G, I, J, O, Q to avoid confusion) after the *Balkenkreuz* identified the *Staffel* or headquarters unit within the *Geschwader*:

A	(Anton)	*Geschwaderstab* and Stabsstaffel
B	(Berta)	*Stab I. Gruppe*
C	(Cäsar)	*Stab II. Gruppe*
D	(Dora)	*Stab III. Gruppe*
E	(Emil)	*Stab IV. Gruppe*
F	(Friedrich)	*Stab V. Gruppe*
H	(Henrich)	*1. Staffel*
K	(Konrad)	*2. Staffel*
L	(Ludwig)	*3. Staffel*
M	(Marta)	*4. Staffel*
N	(Nordpol)	*5. Staffel*
P	(Paula)	*6. Staffel*
R	(Richard)	*7. Staffel*
S	(Siegfried)	*8. Staffel*
T	(Theodor)	*9. Staffel*
U	(Ulrich)	*10. Staffel*
V	(Viktor)	*11. Staffel*
W	(Wilhelm)	*12. Staffel*
X	(Xanthippe)	*13. Staffel*
Y	(Ypsillon)	*14. Staffel*
Z	(Zeppelin)	*15. Staffel*

The code "yellow 9 K + Cäsar Theodor" (9K + CT) was thus clearly the 3rd aircraft of the *9. Staffel* in III./KG 51.

The *Geschwader/Staffel* codes were also applied in black beneath the wings in combination with the *Balkenkreuz*.

As the war went on, the splinter scheme in dark and black green was increasingly replaced by a simple monotone black-green finish – retaining the pale blue wing and fuselage undersides.

Various temporary, usually washable finishes were also used: night black for night raids (especially over England); gray-white for winter operations in Russia/Finland; wave mirror finishes for operations over water; sand-color finishes for tropical use.

It was not unusual for the crosses and codes to be overpainted, making it difficult to determine the nationality of the aircraft. When this occurred, colored fuselage bands in white, red or yellow forward of the tail section were the only means of telling the *Staffeln* apart in the air.

Towards the end of the war the nationality markings and *Balkenkreuze* were simplified, if not to say applied in makeshift fashion. The units simply lacked the time and suitable means to apply textbook markings as per the regulations.

Like the *Staffeln* and even individual pilots, each *Kampfgeschwader* had its own unit emblem, which was worn on the forward fuselage of its aircraft. One can still argue about style, execution and taste, however none of the emblems were approximate representations, instead memorializing of places, events or significant leaders.

The men expressed their pride in their unit and their sense of belonging by displaying their unit emblem everywhere, caring for it lovingly and never forgetting to display it wherever they went.

The edelweiss was a feature of several unit emblems, including those of 8./JG 5 (*Eismeer*), IV./JG 27, III./TG 3 and 2. (H)/14.

Appendix 12
Weapons and Equipment

Defensive Positions

Guns in *Luftwaffe* bomber aircraft were housed in weapons positions, which were generally designated A-, B- or C-positions depending to their location:

A-Stand: gun position in fuselage nose
B-Stand: gun position on top of fuselage, with the
B-1 position facing forwards and the
B-2 position facing rearwards
C-Stand: gun position beneath the fuselage, with the
C-1 position in front, and the
C-2 position in back.
H-Stand: tail gun position.

Gun mounts or turrets were installed to guide the weapons. In the early days, the open *Drehkranz 30*, a cradle seat that enabled the gunner to move his weapon vertically and horizontally, was installed as the *B-Stand*. Arrests or guide rails prevented the gunner from accidentally hitting the tail (tail deflector) or other important parts of his aircraft. The Ju 52 and Ju 86 were equipped with the retractable "dustbin" ventral turret, which could be dangerous and sometimes jammed. In later types this was replaced by an enclosed ventral bath (*C-Stand*) that gave the gunner a certain degree of safety and comfort.

The unarmored *Bola 39* accepted all conventional guns as single weapons, while the armored *Bola 81 Z* was designed for twin guns and offered improved protection against enemy fire.

Enclosed rotating cupola (*Kupla*) and lens mounts (LL) were then the most common standard equipment for nose and dorsal positions, before they were replaced by power turrets.

The electrically powered rotating turret (EDL) reduced the gunner's workload considerably and enabled him to concentrate on defending his aircraft.

Constant improvement and refinement of defensive systems resulted in the remotely controlled barbette (e.g. FDL 131) with sighting periscope (PV-1) and remotely controlled tail barbette (FHL), which were developed during the war.

One unusual weapon was the effective WB 81 weapons container, or as the aircrew called it, the "watering can," which was specially designed for Ju 88s employed in the low-level attack role. The carrier was mounted on an external bomb rack and was fitted with four to six MG 81 machine-guns firing fore and aft. The upper weapons were aligned horizontally, while the lower guns fired at a downward angle. In this way ground targets could be placed under continuous fire when the aircraft was diving, climbing or in level flight.

Guns

After 1933, the Rheinmetall-Borsig and Mauser companies introduced pioneering features in aircraft gun design. Their weapons distinguished themselves through their reliability, simplicity of operation and effectiveness.

The most common machine-gun calibers were 7.9 mm, 13.1 mm and 15.1 mm, for automatic cannon 20 mm and 30 mm.

Large-caliber cannon such as the BK 50 mm, BK 75 mm or even BK 88 mm were not as successful due to insurmountable technical problems.

The guns most commonly used in the bomber aircraft flown by KG 51 were:

Type	Company (mm) (m/sec)	Caliber (rounds per min.)	Rate of Fire	Muzzle Velocity	Used in
MG 15	Rheinmetall	7.9	1,050	755	Do 23, Ju 52, Do 17, He 111
MG 17	Rheinmetall	7.9	1,200	815	Me 410, Ju 88
MG 81 (Z)	Mauser	7.9	1,600	755	Ju 88
MG 131	Rheinmetall	13.1	950	750	Ju 88, Me 410
MG 151/20	Mauser	20	720	760	Me 410
MG FF/M	Oerlikon	20	540	595	He 111
MK 108	Rheinmetall	30	650	520	Me 262

The guns were cocked and fired mechanically, electrically or pneumatically.

Additional weapons combinations were improvised by technically gifted crews (e.g. *Oberleutnant* Dr. Stahl), especially in the He 111 and Ju 88. One of the most noteworthy of these was the "Stahl flamethrower."

Gravity Weapons

Whereas guns were primarily defensive weapons, gravity weapons, or bombs, were the agents of destruction peculiar to bomber aircraft.

Bombs came in a wide variety of size and weight classes for every conceivable type of target, however it should be noted that the *Luftwaffe* achieved an extraordinary level of standardization in its weapons.

There were four major bomb groups, which differed in their effect:

Fragmentation Bombs	SC – fragmentation bomb, cylindrical
	SD – fragmentation bomb, thick-cased
	SB – high-explosive bomb
	SBe – high-explosive bomb, concrete
Incendiaries	B – incendiary bomb
	Flam BC – incendiary, cylindrical
	LC – illumination bomb, cylindrical
Aerial Mines	BM – aerial mine
Armor-Piercing Bombs	PC – armor-piercing bomb, cylindrical
	PD – armor-piercing bomb, thick-cased

Drop containers (AB) could contain leaflets, munitions, rations and fragmentation or incendiary bombs, while bomb dispensers (BSB) and incendiary bomb dispensers (BSK) held only fragmentation or incendiary bombs. The numbers after the weapon designation indicated the type of bomb and weight class in kg.

The bomb fuses used by the *Luftwaffe* were far ahead of their time. Most notable were the electric impact fuses of the EL AZ C 50 series, a glow igniter working on the storage capacitor principle. The fuse could be set just before release, and the bombs were not armed until they left the rack, providing an optimum level of safety.

KG 51 used the following types of bomb during the war:

AB 23
AB 26
BM 1000 "Monika" with braking parachute
BSB 700
Flam BC 250
SB 1000/410 – special version for the Me 410 with elliptical cross-section and braking parachute
SBe 50
SC 10
SC 50
SC 250
SC 500
SC 1000 "Hermann"
SD 2
SD 50
SD 250
PC 500
PC 1000
PC 1400
PC 1800 "Satan"

So-called "Jericho whistles" could be fitted to the fins. When dropped en masse, they produced an ear-shattering noise and were intended to affect the enemy's morale. First made of metal, a switch to papier-mâché was soon made to save valuable materials. As the war went on, this psychological trick was done away with.

Bomb Mounts

Bombs were mounted either inside the fuselage or on the exterior of the airframe beneath the wings or fuselage.

In the bomb bay there were vertical or horizontal cells for dropping bombs in salvo or sequentially, such as:

VeKuMag 6 C 10 (vertical magazine for 6 cylindrical 10-kg bombs)

ElVeMag C 50 (electrically-operated vertical magazine for 5 cylindrical 50-kg bombs)

ESAC 250 (electrically-operated vertical mounting for cylindrical 250-kg bombs)

Outside the fuselage, bombs were mounted on electrically jettisonable horizontal carriers, or weapons racks (so-called ETC – electric carrying device for cylindrical bombs).

Automatic sequential bomb dropping systems (e.g. RAB 14 or Reikow A 16) enabled the bombs to be dropped automatically at designated time intervals, manually or by means of the bombsight (BZG). An emergency jettison safety was always included.

Bombsights

Mechanical-optical bombsights by Goerz-Boykow (e.g. G.V. 219 d, G.F. 218, Lotfernrohr Lotfe C 7 a/b, Lotfe 2 d) were used until 1941, after which they were replaced by gyroscopic single-lens reflex sights (Revi or Lotfe 7 H), that could be coupled with the aircraft's onboard radar.

The Low-Level and Dive-Bombing System (TSA) used in the Me 262 was an extremely advanced aiming system which computed target values from airspeed, altitude and dive angle and displayed them in the aircraft's gunsight. It may be seen as the forerunner of future aiming devices.

Our crews used the proven, reliable and easy to operate robot camera for taking strike assessment photos. The reconnaissance *Schwärme* in the *Kampfgeschwader* used hand-operated cameras (Rb) for battle reconnaissance.

Sources

As noted in the subtitle of this history of *Kampfgeschwader 51*, the author has attempted to put together a chronicle from documents and reports by the *Geschwader* and its members. As he was himself not a member of the wartime generation and did not experience the events at the front, he also had to evaluate and process a great deal of additional literature. In addition to the documents provided by contributors who were former members of the "*Edelweiss Geschwader*," the following works were used to round out the whole:

War Diary III./Kampfgeschwader 51 (copy).
Bartz, Karl: *Als der Himmel brannte*, Hanover 1955.
Baumbach, Werner: *Zu spät?*, Munich 1949.
Bekker, Cajus: *Angriffshöhe 4000*, Oldenburg 1964.
Bley, Wulf: *Deutschland zur Luft*, Stuttgart 1939.
Carell, Paul: *Unternehmen Barbarossa*, Berlin 1963.
— *Verbrannte Erde*, Berlin 1966.
Dahms, Hellmuth Günther: *Der zweite Weltkrieg*, BMVg 1966.
Diakow, J.: *Generaloberst Alexander Löhr*, Freiburg 1964.
Feuchter, Georg W.: *Geschichte des Luftkrieges*, Bonn 1954.
Galland, Adolf: *Die Ersten und die Letzten*, Darmstadt 1953.
Galland-Ries-Ahnert: *Die Deutsche Luftwaffe 1939-1945*, Bad Nauheim, no year.
Jacobsen, Hans-Adolf: *Der zweite Weltkrieg in Chronik und Dokumenten*, Darmstadt 1959.
Mason, Francis K.: *Battle over Britain*, London 1969.
Kens-Nowarra: *Die deutschen Flugzeuge 1933-1945*, Munich 1961.
Ploetz: *Geschichte des Zweiten Weltkrieges*, Würzburg 1960.
Priller, Josef: *Geschichte eines Jagdgeschwaders*, Heidelberg 1962.
Ries, Karl Jr.: *Markierungen und Tarnanstriche der Luftwaffe im Zweiten Weltkriege, Band 1-4*, Mainz 1963.
— *Dora Kürfurst und die Rote 13, Band 1-4*, Mainz 1966.
Roden von, Hans-Detlef Herhudt: *Die Luftwaffe rings um Stalingrad*, Wiesbaden 1950.
Seemen von, Gerhard: *Die Ritterkreuzträger 1939-1945*, Bad Nauheim 1955.
Völker, Karl-Heinz: *Die Deutsche Luftwaffe 1933-1939*, Stuttgart 1967.
Weber, Dr. Theo: *Die Luftschlacht um England*, CH Frauenfeld 1956.

Acknowledgements

The author wishes to thank the following for their assistance, suggestions and support: the German Red Cross, Tracing Department of the German War Graves Commission, German Office for the Notification of Next-of-Kin of Members of the Former German *Wehrmacht* (WAST), the Federal Archives Central Verification Office, the Military History Research Department, Specialized Section VI "Air Forces and Air War History" and the following persons:

Rudolf Abrahamczik
Egon Arz
Wolfgang Baetz
Siegfried Barth
Prof. Dr. Ing. Wilhelm Batel
Helmut Bernhardt
Hans Heinrich Bömer
Dr. Karl Brünner
Wilhelm Buck
Christian Burkhardt
Alfred Delles
Fritzherbert Dierich
Fridl Fath
Karl-Heinz Feldmann
Heinz Fietze
Alfred Fritsch
Hans Grah
Dr. Karl Gundelach
Dr. Hans Gutzmer
Friedrich Hacker
Klaus Häberlen
Hanns Heise
Ernst Hinrichs
Hans Hoiß
Hans Holzwarth
Theo Jäger
Reinhold Joos
Josef Kammhuber
Ledwig Kliebenstein
Dr. Hermann Kölbel
Heinrich Kratzert
Helmut Kroll
Walter Lau
Siegfried Lauterwasser
Ronny Lauer
Günther Löffelbein
Fritz Lutz
Alfred Mahncke
Albert Maser
Wolf Meister
Herbert Meyer
Albert Mittelmann
Hans Moser
Ernst Obermaier
Cornelie Pfeiffer
Ernst Pflüger
Ludwig Piller
Joachim Poetter
Horst Puls
Dr. Else Rath
Bernd Sartor
Friedrich Scheel
Lothar Schilling
Josef Schölß
Adolf Schwachenwald
Gerda Schwiegk-Scholz
Heinrich Schwipp
Wolfgang Seils
Prof. Dr. Otto Stärk
Dr. Karl-Heinz Stahl
Klaus Thoms
Heinz Unrau
Dr. Rolf Woernle
Hans Zeller
Georg Zepf
Uwe Zimmermann
Hans-Joachim Zogel

Photos

The Kommodore of KG 255, Oberst Spang (center, wearing Luftwaffe sword), greeting the young airmen at the new Landsberg garrison in 1937.

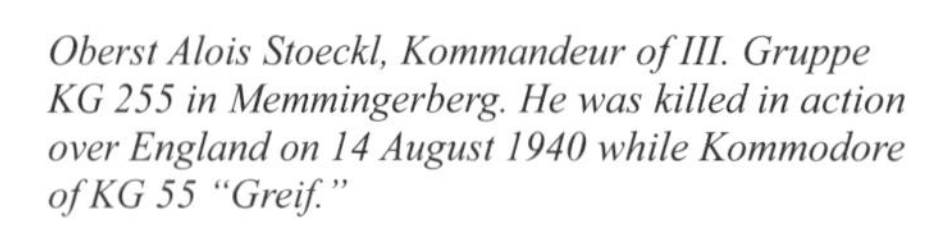
Oberst Alois Stoeckl, Kommandeur of III. Gruppe KG 255 in Memmingerberg. He was killed in action over England on 14 August 1940 while Kommodore of KG 55 "Greif."

KG 153 flew the Do 23, one of the Luftwaffe's first bombers, from Merseburg.

Ju 86, an interim solution.

A Do 17E of KG 255 in flight over Bavaria. It is wearing markings for the 1938 autumn maneuvers, in which the fuselage crosses were replaced by black discs.

In 1939-40 the unit regularly moved to frontline airfields, such as this one in Bad Wörishofen.

Hauptmann Poetter, Staffelkapitän of 7./KG 51, gives instructions to his radio operator, Obfw. Sepp Traut.

A He 111 of the 7. Staffel over the Alpine panorama of the Bavarian mountains.

A contemporary illustration showing all the agencies involved in bomber operations: airfield security, takeoff and landing control officer, base map office, command post, radio and navigation officer, ground control/communications office, airfield operating company, ATC picket boat, ATC coastal boat.

Heinkel He 111H bombers of KG 51 over France en route to a target.

Oberleutnant d.R. Dr. Stahl in his Ju 88 A-1, which was fitted with a flamethrower device of his own design, over Villaroche, October 1940.

Many "functionaries," such as Uffz. Zepr (right) seen here, could not get enough operational sorties. These men were the unofficial reserve for crews who lost a member due to illness.

Generalfeldmarschall Hugo Sperrle in the Zeppelin hangar at Paris-Orly on 12 November 1940. Saluting (left) is Major Marienfeld, Kommandeur of III./KG 51. On the far right is Oberstleutnant Schulz-Heyn, the Geschwaderkommodore.

Hauptmann Kurt von Greiff (left) presents his I. Gruppe to Generalfeldmarschall Sperrle. In the center is Hauptmann Endres, Geschwader adjutant.

A strike assessment photo taken shortly after an attack on the French airfield in Romorantin, 1940.

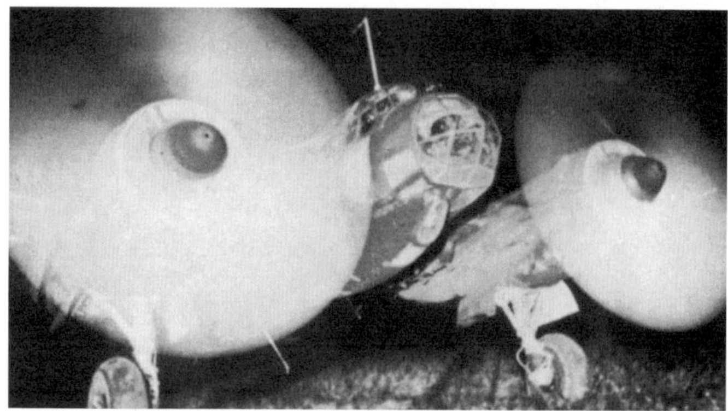

One of KG 51's Ju 88A-1s, running up its engines prior to a night takeoff against targets in England, 1940.

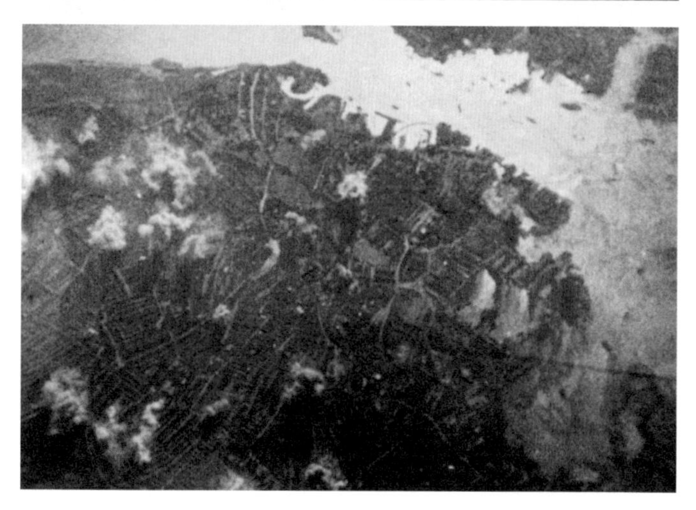

Hits on the port of Portsmouth, 1940.

French prisoners of war help clean away wrecked aircraft in Étampes-Mondésir.

In Étampes-Mondésir, personnel gather before a mission over England, June 1940; from l. to r.: Major Kind, Obfw. Lubrich (†), Obfw. Görres, Oblt. Rath (†), Hptm. Brandt (†). Oblt. Schwegler (†).

The fallen of the Geschwader were buried in the cemetery in Meaux. Major Marienfeld gives the funeral oration. In the background is a band from the armored forces.

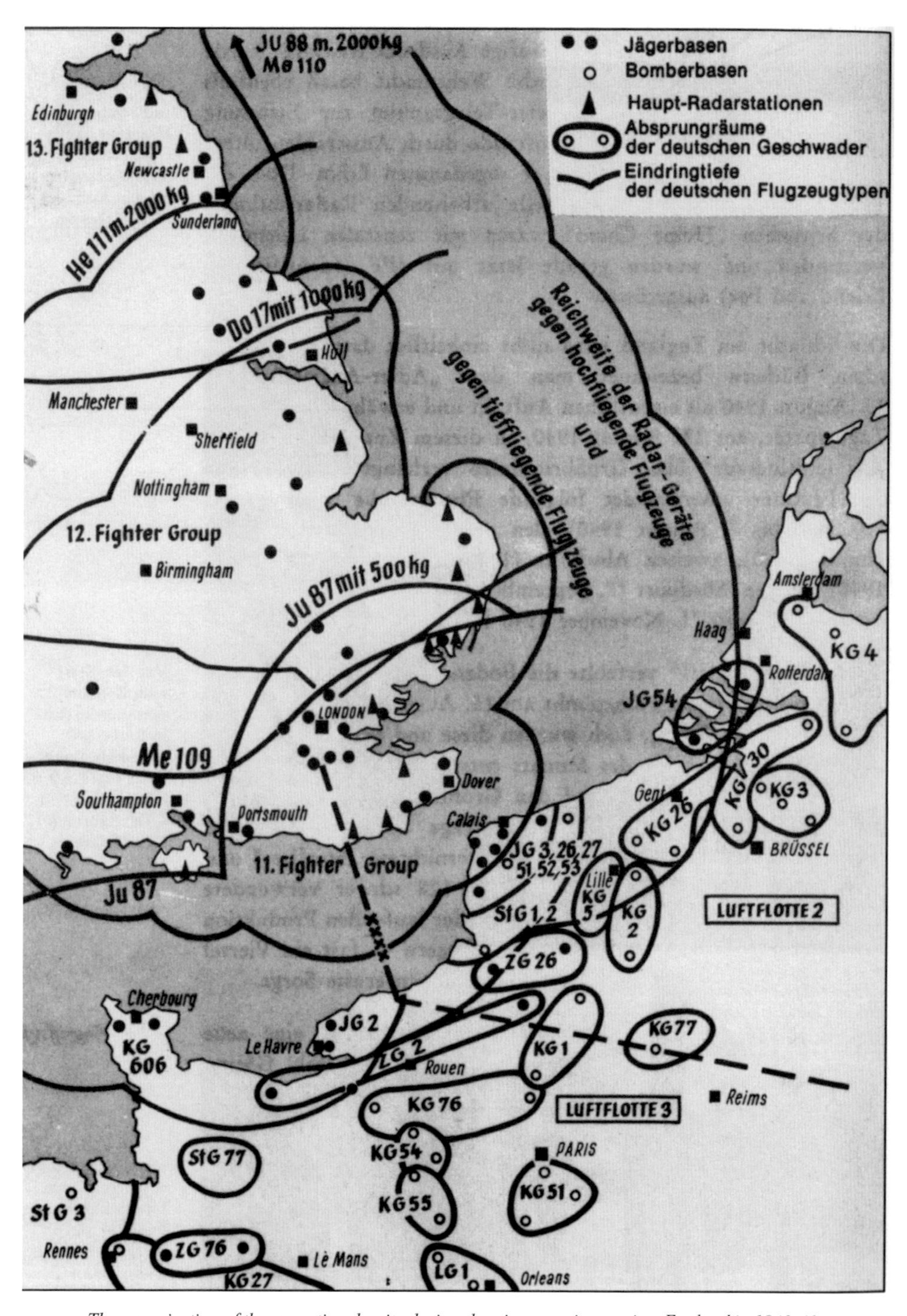

The organization of the operational units during the air campaign against England in 1940-41.

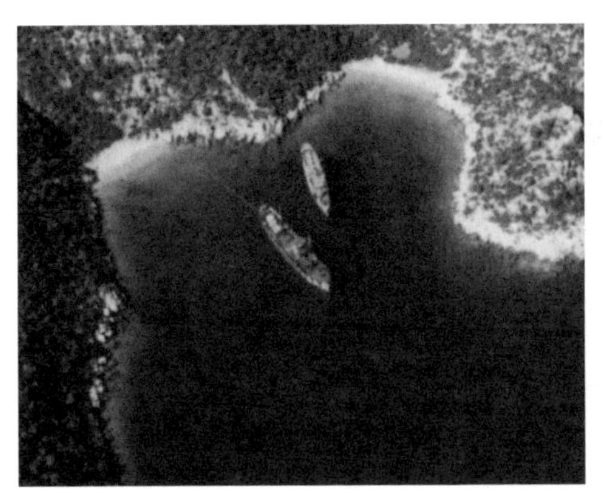

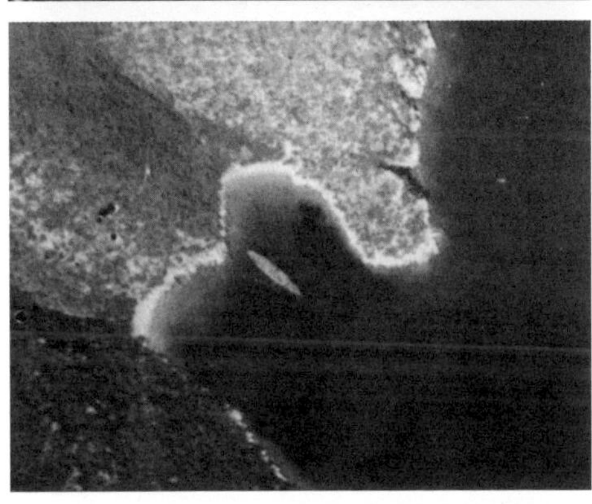

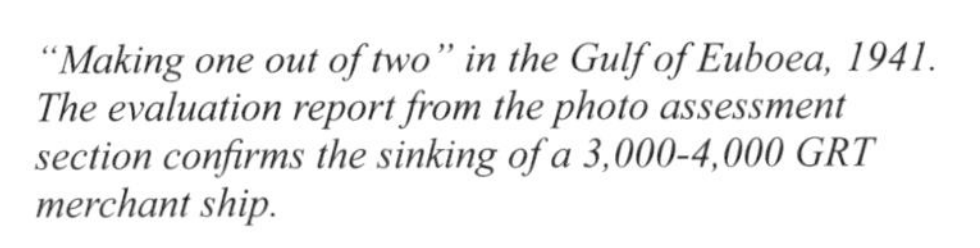

"Making one out of two" in the Gulf of Euboea, 1941. The evaluation report from the photo assessment section confirms the sinking of a 3,000-4,000 GRT merchant ship.

I./K.G. 51 · Bildstelle

Auswertung			Filmkennung	Aufnahme: Tag	Aufnahme: Zeit	Beobachter (Truppenteil)
Auswerter	Tag	Uhrzeit	F 90/41/ I./KG.51	20.4.41	10.30	Aufnehmender: Fw. Görres I./KG.51
Wolsky, Uffz.	23.4.	17.00				

Bild-Nr. Aufnahmeart | Bildmaßstab etwa 1: | Kartenblatt: 1:1000000

Feststellungen (wann? — wo? — wer? — was? — wie?)

2,3,17

Im Nordwestteil des Golfes von Euboea ein Handelsschiff von ca. 3000 - 4000 brt. versenkt.

Flgzgfhr.: Oblt. Schwegler

Beobacht.: Fw. Krüher

Wolsky

Generaloberst Alexander Löhr personally giving directions for the mission against Yugoslavia; from l. to r.: Generaloberst Löhr, Oberstleutnant Schulz-Heyn, Kommodore KG 51, and Major Marienfeld, Kommandeur III./KG 51.

Clusters of incendiaries fall on Belgrade on 6 April 1941.

One of the best-known and successful crews of KG 51; from l. to r.: Oblt. Schwegler. Obfw. Lubrich, Obfw. Görres.

Where is Falimize? Somewhere in Poland in 1941. The troops relied on the walls of signs that lined the advance roads.

The Kommodore in his Me 110 liaison aircraft after landing in Krosno.

Kommodore Oberstleutnant Koester addresses his Geschwader in Nikolayev on the occasion of the first "honor goblets" instituted by Reichsmarschall Göring.

The maintenance personnel prepare their vehicles for the next move.

The technical personnel of the Gruppen travelled across Europe by train, such as here from Paris to Wiener-Neustadt in March 1941.

Whenever the units travelled to new locations, Stabsarzt Dr. Ott, "Buddha," administered vaccinations to ensure the health of the men.

Mud and muck near the German settlement of Strassburg, during the advance into Bessarabia, 1941.

In Balti in 1941, the question arose for Obfw. Kratzert (left) and Obfw. Lubrich (right): "Who's going to slaughter the pig?" Such problems soon caused the plague of mice to be forgotten.

The beautiful gypsy Maria danced in the camp in Balti for bread and nothing else. She and her family lived in caves near the airfield.

SD 2 fragmentation bombs being dropped on Russian airfields and advance roads at the start of the Russian campaign in June 1941.

Hptm. Hahn, Kommandeur of I./KG 51, killed on 3 February 1942 and the crew's grave near Tiraspol.

Burning trains in the Kupyansk railway station, 1941.

Oblt. Unrau's 9K + BL returned from a mission in this condition on 12 August 1941. It was rammed by a Russian fighter over Yevpatoria Bay. The starboard horizontal stabilizer was torn off and the rear fuselage twisted. The crew baled out over Bessarabia. This rare photo was taken by Oblt. Feldmann.

"Florian" radio set with men of the air signals company in action on the Eastern Front.

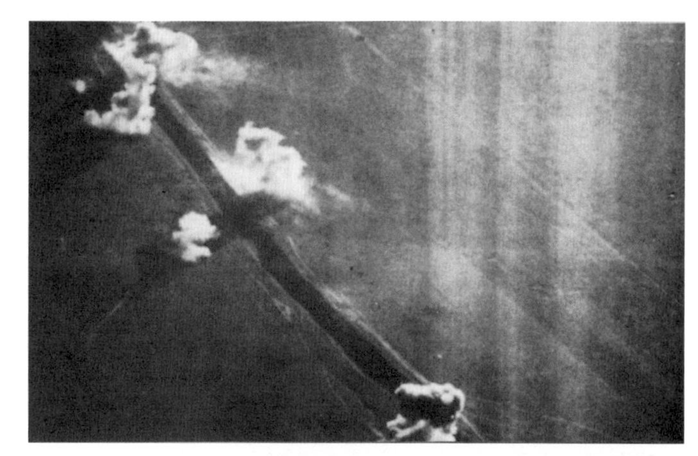

The Tatar Trench near Perekop prior to the conquest of the Crimean Peninsula, June 1942.

Unteroffizier Helmut Bernhard, one of the observers who, with no flying training, landed a Ju 88 after his pilot, Oblt. Hohl, was killed.

Letters home were always hastily written between sorties. Seen here are armorers in Zhitomir.

The harsh winter of 1942 in Zaporozhye, where teams of horses were sometimes used to pull aircraft ...

... was followed by a muddy spring in Nikolayev. Despite all difficulties ...

... flight operations and combat missions were carried out. In the foreground a Ju 88 engine and 50-kg bombs.

Feldwebel Georg Fanderl, I./KG 51's second Knight's Cross winner (24/1/1942), greets Oberleutnant Löffelbein in Tiraspol. On the right is Feldwebel Graichen from the crew of Hauptmann Hahn, killed near Tiraspol on 3 February 1942.

Nikolayev in the winter of 1942. Snowdrifts hindered flight operations considerably.

The Soviet cruiser Krasny Krim, sunk in Sevastopol Harbor by the Fanderl crew.

For a time in the spring of 1942, Hauptmann Werner Baumbach, well known and experienced in anti-shipping operations, flew missions against the Black Sea ports of Novorossisk, Tuapse and Sukhimi with the Geschwader.

The Kommandeur of III./KG 51, Major Rath, conducts a mission briefing during "Operation Neptune" (target: the port of Tuapse). From l. to r.: Obfw. Traut († 22/5/44), Oblt. Seipp († 11/3/43), Major Rath († 22/5/44) and Oblt. Kanz († 11/6//42).

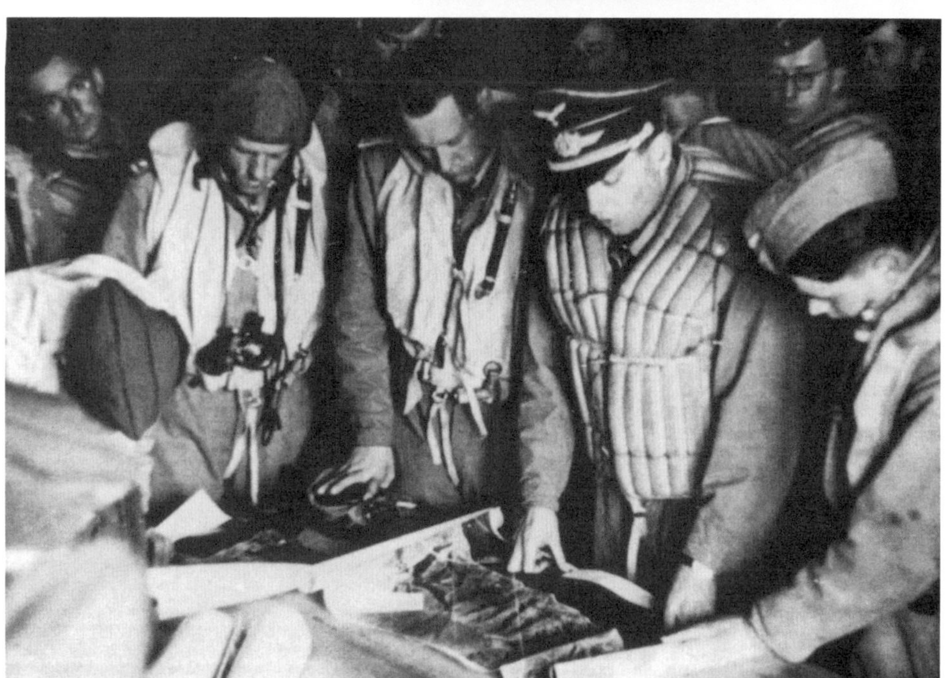

The railroad bridge near Rostov – Bataysk at the time of the spring flooding, 1942.

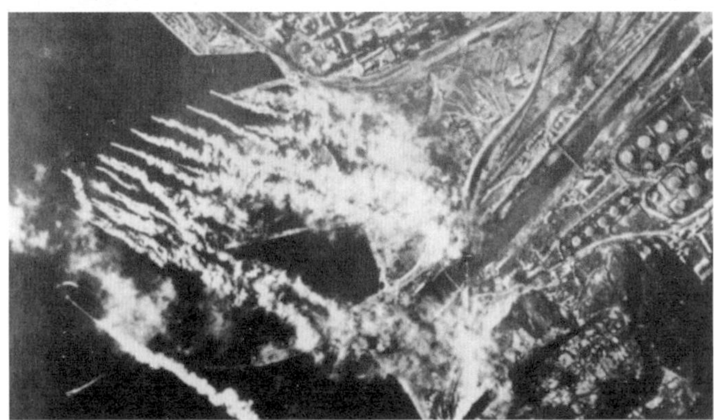

Smoke screen over the port of Tuapse, 1942.

Attack on ships in the port of Tuapse by III./KG 51 on 23 March 1942. At 15:00 the crew of Hptm. Häberlen, Uffz. Ernst, Fw. Böttcher and Uffz. Gallermann in 9K + ED hit a Russian cruiser with two SC 500 and one SC 250 bombs. The submarines escaped damage.

Loading a 1,000 kg bomb.

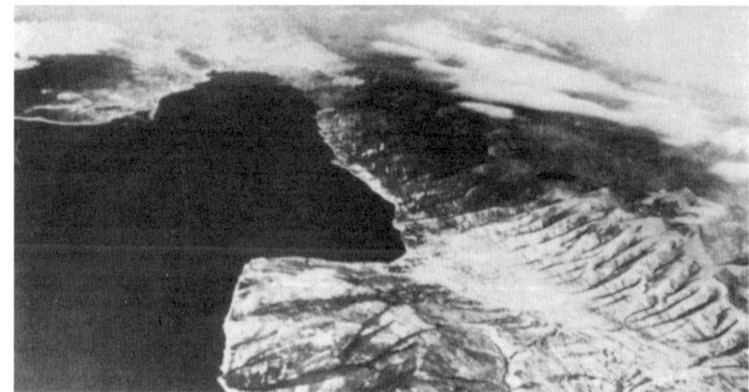

Kabardinka and the protected Bay of Novorossisk looking north, 1942.

A Ju 88 in the flak hell of Novorossisk, 1942.

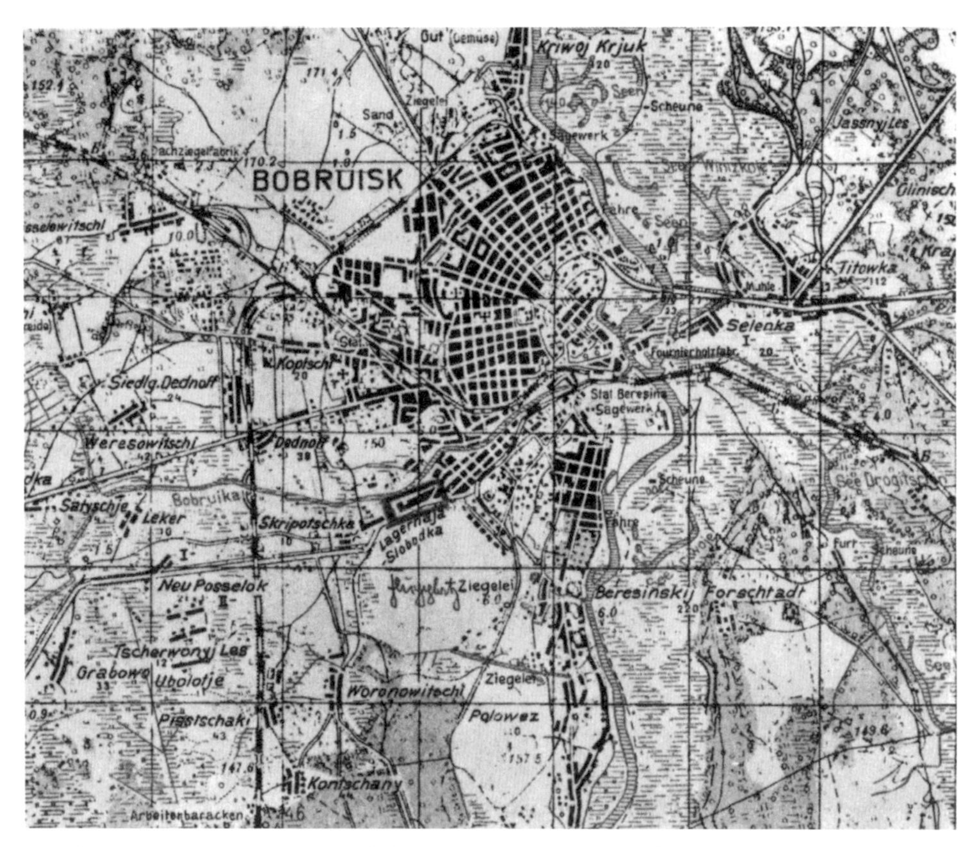

Map of Bobruisk on the Beresina, where the bulk of the new crews were familiarized with conditions at the front by the IV. Gruppe.

"Crash – explosion – fire" – the end of a hopeful crew at the edge of Sechinskaya airfield in 1943. From there, new crews flew their first familiarization missions. Targets were the extensive partisan areas around Roslavl.

The aftermath of a lucky night belly-landing southeast of Taman. A few meters was all that separated the crew from disaster.

Another narrow escape. Despite "stable lamps," there were still difficulties landing in Tatsinskaya.

Wiener-Neustadt: this bomber wanted to taxi home quickly and failed to see a Me 110. Fortunately the aircraft did not belong to the same unit.

Ju 88A-4s of KG 51 over the Crimea. In the background is "Table Mountain" near Simferopol.

Hauptmann Matthias "Teddy" Schwegler, Staffelkapitän of 1./KG 51, in Sarabus. He was awarded the Knight's Cross on 18 December 1942. Schwegler was later killed near Neuses/Ansbach on 18 April 1945.

View of Sevastopol from the north. In the center of the photo is narrow Severnaya Bay, on the right Cape Khersonyes. Visible in the foreground the fortified Sappun Heights, much fought over during the Battle of Sevastopol.

Mounting 164 guns, this flak barge in Severnaya Bay commanded land, air and sea until it was bombed and sunk by Oberleutnant Ernst Hinrichs on 25 June 1942 (top photo taken shortly before the attack, bottom after the bombs struck).

Oberleutnant Ernst Hinrichs of I./KG 51 was awarded the Knight's Cross on 25 July 1942. He hit the troublesome flak barge on his first dive-bombing attack. The ammunition on the barge exploded, destroying it completely.

The remains of the fort at Sevastopol.

A wrecked armored train near Ossadovka, south of Kupyansk, 1942.

Rostov airfield under attack. The Geschwader was later stationed there during the difficult months of 1942-43.

Oberleutnant "Ali" Berger, Kapitän of the 1. Staffel, killed on 27 January 1943. While attempting to bomb a Russian tank on the ice-covered Sea of Azov, his bombs missed and struck the ice. As a result, "Ali" was credited with sinking a tank, a rather rare event in the history of aerial warfare.

Berger crew; from l. to r.: Uffz. Sachs, Oblt. Berger, Obfw. Puls.

Direct hit on a large Russian ammunition ship, 6 km north of Kerch. The photo clearly shows shells of various calibers detonating as a result of the explosion.

With direct flak hits in the wing and tail section, a crew needed luck to get home ...

... it was on the side of the Schlegel crew. From l. to r.: Uffz. Stuhler, Uffz. Haist, Lt. Schlegel, Uffz. Metz.

The coat of arms of the city of Memmingen and the Edelweiss together on the aircraft of Hptm. Häberlen, Gruppenkommandeur of I./KG 51, Russia, winter 1942-1943.

9K + DB, the Ju 88 of Leutnant Geruschke (KIA 3/3/43). Shot down by enemy tanks on 21 February 1943, it had to make a forced landing between the lines. Leutnant Winkel (KIA 21/3/45) landed nearby and, in a courageous act, rescued the crew from its grim situation.

The "Wastel" crew (Lt. Winkel's radio call sign) beneath their Ju 88 A-4. From l. to r.: Leutnant Winkel, Unteroffizier Sieker, Unteroffizier Ziemann, Unteroffizier Schwachenwald, Stabsarzt Dr. Denkhaus, who liked to fly with Winkel.

At the instigation of Major Dierich, Kommandeur of I./KG 51, a cemetery for the fallen of the Geschwader was established in the park of the Tatar castle in Bakhchisary in the Crimea (above left).

Attack on the Bataysk railway station, 1943 (above right).

In Tatsinskaya the men lived in homemade earth bunkers. During the cold winter, cutting wood was one of the most important activities, next to flying.

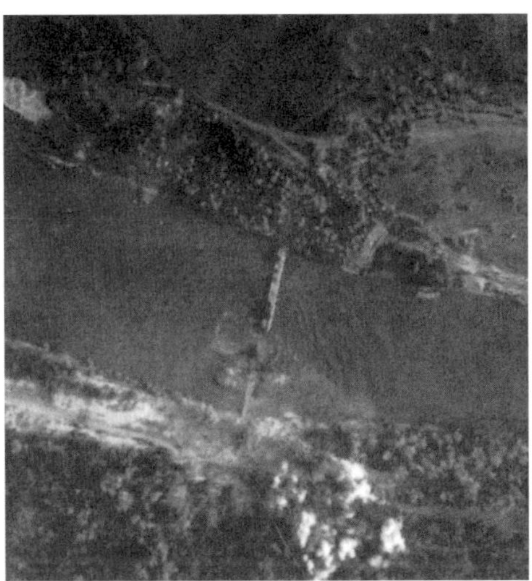

The end of a pontoon bridge over the Don near Kalach. It was used to transport supplies and reinforcements to Stalingrad ...

... Generaloberst von Richthofen commends the assembled Geschwader during a speech in Nikolayev. On the right is Kommodore Major von Friedeburg.

In front of the command post tent in Sarabus, 1942. From l. to r.: Major Ritter, Kommandeur of I./KG 51, Major von Friedeburg, Kommodore KG 51, Hptm. von Bibra, Kommandeur of III./KG 51.

A Ju 88 C-6 Zerstörer used by 7./KG 51 (Eis.) on train-busting sorties in Russia. Note the painted-on "glass nose" and the openings for the automatic cannon.

Tatsinskaya, 1942. Hptm. Schölß (center) and Major Dierich (right), Kommandeur of I./KG 51, discuss the results of a mission against Stalingrad.

Ground personnel in Bagerovo, 1943. Here 500 kg bombs are towed to the aircraft on sledges. In the background are the radio station and Bagerovo flight control.

Armorers shoulder SC 250 bombs onto the wing racks.

Engine change.

50 kg bombs are hoisted into the fuselage bays.

In March 1943 in Zaporozhye, Kommodore Major Frankenberg-Proschlitz congratulates Oberleutnant Löffelbein on the destruction of the railway bridge over the Don near Rychkov. From l. to r.: Hptm. Häberlen, Major von Frankenberg-Proschlitz, Lt. Winkel, Lt. Csurusky, Oblt. Löffelbein.

Major von Frankenberg-Proschlitz (left) with Hptm. Rath and Lt. Stephan in Bagerovo, May 1943.

Kommodore Oberstleutnant Heise greets the Rösch crew in Briansk after the Geschwader's 10,000th combat mission.

Several Knight's Cross Winners of KG 51

Hptm. Rudolf Henne (Knight's Cross on 12/4/1942) died after the war.

Obfw. Albert Spieth (Knight's Cross 24/3/1943), killed in Bobruisk on 4/10/1943.

Oblt. Eberhard Schaefer (Knight's Cross 8/4/1944). Killed in Zamosc on 9/4/1944.

Hptm. Siegfried Barth, known as "Balbo" (Knight's Cross 2/10/1942).

Mission briefing in Balti; from l. to r.: Oblt. Stemmler, Oblt. Barth, Lt. Haberl, operations officer.

Missions over the Aegean ...

... and transfer by the I. and III. Gruppe back to the Reich to take on new assignments.

Rest break in Illesheim for veteran Knight's Cross wearers of KG 51 in 1943. From l. to r.: Hptm. Josef Schölß, Hptm. Klaus Häberlen, Oblt. Dietrich Puttfarken († 23/4/1944).

The first conversion flights on the Me 110 were carried out at the Zerstörer school in Memmingen.

Crews in Illesheim prior to an Me 410 mission, autumn 1943. From l. to r.: Uffz. Hagel, Obfw. Capitain, Fw. Fischer, Hptm. Häberlen, Hptm. Unrau, Obfw. Lösel, Obfw. Puls (far right).

An Me 410 in flight (above right). KG 51 flew this type on missions over England and in the Defense of the Reich.

Hauptmann Klaus Häberlen, Knight's Cross wearer (20/6/1943) and Kommandeur of I./KG 51.

The Reichsmarschall in conversation with Hauptmann Häberlen in Fels am Wagram.

The 210-mm Nebelwerfer rocket (nicknamed Dödel) was supposed to be launched from the Me 410 against American heavy bombers.

The awarding of the Knight's Cross to Hptm. Löffelbein in Hildesheim on 3 October 1943. From l. to r.: Stabsarzt Dr. Bahnsen, Hptm. Löffelbein, Major Schölß, Kommandeur IV./KG 51, Oblt. Dr. Roder, adjutant.

Kommodore Oberstleutnant Hanns Heise, May 1944, in the Saint Georges Motel, France.

From l. to r.: Kommodore Oberstleutnant Meister with adjutant Hptm. Sartor and Hptm. Grundmann, Kommandeur of II./KG 51, July 1944.

A pair of Me 262s of I./KG 51 taking off from Juvincourt near Reims in July 1944, soon after the invasion.

Rheine, September 1944. From l. to r.: Major Wolfgang Schenck, Oberfeldwebel Gerd Gittmann, Oberfeldwebel "Ronny" Lauer, Hauptmann Eberhard Winkel, Oberfeldwebel Adolf Schwachenwald (back to camera).

An Me 262 of the Edelweiss Geschwader in the rainy evening twilight, Hopsten 1944.

In the command post at Rheine, Hauptmann Winkel (right) describes his encounter with enemy fighters to Major Unrau (center), Kommandeur of I./KG 51. Stabsarzt Dr. Denkhaus (left) had previously treated Winkel's injuries.

Critical looks in the command post shelter in Rheine, autumn 1944. From l. to r.: Leutnant Batel, Leutnant Haefner, Leutnant Ritter von Rittersheim (killed 14/1/1945), Hauptmann Abrahamczik, Hauptmann Rösch (killed 28/11/1944), Leutnant Maser.

General der Jagdflieger Adolf Galland discusses Me 262 operations with Major Unrau. (Rheine, 08/10/1944, the day famed Luftwaffe fighter pilot Walter Nowotny was KIA).

The last Christmas of the war, Rheine 1944. From l. to r.: Oblt. Hovestadt, Major Unrau, Stabsint. Hoiß.

Hptm. Hans Gutzmer, Staffelkapitän of 7. Eisenbahnbekämpfungs-staffel (KG 51's train-busting unit). He was awarded the Knight's Cross on 29/2/1944.

Hptm. Winkel and Lt. Gietmann were killed in Giebelstadt on 21/3/1945. Radio operator Obfw. Schwachenwald from Winkel's crew holds the decorations pillow.

"It's as if an angel is pushing" said General Adolf Galland after his first flight in the Me 262. Here is an A-2 version bearing the tactical number 13. These large numbers were worn by aircraft of Luftwaffe training schools to make their aircraft more identifiable and serve as tactical codes. (The swastika was retouched from the original.)

On 8 May 1945, Oberleutnant Wilhelm Batel took off from Saaz (Zatec) in this Me 262, 9K + FB. At 15:28 he made a forced landing in a field near Pommoißel, not far from his father's farm (amateur photo).

Flugbetrieb mit "Silber". Prüf - Nr.

I. Anlassen.
1. Selbstschalter für Generator links und rechts, Anlaßzündung und Meßgeräte eindrücken (Achtung bei allen Flugzeugen nicht gleich angeordnet!).
Beim Anlassen mit Außenbord Fernselbstschalter "Aus".
2. Riedelanlasser 3 - 5 Sekunden tupfen, in Tätigkeit bringen, Umdrehungsanzeigegerät auf kleinen Meßbereich schalten.
Bei 800 U. Zündung drücken. Bei 2000 U. Riedelanlasser loslassen, Bedienhebel mit gedrückter Zündung langsam vorschieben, Brandhahn öffnen, Förderpumpen "Ein", Leerlaufsperre einrasten, bei 3000 U. Zündung loslassen.
3. Tankpumpen einschalten.

II. Nach dem Anlassen.
1. Fernselbstschalter "Ein". Selbstschalter für Wendehorizont, Flossentrimmung, Staurohrheizung (wenn erforderlich) "Ein".
2. Fu.G. 16 "Ein".
3. Für Sprechverkehr am Platz Raste 3.
4. Wendehorizont auf "Los".

III. Abbremsen.
1. Achtung, ob Bremsklötze vorhanden.
2. Jedes Triebwerk einzeln hochfahren.
3. Langsam den Bedienhebel vorschieben, bis 6000 U. (auf Temperatur achten), dann zügig bis Vollast.
4. Bei 8100 U. muß Düsennadel voll ausgefahren sein.(Kontrolle am Gasdifferenzdruck und kann ausgefahrene Düsennadel sehen).
5. Gasdifferenzdruck 0,6 - 0,7.
6. Kraftstoffdruck 60, Schmierstoffdruck 1 - 4, Temperatur nicht über rote Marke.
7. Zügig Bedienhebel zurücknehmen.

IV. Rollen.
1. Kabinendach richtig schließen (Achtung, ob Verschlußhebel eingerastet).
2. Langsam Bedienhebel nach vorn, Temperatur beachten, darf nicht über die rote Marke steigen.
3. Langsam gerade anrollen lassen.
4. Kurven mit Bremsen rollen (darauf achten, daß nicht zu langsam gerollt wird, da sonst Schwierigkeiten mit dem Bugrad).
5. Bremsen müssen einwandfrei ziehen (sonst Flugzeug unklar).

V. Vorbereitung zum Start.
1. Flugzeug am Start gerade hinstellen.
2. Beide Bremsen betätigen.
3. Flossenstellung je nach Betankung bis 3° kopflastig.
4. Landeklappen auf 20°.
5. Sprechprobe mit Bodenstelle.

VI. Start.
1. Stoppuhr drücken.
2. Bedienhebel nach vorn bis 7000 U.
3. Bremsen loslassen, Bedienhebel bis Vollast vorschieben.
4. Anzeigewerte für beide Triebwerke beachten.
5. Steuerknüppel in Normalstellung, Flugzeug rollt gerade aus, bei Abweichen mit Bremsen korrigieren.
6. Bei 180 - 200 km/h Flugzeug vom Boden wegnehmen, nicht zu stark ziehen, da Anstellwinkel zu groß, und kurz wieder nachdrücken.
7. Räder abbremsen.
8. Fahrwerkknopf "Ein" eindrücken, dabei Sperre nach links schieben Knopf springt heraus, wenn Einfahrvorgang beendet. (Fahrt möglichst nicht über 250 km/h beim Fahrwerk einfahren).
9. Drehzahlen auf Reiseflug 8000-8300 U., bei Platzflug 8000 U.
10. Landeklappen "Ein", Fahrt nicht über 350 km/h.
11. Flugzeug in Normallage austrimmen.

VII. Im Fluge.
1. Triebwerkinstrumente beachten.
2. Kraftstoffvorrat beachten.
3. Selbstschalterknöpfe überwachen.

VIII. Vorbereitung zur Landung.
1. Drehzahlen bis 6500 U. zurücknehmen.
2. Fahrt durch Ziehen vermindern (bis 320 - 350 km/h.)
3. Fahrwerkknopf "Aus" drücken (Achtung,beim Fahrwerk ausfahren wird Flugzeug ruckartig schwanzlastig), nachdrücken 300 km/h halten.
4. Schauzeichen für Fahrwerk und Bugrad müssen aufleuchten "Aus" (da sonst keine weitere Kontrolle).
5. Landeklappen auf 200.
6. Kurven mit Fahrwerk "Aus" nicht unter 280 km/h.
7. Steuerdrücke durch Trimmen ausgleichen.

IX. Landung.
1. Normal Gleitwinkel anschweben.
2. Landeklappe ganz ausfahren, 250 km/h halten, in Platznähe 230 - 220 km/h.
3. Am Platzrand ran an den Boden gehen (Aufsetzen mit 200-180 km/h)
4. Bedienhebel zurück auf Leerlaufstellung (Achtung, nicht auf Stopp zurückziehen, da sonst Orkane brennen).
5. Normal den Knüppel durchziehen, bis Flugzeug aufsetzt, Das Bugrad hochhalten, dabei langsam nach vorn übergehen lassen.
6. Ausrollen, wenn erforderlich bremsen, Landeklappe "Ein".

X. Verhalten in besonderen Fällen.
1. Bei Triebwerksausfall Brandhahn zu, Bedienhebel auf Stopp, Förderpumpe aus, mit Seitenrudertrimmung nachtrimmen.
2. Eintriebwerkflug ohne weiteres möglich, kann über laufendes und stehendes Triebwerk kurven, Steigen gut möglich.
3. Eintriebwerklandung ohne weiteres möglich (Achtung, bei links ausgefallenem Triebwerk, Fahrwerk und Landeklappe mit Preßluft ausfahren, Landung normal. Anschweben nicht unter 260 km/h.
4. Durchstarten. Langsam Bedienhebel nach vorn, Fahrwerk einfahren über 300 km/h Landeklappen stufenweise einfahren.
5. Ausstieg. Wenn möglich auf 350 km/h zurückgehen. Kopfhaubenanschluß von Trennstelle lösen, Dach abwerfen, losschnallen. (Die Art des Aussteigens ist jedem Flugzeugführer selbst überlassen).

Many pilots of IV./KG 51 (training Gruppe) used this checklist during their first missions on the Me 262 (codename "Silver"). This helped them master the new and complicated technology of the jet fighter, although the emergency procedures in section X.5 left much up to the pilot.

Generalleutnant Josef Kammhuber, the first Inspector of the Air Force after the war and former Kommodore of KG 51 "Edelweiss," gives the official speech at the dedication of the memorial chapel in Landsberg on 30 September 1956.

The Höschlhof was torn down during construction of the Landsberg air base in 1936; its chapel was preserved as a memorial site to the fallen members of the Geschwader. After the war the chapel had to undergo a complete renovation. The chapel is now the place where young and old of the Geschwader hold their annual reunion on Remembrance day.

May their sacrifice never be forgotten! – And warn the living about the consequences of war.

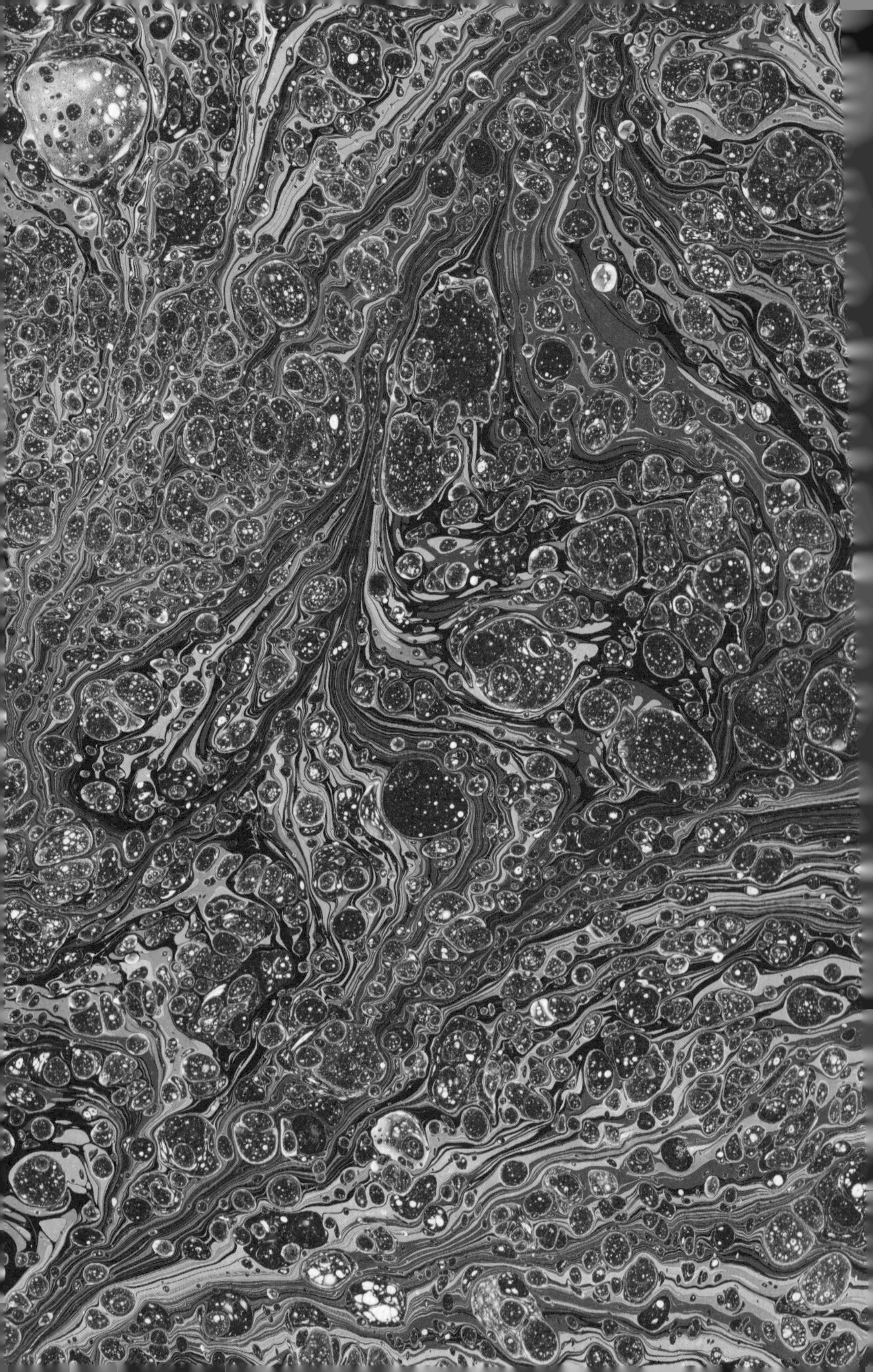